U0509664

日本生物武器作战调查资料

〔日〕近藤昭二　王　选／主编　第二册

社会科学文献出版社
SOCIAL SCIENCES ACADEMIC PRESS (CHINA)

目　录

4　证据——731部队金子顺一、高桥正彦论文集

5 远东国际军事法庭国际检察局调查

4 证据——731部队金子顺一、高桥正彦论文集

4.1　金子顺一论文集

4.1.1　雨下散布ノ基礎的考察（表紙）

资料出处：日本国立国会図書館関西館蔵、博士論文、UT51- 医 29-197。

内容点评：《金子顺一论文集》为日军细菌战部队核心研究人员金子顺一于 1944 年 12 月向东京大学申请医学博士学位提交的论文集。该论文集为战后以来日本国内发现的日本军方两大细菌战重大证据材料之一。

《金子顺一论文集》由 8 篇研究战时细菌战的论文组成，本资料为《陆军军医学校防疫研究报告》第 1 部第 41 号《雨下散布的基础考察》，1941 年 8 月 11 日提交，为 8 篇论文中的主论文。"雨下"指空中散布细菌等物质。限于篇幅，此处仅收入论文封面。

陸軍軍醫學校防疫研究報告
第1部　第41號

雨下撒布ノ基礎的考察

陸軍軍醫學校防疫研究室（部長　石井少將）

陸軍軍醫大尉　金　子　順　一

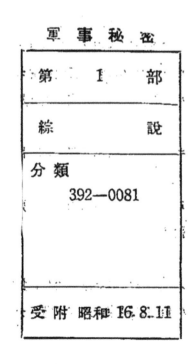

軍　事　秘　密

第　　1　　部
綜　　説
分　類 392—0081
受附　昭和16.8.11

4.1.2 低空雨下試験（表紙）

资料出处：日本国立国会図書館関西館蔵、博士論文、UT51-医29-197。

内容点评：本资料为《陆军军医学校防疫研究报告》第1部第42号，1940年6月7日提交，作者为增田美保、金子顺一，题目:《低空雨下试验》。限于篇幅，此处仅收入论文封面。

陸軍軍醫學校防疫研究報告
第1部　第42號

低　空　雨　下　試　驗

加　茂　部　隊
　　陸軍藥劑大尉　增　田　美　保
　　陸軍軍醫大尉　金　子　順　一

軍　事　秘　密

第　　1　　部
叢　　　報
分　類
392—0081
502—2
受　附　　15．6．7

4.1.3　PX效果略算法

资料出处： 日本国立国会図書館関西館蔵、博士論文、UT51- 医 29-197。

内容点评： 本资料为《陆军军医学校防疫研究报告》第 1 部第 60 号《PX 效果略算法》，1943 年 12 月 14 日提交。"PX"为带鼠疫菌印度客蚤代号。论文以日军对中国各地进行的六次 PX 攻击的相关数据，参照石井四郎的细菌战"ABDEO"（外因、媒介、病原、内因、运用）理论，推算 PX 作为武器的"效果"，即"杀伤力"，也就是一定量的 PX 散布后，引发鼠疫流行，当地感染鼠疫死亡的人数。

陸軍軍醫學校防疫研究報告
第1部 第 60 號

PX 効果略算法

陸軍軍醫學校防疫研究室 （部長 石井少將）

陸軍軍醫少佐 金 子 順 一

軍事秘密

第 1 部
原 著
分 類 385-8 441-9 338-41
受附 昭和 18.12.14

目　　　次

第1　緒　言

兵器ノ具備スベキ條件ノ一トシテ其ノ使用量ト之ニ依ル効果トノ關係ノ明デアル必要性ヲ考ヘネバナラヌ。

例ヘバ一定正面ノ敵陣地制壓ニ要スル弾丸数ヲ予メ算定シテ始メテ細密攻撃計畫ヲ樹立スル事ガ出来ル。

吾人ノ現有兵器中其ノ質及特性ニ於テ最モ優レタル弾種ノ一トシテノPXニ於テモ其ノ効果ヲ予測シ得テ、之ニ基ク製造及運用計畫ヲ築スル事ノ合理的デアルノハ論ヲ俟タヌ。

然ルニPXノ効果ハ其ノ直接罹患致死作用ノミヲ目途トシテモ之ヲ決定スル因子ガ複雑多岐デアルタメ、之ヲ爆理ニヨル理學的作用ノ如ク取扱フ事ハ不可能デアルガ、PXヲ兵器トシテ取扱フ以上ハ少クトモ之ニ依ツテ期待スルベキ効果ヲ何等カノ手段ニ依リ或ル程度迄ハ概算シ得ル事ガ必要デアルト信ズル。

幸ニシテ既往數次ニ渉ル作戦ハ此ノ種ノ問題ノ解決ニ宜要ナ規準ヲ與ヘル。他方昭和十五年以来石井閣下ノ提唱ニヨル細菌戦効果ヲABEDO説ハ爾後ノ経故ヲ経テ盆々其ノ論拠ヲ確立シ来ツタ。

茲ニ命ゼラレテABEDO説ニ基クPXノ効果予想ヲ敢テ試ミタノデアルガ、稍クハ大東亜戦争ニ於ルPXノ赫々タル成果ニ基

キ遂次斯ル考察方法ヲ進展セシメ得ン事ヲ期スルモノデアル。

第2　用字説明

○A（外因，Äuszere Bedingung）

目標地區ニ於ル疫學的外的諸條件ノ總括ヲ云フ。敵ノ直接防疫工作（S）ヲ含ム。

○B（媒体，Bindemittel）

攻撃ニ用フル病原体ヲ終末對照タル人畜ニ結合セシメル媒介体又ハ媒介機序ヲ總稱スル。即チ本篇內容ニ於テハXガ之ニ相當スル。

○E（病原，Erreger）

病原体及其ノ狀態ヲ云フ。一般的ニハ

$$E = f(m, v, r, \mu)$$

デ表ハサレル。即チ「メダイレ」說（石井：昭和八年）デアツテ，玆ニm：量，v：毒力，r：抵抗力，μ：媒質ヲ意味スル。本篇ニ於テハ第3～前提4° ノ通リ，mハPX1,0 圧ニ含マレルP菌量，μハPXノ体組織ニ相當シテ居ルカラ特ニE＝f（v，r）ト考ヘテモ良イ。

○D（內因，Disposition）

當該疫病ニ對スル終末對照ノ罹患素因ノ總括デアル。敵ノ間接的防疫工作トシテノ予防接種ノ効果ヲ抱含スル。但本篇ニ於テハ密集度，住居條件等ノ內第一次感染ニ關與スル部分ハDニ含マシメ，營養疲勞等ノ內ハ二次流行ニ影響スル部分ハAニ入レテ考ヘテ居ル。

○O（運用，Operation）

運用ノ總括。方法ノミナラズ運用器材ノ條件，及又ハEノ運用間自然損耗ヲ來ス因子ヲ含ミ，之ガタメ運用時ノ氣象交感ヲモ考慮スル。（疫學的意義ニ於ケル氣象ハ當然Aニ含マレル。）

○弾種係数

　　攻撃弾種ノ單位量ニ於ケルD×Eヲ云フ。

○運用係数

　　弾種係数ニ○ヲ乗ジタモノ。

　　上記2係数ハ何レモ努力改良ニ依ツテ増加セシメ得ルガ，A及Dハ敵地及敵ノ状況デアツテ目標及時期ニ依リ，自ラ一定シ之ヲ任意ニ變更シ得ズモノデアル。

　　　　　　　　第3　前提及假定

前提1°　　一定條件ニ於ケル効果ハ使用兵器量ニ比例ス。

前提2°　　効果ハ第一次感染ト第二次流行トヨリ成ル。

前提3°　　効果ハA，B，E，D，Oノ函数ナリ。

前提4°　　本篇ニ於テ述ベル効果トハP×1.0瓩ニ對スルモノトス。（前提1°　参照）

　　　　　　　　説　　　明

1）條件ノ相等シイ數多ノ目標ニ同一條件ノ攻撃ヲ併施スレバ各目標ニ於ケル効果ハ何レモ相等シイト考ヘル。此ノ時全効果ヲ綜合的ニ考慮スレバ前提1°ハ明ニ成立スル。之ヲ演繹シテ一目標ニ對シ異ル種々ノ量ヲ使用スル場合ニ効果ハ使用量ニ比例スルモノトス。

2）第一次感染トハ使用シタP×ニ依ル直接効果デアルト解釈シ，之ニ依テ感染獣ヲ生ジ之ニ附着シタ在来ノXガ毒化サレテ発揮スル効果ハ第二次流行ニ算入スル。実際的ニ両者ノ限界ヲ區別スルノハ困難デアルトシテモ概念的ニ2°ハ成立スル。即チ使用P×ノ感染能保持日數ト潜伏期間ヲ加ヘタ時期内ノ効果ノ大部分ヲ第一次感染ト考ヘ第二次流行曲綜ヘ勿発点ヲ攻撃時ニ一致セシメル事ニ依テ該期間内ニ理論上発生スル少數ヲ同期間発生數カラ除去スル。昭和十五年寧波戦例ニ於ケル第一次感染発現状況ヲ例示スレバ第一圖ノ様デアル。

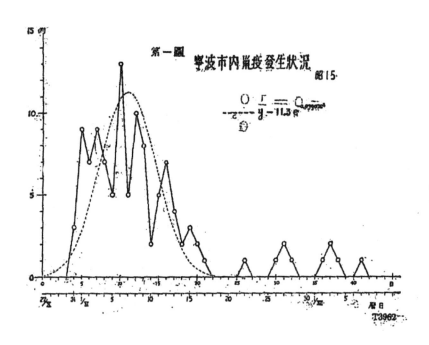

第一圖 寧波市內鼠疫發生狀況 昭15

$$\frac{a}{y=11.3e} \quad \frac{-\left(\frac{x-b}{c}\right)^2}{}$$

3）效果ヲ支配スル無數ノ因子ヲA，B，E，D，Oノ範疇ニ分ツテ然ル後個々ヲ檢討スル所ニ石井說ノ簡明性ガ存スル。尤ヨリ細菌戰ノ效果ノ眞髓ハ他ニ更ニ精神的經濟的ナ恐慌ヲ招來スルニ在ルガ，吾人ハ先ヅ直接罹患致死效果ヲ大ナラシムル樣ニ努力スル事ニ依ツテ任務ヲ完遂シ得ルモノデアル。從ツテ本篇ニ於ケル效果トハ單ニ罹患致死效果ヲ意味スル。

4）前記1°ニ基ヤ效果（R）ハ使用量ニ比例スル故，先ヅPXノ基本量トシテ1，0瓩ヲ選定シ之ニ依ル基本效果ヲ求メ，使用量X瓩ノトキハ效果ハXRデアルト見做ス。本篇ニ於ケル效果トハ此ノ基本效果即チ1，0瓩ノ效果ヲ指ス。

假　定

1°　PX1，0瓩ノ最大效果ハ第一次國染1，000名，第二次流行ヲ含ム全效果ハ其ノ200倍ナリ。即チ1，0瓩ノ最大效果ハ罹患200，000名ナリ。

2°　效果ハA，B，E，D，Oヲ變數トスル時次ノ如ク表ハテル。

$$R = f(A, B, E, D, O,)$$
$$= k, A, B, E, D^{-1}, O,$$

$A, B, E, D^{-1}, O,$ ノ變數ハ各 $0 \sim 10$ ニシテ，最大效果ニ於テハ

$$A = B = E = D = O = 10$$
$$ie \quad maxR = k \times 10^5$$
$$\therefore \quad k = 2,0 \text{（名）}$$

但以下ノ假定ノ成立ノ爲メ $A = 0, 05 \sim 1.0$ トス

3°　第一次感染 $R_{pr} = \varphi(B, E, D, O,)$
$$= k', B, E, D^{-1}, O$$
$$maxR_{pr} = k' \times 10^4$$
$$\therefore k' = 0, 1 \quad \text{（名）}$$

4°　流行係数ハ次ノ如ク定ハサル。
$$Cep = \psi(A)$$
$$= k'' \cdot A$$
$$maxCep = k'' \times 10$$
$$\therefore k'' = 2.0$$

5°　$2^{\circ} \sim 4^{\circ}$ ニ依リ次ノ關係アリ。

$$R = R_{pr} \times Cep$$
$$= k' \cdot B \cdot E \cdot D^{-1} \cdot O \times k'' \cdot A$$
$$k = k' \cdot k''$$

二　説　明

1）従来ノ作戦等ニ依ル上ヨリ効果ノ点ヨリ之ヲ述ツ，之ニ依ツテ明ナ様ニ R_{pr} ノ最大ヲ 1,000 トスルノハ，稍々小サク取ツタモノデアル。流行係数ノ最大ヲ 200 トスルノハ次ニ依ル。

附一表　　　　歷年作戰効果概見表

攻撃目標	撒 PX kg	効 一次	果 二次	果 二次	1.0kg Rp.r	R 殺傷值	Oep
15.6.4 農安	0.0005	8		607	1600	123000	76,9
15.5.4 農安大賚	0.010	12		2424	1200	243600	203.0
15.10.4 衛三郎	8.0	219	9060		26	1,159	44.2
15.10.2 7.	2.0	104	1450		52	777	44.9
16.1.4	1.6	510	2500		194	1,756	9.1
17.8.19 21	0.137	42	9210		321	2,550	70,3

2）f ノ形ニ関シテハ更ニ研究ヲ要スルデアラウガ、前提及
1°ヲ今最モ簡単ニ表現シ得ルモノトシテ2° ノ形ヲ用ヒル。
今細菌ハ効果発現ニ最モ都合良シト考ヘラレル理想限度ヲ
1 0トシ、最モ都合悪シト考ヘラレル場合ヲ0トスル。但
D ハ D⁻¹ ノ範ヲ 0～1 0トスル方ガ便デアル。従ツテ以下
ノ各値ヲ述ベル場合ニハ一般ニ D⁻¹ ノ値ヲ意味スル。

此ノ形ノ意味スル所ハ任意ノ一因数ガ0ナレバ効果ノ皆
無トナル要デアルガ、3° 以下ノ成立ノタメニハ（a＋A）
B・E・D・0 ノ形トスルカ、或ハ A ノ領域ヲ 0・0 5～
1 0トセネバナラヌガ茲デハ後者ヲ採ツタ。即 B＝E＝D⁻¹
＝0＝0、A＝0．0 5ガ最数ノ最少値デアル。

3）R_{pr} ニ於テモ A ノ領域ニ属スル因子ガ作用スルデアラウ
ガ、計算ノ便宜上二次流行ニ関係スル因子ハ総テ A ニ包括
サセ、第一次感染ニ関係スル両外因ハ総テ D ニ含有サセル。
従ツテ茲ニ云フ A 及 D⁻¹ ニハ同ジ因子ヲ含ム可能性ガアル。
然シ R_{pr} ガ大キカレバ C_{ep} ガ小サクナツテモ全効果ニ影響
少ク、C_{ep} ノ大トナル要ハ R_{pr} ノ小サイ基ヲ相殺スルノ
デ、求ニル結果ガ R デアレバ斯ル錯乱ヲ問題トスル必要ハ
ナイ。

第4　効果略算法

假定2°、3° 及4° ニ依リ第一次感染及全効果、従ツ
テ第二次流行数（R－R_{pr}）ノヲ求メ得ル。
此ノ計算ヲ容易ナラシメルタメ次ノ計算図表ヲ提示ー一
（二一四）此ノ図表ノ使用法ハ右ニ記シタ。

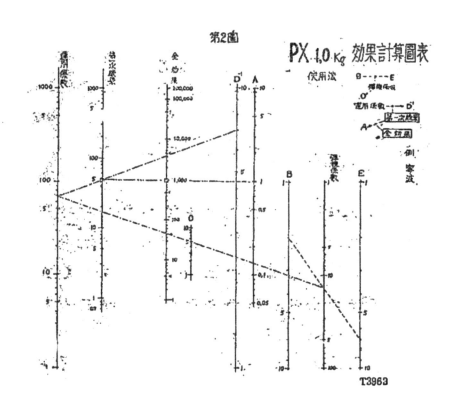

第2圖　PX 1.0 Kg 効果計算圖表

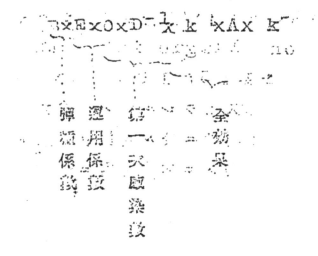

用法ハ次ノ計算ト同等ナアル。

既知効果カラ変数中未知ノモノ若干ヲ逆ニ求ムル場合ニモ同ジ様ニ使用シ得ル。

此處デ各変数ノ常用値ニ就テ説明スル。

A

主トシテ従來ノ流行ノ程度ニ基キ，流行始期ニ使用スレバ殺菌効果ガ大キク，流行閒期ニ於テハ目標ノ氣象及従來ノ流行終熄狀況ニ應シテ多少ノ効果ガアルモノト想定シテAノ値ヲ定ム。最モ「都合惡キ」場合ハ０，０５デアツテ第一次流行ニ止マリ，普通ニハ０，５～２，０トシ，地區ニ依ラハ５，０程度逆ナスル。

敵ノ直接防疫工作ガ絶大ノ効ヲ收メルト考ヘラレレバ０，０５～０，１ノ程度トナル。卽チ直接防疫工作ノミニ依ツテハ之ヲ如何ニ完璧ニスルトモ第一次感染ハ防止シ得ナイ。（之ヲ逆ニ考ヘル時ハ，敵ノ攻擊ヲ全ク無効ニスルニハ友軍ノD^{-1}ヲ絶大ナラシメ，Aニ含マレル直接防疫工作ヲ絶對強化スルノミデハ不完全デアル。卽B及Eガ如何ニ優レタリトモＯヲ等トスレバ効果ハ皆無ニナルノデアル故此ノ意味ニ於テモ防空防諜ノ積極化ガ大キナ効ガアル。）

従來ノ流行ヲ第一次感染ト第二次流行ニ區分スル事ハ容易デハナイ。何レノ流行ニ於テモ元來ハ僅數ノ患鼠又ハ患者ニ基キ，爾後永年ノ流行ヲ總テ第二次流行ト見做ス事モ出來ル。又多クノ自然流行ニ於ケル第一次感染ハ獸授デアルト考ヘラレル。１９００年San Franciscoノ例ニ於テ支那人患者ニ初マル樣ニ見エル流行モ其ノ前ニ鼠ペスト」ガ潜行シテ居ツタモノト見做サレテ居ル。（Hampton: Plague in the U.S., publ. Health Rep. 55, 1143; 1940年）蓋シ一地區ニ於テ「ペスト患者ガ新タニ移入セラレル事ハ稀デアラウ。從ツテC_{ep}ノ想定ニハ流行ノ稍々初期ニ於ル人例ヲR_{prt}ト考ヘルカ或ハ新京ペスト」ノ例ノ如ク初メニ某病院內ニ集簇シ

テ生ジタ数例ヲ取ルカデアルガ、何レモ吾人ノ意味ニ於テノ第二次感染トハ断定シ得ヌ。即チ自然ニ於ケル人ー鼠ノ関係ガ此ノ問題ヲ複雑ニシテ居リ、又自然ニ於テハ決シテＰＸヲ鼠ペストト」以外カラ忽然ト大致ニ現ハレル事例ナイノデアル。茲ニ於テＣepノ確実ナ撤點ハ既往ノ経験以外ニハ求メ得ナイ。然シ乍ラＡノ判定ニ當ツテハ既往ノ流行記録ヲ参照スル事ハ絶対必要デアル。即チ従來大流行ノアツタ場所、特ニ夫ガ持續シタ場所ハソノ流行ノ大小ニ應ジテ多少ノ「ペスト毒因ガアル譯デアル。大流行ノ地デハＡハ大キク、小サイ流行シカ起ラヌ土地デハ之ガ小サイト考ヘルノガ至當デアル。

　従來流行記録ノ無イ個所ニ於ケルＡノ判定ニハ特ニ慎重ナルヲ要スルガ、之ニ關シテハ第7デ論ヘル。

　Ａヲ各因子ニ分解シテ流行ノ本質ヲ確カメ、之ヲ應用シテ細菌戰ノ至大効果ヲ求メル事ツ今後吾人ノ責務デアル。

　　　　　　　　　　　　Ｂ

　ＰＸヲ直接秤量スルノガ容易デナイ爲ニＰＸ量トシテ原Ｘ量ヲ表示サレル場合ガアル事ヲ考慮シテ次ノ様ニ表ハス。

　Ｂ＝毒化生存率×仕上率×有効率×１０（使用時）
即チ毒化生存率＝１ー（自然損耗率＋毒化損耗率）、
仕上率＝保菌率（＝従來ノ毒化率）、有効率＝保菌Ｘ中感染能保持率デアル。

　従來ノ諸資料ヲ綜合スレバ大量生産時ノ最大値ハ5，０ノ程度デアラウ。一般ニ仕上完了後5〜１０日位デハＢハ1〜3ト見做スベキデアル。使用時ノ氣象ニ依ルＰＸノ有効生命ノ伸縮ハ０ニ含メテ考ヘル。

　　　　　　　　　　　　Ｅ

　ＰＸニ含マレルＰ菌ノ質ニ関スルモノデアルガ所謂Infectivity ヲＢノ有効率ニ含メテ考ヘレバＥハ毒化ニ使用サレ

タ原菌株ノ質ヲ以テ代表サセ得ル。使用時ノ氣象ガPX体内ノ菌ヲ急ニ遷性サセル様ナ狀況ガアレバBノ有効率トハ離レテEヲ減少セシムベキデアラウ。

現在使用セラレルP菌デハE＝7，0〜8，0ト定メル。

$$D^{-1}$$

先天的及ビ後天的ノ個人的及ビ集團的免疫度，終末對照ノ生活條件ヲ考慮シ，一般ニ6，0〜8，0ヲ基準トスル。特別ナ營養不及，疲勞蓄積等ノ條件ガアレバ1〜2増加シ，後方基地ニ於テ一般狀況良好ナ生活ヲ行フ場合ハ1〜2減少，更ニ特異的予防處理ノ施サレタ場合ハ1〜2ヲ減ズル。但如何ニ体質愰瘻デアリ，完全免疫ガ行ハレタ場合デモ一般ニ$D^{-1}=0$トナル事ハ考ヘラレナイ。

$$0$$

使用PXヲ終末對照ニ到達セシメル能率ニ相當スル。
謀略的使用ニ於テ終末對照ニ近迫シテ用ヒ得ル場合ヲ10トスル。一般ニ

0＝運用難易度×運用間生殘率×有効濃度形成能率×到達能率×10

運用間生殘率ハ器材ノ機能不全ニ依ツテ致死又ハ無効化セラレタ部分ヲ云ヒ，有効濃度形成能率ハ最少有効濃度（假＝10四/㎡トス）ヲ形成スル面積ト使用量ヲ以テ一樣ニ有効濃度ヲ構成シ得ル計算上ノ面積トノ比，到達能率ハ目標捕捉度及兩後ノ到達難易性ヲ意味スル。

PXノ移動能ハ一夜30米ノ程度ニ過ギヌ（貴室院）故ニ初發傳染惹起ノタメニハ必ズ最終對照ヲ含ム地域ニ命中セシメル必要ガアル。又著地後目標ノ狀況ニ依テ無効果スル部分ノ多少ヲ顧慮セネバナラナイ。例ヘバ日中灼熱シタ補裝又ハ屋根ニ落

ヲ、或ハ水上ニ落遷シ、時ニハ濠ニ圍マレタ交道ノナイ土地ニ
落デルモノハ恐ラク遂ニ無効化スルデアラウシ、地上ニ落遷シ
タモノガ高床住居内へ侵入シ難イ事モアラウ。地上運用又ハ謀
略的使用ニ於テハ狀況ガ有利デアル事ガ多イ。

上式ニ依ルＯノ算出例ハ次ノ樣デアル。

Ｏ市街・低撒＝０，９ｘ０，９ｘ０，８ｘ０，８ｘ１０＝５，２
Ｏ市街・高撒＝１，０ｘ０，８ｘ０，２ｘ０，５ｘ１０＝０，８
Ｏ市街・爆撃＝１，０ｘ０，５ｘ０，８ｘ０，８ｘ１０＝３，２
Ｏ市街・謀略＝１，０ｘ１，０ｘ１，０ｘ１，０ｘ１０＝１０，０
Ｏ野戰・低撒＝０，９ｘ０，９ｘ０，８ｘ０，５ｘ１０＝３，２

第5 効果發現狀況

第二次流行ニ導入シ得タ場合ハ通常ハ爾後多年ニ涉リ大小ノ流行
ヲ繼續スルデアラウ。然シ前提ニ基イテ最大効果ヲ限定スル場合ニ
全効果ヲ數次ニ分割スル事ハ必ズシモ容易デハナイ故，効果ハ使用
直後發現シ一回ノ流行ニヨッテ終結スルト假想スル。此ノ時流行ノ
形ハ確率曲線ノ型デアルト見做ス。玆ニ從來ノ二三ノ流行例ヲ示セ
バ第三圖ノ樣デアル。今次二次流行ニ於ケル毎週患者發生數ヲ

$$y = A e^{-b^2 x^2} \quad (x：週)$$

トシ、流行ノ始終ヲ $y \leqq 0$，７デ規定シ、流行期ヲ２４週，３６週
及ビ４８週トスル時，全數１９９，０００（＝２００，０００－１，
０００）ノ毎週發生數ハ第三圖及ビ第二表ニ示ス通リデアル。

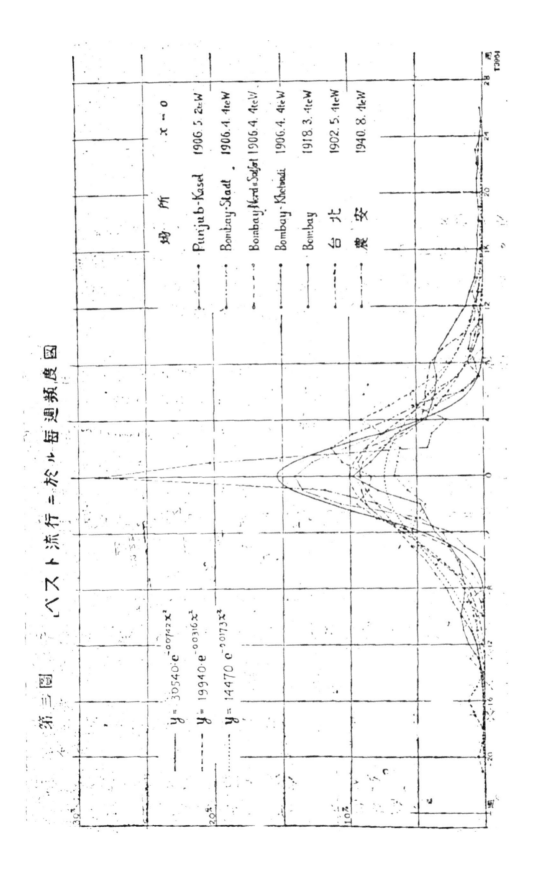

第二表　$y = A \cdot e^{-b^2 x^2}$，$\displaystyle\int_{-\infty}^{+\infty} = 199,000$

±x	A=30540, b²=0.0712 y	%	A=19940, b²=0.0316 y	%	A=14770, b²=0.0173 y	%
0	30540	15.4	19940	10.0	14770	7.41
1	28350	14.2	19320	9.72	14500	7.27
2	22700	11.4	17590	8.84	13790	6.92
3	15660	7.85	15000	7.53	12650	6.35
4	9310	4.68	12050	6.04	11200	5.62
5	4775	2.40	9050	4.55	9580	4.81
6	2115	1.06	6400	3.22	7920	3.97
7	806	0.405	4230	2.13	6340	3.19
8	265.8	0.133	2460	1.24	4890	2.46
9	74.4	0.038	1543	0.774	3630	1.82
10	18.3	0.0092	847	0.426	2540	1.28
11	3.85	0.0019	437	0.220	1820	0.913
12	0.70	0.00035	209	0.105	1224	0.614
13	0.091	0.000046	95.5	0.048	705	0.400
14			40.7	0.021	498	0.251
15			16.2	0.0081	303	0.152
16			6.10	0.0031	177	0.089
17			2.15	0.0011	99.3	0.050
18			0.70	0.00035	54.0	0.027
19			0.22	0.00011	28.8	0.015
20					14.7	0.0074
21					7.24	0.0036
22					3.43	0.0017
23					1.58	0.00079
24					0.70	0.00035
25					0.30	0.00015

T3965

註：

$$全数 Y = 2A \int_0^\infty e^{-b^2 x^2} dx$$

$$= \frac{A}{b}\sqrt{\pi} = 199,000$$

$$\therefore A = \frac{b}{\sqrt{\pi}} \times 199,000$$

又

$$y = A e^{-b^2 x_t^2} \leq 0.7 \quad (x_t = \pm12, \pm18, \pm24)$$

$$\therefore \frac{b}{\sqrt{\pi}} \times 199,000 \cdot e^{-b^2 x_t^2} \leq 0.7$$

$$Log \frac{199,000}{0.7\sqrt{\pi}} + Log\, b \leq b^2 x_t^2$$

ヨリ b ヲ求メ，之ヨリ A ノ値ヲ定ム。

第一次流行ニ於シテ 各期ノ計算ヲ行ヒ

$$Y_{pr} = 500 (又ハ1000)$$

$$x = \pm 2 ニ於テ \quad y \leq 0.7$$

トヲカバ第三図中ニ示ス第一次以後曲線ヲ得ル。

以下ハ x = ±18ニ於テ y ≤ 0.7 ノ形，即チ最大場果ノ流
行期36週ノ形ニ就キ得々 b ヲ以テ小サイ流行ニモアテハメル。
然ルトキハ第二次流行並ニ N ノ場合

$$y_N = A_N \, e^{-0.0316 x^2}$$

$$A_N = 19,940 \times \frac{N}{199,000}$$

ト置キ，$y \leq 0,7$ ヲ以テ同様ニ流行ノ始終トスル。於ル時ニ
Nト流行期間 d（$= 2 x_t$）ノ関係ハ第四圖ノ通リデアリ，Nノ
二三ノ値ニ對スル發生曲線ハ第五圖ノ様ニナル。 第二次流行
ノ始ハ第一次爛熟ノ始，即チ交會時ニ一致セシメル故第一次爛
熟期間ノ虫候發生ハ兩者ノ和トナルガ，此ノ時期ニハ第二次
流行虫數ハ極微少デアルカラ曲線ノ形ハ第五圖ニ見ル通リ大差
ハナイ。

註：

Nト d ヲ関係ヲ求メル場合ニ $b^2 = 0,0316$ トオイタ故ニ
$d = 0$ ニ於テモ　$N \sim 0$ ニナラナイ。即チ

$$N = \int = \frac{A}{b} \sqrt{\pi}$$

$$\therefore A \fallingdotseq 0,10 \, N$$

$$y = A, e^{-0.0316 \, x_t^2}$$

$$= 0,10 N \cdot e^{-0.0316 \left(\frac{d}{2}\right)^2} = 0,7$$

$$i e \quad x_t = \frac{d}{2} = 0 \qquad \text{ニ於テ}$$

$$N_{d=0} = 7,0$$

之ハ N ノ値ニ無關係ニ $b^2 = 0.0316$ ナル同一値ヲ用ヰル
裏ガ不適切ナ事ヲ示スモノデアルガ考察ノ順序トシテ先ヅ不問
トスル。簡單ニ修正スルニハ

$$N' = N - 7.0 \quad \text{トシ}$$
$$A' = 0.10 N',$$

ヲ用フルガヨイ。

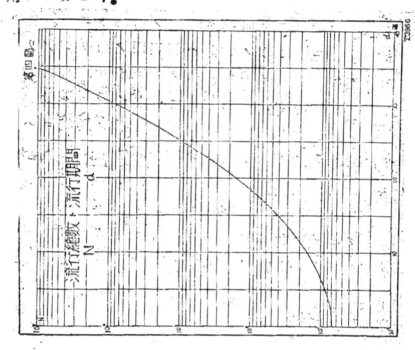

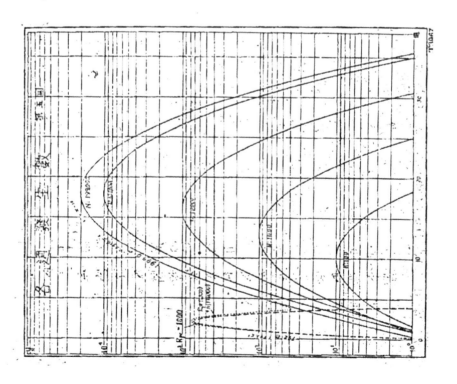

第6　既往作戰ニ於ケル變數值

　第一表及ビ第4ニ依ツテ既往作戰ヲ解析スレバ第三表ニ見ル變數值ヲ得ル。

　Ｂ，Ｅ，Ｏノ値ノ推定ニ就テノ理由ハ各作戰ノ狀況ヲ詳記スル事ニナルノデ省略スル。細部ハ各作戰詳報ヲ細密ニ參照サレタイ。

第三表

区分	B	E	O	D-1	Rpr	A	R
腹·水	8.0	8.0	9.0	9.0	5 1 8（1600）	8.0	82900（123000）
腹·水	8.0	8.0	9.0	9.0	5 1 8（1200）	8.0	82900（243600）
脾·腺	1.5	7.0	4.0	7.0	2 9（26）	2.0	1175（1159）
脾·波	2.0	7.0	5.0	7.0	4 9（52）	1.0	980（777）
常·德	3.0	8.0	5.0	7.0	8 4（194）	1.0	1680（1756）
腐·广·玉	6.0	8.0	9.0	7.5	3 2 4（321）	3.0	19430（22550）

（　）内ハ総一表ノ値

第7　目標地區ニ於ケル予想變數値

第2及第4ニ從ヒテ變數値ヲ予想スル。B，E八決定ニ大ナル困難ガナイ。C八作戰ノ困難サヲ考慮シ且目標ニヨリ用法ノ異ル專ニ留意シテ判定スル。D^{-1}八各地區ニ於ケル生活狀況ニ基イテ決定スル。

最モ重大ナルハA／予想デアル。從來ノ流行ノ程度ノ明瞭ナ場所ニ就テハ其ノ大小ニ從ツテ判定シ，流行前驅期又ハ初期ニ於テ最大値ヲ與ヘル。

從來流行記錄ノナイ場所ニ就テハ先ヅ流行ガ起リ得ルカ否カヲ判定シ，更ニ起リ得ル流行ノ程度ヲ推定セネバナラナイ。即チ該地區ノ氣象的生物的狀況ヲ他ノ流行既知ノ場所ト比較シテ流行ノ成否，流行期及其ノ程度ヲ判定類推スル。然シ流行ノ程度ニ到ツテハ極メテ判定困難デアル。

此處ニ各種資料ヲ綜合シタ予想變數値表及之ニヨルPXノ效果ノ一案ヲ提示スル。（第四表）又特ニAニ關聯シテ各地流行期推定圖ヲ示ス。（第六圖）第六圖ハ發生頻度デハナク發生數ヲモ示ス如クシタタメ一定ノ基準ニ據ラズニ描イテアル。

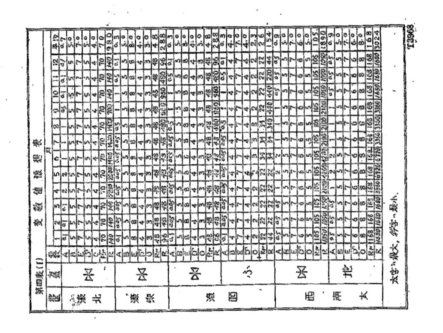

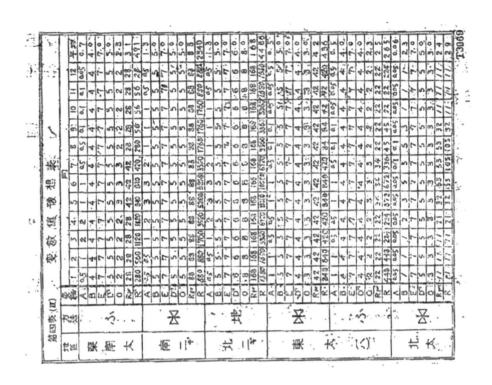

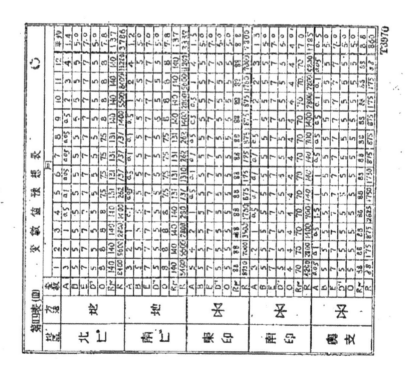

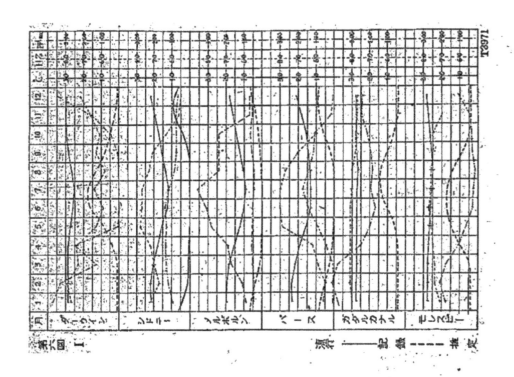

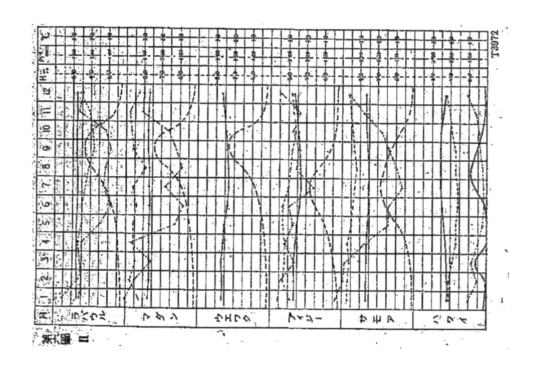

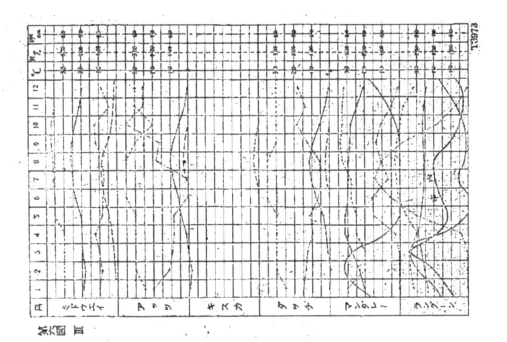

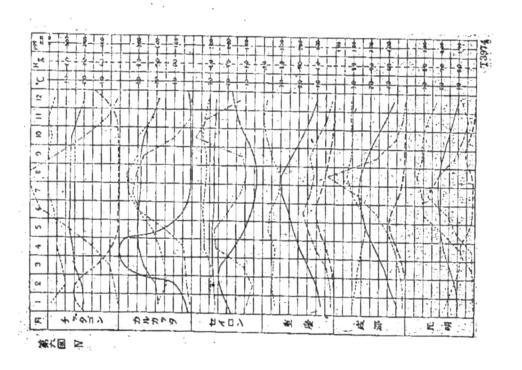

次ニ参考キシテ近年ニ於ル各地『ペスト』年別發生圖ヲ掲グ
ダ。（第七圖）

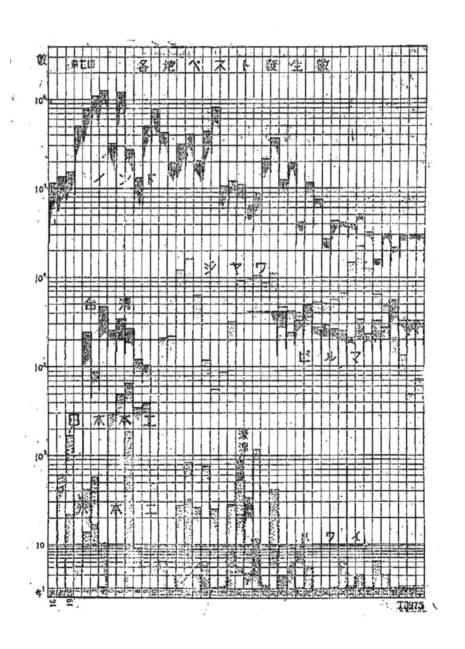

尤ヨリ前記数値ノ判定規準ハ記録ノ明カナ地ノ平均統計ニ準
拠スルモノデアルノデ，使用時ノ状況ガ平均カラ偏倚スルホド
適合性ハ不良ニナルデアラウ。然ルニ従来ノ記録ニ依レバ年中
流行ノ持續スル地デハ最大發生月ハ移動シ易イガ（例ヘバ
コロンボ）著シイ流行期ノアル地デハ山ト谷ノ配置月別ニ概ネ
一定シテ居ル（例カルカツタ、ラングーン）　特ニ興味アルノ
ハ、ジヤワ、ノ初發年1911年ノ曲線ガ他ノ年ヲ懸絶シテ居
ル事デアル。之ヲ1911年ノ状態ガ著シク偏シテ居タ事ニ歸
スルベキデナク（當年ノ諸元ヲ得ラレヌデ確言ハ留保スルガ）
斯ル年中流行ノアル土地デハ攻襲ニ依ツテ随時効果ヲ得ル事ノ
一證ト見做シタイ。

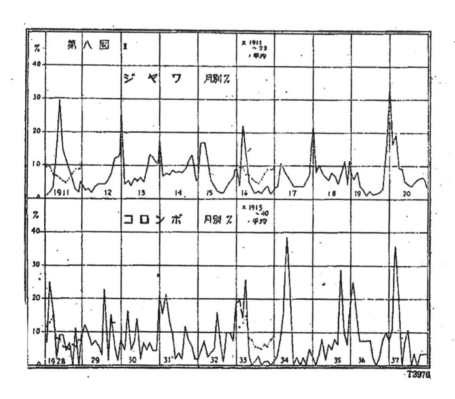

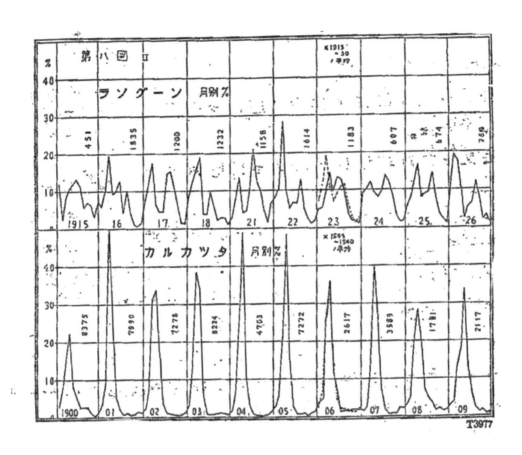

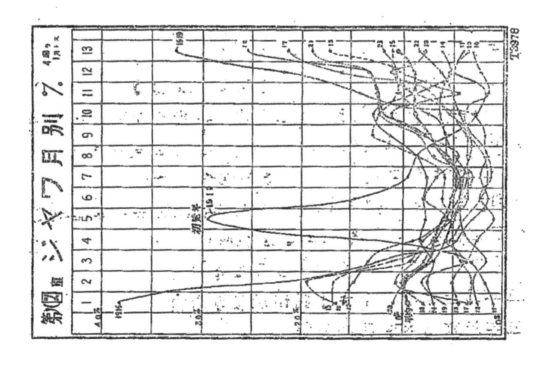

第8　結及参考文献

結

茲ニ石井說ニ基キ既往ノ作戰ノ經驗ヲ參照シテＰＸノ效果ノ計算法ヲ提示シタ。

更ニ同法ヲ予想目標地區ニ於テモ應用スベク推理ノ擴張ヲ行ツタ。

之ニ依レバＰＸ１,０瓲ノ效果ハ次ノ樣デアル。

第一次感染 (最少　　　　　　　１１名（北太冬）
　　　　　　　最大　　　　　　１６８名（西南太ニーギ）

全　效果 (最少　　　　　　　１１名（北太冬）
　　　　　　最大　　　　１１,２００名（ビ１２月）

斯ル推定ガ如何ニ實際ニ卽應スルカ，如何ニ改良スベキカハ大東亞戰ニ於ル今後ノ效果ノ檢討ニ俟タネバナラヌガ，茲ニ考察シタ程度ヲ遙ニ凌駕スル大效果ヲ以テ上記推定ヲ根底カラ再檢討スベキ秋ノ來ラン事ヲ希ツテ止マヌ。

主要參考文獻

澁見：「ホ」號作戰效果情報　　　　　（昭１８.１１）

石井：　特殊戰原則　　　　　　　　　（昭１５.１２）

金子：　甲「フ」目標調査　　　　（防研報告第１部第４５號）

貴寶院，高安：印度及南海方面敵狀判斷（昭１８.９）

田中：　新醫學兵器ノ完成　　　　　　（昭１６.４）

內藤：　印度ニ於ケル傳染病史槪要（南防業報丙第４４號）

〃：　昭１７.１１廣盦「ペスト」流行ニ於ケル死者數ノ推
　　　定計算　　　　　　（昭１８.１１）

昭和十五年乃至十七年「ホ」號作戰戰斗詳報

昭和十五年新京ペスト防疫詳報

4.1.4　微粒ニヨル紙上斑痕ニ就テ（表紙）

资料出处：日本国立国会図書館関西館蔵、博士論文、UT51- 医 29-197。

内容点评：本资料为《陆军军医学校防疫研究报告》第 1 部第 62 号《关于滴粒在纸上的瘢痕》，1944 年 2 月 7 日提交，作者为金子顺一、小酒井望。此处仅收入其封面。

陸軍軍醫學校防疫研究報告
第1部　第62號

滴粒ニヨル紙上斑痕ニ就テ

陸軍軍醫學校防疫研究室（部長　石井少將）
　　　陸軍軍醫少佐　金　子　順　一
　　　陸軍軍醫中尉　小酒井　　　望

軍事秘密

第　1　部

原　著

分類

392-0081

受附　昭和　　19年

4.1.5 X.cheopis ノ落下状態ノ撮影（表紙）

资料出处：日本国立国会図書館関西館蔵、博士論文、UT51- 医 29-197。

内容点评：本资料为《陆军军医学校防疫研究报告》第 1 部第 63 号《X. cheopis 落下状态摄影》，1944 年 2 月 24 日提交，作者为金子顺一、矢田博。此处仅收入其封面。

陸軍軍醫學校防疫研究報告
第1部　第63號

X.cheopis　ノ落下狀態ノ撮影

陸軍軍醫學校防疫研究室（部長　石井少將）

陸軍軍醫少佐　　金　子　順　一

矢　田　博

軍 事 秘 密

第　　1　　部
原　　　　著
分　類 385-1 385-8
受附 昭和 19224

4.1.6　X.航空撒布ニ於ケル算定地上濃度（表紙）

资料出处：日本国立国会図書館関西館蔵、博士論文、UT51- 医 29-197。

内容点评：本资料为《陆军军医学校防疫研究报告》第 1 部第 81 号《有关 X. 高空散布地面浓度的测定》，1944 年 6 月 16 日提交，作者为金子顺一、小酒井望。此处仅收入其封面。

陸軍軍醫學校防疫研究報告
第1部　第 8 1 號

X.高空散布ニ於ケル算定地上濃度

陸軍軍醫學校防疫研究室（部長　石井少將）

陸軍軍醫少佐　　金　子　順　一
陸軍軍醫中尉　　小酒井　　望

軍 事 秘 密

第　1　部
原　著
分　類
38568
受附 昭和 19・6・16

4.1.7　火薬力ニ依ル液ノ飛散状況（表紙）

资料出处：日本国立国会図書館関西館蔵、博士論文、UT51-医 29-197。

内容点评：本资料为《陆军军医学校防疫研究报告》第 1 部第 82 号《液体借火药力飞散的状况》，1944 年 7 月 1 日提交，作者为金子顺一、小酒井望。此处仅收入其封面。

陸軍軍醫學校防疫研究報告
第1部　第一八二號

火藥力ニセル液ノ飛散狀態

南軍醫學校防疫研究室

軍事秘密

| 第 1 部 |
| 原　著 |
| 分　類 |
| 392-0085 |
| 受附 昭和19.7.1 |

4.1.8 しろねずみヨリ分離セル「ゲルトネル」菌ノ菌型（表紙）

资料出处：日本国立国会図書館関西館蔵、博士論文、UT51- 医 29-197。

内容点评：本资料为《陆军军医学校防疫研究报告》第 2 部第 791 号《从白鼠分离的肠炎沙门氏菌菌型》，1944 年 1 月 17 日提交，作者为浅见淳、金子顺一、丸山正夫。此处仅收入其封面。

陸軍軍醫學校防疫研究報告
第2部 第791號

しろねずみヨリ分離セル「ゲルトネル菌ノ菌型

陸軍軍醫學校防疫研究室（部長 石井少將）

陸軍軍醫少佐 　浅　見　　淳

同 　　　　　 金　子　順　一

　　　　　　　 丸　山　正　夫

第　　2　　部
原　　　　著
分類 　　434—8 　　381—3
受附 昭和 19. 1. 17

4.2 高桥正彦论文集

4.2.1 「ペスト」皮膚反応

资料出处：日本国立国会図書館関西館蔵、博士論文。

内容点评：《高桥正彦论文集》为高桥正彦申请医学博士学位而提交的论文。本资料为《陆军军医学校防疫研究报告》第 2 部第 381 号《关于鼠疫的皮肤反应》，1942 年 9 月 1 日提交。

陸軍軍醫學校防疫研究報告
第2部 第381號

「ペスト」皮膚反應ニ就テ

陸軍軍醫學校軍陣防疫學教室（主任 增田大佐）
陸軍軍醫少佐 高 橋 正 彦

第 2 部
原 著
分 類   441—6   537—441
受附 17. 9. 1

擔任指導 石 井 少 將

目 次

緒 論

人又ハ動物ハ種々ノ微生物ノ自然感染ヲ受ケタル際、其ノ過程ニ於テ所謂感作セラレテ細菌性「アレルギー」ノ狀態トナリ、耐過後モ其ノ狀態ヲ持續スルモノナリ。又實驗的ニモ各種ノ生菌或ハ死菌ヲ接種スルコトニヨリテ、一定期間ノ後ニ細菌性「アレルギー」ノ狀態ヲ作リ得ルモノナリ。斯カル狀態ニ在ル人或ハ動物ニ極メテ小量ノ「アレルゲン」即チ細菌體、菌體成分或ハ其代謝產物等ヲ皮膚或ハ皮內ニ接種スルトキハ、ソレニ對シ、接種局所ニ特異性過敏反應ヲ出現ス、之ヲ「アレルギー性皮膚反應ト稱ス。

此レト同類ノ皮膚反應ハ1873年 Blackley[1] ガ始メテ「アレルギー性疾患タル枯草熱患者ノ診斷ニ試ミタルモノニシテ、其ノ後 Walker[2][3] ニヨウテ其ノ他ノ「アレルギー性疾患ノ診斷ニ用ヒラレタルモ、一方各種ノ細菌性疾患ニ就テモ、「アレルギー性皮膚反應ガ檢査セラレ、ソレガ診斷ノ助トナリ得ベキコト明ニセラレタリ。

後者ノ開拓者ハ Pirquet ニシテ、Pirquet[4][5][6] ハ先ヅ痘瘡ニ就テ研究シ、痘瘡ヲ經過セルモノ、又ハ種痘ヲ受ケタルコトアルモノニ、再種痘ヲ行フトキハ、初種痘ノ場合ト異ナリ、數時間ニシ

テ局所ニ發赤腫脹丘疹ヲ生ジ、1日乃至2日ニシテ最高ニ達スルヲ觀察シ、此ノ皮膚反應ハ、痘瘡ト之ニ對シテ「アレルギー」狀態ニナリ居ル者トノ間ニ起ル特異性反應ニシテ、其ノ强弱ハ免疫ノ强弱トニ一致ス。即チ其ノ者ニ存スル抗體ト密接ナル關係ノ存スルコトヲ述べ、之ニ依リテ未種痘者ト既種痘者ノ識別及既往ニ痘瘡ニ罹患セルコトノ有無ヲ知ルコトノ可能ナルバカリデナク、痘瘡免疫ノ程度ノ推定モ亦可能ナルコトヲ論ゼリ。次デ Pirquet [7] ハ結核ニ就テモ同樣ノ研究ヲナシ「ツベルクリン」皮膚反應ハ一種ノ「アレルギー性反應ニシテ、一旦結核菌ノ侵襲ヲ受ケタルモノハ、其ノ病竈ガ現在活動性ノモノデアレ、非活動性ノモノデアレ、何レモ陽性ニ出現スルモノナリ。從ツテ結核ノ診斷殊ニ乳兒及幼兒ノ結核診斷ニハ相當價値アルモノナリト述べタリ。其ノ後之ヲ追試或ハ補遺セル業績極メテ多シ。即チ痘瘡ニ就テハ Tieche, [8][9][10] 城井等ハ皮膚反應ガ痘瘡診斷ニ用ヒ得ベキコトヲ述べ、結核ニ就テハ Moro, [11] Mantoux, [12] Hart, [13] Groer, [14] Johnston, [15] Lloyd, [16] Opie [17] 等ハ「ツベルクリン反應ノ診斷的價値ニ就テ論述セリ。

尚其ノ他ノ細菌性疾患ニ就テモ、「アレルギー性皮膚反應ヲ檢査シ、其ガ診斷的價値アルコトヲ結論セルモノ多シ。今其ノ代表的ノモノヲ述べレバ、淋疾ニ於ケル「ゴノコタチン反應(Bruck, [18] Iron, [19] 綱谷, [20] 吉永 [21]) 波狀熱ニ於ケル「メルチン」及「アボルチン反應 (M'Fadyean, [22] Huddleson, [23] Burnet [24]) 鼻疽ニ於ケル「マレイン反應(Nocard, [25] Hutyra, [26] Reinhardt [27])、葡萄狀球菌ノ浸出液ニヨル皮膚反應(Coenen, [28] Jullianelle [29])黴毒ニ於ケル「ルエチン反應 (Noguchi [30])、軟性下疳ニ於ケル伊東氏反應(Ito, [31] Cole, [32] Reenstierna [33])、第4性病ニ於ケル「フライ反應 (Frei [34])、ワイル氏病ニ於ケル「ワイリン反應 (Jacobsthal [35])、腸チブス」ニ於ケル「チイフオイデン反應 (Chantemesse, [36] Gay, [37] Force [38]) 等ナリ。

上述セル各皮膚反應ハ臨床上疾病ノ診斷ニ大ナル意義ヲ有スルモノナルモ、此ノ反應ハ、其ノ疾病ガ "manifest" デアルトキバカリデナク耐過後ニモ仔存シテキルコトアリ、又豫防接種ヲセルモノニ於テモ陽性ニ出現スルコトアルタメ、此ノ「アレルギー性反應ノミヲ以テ診斷ヲ下スコトノ不可能ナルコトハ一般ノ認ムル處ナリ、例ヘバ結核ニ就テ、幼年ニ於テハ「ツベルクリン反應陽性ナレバ、結核ガ "manifest" ナルコトヲ意味シ、從ツテ他ノ臨床所見ト共ニ、此ノ反應モ重大ナル意義ヲ持ツモ、成人ニ於テハ陽性ハ必ズシモ結核ガ "manifest" ナルコトヲ意味スルモノニハアラズト謂フモノアリ。

前述セル如ク生體ガ細菌ニ對シテ活動性免疫ヲ獲得シツツアル間ニ（ソレハ細菌ノ自然感染ニヨル場合ト、人工的ニ生菌或ハ死菌ヲ接種スルコトニヨル場合トアリ）組織ハ其ノ細菌體成分ニ對シテ過敏性トナリ所謂「アレルギー性反應ヲ呈スルモノナリ、從ツテ細菌性アレルギート免疫（感染防禦ヲ意味ス）トノ間ニ何等カノ關係ノ存スルコトナキヤニ關シテ「アレルギー性皮膚反應ヲ通ジテ、細菌性アレルギー」ト免疫トノ關係ヲ研究セル業績ハ極メテ多シ、然レトモ未ダ結論ニ達セザルハ、「アレルギー性反應ノ本態ガ不明ナルタメナリ。此ノ本態ニ關シテハ、多數ノ研究者ハ「アレルギー性反應ガ特異性デアル點ヨリ、之ヲ一種ノ抗原抗體反應ナリト説明セリ (Pirquet, [39] Wassermann, [40] Pickert, [41] Zinsser, [42] Keller [43])。

而シテ「アレルギー」ト免疫トノ關係ニ就テ見ルニ兩者ハ必ズシモ平行スルモノニアラズシテ、オ互ニ他ノ存在ト關係ナクモ存在シ得ルモノナルコトヲ觀察セルモノアリ。即チ結核ニ於ケル Römer[44], Fischl[45], Philibert[46] 肺尖ニ於ケル Mackenzie[47] 等ハソレナリ。Kraus[48] ノ如キモ結核ノ免疫ト「アレルギー」トノ關係ヲ詳細ニ研究セル結果、現在ノ知識ニ於テハ兩者ヲ同一視スルコトハ適當ナラスト述ベタリ。

然レドモ「アレルギー」ト免疫トハ其ノ本態ハ同一ナラザルモ極メテ密接ナル關係アリ。「アレルギー反應ハ免疫ノ一隨伴現象ト云ヒ得ベク、從ツテ或ル程度免疫ノ「インヂイカトール」トナリ得ルモノナリト云ヒ得ベシ。此ノ免疫ト「アレルギー」トノ關係ニ就テハ結核ニ於テ最モ詳細ニ研究セラレアリ。今其ノ概要ヲ述ブレバ、先ヅ Koch[49] ハ海猽ニ就テ實驗セル結果、「ツベルクリン」ニ對シ高キ感受性ヲ有スル海猽ハ、低キ感受性ヲ有スル海猽ヨリモ、結核菌ノ再感染ニ對シ罹患シ難キコトヲ述べ、其ノ後此ノ成績ヲ追試承認セルモノ多シ。Heimbeck[50] ハ病院ノ看護婦ニ就テ詳細ナル觀察ヲナシ「ツベルクリン反應陽性中ヨリノ結核患者ノ發生ハ「ツベルクリン反應陰性者中ヨリノソレニ比シテ極メテ少ナキコト、及「ツベルクリン反應陰性者ニ B.C.G ヲ接種スルトキハ「ツベルクリン反應陽性トナリ。ソノ中ヨリノ結核患者ノ發生ハ極メテ減少セルコトヲ報告セリ。Schell[51] モ亦「ツベルクリン」陰性者ハソノ陽性者ニ比シテ結核發病ニ對スル抵抗ノ弱キコトヲ指摘セリ、然レドモ一方、Jacobson[52] ハ此ノ問題ニ關シテハ結論ヲ下シ得ズト報告シ、Schipman[53], ハカルフオルニアニ於ケル調査ノ結果ハ「ツベルクリン」陽性者ニ於テ反ツテ結核發病率ノ高カリシコトヲ報告セリ。其ノ他「アレルギー」ト免疫トノ關係ヲ「ツベルクリン反應ノ成績ト臨床的觀察ノ成績ヨリ考察シテ、ソレニ就テ何等カノ結論ヲ得ント努メタル研究者ハ極メテ多キモ、尚現在ニ於テハ確タル結論ニ到達シアラズ。動物實驗ニヨツテモ、此ノ問題ハ詳細ニ研究セラレタリ、即チ Zinsser[54] ハ結核死菌ヲ以テ海猽ヲ免疫セルニ「ツベルクリン反應陽性トナリ再感染ニ對シテ其ノ罹患ノ程度輕度ニシテ且長ク生存シ得ルコトヲ實證セリ、然レドモ「アレルギー」ト免疫トノ關係ハ明瞭ニナシ得ザリシト述ベタリ、Willis[55] ハ結核菌ノ無毒性生菌ヲ海猽ニ接種セルニ、其ノ皮膚反應消失セル後モ尚再感染ニ對シ抵抗ノ存スルコトヲ述べ、Julianelle[56] ハ結核菌ヨリ分離セル純粹ナル蛋白質ヲ以テ海猽ヲ免疫スルトキハ皮膚ノ「アレルギー性ハ生ズルモ、免疫ハ得ラレザリシコトヲ述べ、Seibert[57] ハ海猽ニツキ、加熱殺菌セル結核菌ヲ靜脈內ニ注射スルトキハ "relative Immunität" ハ得ラレルモ皮膚ニハ「ツベルクリン・アレルギー」ノ證明セラレザルコトヲ實驗シ、又 Rich, Siegel[58][59] ハ結核海猽ニ「ツベルクリン」ヲ增量的ニ注射スルト遂ニハ除感作セラレテ「ツベルクリン反應ハ出現セザルニ到ルモ、此ノ海猽ハ依然トシテ免疫ノ消失シ居ラザルコトヲ述べ、Sewall[60] モ亦海猽ヲ以テ實驗シ「アレルギー」ハ感染ニ對スル防禦力ノ增強ナシニ現ハレ、免疫ハ又「アレルギー」ノ出現ナシニ現ハレルコトアリト述ベタリ。以上ノ動物實驗ノ成績ヨリ考察スルモ細菌性アレルギー」ト免疫トヲ同一視スルコトハ適當デナク、別箇ノモノナリト考ヘルヲ至當トスルナラン、然レドモ其ノ本態ハ不明ナルモ其ノ兩者ノ間ニ密接ナル關係ノ存スルコトハ又何人モ否定シ得ザル處ナリ。

以上述ベタル人體ニ就テノ臨床觀察ノ成績及動物實驗ノ成績ヲ綜合シテ、結核ニ於テハ「アレルギー」ハ免疫ノ過程ニ於ケル一狀態ニシテ、一般ニ此ノ狀態ニアルモノハ、既往ニ於テ全然結核菌ノ浸襲ヲ受ケタルコトナキモノヨリモ結核ニ對シ發病シ難キモノナリト云フコトヲ得ベシ、然レドモ多數ノ例外アリ、即チ不顯性ノ活動性病竈ヲモツモノニ於テハ反ツテ「ツベルクリン」陰性ノモノヨリモ發病シ易ク、又「ツベルクリン反應ガ陽性ニ轉化セル際ニ、之ヲ不良ナル環境ニ置クトキハ結核ニ發病スルモノ多キハ一般ニ觀察セラレアル處ナリ。

以上ノ如ク「アレルギー」ト結核發病トノ關係ハ極メテ複雜ニシテ、ソレニハ他ノ多數ノ要素特ニ病竈ノ狀態、感染ノ機會、環境等ガ重大ナル關係ヲモツモノナリ、故ニ「アレルギー」ト免疫トノ關係ノ鮮明スルタメニハ更ニ詳細ナル研究ヲ要スルナリ。

以上ノ他、「アレルギー」ト免疫トノ關係ニ就テハ、Pirquet ハ痘瘡ニ就テ、Mackenzie, Julianelle, Francis and Tillet ハ肺尖ニ就テ研究シアルモ、何レモ其ノ關係ヲ明膫ニセルモノナシ。

前述セル如ク「アレルギー性皮膚反應ハ不顯性感染ヲナセルモノニ於テモ陽性ニ出現スルモノナリ、故ニ之ヲ團體生活ヲナス多衆ニ就テ試ミ、病毒侵潤ノ程度ヲ知リ、以テ疾病ノ豫防ニ資セントシ試ミタルモノ多シ、殊ニ結核ニ於ケル「ツベルクリン反應ハ、地方的、職業別、生活樣式別、性別、年齡別等ニ詳細ニ調査セラレ、ソレニヨツテ結核病毒汚染ノ程度ヲ推論シ、結核發病トノ關係ヲ考察シ、以テ結核豫防ニ資スルガ如キ研究極メテ多シ。(Pirquet, Mantoux, Calmette, Dow, Scheel, Myers, Myers, Brink, Cummins, Drolet, 小林、太田、杉山)、鼻疽ニ於ケル「マレイン反應モ此ノ目的ニ使用セラレ (Babes, M'Fadyean, Bonome, 並河)、波狀熱ニ於ケル「メルチン」及「アボルチン反應モ此ノ目的ニ使用セラル (Simpson, Straube, Reinsford, Heathman, Goldstein, Taylor)。

「ペスト」ニ關スル皮膚反應ニ就テハ尼子ノ記載アルノミナリ、氏ハ明治38年ノ神戸ニ於ケル「ペスト流行時ニ桃山病院ニ收容セル「ペスト患者ニツキ、皮膚反應及眼反應ヲ行ヒ、同時ニ對照トシテ凝集反應及補體結合反應ヲ行ヘリ、其ノ結果皮膚反應及眼反應ハ「ペスト患者ノ約半數ニ於テ陽性ニ出現スルコトヲ明カニシ、次デ兩者ノ反應ノ强サト凝集反應及補體結合反應トノ間ニハ一定ノ關係ナク、凝集反應ト補體結合反應モ亦併行セサルコトヲ述べ、此ノ皮膚反應及眼反應ハ「ペスト診斷上實際的價値ナシト結論セリ。

余ハ「ペスト皮膚反應ヲ健常者、「ペスト豫防接種ヲナセルモノ、「ペスト患者及治癒者ニ就キ詳細ニ觀察シ、其ノ診斷的價値アルヲ知リ、又免疫トノ關係ニツイテ若干知見ヲ補遺スルヲ得タリ、更ラニ昭和15年ノ晨安「ペスト流行時ニ流行地域內住民ニ就テ調査シ、皮膚反應ト不顯性感染及大衆免疫トノ關係ニツキ極メテ興味深キ成績ヲ得タルニ依リ茲ニ報告シテ諸賢ノ批判ヲ仰ハントス。

第1章 「ベスト」豫防接種者及健常者ニ於テノ成績

第1節 豫 備 試 驗

余ハ「ベスト」弱毒株（P$_1$株、S型菌）ノ37°C45時間培養菌ヲ以テ、$^{1mg}/_{cc}$濃度ノ生理的食鹽水ニヨル菌浮游液ヲ作リ、之ヲ60°Cニテ60分間加熱セル後、其ノ死滅セルコトヲ確メ、之ヲ抗原トシテ、頻回ニ「ベスト・インムノーゲン」ノ豫防接種ヲ受ケタル「ベスト室勤務者（凡ソ1ヶ月1回ノ割合ニテ20回以上ニ亘リテ豫防接種ヲナセルモノナリ）及全然「ベスト」ノ豫防接種ヲ受ケタルコトナキモノニツイテ皮膚反應ヲ檢査セリ。

其ノ檢査術式ハ抗原0.1ccヲ「ツベルクリン注射器ヲ以テ結核ニ於ケルマンツウー氏反應ノ術式ニナラヒ、背部ノ肩胛間部ノ皮内或ハ上膊外側皮内ニ注射シテ、局所ノ所見ヲ觀察セリ、對照トシテ之ヨリ約3乃至5cmヲ距テテ生理的食鹽水0.1ccヲ注射セリ、局所ノ所見ハ多クハ單ナル發赤ノミニシテ腫脹硬結ヲ缺クヲ常トセリ、故ニ發赤ヲ對照トシテ、發赤出現ノ時期、發赤ノ大キサ、其ノ消退ノ時間等ヲ詳細ニ觀察セリ、其ノ成績ハ第1表ニ示セルガ如シ。

第1表　頻回豫防接種セルモノ及健常者ニ於テノ詳細ナル觀察

區分	性	檢査人員	年齡	5分	10″	20″	30″	40″	50″	60″	70″	80″	90″	2時間	3″	4″	5″	6″	7″	8″	1日	2日	成績判定
頻回免疫セラレシモノ	男	1	28	4.2	4.1	4.7	4.1	3.5	3.1	3.2	3.0	2.0	—	—	—	—	—	—	—	—	—	—	卅
	〃	2	30	4.5	5.0	4.5	4.5	3.5	3.5	2.5	2.0	2.0	2.0	1.5	1.5	1.5	2.0	2.5	2.5	2.5	3.0	1.5	卅
	〃	3	27	1.2	1.5	1.5	1.5	1.5	1.5	1.2	1.2	1.0	1.0	—	—	—	1.5	1.5	1.5	2.0	2.0	1.5	土
	〃	4	31	4.5	4.5	5.0	4.0	4.0	2.5	2.0	2.0	2.0	—	—	1.5	2.0	2.0	2.5	2.5	2.5	2.5	1.5	卅
	〃	5	42	1.3	1.5	1.5	1.8	1.5	1.5	1.2	1.5	1.2	1.2	1.2	1.2	1.5	1.5	1.5	1.5	1.5	2.0	1.0	土
	〃	6	22	6.0	5.0	6.5	5.5	4.5	3.5	3.0	3.0	3.0	2.0	1.5	1.5	2.0	2.0	2.0	2.0	2.0	2.0	1.5	卅
	〃	7	23	2.5	2.5	2.5	2.5	2.0	2.0	1.0	—	—	—	—	—	1.5	1.5	2.0	2.0	2.0	2.0	1.0	+
	〃	8	25	—	—	—	—	—	—	—	—	—	—	—	1.5	1.5	1.5	1.5	2.0	2.0	1.0	—	—
	〃	9	27	1.3	1.5	1.5	1.5	1.5	1.2	1.0	1.0	1.0	1.0	1.0	1.0	1.2	1.5	1.5	2.0	2.0	2.5	1.0	—
	〃	10	28	3.0	3.0	2.5	2.5	2.5	2.5	2.0	2.0	2.0	1.0	1.5	2.5	2.5	2.5	3.5	3.5	3.5	2.5	1.5	+
	〃	11	32	—	—	—	—	—	—	—	—	—	—	—	—	—	—	—	—	—	—	—	—
	〃	12	43	2.2	2.5	2.5	2.0	2.0	1.5	1.5	—	—	—	—	1.5	1.5	2.0	2.5	2.5	2.5	—	1.0	+
	〃	13	35	3.5	4.0	4.0	3.0	2.5	2.0	2.0	2.0	2.0	2.0	—	—	—	—	—	—	—	—	—	卅
	〃	14	22	2.5	2.5	3.5	3.0	2.5	2.5	2.0	2.0	2.0	1.5	1.5	1.5	1.5	2.0	2.0	2.0	2.0	2.0	1.5	卅
	〃	15	19	1.5	2.0	2.0	1.5	1.5	1.5	1.5	1.5	1.5	1.5	1.5	1.5	1.5	1.5	1.5	1.5	1.5	2.0	1.5	土
健常ナルモノ	男	1	23	—	—	—	—	—	—	—	—	—	—	—	1.5	1.5	1.5	1.5	1.5	1.5	2.0	1.0	—
	〃	2	27	—	—	—	—	—	—	—	—	—	—	—	1.5	1.5	1.5	1.5	1.5	1.5	—	—	—
	〃	3	36	—	—	—	—	—	—	—	—	—	—	—	—	—	—	—	—	—	—	—	—
	〃	4	32	—	—	—	—	—	—	—	—	—	—	—	1.5	1.5	1.5	1.5	2.0	2.0	2.0	2.0	—
	〃	5	33	—	—	—	—	—	—	—	—	—	—	—	1.5	2.0	2.5	2.5	3.0	3.0	3.0	—	—
	〃	6	41	—	—	—	—	—	—	—	—	—	—	—	1.5	1.5	1.5	1.5	1.5	1.5	1.5	—	—
	〃	7	26	—	—	—	—	—	—	—	—	—	—	—	1.5	1.5	1.5	2.0	2.0	1.5	—	—	—
	〃	8	22	—	—	—	—	—	—	—	—	—	—	—	1.5	1.5	2.0	2.0	2.0	2.0	2.0	1.5	—
	〃	9	21	—	—	—	—	—	—	—	—	—	—	—	—	1.5	1.5	1.5	1.5	2.0	—	—	—
	〃	10	18	—	—	—	—	—	—	—	—	—	—	1.5	1.5	1.5	1.5	1.5	1.5	1.5	2.0	—	—
	〃	11	18	—	—	—	—	—	—	—	—	—	—	—	1.5	1.5	1.5	1.5	—	—	—	—	—
	〃	12	28	—	—	—	—	—	—	—	—	—	—	—	1.5	1.5	1.5	1.5	2.0	2.0	1.5	—	—
	〃	13	26	—	—	—	—	—	—	—	—	—	—	—	1.5	1.5	1.5	1.5	2.0	2.0	2.5	1.5	—
	〃	14	32	—	—	—	—	—	—	—	—	—	—	—	1.5	2.0	2.0	2.0	—	—	—	—	—
	〃	15	25	—	—	—	—	—	—	—	—	—	—	—	1.0	1.2	1.5	1.5	1.5	1.5	1.0	—	—

備考　1. 數字ハ發赤ノ直徑ヲcmニテ示セルモノナリ
　　　2. (—)ハ發赤ヲ現ハサザルモノヲ示ス

　　第1表ニ示セルガ如ク、「ペスト」豫防接種ヲ頻回ニ受ケタルモノハ大部分ニ於テ（約60%）抗原接種後5分間以內ニ接種局所ニ直徑6cmニ及ブ發赤出現シ、此ノ發赤ハ次第ニ著明トナリ、20分乃至30分ニテ最高ニ達シ、ソレヨリ次第ニ褪色縮少シ、早キハ40分、遲クモ2時間ニシテ多クハ消失スルヲ見ル、此ノ際疼痛、瘙痒ハ認メラレズ、ソレヨリ更ラニ觀察ヲ積クル時ハ、早キハ3時間目頃ヨリ再ビ輕度ノ發赤出現シ始メ、輕度ノ疼痛ヲ伴ヒ、コノモノハ24時間後ニ於テ最モ著明ニ認メラレ、48時間ニシテ多クハ再ビ消褪スルモノナリ。

　　「ペスト」ノ豫防接種ヲ受ケタルコトナキ健常者ニ於テハ、抗原ヲ接種スルモ接種直後ニハ其ノ局所ニ何等ノ所見ヲ呈セズ、唯一部ニ於テ接種後約3時間目頃ヨリ輕度ノ發赤現ハレ、輕度ノ疼痛ヲ作ヒ、24時間後ニ於テ最モ著明ニシテ、48時間後ニハ多クハ消失スルヲ認メタリ、對照ニ用ヒタル食鹽水ハ兩者ニ於テ何レモ接種局所ニ何等ノ所見ヲ呈セザリキ。

　　此ノ成績ヨリ觀察スレバ「ペスト」豫防接種者ニ於テ、抗原接種後卽時ニ現ハレル反應ハ「ペスト菌ニヨツテ感作セラレタル個體ニ特異性ニ現ハレル所謂「アレルギー」反應ナリト考ヘルコトヲ得、而シテ24時間後ニ認メラレル局所ノ反應ハ健常者ニ於テモ認メラレルモノナル故「ペスト菌毒素ニヨル反應ナリト考ヘルコトヲ得ベシ。

　　茲ニ於テ余ハ「ペスト・アレルギー反應ト考ヘラレル前述ノ皮膚反應ヲ「ペスト患者ニ試ミテ診斷的價値ノ有無ヲ檢シ、又「ペスト・ワクチン接種者ニ就キ多數ノ觀察ヲナシ之ト免疫トノ關係ヲ知ラントセリ。

　　檢査術式ハ前述セル所ニヨリ、成績ノ判定ハ、抗原接種後20分乃至30分後ノ發赤ノ大サヲ測定シ、其ノ直徑1.0cm以下ヲ（一）トシ、1.1～1.9cmヲ（±）、2.0～2.9cmヲ（十）、3.0～3.9cmヲ（卅）、4.0cm以上ヲ（卌）トナセリ。

第2節　各種抗原ヲ以テセル成績

　　各種細菌性疾患ノ「アレルギー性皮膚反應ヲ檢査スルタメニハ其ノ抗原トシテ其ノ菌體及菌體ヨリ抽出セル Nucleoproteide 或ハ Polysaccharide 等ガ用ヒラレ、其ノ抗原ノ種類ニヨリ反應ノ特異性ノ異ナルコトハ、結核、肺尖、波狀熱、淋疾等ニ就テ發表セラレアル處ナリ、而シテ診斷ノ目的ニハ最モ特異性高キ抗原ヲ選定スルコト必要ナリ、余ハ此ノ目的ノ爲、下記ノ如キ各種ノ抗原ヲ用ヒテ頻回免疫セルモノ及健常者ニツキ皮膚反應ヲ檢セルニ第2表ノ如キ成績ヲ得タリ。

抗原ノ種類

a) 猛毒株(No. 105株)S型37°C 45時間培養菌、$1^{mg}/_{cc}$、菌液60°C 60分加熱殺菌セルモノノ上清。

b) 猛毒株(No. 105株)S型37°C 45時間培養菌、$1^{mg}/_{cc}$、菌液60°C 60分加熱殺菌セルモノ。

c) 猛毒株(No. 105株)R型37°C 45時間培養菌、$1^{mg}/_{cc}$、菌液60°C 60分加熱殺菌セルモノ。

d) 弱毒株(P₁株)S型37°C 45時間培養菌、$1^{mg}/_{cc}$、菌液60°C 60分加熱殺菌セルモノノ上清。

e) 弱毒株(P₁株)S型37° 45時間培養菌、¹ᵐᵍ/cc、菌液60°C 60分加熱殺菌セルモノ。

f) 弱毒株(P₁株)R型37°C 45時間培養菌、¹ᵐᵍ/cc、菌液60°C 60分加熱殺菌セルモノ。

g) 弱毒株(P₁株)S型4°C 7 日間培養菌、¹ᵐᵍ/cc、菌液60°C 60分加熱殺菌セルモノ。

h) 弱毒株(P₁株)S型37°C 45時間培養菌、¹ᵐᵍ cc、菌液、生菌ノママ。

i) 弱毒株(P₁株)R型37°C 45時間培養菌、¹ᵐᵍ/cc、菌液、生菌ノママ。

第2表ニ於テ見ル如ク上述ノ各抗原ノ間ニハ殆ンド其ノ抗原性及特異性ニ毫モ差ヲ認ムルコトヲ得ズ、即チ猛毒株 .弱毒株、S型、R型ノ間ニ抗原性ノ差異ヲ認メズ、又菌體成分ト上清トノ間及37℃培養菌ト4℃培養菌（所謂「エンヴエロープ」ヲ有セズ）トノ間ニモ差異ナク、S型及R型ノ弱毒株生菌ヲ以テスルモ同様ノ抗原性ヲ保有スルヲ認メタリ、但シ弱毒生菌ヲ抗元ニ使用セルトキハ注射直後ノ反應ハ死菌抗原ノ場合ト同様ナルモ24時間後ニ於ケル發赤、腫脹、疼痛等ノ局所反應ハ健常者ニ於テ著明ニシテ、頻回免疫セルモノニ於テハ極メテ輕度ナルカ、又ハ消褪シテ何等ノ所見ヲモ呈セザルモノ多カリキ、健常者ニ就テノ成績ニ於テモ各種抗原ノ間ニ非特異性ノ陽性反應ヲ現ハスモノナカリキ、2例陽性ニ現ハレタルモノハ對照ニ用ヒタル食盥水ニ於テモ發赤ノ出現セルモノニシテ皮膚ノ特異的過敏性ニ起因スルモノト考ヘラル、尚對照トシテ腸チフス菌ヲ加熱殺菌セルモノ、及「コレラ菌ヲ加熱殺菌セルモノヲ抗原トシテ「ペスト皮膚反應陽性者ニ試ミタルモ發赤反應ノ陽性ニ出現セルモノヲ認メザリキ。（表略ス）

又抗原ノ菌量ト抗原性トノ關係ヲ檢査セルニ其ノ成績ハ第3表ニ示セルガ如シ。

第3表 抗原性ト菌量トノ關係

検人委員	性	年齢	抗 原 菌 量						對 照	
			2mg/cc	1mg/cc	1mg/cc上清	0.5mg/cc	0.25mg/cc	0.1mg/cc	生理的食盥水	0.5%石炭酸食盥水
1	男	26	＃	＃	＃	＃	＃	上	-	-
2	〃	23	＃	＃	＃	＃	＃	＃	-	-
3	〃	27	＃	＃	＃	＃	＃	+	-	-
4	〃	28	＃	＃	＃	＃	＃	＃	-	-
5	〃	31	-	-	-	-	-	-	-	-
6	〃	35	+	±	+	+	+	±	-	-
7	〃	25	±	±	±	±	±	±	-	-
8	〃	27	＃	＃	＃	＃	＃	＃	-	-
9	〃	29	＃	＃	＃	＃	＃	＃	-	-
10	〃	30	＃	＃	＃	＃	＃	+	-	-

備考　1．P₁株37℃24時間培養菌各濃度食盥水菌液60℃60分殺菌セルモノヲ抗原トス
　　　2．＃ ＃ + ± - ノ記號ハ第2表ト同様ナリ

本表ニ於テ見ル如ク皮膚反應ノ抗原トシテハ或ル一定量ノ菌量ヲ必要トスルモノナリ、然レドモ發赤ノ大サ及陽性率ハ一定ノ菌量以上ニ於テハ其ノ量ニ比例セザルコトヲ認メタリ。

次ニ消毒藥及過熱ノ抗原性ニ及ス影響ヲ檢査セルニ皮膚反應抗原性ハ0.5%石炭酸或ハ煮沸（100℃、20分間）ニ依リテハ減弱セルコトヲ認メタリ（表略ス）。抗原ノ選擇ニ就テハ更ニ菌體成分ニツキ種々ナル「フラクション」ヲ作リ、ソノ内ノ何レノ成分ガ特異性反應ヲ呈スルモノナルカヲ究明シ、以テ最モ特異性高キ抗原ヲ用ヒルコト必要ナルベシ。

381—9／2

第2表 各種抗元ヲ以テセル成績

区分	検人委員	性	年齢	a抗原	b 〃	c 〃	d 〃	e 〃	f 〃	g 〃	h 〃	i 〃	静脈
類固免疫セルモノ	1	男	28	++	++	+	++	+	+++	++	++	++	−
	2	〃	30	++	++	++	++	+	+++	++	++	++	
	3	〃	27	+	±	+	±	±	±	+	+	+	
	4	〃	31	+++	++	++	++	+	+++	++	++	++	
	5	〃	42	±	±	±	±	+	±	±	±	±	−
	6	〃	22	++	++	++	++	++	++	++	++	+	−
	7	〃	23	+	±	+	+	+	+	+	+	+	−
	8	〃	25	−	−	−	−	−	−	−	−	−	
	9	〃	27	−	−	±	−	±	−	±	±	±	±
	10	〃	28	+	+	±	+	+	+	+	+	+	
	11	〃	32	−	−	−	−	−	−	−	−	−	
	12	〃	43	+	+	+	+	±	+	+	+	±	
	13	〃	35	++	++	++	++	++	++	++	++	++	
	14	〃	22	+++	++	+++	++	++	+++	++	+++	++	
	15	〃	19	+	+	±	±	+	+	+	+	+	
	16	〃	21	++	++	++	+	+++	+++	+++	++	++	
	17	〃	25	+	+	±	++	+	+++	++	++	++	
	18	〃	26	±	+	±	+	+	+	+	+	+	
	19	〃	26	+	±	±	±	±	±	±	±	±	
	20	〃	28	+	+	+	+	+	+	+	+	+	
健常ナルモノ	1	男	23	−	−	−	−	−	−	−	−	−	
	2	〃	27	−	−	−	−	−	−	−	−	−	
	3	〃	32	−	−	−	−	−	−	−	−	−	
	4	〃	33	−	−	−	−	−	−	−	−	−	
	5	〃	45	−	−	−	−	−	−	−	−	−	
	6	〃	21	+	±	±	+	±	±	+	+	+	+
	7	〃	23	−	−	−	−	−	−	−	−	−	
	8	〃	26	−	−	−	−	−	−	−	−	−	
	9	〃	22	−	−	−	−	−	−	−	−	−	
	10	〃	23	−	−	−	−	−	−	−	−	−	
	11	〃	25	±	±	−	−	−	±	−	−	−	
	12	〃	28	−	−	±	±	−	±	−	−	−	
	13	〃	29	−	−	−	−	−	−	−	−	−	
	14	〃	30	−	±	±	±	−	−	−	−	−	
	15	〃	24	±	±	±	±	+	+	±	±	±	±
	16	〃	27	−	−	−	±	−	−	−	−	−	
	17	〃	22	−	−	±	−	−	−	−	−	−	
	18	〃	19	−	−	−	−	−	−	±	−	−	
	19	〃	27	+	+	+	+	+	+	+	±	±	+
	20	〃	26	−	−	±	±	−	−	−	−	−	
	21	〃	25	−	−	−	−	−	−	−	−	−	
	22	〃	23	−	−	−	−	−	−	−	−	−	
	23	〃	25	−	−	−	−	−	−	−	−	−	
	24	〃	26	−	−	−	−	−	−	−	−	−	
	25	〃	31	−	−	−	−	−	−	−	−	⊥	

備考　− 膿疹ノ直径(平均セルモノ)1.0cm以下ノモノ
　　　± 膿疹ノ直径　1.1～1.9cm
　　　十 膿疹ノ直径　2.0～2.9cm
　　　艹 〃 〃　3.0～3.9cm
　　　艹 〃 〃　4.0cm以上ノモノ

余ノ實驗シタル範圍內ニ於テハ各抗原トモ大體同樣ノ抗原性ヲ有スルコトヲ認メタリ、依ツテ皮膚反應抗原トシテハ、「ペスト菌37°C 45時間培養菌ヲ以テ $1^{mg}/_{cc}$ 食鹽水菌液ヲ作リ、之ヲ60°C ニテ60分間加熱殺菌シ、菌生存試驗及雜菌試驗ヲ行ヒ合格セルモノニ0.4%ノ割合ニ石炭酸ヲ加ヘタルモノヲ使用スルコトトセリ。

第3節　豫防接種者ニ就テノ檢査成績

「ペスト・インムノーゲン」ヲ1回接種セルモノ及2回接種（2週間間隔）セルモノニ就キ、最終接種後約1ケ月ヲ經テ皮膚反應ヲ檢査セルニ、其ノ成績ハ第4表ノ如シ、即チ1回接種者ハ其ノ陽性率7.9%ナルニ比シ、2回接種者ハ其ノ陽性率15.8%ニシテ、明ニ豫防接種ニヨリテ陽性率ノ高クナルヲ認ムルコトヲ得タリ。

第4表　「ペスト・インムノーゲン接種者ニ就テノ檢査成績

區別	豫防接種回數	檢査人員	檢査成績 ⧻	⧻	+	±	-
I	1回	101人		2	6	10	83
			8 (7.9%)			93(92.1%)	
II	2回	63人	1	3	6	10	43
			10(15.8%)			53(84.2%)	

尙昭和15年10月下旬新京ニ於ケル「ペスト流行時ニ住民ニ就テ檢査セル成績ハ第5表ニ示ス如シ。

第5表　新京流行時ニ於ケル検査成績（検査月日、昭和15年11月6日及7日）

区別	構成人員	勤務種別	豫防接種状況	検査人員	検　査　成　績				
					＋	＃	＋	±	－
I	市民（患者発生地域外ノ義勇奉公隊員）	1～2日間防投薬務ノ援助ス	1回（10月上旬）	169人	1	8 12(7.1%)	3	23	134 157(92.9%)
II	市民（「ペスト患者隔離所勤務員）	「ペスト患者及健康罹病者ノ看護	1回（10月上旬）	71人		2 6(8.4%)	4	18	47 65(91.6%)
III	学生（哈爾大及新京醫大）	検診及検索業務ノ援助	1回（10月中旬）	45人	1	1 3(6.6%)	1	24	18 42(93.4%)
IV	軍隊 1（派遣セラレタルモノ）	検診治療	1回（10月中旬）	164人	1	3 14(8.5%)	10	24	126 150(91.5%)
V	軍隊 1（加茂部隊関係者）	検索事務	2回（9月中旬及下旬）中ニハ3回セルモノアリ	114人	5	4 24(21%)	15	26	64 90(79%)

備考　接種セルワクチンハ主トシテ「ペスト・インムノーゲン」ナルモ、中ニハ衛生技術廠製
　　　ペスト・ワクチン」ヲ用ヒタルモノモアリ

之ニ依ツテ見ルモ「ペスト皮膚反應ノ陽性率ハ豫防接種ノ回數ニ比例スルコト認メラル、此ノ際ニハ住民ニ就テハ「ペスト・インムノーゲン」ト普通「ペスト・ワクチン」混用セラレタルタメ「ワクチン別ニコル詳細ナル觀察ヲナシ得ザリシモ、概ネ皮膚反應ノ陽性率ハ豫防接種回數ノ多キモノニ於テ高キコトヲ認ムルヲ得タリ。

又「ペスト・インムノーゲン」ヲ2乃至3回接種セルモノ及「ペスト豫防接種ヲ受ケタルコトナキ健常者ニ就テ、二、三ノ抗原ヲ用ヒテ皮膚反應ヲ検査セル成績ハ第6表及第7表ニ示セルガ如シ。

第6表　「ベスト・インムノーゲン接種者ニツキ、二、三ノ抗原ヲ
以テセル検査成績

区別	抗原	検査人員	検	査	成	績	
			┼┼	┼	+	±	
I	a	143人	6	11	17	47	62
				34(23.7%)		109(76.3%)	
II	b	158人	11	9	20	61	57
				40(25.3%)		118(74.7%)	
III	c	146人	7	14	16	58	51
				37(25.4%)		109(74.6%)	
IV	d	142人	14	56	41	24	7
				111(78.2%)		31(21.8%)	
V	e	154人			4	26	124
				4(2.6%)		150(97.4%)	
VI	f	152人			2	14	136
				2(1.3%)		150(98.7%)	

備考　抗原　a……P₁株S型37°C 45時間培養　1mg/cc 生菌
b……P₁株S型37°C 45時間培養　1mg/cc 60°C 60分死菌
c……同上ノ上済
d……「ベスト治療用馬血清
e……腸チフス菌37°C 24時間培養　1mg/cc 60°C 60分死菌
f……生理的食塩水

第7表　健常者ニツキ、二、三抗原ヲ以テセル偽陽性反應検査成績

区別	抗原	検査人員	検	査	成	績	
			┼┼	┼	+	±	
I	a	160人		1	5	10	144
				6(3.8%)		154(96.2)%	
II	b	160人		2	5	13	140
				7(4.4%)		153(95.6%)	
III	c	160人		1	6	15	138
				7(4.4%)		153(95.6%)	
III	d	135人	13	54	40	20	8
				107(79.3%)		28(20.7%)	
V	e	153人		1	3	14	135
				4(2.6%)		149(97.4%)	

備考　抗原　a……P₁株S型37°C 45時間培養　1mg/cc 生菌　b……同上 1mg/cc 60°C 60分死菌
c……同上ノ上済　d……「ベスト治療用馬血清　e……生理的食塩水

之ニヨツテ観レバ前章ノ成績ト同様ニ各抗原ノ間ニ抗原性ノ遑異ヲ認ムルコトヲ得ザリキ、但シ健常者ニ於テモ3乃至5％内外ノ發赤陽性者ヲ認メタリ、之ハ非特異性低陽性反應ニシテ、斯カルモノハ食鹽水ニヨツテモ、接種局所ニ發赤ノ出現スルモノニシテ、其ノ本態ハ不明ナルモ、皮膚ノ特異的過敏性ニヨルモノナラント考ヘラル。

以上ノ檢査成績ヨリ「ベスト皮膚反應ハ若干ノ非特異性反應(低陽性反應)ハアルモ、概ネ「ベスト菌ニヨリテ感作セラレタル個體ニ於テ陽性ニ出現スル特異性「アレルギー反應ナリト考ヘラル。

第4節　小　　括

「ベスト・インムノーゲン」類同接種者及健常者(「ベスト豫防接種ヲ受ケタルコトナキモノ)ニ就テ「ベスト菌抗原ヲ以テ、抗原皮内接種ニヨル皮膚反應ヲ詳細ニ觀察セル結果、「ベスト菌ニ依ツテ感作セラレタルト考ヘラレル個體ニ於テハ接種直後ニ特異性過敏反應ノ出現スルコトヲ觀察セリ、而シテ「ベスト菌ヨリ作レル種々ノ抗原ヲ用ヒテ其ノ抗原性ヲ檢査セルニ、其ノ間ニ特ニ特異性ノ高キモノヲ見出シ得ザリキ、又「ベスト菌以外ノ細菌卽チ腸チフス菌、「コレラ菌等ヲ抗原トシテ檢査セル場合ニハ陽性反應ノ出現セザルコトヲ認メタリ、之ニ依リテ余ノ試ミタル皮膚反應ハ「ベスト菌トソレニ依リテ感作セラレタル個體トノ間ニ起ル特異性「アレルギー反應ナリト考ヘラル。

尚本ベスト皮膚反應ハ其ノ反應ノ出現及消失ノ時間的關係ニ於テ結核其ノ他ノモノニ比シテ極メテ早期ニ出現シ且ツ短時間ニ消失スルヲ特徴トスルモ、「アレルギー性反應ノ中ニハ例ヘバ血清病ニ於テ見ル血清注射直後ニ起ル Pirquet 氏等ノ所謂卽時反應ノ如ク極メテ速カニ出現スルモノノ在スル點ヨリ考察スレバ本皮膚反應ヲ「アレルギー性反應ト考フルモ支障ナカラン。

上述セル實驗成績ヨリ「ベスト」皮膚反應用抗原トシテハ第2節ニ述ベタルガ如キモノヲ用ヒ、檢査術式ハ結核ニ於ケルマンツウー氏反應ニナラヒ、成績ノ判定ハ第1節ニ述ベタルガ如キ標準ニヨルコトト定メタリ。

此ノ方法ニ從ツテ多數ニ就キ檢査セル結果、「ベスト」皮膚反應ノ陽性率ハ「ベスト・ワクチン」ノ接種回數ノ多キ者ニ於テ高ク、尚健常者ニ於テモ3乃至5％内外ノ低陽性者ヲ出スコトヲ認メタリ。

第2章　「ベスト患者ニ就テノ成績

第1節　「ベスト治癒者ニ就テノ成績

昭和15年度農安ニ於ケル「ベスト流行時ニ、菌檢索ニヨリ「ベスト」ト診斷サレ、看護治療ノ結果恢復セル「ベスト治癒者8名ニ就キ、前章ニ述ベタル術式ニ從ツテ皮膚反應ヲ行ヒ、詳細ニ觀察セル成績ハ第8表ニ示セルガ如シ。

第8表　「ペスト恢復患者ニ就テノ詳細ナル觀察」（於鼠安）（11月3日）

檢査人員	性	年齢	科名	日	8分	10	20	30	40	50	60	70	80	90秒	2時間	3	4	5	6	7	8	1日	2日	成績判定
1	女	35	腺ペスト	89日	5.0	6.5	6.5	6.0	5.0	4.5	4.5	4.5	1.4	1.2	1.2	—	—	—	—	—	—	2.5	2.0	艹
2	男	27	腺ペスト	61日	5.0	5.5	5.5	5.0	5.0	3.0	1.5	1.2	1.2	1.2	1.0	—	—	—	—	—	—	—	—	艹
3	〃	36	皮膚ペスト	57日	4.0	4.5	4.5	4.0	4.0	4.0	3.0	2.0	2.0	1.5	1.5	—	—	—	—	1.5	2.0	2.0	—	艹
4	女	59	腺ペスト	51日	4.5	4.5	5.0	4.5	3.5	2.0	2.5	1.5	—	—	—	—	—	—	—	—	—	—	—	艹
5	男	55	腺ペスト	46日	3.5	4.0	4.0	3.5	3.5	3.5	3.5	3.5	1.5	—	—	—	—	—	—	1.5	2.0	1.5	—	艹
6	女	26	腺ペスト	43日	3.0	3.5	3.5	3.5	3.0	3.0	2.0	1.5	1.5	—	—	—	1.5	1.5	1.5	1.5	2.0	1.5	—	艹
7	〃	26	腺ペスト	45日	4.8	4.5	5.0	5.0	5.0	4.5	4.5	2.0	1.5	—	—	—	—	—	—	—	—	—	—	艹
8	男	5	腺ペスト	26日	3.0	3.5	3.5	4.0	4.0	3.0	2.0	1.5	—	—	1.5	1.5	1.5	1.5	1.5	2.0	2.0	—	—	艹

備考　1．數字ハ圓赤ノ直徑（平均セルモノ）ヲcmニテ示セルモノナリ
　　　2．一ハ圓赤ヲ現ハサザルモノヲ示ス

本表ニ於テ見ル如ク「ペスト恢復者ニ於テハ抗原接種後、即時ニ接種局所ニ高度ノ發赤出現シ、20分乃至30分ニテ最高ニ達シ、ソレヨリ次第ニ消褪縮小シ、早キハ1時間遲クモ2時間ニシテ其ノ消褪スルヲ認メタリ、尚觀察ヲ被クルトキハ、4乃至6時間ニシテ輕度ノ發赤出現シ、24時間ニシテ最高ニ達シ2日ニシテ次第ニ消褪スルモノヲ一部ニ於テ認メタリ、此ノ成績ハ前章ニ於テ「ペスト豫防接種者ニ就テ觀察セル成績ト同樣ナルモノナリ、然レドモ其ノ陽性率ハ豫防接種者ニ於テハ、50％內外ナルニ比シ、「ペスト治癒者ニ於テハ、其ノ陽性率100％ナリキ。

尚各種抗原ヲ用ヒテ「ペスト治癒者ニ就キ皮膚反應ヲ檢査セル成績ハ第9表ニ示セルガ如シ。

第9表　「ペスト恢復患者ニ就キ二、三ノ抗原ヲ以テセル成績

檢査人口	性	年齡	病　名	病日	抗 原 a	b	c	對 d	照 e	f	凝集反應	沈降反應	補合體結應
1	女	35	右腋腺ペスト」(中)	91日	+		+	+	−	−	+40	+4	+20
2	男	27	左鼠蹊腺「ペ」(重)	63日	+		+	+	−	−	+80	+4	+40
3	男	36	皮　膚「ペ」(輕)	59日	+		+	+	±	−	+40	+1	+20
4	女	59	左鼠蹊腺「ペ」(重)	53日	−		+	+	−	−	−	−	−
5	女	55	右腋腺「ペ」(中)	48日	+		+	+	−	−	+160	+8	+80
6	女	26	右頸腺「ペ」(中)	47日	−			+	±	−	+40	+2	+10
7	男	6	左膝窩腺「ペ」(中)	47日	+	+	+	+	−	−	+40	+2	+10
8	女	26	右腋腺「ペ」(輕)	45日	+	+	+	+	±	−	−	+2	+10
9	男	54	右鼠蹊腺「ペ」(輕)	30日	+	+	+	+	±	−	−	−	−
10	男	5	右腋腺「ペ」(輕)	28日	+		+	+	−	−	+20	+2	+20
11	女	42	右膝窩腺「ペ」(重)	23日	+	+	+	+	−	−	+20	+1	+5
12	男	15	右腋腺「ペ」(輕)	22日	+	+	++	+	−	−	+20	+1	+5
13	女	17	右鼠蹊腺「ペ」(輕)	22日	+	+	+	+	±	−	+20	+1	+10
14	男	35	右鼠蹊腺「ペ」(輕)	21日	+	+	+	+	−	−	−	−	−
15	女	14	左腋腺「ペ」(輕)	17日	+	+	+	+	±	−	−	−	−
16	男	15	左鼠蹊腺「ペ」(輕)	27日	+	+	+	+	−	−	−	−	−
17	女	39	右鼠蹊腺「ペ」(中)	88日	+	+	+	+	−	−	/	/	/
18	男	33	皮　膚「ペ」(輕)	81日	+	+	+	+	−	−	/	/	/
19	女	4	右鼠蹊腺「ペ」(中)	76日	+	+	+	+	−	−	/	/	/

備考　1. 抗原　a……P株S型37℃45時間培養 $1mg/cc$ 生菌　　b……同上 $1mg/cc$ 60℃60分死菌　　c……同上ノ上清　　d……「ペスト」治療用馬血清　　e……腸チフス菌37℃24時間培養 $1mg/cc$ 60℃60分死菌　　f……生理的食鹽水

2. 病名ノ(中)ハ中等症、(重)ハ重症、(輕)ハ輕症ヲ示ス

3. 凝集反應 +40 ハ血清稀釋ニヨル最高凝集價 1:40 ナルコトヲ示ス

4. 沈降反應 +4 ハ抗元稀釋ニヨリ 1:4 マデ陽性ナルコトヲ示ス

5. 補體結合反應 +20 ハ血清稀釋ニテ 1:20 マデ k、或sp、陽性ナルコトヲ示ス

此ノ成績ニヨツテモ已ニ前章ニ述ベタルガ如ク、各種抗原ノ間ニ抗原性ノ差異ヲ認ムルコトヲ得ザリキ、對照トミテ用ヒタル腸チフス菌及食鹽水ニヨツテハ陽性反應ヲ示セルモノナカリキ。

尚同時ニ檢査セル患者血清ノ凝集反應、沈降反應及補體結合反應ノ檢査成績ヲ比較スレバ、「ペスト皮膚反應ハ最モ陽性率高ク、「ペスト治癒者ニ於テハ100％陽性ニ出現スルヲ認メタリ。

第2節　病日ト皮膚反應出現ノ關係ニ就テ

「ペスト皮膚反應ハ「ペスト治癒者ニ於テハ100％陽性ニ出現スルモノナルコトハ前節ニ於テ述ベタル如クナルモ、此ノ反應ノ陽性出現ト病日トノ關係ヲ知ルコトハ、皮膚反應ノ診斷的價値ヲ云々スル上ニ於テ極メテ必要ナリ。依ツテ「ペスト患者ニ就キ皮膚反應ヲ病日ヲ追ヒテ檢査セリ、然レドモ「ペスト」ハ一般ニ病狀激烈經過急激ナルタメ充分ナル觀察ヲナスコト困難ニシテ僅カニ數例ニ就テ檢査セルノミ。其ノ成績ハ第10表ノ如シ。

第10表　「ペスト患者ニ就テノ成績（於農安10.20～11.9）

檢査人員	性	年齢	病名	豫防接種轉歸	病日 1	2	3	4	5	6	7	8	9	10	11	12	13	14	15	16	17	18	19
1	男	45	腺「ペスト」	13/7 15/9 死								+							+	死			
2	女	15	腺「ペスト」	13/7 13/9 治癒								±		+	+							++	
3	男	31	腺「ペスト」	12/7;13/9 22/10											±								
5	男	26	腺「ペスト」	不明 死								− 死											
6	男	35	腺「ペスト」	〃 死			± 死																
7	女	26	腺「ペスト」	〃 治癒					±				±				+				++		++
8	男	32	腺「ペスト」	〃 〃															+			++	

備考　豫防接種、13/7ハ7月13日ニ接種セルコトヲ示ス

第11表　「ペスト容疑患者ニ就テノ成績（於農安10.20～11.9）

檢査人員	性	年齢	科名	豫防接種轉歸	病日 1	2	3	4	5	6	7	8	9	10	11	12	13	14	15	16	17	18	19
1	男	38	急性氣管支炎	13/7 5/9 治癒			±		±			±						±				±	
2	男	10	〃	13/7 4/9 〃						±								±					
3	男	49	右眼瞼炎	13/7 〃																−		− ±	
4	男	14	豫防接種反應熱	13/7 26/10 〃	+	+				+				+							±		
5	男	6	張熱眼瞼	13/7 23/10 〃				±						±								±	
6	男	15	〃	14/7 22/10 〃		±					±							±				±	
7	女	9	張熱	13/7 〃		−				−			−								−	±	
8	男	6	〃	5/9 24/10 〃				±			±											+	
9	男	9	〃	13/7 5/9 20/10 〃	+		+		+				+				++				++		

備考　豫防接種、13/7ハ7月13日ニ接種セルコトヲ示ス

観察数少キタメニ、本表ノ成績ノミニヨツテ結論ヲ下スハ困難ナルモ、此ノ成績ヨリ判断スレ
バ皮膚反應ハ概ネ第9病日頃ヨリ弱陽性ニ出現シ、次第ニ強陽性トナリ、第3週乃至第4週ニ於
テ最高ニ達シ、ソレヨリ相當ノ期間陽性ニ出現スルモノノ如ク考ヘラル、然レドモ發病ノ當初ニ
於テハ陽性ニ出現スルコトナク、從ツテ「ベスト」ノ早期診斷ニハ有効ナラザルナリ。

又他ノ原因ニヨリテ發熱セル患者ニ就テ檢査セルニ、此レ等ノ者ニ於テハ發病後2週乃至3週
經過セルモ皮膚反應ノ陽性ニ出現スルモノナカリキ（第11表）。故ニ「ベスト流行時ニ不明ノ高熱
ヲ持續シ而モ臨床的ニハ明確ニ「ベスト」タルコト認メ難ク、又菌檢索、血清反應檢査等ニヨリ
テ診斷不可能ナルトキニモ、此ノ皮膚反應ニヨツテ概ネソレガ「ベスト」ナルカ否カヲ推定シ得ル
モノナリ。而シテ「ベスト豫防接種ニヨル陽性反應及皮膚ノ特異的過敏性ニ基ク考ヘラレル假
陽性反應ヲ除外シ得レバ「ベスト」ト斷定スルモ支障ナキモノナリ（本章第3節參照）、以上ノ意味
ニ於テ「ベスト皮膚反應ハ診斷的價値アリト云フコトヲ得ベシ。

第3節 他ノ傳染性熱性患者ニ就テノ成績

他ノ傳染性熱性疾患ノ患者及治癒者ニ就キ「ベスト皮膚反應ヲ檢査セル成績ハ第12表ニ示セル
ガ如シ。

第12表 他ノ傳染病患者ニ就テノ成績

檢査人員	性	年齢	病 名	病日	檢査成績		
					「ベスト抗原	食塩	水
1	男	26	赤 痢	25日	—		—
2	男	23	赤 痢	34日	—		—
3	男	15	赤 痢	35日	—		—
4	女	28	赤 痢	22日	—		—
5	女	29	赤 痢	52日	—		—
6	男	30	腸チフス」	36日	—		—
7	女	18	腸チフス」	53日	—		—
8	男	24	腸チフス」	72日	—		—
9	男	27	腸チフス」	82日	±		—
10	女	28	腸チフス」	56日	—		—
11	女	26	腸チフス」	38日	—		—
12	男	32	腸チフス」	56日	—		—
13	男	45	腸チフス」	92日	±		±
14	男	28	腸チフス」	78日	—		—
15	女	22	腸チフス」	72日	—		—

本表ニ於テ明ナル如ク、「ペスト皮膚反應」ハ「ペスト以外ノ熱性疾患ニ就テハ陽性ニ出現セルモノナシ、而シテ前述セル如ク「ペスト」治癒者ニ於テハ100%陽性ニ出現スルモノナレバ、極メテ特異性高キ反應ナリト云フコトヲ得ベシ。

第4節 小 括

余ハ「ペスト」治癒者ニ就キ「ペスト皮膚反應ヲ檢査セルニ、其ノ陽性率100%ナルコトヲ認メタリ、更ラニ「ペスト患者ニ就テ檢査セルニ、發病ノ當初ニ於テハ陰性ナルモ、第9病日ノ頃ヨリ弱陽性ニ出現シ、ソレヨリ次第ニ強陽性トナリ第3週乃至第4週ニ於テ最高ニ達シ、ソレヨリ尚相當期間陽性ニ出現スルモノナルコトヲ認メタリ、「ペスト菌以外ノ腸チフス菌ヲ抗原トセル場合ニ於テハ陽性反應ヲ呈スルモノナカリキ。

又他ノ傳染性疾患即チ腸チフス」、赤痢、肺炎、氣管枝炎等ノ患者及治癒者ニ就テ檢査セルニ何レモ陽性反應ヲ呈スルモノナキヲ認メタリ、即チ「ペスト皮膚反應」ハ「ペスト患者ニ於テ極メテ高キ特異性ヲ示スモノナリト云フヲ得ベシ、然レドモ前章ニ於テ述ベタル如ク、此ノ反應ハ「ペスト菌ニテ人工的ニ感作セラレタル個體（「ペスト豫防接種ヲナセルモノ）ニ於テモ陽性ニ出現スルモノニシテ、又皮膚ノ特異的過敏性ヲ有スルト考ヘラレル者ニ於テモ僞陽性反應ヲ呈スルモノナリ（之ハ食鹽水ヲ對照ニ用ヒテ檢査スルコトニヨリ除外スルコトヲ得）、從ツテ「ペスト皮膚反應ニヨツテ「ペスト」ヲ診斷セントスルトキニハ、是等ノ點ヲ特ニ考慮セザレバ誤チニ陷ルコトアルベシ。

第3章 「ペス 流行地ニ於ケル檢査成績

昭和15年6月ヨリ11月ニ至ル農安「ペスト流行時ニ其ノ流行ノ根元地タル農安街ニ於ケル住民ニツキ「ペスト皮膚反應ヲ檢査シ、之ヲ地域別、性別及年齡別ニ觀察セルニ極メテ興味深キ成績ヲ得タリ。

尚參考ニ資スル爲メ茲ニ農安ニ於ケル「ペスト流行ノ概況ト豫防接種實施ノ概況ヲ述ベントス。

昭和15年農安ニ於ケル「ペスト流行ノ概況

農安街ハ戸數5600餘、人口31000餘人ノ滿洲的ノ都市ニシテ、所謂滿洲ペスト」常在地帶ノ東部ニ位シ、農産物ノ集散市場ナリ、數年來縣城内ニハ「ペスト患者ノ發生ヲ見ザリシモ本年6月中旬西大街農安醫院附近ヨリ「ペスト患者初發シ、ソレヨリ相次イデ患者ノ發生ヲ見、流行地域ハ漸次擴大セラレ、遂ニ全縣城内ヨリ縣城外ノ諸部落ニ迄及ビ、9月ノ候患者最モ多發シ、10月ニハ稍々其ノ疫勢ヲ弱メ、11月ニ至リテ殆ド終熄セリ。

豫防接種實施ノ概況

流行發生前ニハ豫防接種ハ實施セザリキ、而シテ流行發生後直チニ第1回ヲ7月13日ヨリ7月20日ニ至ル間ニ實施セリ、其ノ間ニ使用セル「ワクチン」ハ「ペスト・インムノーゲン」ニシテ、謹

防接種普及ノ程度ハ全住民ノ約$\frac{2}{3}$ト考ヘラル。

第2回ハ9月3日ヨリ9月9日ノ間ニ實施セラレ、其ノ時使用セル「ワクチン」ハ第1回ト同様ノモノナリ。此ノ時ハ主トシテ患者多發地區ノ住民ニノミ實施セラレタリ。第3回ハ10月21日ヨリ10月25日ノ間ニ實施セラレタリ、此ノ時使用セル「ワクチン」ハ前回ト同様ニ「ペスト・インムノーゲン」ニシテ、實施セル範圍ハ全地域ニ亘リ、殆ド全住民ニ普及サレタリ。

第1節 地域別檢査成績

農安縣街ニ於テ凡ソ30戸乃至50戸ヲ一檢査單位トシ（牌ヲ單位トシテ區分セリ）、各地域ニ亘リ適當ナル檢査區域16ケ所ヲ選定シ、11月1日ヨリ11月5日ニ至ル間ニ於テ其ノ住民ニツキ「ペスト皮膚反應ヲ檢査セリ、檢査時使用セル抗原ハ第1章ニ述ベタル方法ニ從ツテ作リタルモノニシテ、其ノ檢査術式ハ第1章ニ述ベタル方法ニ從ヘリ。

其ノ地域別檢査成績ハ第13表ニ示ス如シ。

第13表　地域別検査成績(於農安 ¹/ₓᵢ～⁵/ₓᵢ)

区分	検査区域	\[ペスト\]患者發生状況 6月	7月	8月	9月	10月	計	豫防接種	検査人口	検査成績 卌	丗	+	±	-
患者多發地區	1		4	20			24	2回 / 1回	94人	21	34 / 77(81.9%)	22	9 / 17(18.1%)	8
	2		7	3			10	2回 / 1回	56人	12	18 / 41(73.2%)	11	6 / 15(26.8%)	9
	3		6		5(上旬)		11	2回 / 1回	169人	31	45 / 106(62.7%)	30	36 / 63(27.3%)	27
	4		3(1)	2(1)	1(上旬)	6(2)		2回 / 1回	281人	72	64 / 183(65.1%)	47	70 / 98(34.9%)	28
	5			2	1(上旬)		3	2回 / 1回	24人	12	7 / 20(83.3%)	1	2 / 4(16.7%)	2
	6			2	1(上旬)		3	2回 / 1回	141人	41	33 / 105(74.4%)	31	35 / 36(25.6%)	1
患者散發地區	1			4			4	3回 / 1回	166人	22	18 / 64(38.5%)	24	49 / 102(61.5%)	53
	2		6				6	1回 / 1回	97人	4	17 / 32(33%)	11	31 / 65(67%)	34
	3		1(1)		1(1)		2回 / 1回		177人	12	24 / 57(32.2%)	21	19 / 120(67.8%)	101
	4		(1)		0(1)		2回 / 1回		48人	2	5 / 17(35.4%)	10	10 / 31(64.6%)	21
	5		(1)		0(1)		2回 / 1回		59人	4	3 / 17(28.8%)	10	13 / 42(71.2%)	29
患者非發生地區	1						0	1回 / 1回	168人	2	1 / 11(6.6%)	8	81 / 157(93.4%)	76
	2						0	1回 / 1回	103人		5 / 15(14.5%)	10	76 / 88(85.5%)	12
	3						0	1回 / 1回	82人		4 / 8(9.8%)	4	17 / 74(90.2%)	57
	4						0	2回 / 1回	80人		1 / 11(13.7%)	10	47 / 69(86.3%)	22
	5						0	2回 / 1回	38人	1	1 / 6(15.8%)	4	11 / 32(84.2%)	21
現患多發地區	1			1	4		5	1回 / 1回	39人	2	6 / 16(41%)	8	10 / 23(59%)	13
	2				7		7	2回 / 1回	123人	12	14 / 42(34.1%)	16	26 / 81(65.9%)	55

備考　1.「ペスト」患者發生ノ(　)ハ推定「ペスト患者数ヲ示ス

即チ患者多發地區ニ於テハ6ケ所ヲ選定シ検査セルニ各箇所トモ皮膚反應賜性率ハ60%乃至80

532

％ナリキ、斯ル地域ニ於テハ7月及8月ノ候最モ患者多發シ、10月ニ至レバ其ノ發生数ノ漸次減少シ来タルヲ見得ベシ、殊ニ1及2ノ箇所ニ於テハ其ノ傾向著明ナリ。

患者ノ散發セル地區ニ於テハ5ケ所ヲ選定シ検査セルニ各箇所トモ皮膚反應ノ陽性率ハ30％内外ナリキ、患者ノ發生セザリシ地區ニツイテハ5ケ所ヲ選定シテ検査セルニ各箇所トモ皮膚反應ノ陽性率ハ7％乃至15％ノ間ニアリキ。

而シテ皮膚反應検査當時最モ患者ノ多發シアル地區ニ就テハ2ケ所ヲ選定シ検査セルニ、其ノ陽性率ハ30％乃至40％ノ間ニアリキ、此ノ地域ハ9月ノ下旬ヨリ患者發生シ、10月ニハ相當数ノ患者ヲ出シ、11月検査當時尚患者ノ發生止マザル地區ニシテ、斯ル地區ニ於テ皮膚反應ノ陽性率30％内外ナルコトハ、7月及8月ノ候患者多發セルニ10月ニ至リテハ殆ド患者ノ發生ヲ見ザルニ至リシ地區ニ於テ、其ノ陽性率70％内外ナリシコトト、比較考察スルトキハ、皮膚反應ノ陽性率ト流行ノ消長トノ間ニ一定ノ關係ノ存スベキコトヲ思ハセルモノニシテ。極メテ興味深キ成績ナリト考ヘラル。

上述セル成績ヲ総括シテ示セバ第14表ノ如シ。

第14表　総括セル成績

區分	患者發生状況 7月	8月	9月	10月	計	豫防接種 7月	10月	検査人口	検査成績 −	+	±	計	±	−	計
患疑者地多區	14 (1)	31 (1)	4 (上旬)	8 (2)	57人	2回	1回	765人	189 24.7％	201 26.3％	142 18.5％	532 69.5％	158 20.6％	75 9.9％	233 30.5％
患發者地散區		10	1 (3)		11人 (3)	2回	1回	547人	44 8.0％	67 12.2％	76 13.9％	187 34.1％	122 22.3％	238 43.6％	360 65.9％
患左者地非發區一				0		2回	1回	471人	3 0.6％	12 2.5％	36 7.6％	51 10.7％	232 49.2％	188 40.1％	420 89.3％
現發患地多區			1	11	12人	2回	1回	162人	14 8.6％	20 12.3％	24 14.8％	58 35.7％	36 22.2％	68 42.1％	104 64.3％

備考　患者發生ノ（　）内ハ推定ペスト患者ノ数ヲ示ス

又鑫安縣城外ノ部落ニツキ、患者發生セル部落ト發生セザリシ部落ニ於テ皮膚反應ヲ検査セルニ第15表ノ如キ成績ヲ得タリ、之ニ依ツテ見ルモ患者發生部落ハ非發生部落ニ比シ、皮膚反應ノ陽性率極メテ高キコトヲ認メ得ルナリ。

第15表　部落民ニ就テノ検査成績（²/XI）

区分	検査地域	患者発生状況						予防接種				検査人口	検査成績				
		6月	7月	8月	9月	10月	計	7月	8月	9月	10月		卌	卅	十	±	―
患者非発生部落	1				0 1回				2回			73人		1	6	42	24
														7(9.6%)		66(90.4%)	
	2				0 1回				1回			139人	1	2	9	88	39
														12(8.6%)		127(91.4%)	
患者発生部落	1		6	5 11人 (上旬) (20～27)			2回					163人	24	6	16	70	52
														46(27.4%)		122(72.6%)	

第16表　患者発生家族ト非発生家族ニ就テノ成績

区分		患者発生状況						予防接種				検査人口	検査成績				
		6月	7月	8月	9月	10月	計	7月	8月	9月	10月		卌	卅	十	±	―
患者発生部落	患者発生家族		6	5 11人 (上旬)			2回					32人	17	2	1	7	5
														20(62.5%)		12(37.5%)	
	患者非発生家族				0		2回					136人	7	4	15	63	47
														26(19.1%)		110(80.9%)	
患者多発地区(1)及(2)	患者発生家族	11	23	34人 2回			1回					51人	15	18	14	3	1
														47(92.1%)		4(7.9%)	
	患者非発生家族				0		2回		1回			99人	18	34	19	12	16
														71(71.7%)		28(28.3%)	

更ニ上述ノ検査成績ヲ、患者発生家族ト患者非発生家族トニ区別シテ、其ノ陽性率ヲ比較スル＝其ノ成績第16表ノ如シ、即チ患者発生家族ノ陽性率ハ非発生家族ノソレニ比シ極メテ高シ。

以上ノ成績ヲ呈シタル各被検人員ハ総テ「ペスト・インムノーゲン」ヲ1回乃至2回ニワタリ接種セラレタルモノナリ。従ツテ各群別陽性率ノ差ハ之ヲ「ワクチン」ノ接種回数ニヨルモノト云フコトヲ得ズ、他ニ説明ヲ求メザルベカラズ、余ハ之ヲ不顕性感染ニヨツテ説明スルヲ最モ合理的ナリト考ヘルモノナリ。即チ「ペスト患者多発地区ハ「ペスト病毒ノ最モ濃厚ニ浸淫セル地区ニシテ斯ル地区ニ於テハ「ペスト菌ヲ有スル鼠多数棲息シ、従ツテ「ペスト有菌蚤多ク、住民ノ感染ノ危険ニ暴露セラルルコト極メテ多キハ否定シ得ザル処ナリ、之ニヨリテ患者ノ多発ヲ説明シ得ルナリ、而シテ又「ペスト菌ノ体内侵入ヲ受ケタルモノ（主トシテ有菌蚤ノ刺螫ニヨルナルベシ）

ノ内ニハ、其ノ侵入菌最少キカ或ハ個體ノ「ペスト菌ニ對スル抵抗強キタメ」、發病セズニ經過スル所謂不顯性感染ナルモノノ相當多數ニ存スルコトハ想像スルニ難カラズ。斯ルモノハ其ノ「ペスト菌ノ侵入ニヨリテ感作セラレ、所謂「アレルギー」ノ狀態トナリ、從ツテ皮膚反應陽性ニ出現スルモノナラン。患者多發地區ニ於テハ、斯ク不顯性感染ニテ經過セルモノ多キタメニ皮膚反應ノ陽性率高キナリト說明スルヲ最モ至當ト思惟ス。

上述セル說明ニヨリテ、患者ノ散發セル地區ニ於テハ皮膚反應ノ陽性率30%內外ナルコト及患者ノ發生セザル地區ニ於テハ10%內外ナルコトモ充分理解シ得ラル。又之ニヨリテ患者ノ發生家族ニ於テ其ノ陽性率極メテ高キコトモ說明シ得ラル。即チ從來コリ謂ハレツル如ク、「ペスト」ハ好ンデ非衛生的環境ニ在ル家屋ニ發生スルモノニシテ、斯ル家屋ニ住ムモノハ最モ屢々感染ノ機會ヲ受クルモノナルコトヲ知ルヲ得ベシ。而シテ其ノ內ノ或ル者ハ發病シ、或ル者ハ不顯菌感染ニ經過スルモノナリト云フヲ得ベシ。

第2節　性別、年齡別檢査成績

第1節ニ述ベタル成績ヲ更ニ性別、年齡別ニ觀察セルニ第17表(其ノ1、其ノ2、其ノ3)ノ如キ成績ヲ得タリ。

第17表（其ノ1）　患者多發地區ニ於ケル性別、年齢別成績

區分	年齢	男 検査人員	卅	廾	+	計	±	-	計	女 検査人員	卅	廾	+	計	±	-	計
1	5歳以下	3	1			2 (66.7%)		1	1	0							
2	6~10歳	17	2	7	4	13 (76.5%)	2	2	4	9	2	6	0	8 (88.8%)		1	1
3	11~15〃	74	24	16	18	58 (78.3%)	8	8	16	29	8	11	4	23 (79.3%)	4	2	6
4	16~20〃	63	24	19	7	50 (79.3%)	11	2	13	23	7	11	2	20 (86.9%)	2	1	3
5	21~30〃	104	35	32	16	83 (79.8%)	16	5	21	41	7	9	11	27 (65.9%)	5	9	14
6	31~40〃	135	37	37	24	98 (72.6%)	27	10	37	33	10	5	6	21 (63.9%)	8	4	12
7	41~50〃	91	14	20	14	48 (52.7%)	31	12	43	29	3	5	10	18 (62.1%)	9	2	11
8	51~60〃	47	5	10	10	25 (53.2%)	16	6	22	23	5	4	3	12 (52.2%)	7	4	11
9	61歳以上	29	1	5	7	13 (44.8%)	12	4	16	10	1	4	3	8 (80%)	1	1	2
10	計	563	143	146	101	390 (69.2%)	123	50	173	197	43	55	39	137 (69.5%)	36	24	60

第17表（其ノ2）　患者散發地區ニ於ケル性別、年齢別成績

區分	年齢	男 検査人員	卅	廾	+	計	±	-	計	女 検査人員	卅	廾	+	計	±	-	計
1	5歳以下	7			3	3 (42.9%)		4	4	5			1	1 (20%)	1	3	4
2	6~10歳	36	1	1	6	8 (22.2%)	11	17	28	30	1	2	4	7 (23.3%)	11	12	23
3	11~15〃	50	8	6	3	17 (34%)	10	23	33	42	2	6	8	16 (38.1%)	10	16	26
4	16~20〃	50	6	9	9	24 (48%)	8	18	26	16	4	2	3	9 (56.2%)	4	3	7
5	21~30〃	63	3	10	11	24 (38.1%)	10	29	39	48	2	3	6	11 (22.9%)	15	22	37
6	31~40〃	93	12	19	16	47 (50.5%)	17	29	46	43	1	5	5	11 (25.6%)	7	25	32
7	41~50〃	71	7	10	8	25 (35.2%)	16	30	46	28	2	7	3	12 (42.8%)	4	12	16
8	51~60〃	46	3	3	3	9 (19.6%)	11	26	37	23	2	4	0	6 (26.1%)	7	10	17
9	61歳以上	33	2	1	4	7 (21.2%)	7	19	26	16	2	0	4	6 (37.5%)	4	6	10
10	計	449	42	59	63	164 (36.5%)	90	195	285	251	16	29	34	79 (31.4%)	63	109	172

第17表（其ノ3）　患者非發生地區ニ於ケル性別、年齢別成績

區分	年齢	男 検査人員	卅	廾	+	計	±	-	計	女 検査人員	卅	廾	+	計	±	-	計
1	5歳以下	18				0 (0%)	8	10	18	7				0 (0%)	2	5	7
2	6~10歳	34		1		1 (2.9%)	13	20	33	24				0 (0%)	8	16	24
3	11~15〃	45		1	2	3 (6.6%)	19	23	42	28			5	5 (17.8%)	14	9	23
4	16~20〃	28	1	2	2	5 (17.8%)	15	8	23	32		1	3	4 (12.5%)	18	10	28
5	21~30〃	71	2	4	5	11 (15.5%)	39	21	60	50			3	3 (6%)	29	18	47
6	31~40〃	78		3	11	14 (17.9%)	41	23	64	44	1	2	1	4 (9.1%)	19	21	40
7	41~50〃	57			8	8 (14.0%)	36	13	49	46		1	8	9 (19.5%)	29	8	37
8	51~60〃	45				0 (0%)	30	15	45	29			3	3 (10.3%)	17	9	26
9	61歳以上	17				0 (0%)	12	5	17	18			1	1 (5.5%)	9	8	17
10	計	393	9	11	28	42 (10.7%)	219	133	351	288	1	4	24	29 (10.1%)	145	104	259

即チ患者多發地區ニ於テハ、皮膚反應陽性率ハ、男女ノ間ニ差ナク、又男女共ニ年齢別ニミルモ大ナル差ヲ認ムルコトヲ得ザリキ。但シ男41歳以上ニ於テ其ノ陽性率稍々低キ傾向認メラル。

患者散發セル地區ニ於テモ、其ノ陽性率ハ性別、年齢別ニ大ナル差ヲ認メザルナリ。但シ男41歳以上ニ於テ其ノ陽性率稍々低キ傾向認メラル。

患者ノ發生セザル地區ニ於テモ其ノ陽性率ハ性別、年齢別ノ差ヲ認ムルヲ得ズ。但シ男41歳以上ニ於テ其ノ陽性率低キ傾向認メラル。

以上ノ成績ヨリ患者發生地區ニ於テハ、其ノ住民ハ性別、年齢別ニ關係ナク、殆ド平等ニ「ペスト性」ノ侵襲ヲ受クルモノナリト考ヘラル。即チ住民ハ平等ノ感染機會ニ暴露セラレアルモノト考ヘラル。

患者發生セザル地區ニ於テハ主トシテ其ノ陽性率ハ豫防接種ニヨリテ獲得セルモノニシテ、之ニ就テモ性別、年齢別ノ差ハ殆ド認メラレズ、但シ男41歳以上ニ於テハ何レノ地域ノ檢査成績モ陽性率ノ稍々低キ傾向ヲ認メタリ。然レドモ之ニ就テハ如何ナル原因ニヨルモノナルカ説明シ得ズ。

参考ノタメ、農安街ニ發生セル「ペスト患者ノ性別、年齢別ノ統計表ヲ示セバ第18表（其ノ1、其ノ2）ノ如クニシテ其ノ患者發生率ハ男女ノ間ニ大ナル差ヲ認メズ、又年齢別ニミルモ大ナル差ヲ認メ得ザルナリ。

第18表（其ノ1）　性別、年齢別、患者發生率（農安）

年齢別患者數：年齢別人口（%）

年　一　齢	男	女	計
1～10歳	0.8%	0.9%	0.9%
11～20	1.7	1.2	1.4
21～30	1.3	1.7	1.5
31～40	2.5	2.3	2.4
41～50	1.8	0.8	1.4
51～60	3.6	1.7	2.8
61～70	2.5	1.8	2.2
71歳以上	2.1	1.0	1.6
平　均	2.0	1.4	1.7

第18表(其ノ2)　性別、年齢別、患者發生數(農安)

年齢	男		女		計	
	實數	%	實數	%	實數	%
1～5歳	8	12.2	14	18.1	22	14.7
6～10	17		13		30	
11～15	14	15.6	14	16.8	28	16.7
16～20	18		11		29	
21～30	20	9.8	31	20.8	51	14.4
31～40	47	23.0	35	23.5	82	23.2
41～50	27	13.2	9	6.0	36	10.2
51～60	34	16.6	12	8.0	46	13.3
61～70	15	7.3	8	5.4	23	6.5
71歳以上	4	1.9	2	1.3	6	1.7
計	204	100	149	100	353	100

以上ヲ綜括スレバ、「ペスト」流行地ニ於テハ性別、年齢別ニハ大ナル關係ナク、平等ニ「ペスト」病毒ノ侵襲ヲ受クルモノナリ、從ツテ患者ノ發生率モ性別、年齢別ニ大ナル關係ヲ有セザルコト認メラル、但シ前節ニ述ベタル如ク、地域別ニハ極メテ大ナル差ヲ認メ得ルモノナリ、今次ノ調査ハ極メテ短期間ニナサレタルモノニシテ、其ノ檢査總數モ比較的少キタメ、「ペスト皮膚反應」ト「ペスト」流行トノ關係ヲ鮮明スルニハ充分ナラザルナリ、將來流行ノ各時期ニ於テ、地域別ハ勿論、性別、年齢別、職業別等ニ就テ詳細ニ調査シ、又「ワクチン接種トノ關係ヲ考慮ニ入レテ觀察セバ、「ペスト皮膚反應」ガ「ペスト流行ニ關シテ持ツ意義ハ漸次鮮明セラルルニ至ルベシト考ヘラル。

第3節　小　括

昭和15年農安「ペスト」流行時ニ、農安街及其ノ附近ニ於テ「ペスト患者多發地區、中等度發生地區、非發生地區、現患多發地區ニ區分シテ、「ペスト皮膚反應ヲ檢査シタル結果、患者發生地區ニ於テハ其ノ陽性率極メテ高キコトヲ證明シ、之ハ「ペスト」ノ不顯性感染ニヨルモノナリト說明シ、又「ペスト皮膚反應」ノ疫學的意義ニ關シ考察セリ。

第4章　總括及考察

余ハ結核ニ於ケルマンツウー氏反應ノ術式ニナラヒ、「ペスト菌ヨリ作リタル抗原ヲ用ヒテ「ペスト患者、「ペスト・ワクチン接種者及健常者（「ペスト・ワクチン」ノ接種ヲ受ケタルコトナキモノ）ニ就キ皮內接種ニヨル局所反應ヲ詳細ニ觀察セル結果、「ペスト菌ノ自然感染ヲ受ケタルモ

ノハ勿論、人工的ニ「ペスト菌ヲ接種セラレタルモノモ「ペスト菌ニ對シテ所謂「アレルギー」状態トナリ、斯ル者ニ於テハ抗原接種局所ニ特異性過敏反應ヲ呈スルヲ見タリ。

抗原ニ就テハ「ペスト菌ヨリ種々ナルモノヲ作リ檢査セルモ、各抗原ノ特異性ニ關シテハ大ナル差異ヲ認メザリキ、故ニ皮膚反應用抗原トシテハ「ペスト菌弱毒株ノ37°C45時間培養菌ヲ以テ$^{1mg}/_{cc}$濃度ノ食鹽水菌浮遊液ヲ作リ、之ヲ60°Cニテ60分間加熱殺菌セルモノニ、0.4％ノ割合ニ石炭酸ヲ加ヘタルモノヲ使用セリ、其ノ檢査術式ハマンツウー氏反應ノ術式ニ從ヒ、抗原0.1ccヲ肩胛間部或ハ上膊外側ノ皮內ニ接種シ、接種局所ノ所見ヲ觀察セリ、成績ノ判定ハ抗原接種後20分乃至30分後ノ局所ニ現ハレタル發赤ノ大サヲ測定シ、其ノ直徑1.0cm以下(－)、1.1cm～1.9cm(±)、2.0cm～2.9cm(＋)、3.0cm～3.9cm(＃)、4.0cm以上(＃)トセリ。

對照トシテ生理的食鹽水0.1ccヲ抗原接種局所ヨリ約3cm～5cm距テテ接種シ、之ニヨツチ發赤ノ出現スルモノハ皮膚ノ特異的過敏性ニヨルモノナリト考ヘテ、成績判定上特ニ注意セリ、多數ノ健常者ニツキ檢査セルニ、斯ル偽陽性反應ヲ呈スルモノハ健常者ニ於テ3～5％內外存スルコトヲ知レリ。

上述ノ檢査術式ニ從ツテ「ペスト患者ニツキ皮膚反應ヲ觀察セルニ、此ノ反應ハ發病ノ初期ニ於テハ陽性ニ出現セザルモ、第9病日頃ヨリ弱陽性ニ出現シ、ソレヨリ次第ニ強陽性トナリ第3週乃至第4週ニ於テハ最高ノ陽性反應ヲ呈シ、ソレヨリ尚相當長期間ニ亘リテ陽性ニ出現スルモノナルコトヲ認メタリ、而シテ此ノ皮膚反應ハ他ノ傳染性熱性疾患ニ於テハ陽性反應ヲ呈スルコトナク、從ツテ「ペスト患者ニ對シ極メテ高キ特異性ヲ有スルモノナリト云ヒ得ベク、診斷的價値大ナリト考ヘラル、勿論前述セル如ク此ノ反應ハ「ペスト菌ニヨツテ人工的ニ感作セラレタルモノ即チ「ペスト・ワクチン接種者ニ於テモ陽性ニ出現スルモノニシテ、又皮膚ノ特異的過敏性ヲ有スルト考ヘラレルモノニ於テモ低陽性反應ヲ呈スルモノナリ（之ハ食鹽水ヲ對照トシテ接種スルトキ之ニ對シ發赤ヲ現ハスモノニシテ、此ノ方法ニヨリ除外シ得ルモノナリ、健常者ニ就テ3％乃至5％內外存在スルモノナリ）、故ニ「ペスト皮膚反應ニヨリテ「ペスト」ヲ診斷セントスルトキニハ、此ノ點ヲ考慮セザルベカラズ、然レドモ「ペスト患者ニ於テハ100％ニ陽性ニ出現スルモノナリ、故ニ流行時ニ於テ臨床的、細菌學的故ニ血淸學的ニ診斷ノ困難ナル症例等ニツイテハ、此ノ皮膚反應ニヨリテ或ル程度「ペスト」ノ診斷ヲ可能ニナシ得ルモノナリ。

一般ニ「ペスト」ノ診斷ハ主トシテ臨床的所見及菌檢索ニヨリテ可能ナルモ、中ニハ此レ等ノ方法ニヨリテ診斷ノ困難ナル症例アリ、ソレニ就テハ從來ヨリ血淸學的診斷利用セラレタリ、然レドモ其ノ內渡集反應ハ Zabolotony 及 Schtschastny [83] ノ述ベタル如ク其ノ出現ハ早クモ第7病日乃至第10病日ニシテ而モ其ノ陽性率ハ50％內外ニ過ギザルタメ診斷的價値少ナシト云ハザルヲ得ズ、補體結合反應ニ就テハ Amako, Moses, Scktschastny [84][85][86] 等ノ檢査成績アリ、此ノ反應ハ早キハ第5病日頃ヨリ出現スルモノアルモ、多クハ第2週以後ニ始メテ陽性ニナルモノニシテ而モ其ノ陽性率ハ約50％內外ナリ、故ニ診斷的價値少ナシト云ハザルヲ得ズ、然レドモ此ノ補體結合反應ハ Jaltrain, Simard, 及 Dickie [88][89][90] 等ノ云フ如ク、偽陽性反應ヲ呈スルモノ又ハ弱陽性者

ノ意義ハ大ナリ、又凝集反應陰性ナルトキニモ、本反應ノ陽性ニ出現スルコトアリ、故ニ試ムベキ診斷法ト云フヲ得ベシ、其ノ他溶菌素及「オプソニン」ニ就テハ Row[(91)] 及 Weinstein[(92)] 等ガ其ノ反應ノ特異性ナルヲ認メ診斷ニ用ヒ得ベシト述ベアルモ、其ノ檢查術式複雜ニシテ熟練ヲ要シ且其ノ成績ハ必ズシモ一定セザル場合多シ。以上述ベタル如ク、血淸診斷ニヨリテモ「ベスト」ノ診斷不可能ナル場合相當多シ、然ルニ皮膚反應ハ「ベスト患者ニ於テハ100%陽性ニ出現スルモノナル故ニ斯ル際ニハ診斷的價値大ナリト云フヲ得ベシ、Amako[(84)] ハ「ベスト患者ニ就キ「ベスト皮膚反應ヲ試ミ、6時間乃至24時間後ノ接種局所ノ所見ヲ檢シ、ソレガ50%陽性ニ出現スルニ過ギザルタメ診斷的價値少ナシト結論セリ、同氏ハ「ベスト強毒菌ヲ2週間「ブイヨン」ニ培養シタル後其ノ上淸ニ純「アルコールヲ入レテ沈澱セシメ、ソレヲ眞空ニテ乾燥粉末トシ、其ノ1gmヲ100ccノ生理的食鹽水ニ溶解シ、ソレヲ抗原トシテ使用セリ、其ノ檢查術式ヲ見ルニ、氏ハ此ノ抗原中ニ浸シタル小刀ノ尖ヲ以テ上膊ノ皮膚ヲ傷ツケ、6, 12, 24時間後ノ接種局所ノ所見ヲ檢查セリ「ベスト患者9名及「ベスト恢復者10名ニ就キ檢查シタルモ詳細ナル局所所見ノ觀察成績記載シアラズ、又病日トノ關係ヲ深ク考慮シアラザルタメ、余ノ檢查成績トハ比較考察シ得ザルモ、氏ノ觀察セル局々見ハ、余ガ「ベスト・ワクチン接種者及「ベスト恢復者ニ就テ觀察セル3乃至4時間後ニ出現シ、24時間後ニ最モ著明ニ現レル局所々見(余ハ之ヲ非特異性ノモノト判定セリ)ト一致スルモノナラズヤト思惟セラルルモ、其ノ抗原故ニ檢查術式ヲ異ニスル故ニ、直ニ斯ク判定スルハ早計ナリト思考ス、何レニセヨ余ノ檢查方法ニヨルトキハ「ベスト皮膚反應ハ第9病日以後ニ於テハ100%陽性ニ出現スルモノナリ、從ツテ診斷的價値高シト云フヲ得ベシ。ソレニ反シ余ノ檢查セル成績ニ於テモ各種免疫血淸反應ハ約60%ニ於テ陽性ニ出現スルニ過ギザリキ、故ニ其ノ診斷的價値少ナシト云ハザルヲ得ズ。

「アレルギー」ト免疫(感染防禦ヲ意味ス)トノ關係ニ就テハ結論ニ於テ詳述セル如ク、結核、痘瘡、肺尖等ニ就テ深ク研究セラレアルモ、未ダ充分ニ鮮明セラレズ、然レドモ「アレルギー」ト免疫ガ密接ナル關係ヲ有シ「アレルギー」ガ免疫ノ一過程ヲ示スモノナルコトハ一般ニ認メラルル處ナリ。

「ベスト皮膚反應ニ就テ考察スルニ「ベスト」ニ發病耐過セルモノニ於テハ皮膚反應ノ陽性率100%ナルコトヲ認メタリ、而シテ斯ル「ベスト發病耐過者ハ殆ド完全ニ近キ免疫ヲ獲得シ、再感染ニヨリテモ發病セザルモノナルコトハ以前ヨリ知ラレタル事實ナリ。

又「ベスト・ワクチン」ノ接種ヲ受ケタルモノニ就テハ皮膚反應ノ陽性率ハ非接種者ニ比シテ極メテ高ク、而モ其ノ陽性率ハ豫防接種ノ回數ニ比例スルヲ觀察セリ、即チ1回乃至2回ノ豫防接種者ニ於テハ其ノ陽性率ハ10〜20%內外ナルニ、頻回ニ豫防接種ヲ受ケタルモノハ其ノ陽性率ハ實ニ50〜60%ノ高キニ登ルヲ見タリ、而シテ一方「ベスト・ワクチン」ノ接種ガ「ベスト」ノ感染防禦ニ有効ナルコトハ多數ノ研究者ニヨリテ認メラルル處ナリ、殊ニ本試驗ニ用ヒタル「ベスト・インムノーゲン」ガ從來ノ「ベスト・ワクチン」ニ比シテ更ニ有効ナルコトハ倉內[(93)]、春日[(94)]等ノ等シク證明セル處ナリ、而モ感染防禦力ハ接種回數ニ比例シテ高クナルモノニシテ、此ノ點ヲ皮膚反

應ノ陽性率ガ「ペスト・ワクチン」ノ接種回數ニ比例シテ上昇スルコトト對照シテ考察スルトキハ「ペスト皮膚反應ハ免疫ト併行スルモノナリトハ云ヒ得ザルトモ、或ル程度「ペスト免疫獲得」ノ程度ヲ表現スルモノナリト考へ得ベシ。

流行地帶ニ於ケル檢査成績ヲ觀察スルニ、患者多發地區ニ於テハ皮膚反應ノ陽性率極メテ高シ、之ハ既ニ前述セル如ク、患者多發地區ハ最モ濃厚ニ「ペスト病竈ニヨリテ汚染セラレ、其ノ内ニ不顯性感染ニテ經過セルモノ極メテ多キタメナリト説明スルガ最モ合理的ナリト考ヘラル、而シテ流行初期ニ於テ患者多發セル地區ハ流行末期ニ於テハ皮膚反應陽性率高クナリ、他地域(皮膚反應陽性率低シ)ニ於テハ尚「ペスト患者ノ發生頻數ナルニ拘ラズ此ノ地域ニハ患者ノ發生ヲ見ザルニ至ル事實ヨリ觀察スルニ、之ニハ感染機會トイフ要素ヲ除外視シ得ズ、又斯ル地域ニ於テハ本々「ペスト」ニ自然抵抗性ヲ有スルモノガ多ク殘存スルニ因ルモノナルコトハ否定シ得ザルモ、一方不顯性感染ニ因ツテ免疫ヲ獲得スルモノ次第ニ多クナリ、從ツテ再感染ノ機會アルモ、感染發病スルモノ漸次減少スルモノナリト説明スルヲ得ベシ、即チ此ノ事ハ皮膚反應ノ陽性率ハ或ル程度「ペスト」ニ對スル免疫獲得ノ程度ヲ現ハスモノナリト云フ前述ノ考察ヲ裏書キスル事實ナリト謂ヒ得ベシ。

尚滿洲其他各地ニ於ケル「ペスト」ノ流行ヲ年別ニ觀察スルニ、數年ヲ一期トスル流行ノ波ヲ認メ得ルモノナリ、之ハ「ペスト」ノ關係獸類及昆蟲ノ繁殖ノ消長(流行年ニハ減少スル從ツテ其ノ翌年ハ少ナイ)及鼠族ノ獲得セル抵抗性(流行年ニ「ペスト菌ノ浸襲ヲ受ケ、免疫ヲ獲得スル)ト密接ナル關係ノ在スルコトハ勿論ナルモ、一ツニハ大流行ノ時ニハ住民ガ「ペスト病竈ニ濃厚ニ汚染セラレ其ノ内不顯性感染ニ經過シ、ソレニヨツテ免疫ヲ獲得ヘルモノ多ク、從ツテ翌年及翌々年ハタトヘ新病竈ノ浸襲アルモ大ナル流行ヲ惹起スルコトナシト推論スルモ可ナラン、(尚將来ノ研究及檢探ヲ要ス)。

斯ノ如ク皮膚反應ガ果シテ大衆ノ獲得セル免疫ノ程度ヲ示スモノナルカ否カ、又皮膚反應陽性者ニ於テハ、其ノ陰性者ニ比シテ、平等ノ感染機會ニ曝露セラレタル際、罹患發病スルモノ少キカ否カ、又皮膚反應ノ陽性率ガ或ル一定ノ%ニ達シタル住民ニ於テハ「ペスト」ノ流行ヲ抑壓シ得ルモノナリヤ否ヤ、等ノ問題ハ長期ニ亘リ多數ノ住民ニ就テノミナラズ、地域別ニ廣ク調査スルコトニヨリ次第ニ鮮明セラレルニ至ルベク、皮膚反應ヲ通ジテ見クル不顯性感染ノ問題、大衆免疫ノ問題、「ペスト流行ノ發生、終熄ノ本旃ニ關スル問題等ハ極メテ興味深キ研究題目ト云ヒ得ベシ。

又、Opie[95]等ハ結核ニ就テ「ツベルクリン反應陽性者ニ於テハ、ソノ病竈ガ非活動性ノモノカラデモ結核菌ヲ檢出シ得ルモノナリト云ヘリ、「ペスト菌保有者ニ就テハ Leger[96][97], Tanon[98], Uriarte[99], Durand[100], Boston[101] 等ハ「ペスト患者ノ發生セル周圍ノ人達ニ就キ「ペスト菌ノ檢索ヲ行ヒ、僅ニ腫脹セル腺腫ヨリ「ペスト菌ヲ檢出シ得タリ、氏等ハ斯ル腺腫ハ壓痛ヲ伴ヘザルコト多ク且ツ菌保有者ハ何等一般症狀ヲ呈セザルモノ多キタメニ其ノ檢出ノ困難ナルコトヲ述ベタリ、Uriarte[102]ハ菌保有症ノ檢出ニハ腺腫ヲ穿刺スルヨリ切開スル方法ガ菌檢出ノ良好ナルコトヲ

述ベタリ、又 Nikanorov ハ全ク健康ニ見エル人ノ血液中ヨリ「ペスト菌ヲ證明シ、斯カルモノ
ガ傳染源トナル危険ノ大ナルコトヲ述ベタリ。其ノ他 Christie ハ15日間ニ11人ニ「ペスト」ヲ感
染セシメタル一健康婦人ニ就テ報告シ、Zlatogoroff 等ハ肺ペスト患者ノ看護人21人ノ咽頭液
ヨリ1例ニ於テ「ペスト菌ヲ檢出シ、Wu lien-Te ハ満洲ニ於ケル肺ペスト」ノ流行時ニ略痰中
ニ「ペスト菌ヲ排出セル2例ノ健康菌保有者ヲ報告セリ。Gotschlich 等ハ「ペスト恢復者ガ2～
3ケ月ニ亘リ、全然一般症状ヲ認メザルニ拘ラズ、其ノ略痰中ニ「ペスト菌ヲ排出スルヲ認メタ
リ。

以上ノ如ク「ペスト菌保有者ニ就テノ若干ノ報告ハアルモ、尚其ノ流行學的意義ハ全然鮮明セラ
レアラザル状況ナリ。コレ大衆ニ就キ々其ノ血液ヲ培養シ、或ハ腺腫ヲ穿刺シテ「ペスト菌ヲ
檢出スル手技ノ極メテ煩雜ニシテ且ツ困難ナルタメナリ。然ルニ此ノ問題ノ解決ハ「ペスト防疫
上極メテ肝要ナルコトハ言ヲ俟タザル處ナリ。余ノ考案セル「ペスト皮膚反應ハ「ペスト菌ヲ保
有スルモノニ於テハ必ズ陽性ニ出現スル筈ナリ。勿論コレハ生菌ヲ保有セザル「ペスト恢復患者
及「ペスト・ワクチン」ヲ接種セルモノニ於テモ陽性ニ出現スルコトハ前述セル處ナルモ、多數ノ
人ニ就キ「ペスト菌保有者ヲ檢出セントスルトキ。先ヅ皮膚反應ヲ行ヒテ陽性者ヲ檢出シ、次ニ
其ノ陽性者ノミニ就テ腺腫或ハ血液ニツキ菌檢索ヲ實施スルモ、滿遺者ヲ出スコトナク、菌保有
者ヲ檢出シ得ル理由ナリ。從ツテ此ノ方法ニヨリ大イニ勞力ヲ省キ且ツ比較的容易ニ「ペスト菌
保有症ヲ檢出シ得ルト云ヒ得ベシ。

又皮膚反應ガ「ペスト免疫ノ「インデイカトール」トナリ得ルコト鮮明セラルレバ、之ニヨリテ
「ペスト・ワクチン」ノ効果ヲ制定スルコト可能トナリ得ベシ。是等ノ問題ハ將來ニ殘サレタル研
究題目ナリト考ヘラル。其ノ他「ペスト皮膚反應ノ本態ニ關シテハ實驗スル處少ナカリシモ、結
核菌、肺尖菌及淋菌等ニ就テ研究セラレアル如ク、菌體成分ノ内如何ナル部分ガ特異性抗原性ヲ
有スルモノカ、除感作ヲナシ得ルモノナルカ、又被働性感作ノ成立シ得ルモノナルカ、等ハ將來
究メラレベキ研究問題ナリト考ヘラル。

以上ノ如ク「ペスト皮膚反應ニ關シテハ將來尚研究スベキ多數ノ問題ヲ殘シアルモ、本反應ハ
「ペスト菌ノ自然感染或ハ人工的接種ニヨリテ「ペスト菌ニ感作セラレタル個體ニ於テ特異性ニ出
現スル「アレルギー反應ナリト云ヒ得ベシ。從ツテ之ハ「ペスト診斷ノ一補助的方法トナリ。又
免疫ト一定ノ關係ヲ有スルモノナリト云ヒ得ベシ。

結　論

余ハ「ペスト皮膚反應ノ抗原及檢査術式ヲ考案シ、ソレニヨリテ「ペスト患者及「ペスト・ワ
クチン接種者ノ皮膚反應ヲ詳細ニ觀察シ、更ニ「ペスト流行地ニ於テ多數ニツキ檢査セル結果次
ノ如キ結論ヲ得タリ。

1.「ペスト皮膚反應ハ「ペスト菌ノ自然感染或ハ人工的接種ニヨリテ「ペスト菌ニ感作セラレタ
ル個體ニ特異性ニ現ハルル「アレルギー性反應ナリト考ヘラル。

2. 「ペスト皮膚反應ハ「ペスト」ニ發病耐過セルモノニ於テハ100%陽性ニ出現スルモノナリ、從ツテ「ペスト血淸診斷ヨリハ共ノ診斷的價値大ナリト云ヒ得ベシ。

3. 「ペスト皮膚反應ハ「ペスト・ワクチン」ヲ接種セルモノニ就テ檢スルニ、接種回數ニ比例シテ其ノ陽性率ノ高上スルヲ認ム、故ニ或ル程度「ペスト免疫ノ程度ヲ現ハスモノナリト考ヘラル。

4. 「ペスト皮膚反應ハ不顯性感染ニ經過セルモノニ於テモ陽性ニ出現スルモノナリト考ヘラル、從ツテ流行地ニ於ケル「ペスト病毒浸染ノ程度ヲ表スモノナリト云ヒ得ベシ。

附　記

余ハ「ペスト皮膚反應ヲ檢出セル際、抗原接種ニヨリテ接種局所ニ作ラレル「クワドラ」ノ吸收サルルニ要スル時間ヲ詳細ニ觀察セルニ、「ペスト」ニ發病耐過セルモノ及「ペスト・ワクチン」ヲ接種セルモノニ於テハ、健常者ニ比シ、其ノ吸收時間極メテ延長スルヲ認メタリ、食鹽水其ノ他ノ液體ヲ皮内接種スルコトニヨリテ生ジタル「クワドラ」ノ吸收ノ速度ガ網狀織内被細胞系統ノ機能ニ深キ關係アルコトハ今日一般ニ認メラルル處ナリ、此ノ事ヨリ前述セル成績ヲ考察スルトキハ、「クワドラ」ノ吸收時間ト免疫トノ間ニ何等カノ關係ノ存スルコトヲ想像シ得ベシ。余ハ之ニ就テ何等說明シ得ル知識ヲ有セザルモ、研究者ノ參考トナルベキヲ思ヒ、觀察セル事實ヲ附記スルモノナリ。

引　用　文　蔵

1) **Blackley** : Experimental Researches on the causes and nature of catarrhs aestivus, London, (1873).

2) **Walker, J.C.** : Jl. med. Res., (1917), **37**, 51.

3) **Walker, J.C.** : Boston Med. Surg. Jl., (1918), **179**, 228.

4) **Pirquet, C.V.** : Wien. kl. Wochschr., (1906), **29**, 855 u. 1407.

5) **Pirquet, C.V.** : Zschr. Immunitätsf., (1911), **10**, 51.

6) **Pirquet, C.V.** : Münch. med. Wochschr., (1911), **58**, 937.

7) **Pirquet, C.V.** : Berl. kl. Wochschr., (1907), **48**, 644 u. 699.

8) **Tieche** : Korrespond. Bl. Schw. Arzte, (1912), **42**, 626. u. (1913), **44**, 1121.

9) **Tieche** : Schweiz. med. Wochschr., (1924), **16**, 36.

10) 飯井，石島 : 日本傳染病學會雜誌、(昭9, 7), **8**, 999.

11) **Moro** : Jahreskurse f. ärztl. Forthildung, H. 6, (1910).

12) **Mantoux, C.** : Presse méd., (1910), **18**, 10.

13) **Hart, P.D'A.** : Spec. Rep. Ser. med. Res. Coun., London, No. 164, (1932).

14) **Groer, F.V.** : Wien. med. Wochschr., Sonder Abdruck. No. 39. (1932).

15) **Johnston, J.A., Howard, D.J., & Moraney, J.** : Amer. Rev. Tuberc., (1934), **29**, 652.

16) Lloyd, W.F. & Macpherson, A.M.C. : Brit. med. Jl., (1933), 1. 818.

17) Opie, E.L. : Amer, Rev. Tuberrc., (1935), 32, 617.

18) Bruck, C. : Dtsch. med. Wochschr, (1909), 35, 470.

19) Iron, E.E. : Jl. infect. Dis., (1912), 11, 77.

20) 細谷：東京醫事新誌, (昭13, 10), 3106. 1. 及 (昭14. 10). 3156, 1. 及 (昭14. 11), 3160, 3.

21) 吉永：醫事公論, (昭13, 11). 1373. 6.

22) M'Fadyean & stockmann : Rep. Comm. on Epid. Abortion, append to Part I, London, (1909).

23) Huddleson & Iohnson : Amer. Jl. trop. Med., (1933), 73. 485.

24) Burnet. E. : Arch. Inst. Pasteur, Abrique nord., (1922), 2, 187

25) Nocard. E. : Jl. comp. Path., (1895), 8. 227.

26) Hutyra, F. & Merek, J. : Special Pathology and Therapeutics of the Diseases of Domestic amimals, (1926).

27) Reinhardt. R. : Berl. tierärztl. Wochschr., (1919), 35, 453 u. 465.

28) Coenen, H. : Beitr. kl. Chir., (1908), 60, 402.

29) Jullianelle & Hartmann : Jl. exp. Med., (1935), 62, 11. 23. 31., (1936), 64, 149.

30) Noguchi : Jl. exp. Med., (1911), 14, 557.

31) Ito, T. : Arch. Derm., (1913), 116. 341.

32) Cole, H.N. & Levin, E.A. : Jl. amer. med. Assoc., (1935), 105, 2040.

33) Reenstierna, J. : Arch. Derm., (1924), 147, 362.

34) Frei, W. : Kl. Wochschr., (1925), 4, 2148.

35) Jacobsthal : Münch. med. Wochschr., (1917), 63, 87.

36) Chantemesse, A. : Dtsch. med. Wochschr., (1907), 33. 1572.

37) Gay & Force : Univ. Calif. in Path., (1913), 2, 127.

38) Force & Stevens : Ann. int. Med. (Am.), (1917), 1', 440.

39) Pirquet, C.V. : Wien. kl. Wochschschr., (1906), 19, 1407.

40) Wassermann, A. & Bruck, C. : Dtsch. med. Wochschr., (1906), 32, 449.

41) Pickert, M., & Löwenstein, E. : Dtsch. med. Wochschr., (1908), 34. 2262.

42) Zinsser & Müller Jl. exp. Med., (1925), 41, 159.

43) Keller, W. : Kl. Wochschr. Jahrg., (1927), 6, 2460.

44) Römer, P.H. : Beitr. kl. Tuberc., (1909), 13, 1.

45) Fischl, F. : Arch. Derm., (1925), 148, 402.

46) Philibert, A. et Cordey, F. : Ann. de Méd., (1925), 17, 5.

47）Mackenzie, G.M. : Jl. exp. Med., (1925), **41**, 53.

48）Krause, A.K. : Amer. Rev. Tuberc., (1928), **18**, 232.

19）Koch, R. : Dtsch. med. Wochschr., (1890), **16**, 1029., (1897), **23**, 209.

50）Heimbeck, J. : Lancet, (1927), II, 290., Presse méd., (1932), **40**, 528., Med. Kl., (1933), **29**, 1731.

51）Scheel. O. : Bull. acad. Med., (1935), **114**, 149.

52）Jacobson, C.T. : Hospitalstidende, (1932), **76**, 763.

53）Schipman, S.J. & Davis, E. : Amer. Rev. Tuberc., (1933), **27**, 474.

54）Zinsser, H., Hugh, K.W. & Jennings, F.B., Jl. Immunol., (1925), **10**, 719.

55）Willis, H. St. : Amer. Rev. Tuberc., (1928), **17**, 240.

56）Jullianelle : Jl. exp. Med., (1930), **51**, 441. 449. 463. 633. 643.

57）Seibert : Proc. Soc. exp. Biol. Med., (1933), **30**, 1274.

58）Rich, A.R. : Bull. Johnshopkins Hosp. Baltim., (1933), **52**, 203.

59）Siegel : Beitr. Klin. Tuberc., (1934), **84**, 311.

60）Sewall. H. Savitsch. E.D. & Butler, C.P. : Amer. Rev. Tuberc., (1934), **29**, 373.

61）Francis T. & Tillett, W.S. : Jl. exp. Med., (1930), **52**, 573., (1931), **54**, 584.

62）Pirquet, C.V. : Jl. amer. med. Assoc., (1911), **52**, 675.

63）Calmette, A., Grysez, V. & Letuelle, R. : Presse méd., (1911), **19**, 651.

64）Low, D.J. & Lloyd, W.E. : Brit. med. Jl., (1931), II, 183.

65）Scheel, O. : Ann. Inst. Pasteur, (1929), **43**, 394.

66）Myers, J.A. : Amer. Rev. Tuberc., (1930), **21**, 479.

67）Myers, J.A., Diehl, H.S. & Lees, H.D. : Jl. amer. med. Assoc., (1934), **102**, 2086.

68）Brink, G.C., Brown, M.H. & Gray, K.G. : Canad. publ. Health Jl., (1933), **24**, 471.

69）Cummins, S.L. & Evans, A. C. : Brit. med. Jl., (1933), **I**, 815.

70）Drolet, G.J. : Amer. Rev. Tuberc., (1934), **30**, 1.

71）小林 : 結核. (昭6, 10), **9**, 1291.

72）太田、相澤、岡 : 結核、(昭7, 6), **10**, 410.

73）杉山、斎藤 : 陸軍軍醫團雑誌、(昭9), **249**, 325.

74）Babes : Arch. Med. exp. T., (1891), **3**, 619.

75）M'Fadyean : Jl. comp, Path., (1893), **6**, 36.

76）Bonome : Dtsch. med. Wochschr., (1894), **20**, 703. 725. 744.

381—34

77）益河、栗原：陸軍軍醫團雜誌. (昭10), 310, 569.

78）Simpson, W.M. : Ann. int. Med. (Am.), (1930), 4, 238.

79）Straube, G. : Med. Klin. (1932), 28, 1501.

80）Rainsford, S.G. : Jl. R. nav. med. Serv., (1933), 19, 1.

81）Heathman, L.S. : Jl. infect. Dis., (1934), 55, 243.

82）Goldstein, J.D. : Jl clin. Invest., (1934), 13, 209.

83）Taylor. R.M., Leisbonne, M. & Vidal, L.F. : Mouvement San., (1945), 12, 51,

84）Amako, T. : Zentbl. Bakt., I. Orig., (1909), 51, 674.

85）Zabolotony : Dtsch. med. Wochschr., (1897), 23, 392.

86）Schtschastny : Die Pest in Odessa, 1910, St. Petersburg, (1912).

87）Moses : Mem. Inst. Oswaldo Cruz, 1, quot. by Dieudonne & Otto, (1909),

88）Jaltrain, E. : C.R. acad. Sci. Paris, (1920), 171, 413.

89）Simard : Bull. Off. internat. d'Hyg Publi., (1921), 13, 964.

90）Dickie, W.M. : Proc. conf. State & prev. Health auth. North America, 30,
    quot. Trop. Dis. Bull. (1926), 25, 314.

91）Row. R. : Brit. med. Jl., (1902), II, 1895., (1903), I, 1076.

92）Weinstein : Westn. obschtsch. Hygieni, St. Petersburg, (1909).

93）倉內、其ノ他：細菌學雜誌, (昭12), 493, 121.

94）春日：東京醫事新誌, (昭12. 7), 3041. 1.

95）Opie, E.L. & Aronson. J.D. : Arch. path. Lab. Med., (1927), 4, 1.

96）Leger, M. & baury, A. : C.R. acad. Sci., Paris, (1922), 175, 734.

97）Leger, M. & Baury, A. : Bull. Soc. Path. exot., (1923), 16. 54.

98）Tanon, L. & Cambessedes : Rev. Méd. Hyg. trop., (1923), 15, 65.

99）Uriarte, L. : C.R. Soc. Biol., Paris, (1924), 91, 1039.

100）Durand, P. & Consell. E. : Arch. Inst. Pasteur, Tunis, (1927), 16, 92.

101）Boston, H.M. : Lancet, Lond., (1927), 1, 870.

102）Uriarte, L. : C.R. Soc. Biol., Paris, (1925), 92, 901.

103）Nikanorov, S, M. : Seuchen bekämpfung der Infektionskrankheiten, (1927),
    4, 140.

104）Christie : J. trop. Med. Hyg., (1911), 14, 147.

105）Zlatogoroff & Padlewski : Zur Bakteriologie der Lungenpest, Moskau, (1912).

106）Wu lien-Teh : Manch. Plague prev. Serv. Rep., (1926), 5, 1.

107）Gotschlich, E. : Zshr. Hyg., (1899), 32, 402,

（昭和16年8月15日脫稿）

4.2.2　昭和 15 年農安及新京ニ発生セル「ペスト」流行ニ就テ　第 1 編 流行ノ疫学的観察（其ノ 1）農安ノ流行ニ就テ

资料出处： 日本国立国会図書館関西館蔵、博士論文。

内容点评： 本资料为《陆军军医学校防疫研究报告》第 2 部第 514 号《关于昭和 15 年农安及新京发生的鼠疫流行　第 1 编　流行的疫学观察（其 1）关于农安的流行》，1943 年 4 月 12 日提交。

高桥有关 1940 年农安和"新京"鼠疫诸论文，涉及各个领域，内容详尽，为 1940 年日军对农安等地实施鼠疫跳蚤攻击后鼠疫流行的全面观察和研究。

陸軍軍醫學校防疫研究報告
第2部　第514號

昭和15年農安及新京ニ發生セル「ペスト」流行ニ就テ

第1編　流行ノ疫學的觀察（其ノ1）
農安ノ流行ニ就テ

陸軍軍醫學校軍陣防疫學教室（主任　增

陸軍軍醫少佐　高　橋

第　2　部
原　　著
分　類
441—2
333—41
受附 昭和18.4.12

514—2

担任指導　陸軍軍醫少將　石　　井　　四　　郎

　本報告ハ昭和15年9月下旬新京ニ「ペスト」ノ流行ガ發生シタル際ニ其ノ防疫ヲ擔當シタ加茂部
隊(部隊長　石井大佐)關係者ノ研究調査シタ業績ノ内參考トナルベキ事項ヲ綜合シタモノデアル、
玆ニ研究資料ヲ提供セラレタ關係者各位ニ對シ衷心ヨリ感謝スル次第デアル。

目　　　　次

緒　　　言

第1章　患者ノ發生狀況及流行狀態

第2章　流行ノ疫學的觀察

　　第1節　流行ノ季節的消長

　　第2節　流行ノ環境衞生學的觀察

　　第3節　流行ノ統計的觀察

第3章　傳染經路ニ關スル考察

総　　　括

文　　　献

緒　　　言

　「ペスト」ノ疫學ニ關スル正確ナ概念ヲ得ルコトハ「ペスト」ノ防疫ヲ科學的且合理的ニ實施スル
上ニ極メテ必要デアル、而シテ「ペスト」ノ疫學ノ概念ヲ得ルーツノ方法トシテハ先ヅ各ミノ流行
ヲ詳細ニ觀察調査シテ、其ヲ詳細ニ記録ニ止メテ置キ、然ル後ニ多數ノ流行ニ就テ觀察サレタ成
績ヲ總括シ考察スルコトガ必要デアル、此ノ意味ニ於テ昭和15年農安ニ發生セル「ペスト」ノ流行
ニ就テ調査シ得タ事項ヲ取擢メテ記載シ、其ニ就テ若干ノ疫學的考察ヲ試ミントスル次第デアル、
尚農安ハ滿洲ノ「ペスト」常在地域內ニ在ル滿人都市デアルタメニ此ノ地ニ於ケル「ペスト流行ノ
狀態ヲ觀察スレバ其ノ成績ヨリ滿洲ノ「ペスト」常在地域ニ於ケル「ペスト流行ノ狀態ヲ概ネ推論
シ得ルモノト信ジ、調査ノ不備ヲ顧ミズ、玆ニ報告シテ諸賢ノ批判ヲ乞フ次第デアル。

第1章　患者ノ發生狀況及流行狀態

　今次流行ニ於テハ「ペスト患者ノ發生當初ノ狀況ハ明瞭デナイケレドモ住民ヨリ聽取シテ調査
セル處ニ據ルト、6月中旬西大街ニ在ル農安醫院附近ニテ2,3人ノモノガ不明ノ急性疾患ニテ死
亡シタノヲ診療シタ農安醫院醫師李奎芳ガ6月30日ニ發病シ、7月2日ニ死亡シタコトヨリ始メ
テ「ペスト患者ノ發生ガ公ニサレ、次デ7月9日發病シ同月11日ニ死亡シタ吳元林ニ就テ菌檢索
ノ結果「ペスト」デアルコトガ決定サレタノデアル、從ツテ流行發生當初ノ患者ノ狀況ハ不明デア
ルケレドモ前郭族調査所ニテ調査セル處ニ據ルト患者ノ發生狀況ハ大體第1表ニ示ス如クニシテ

6月17日ニ死亡セル陳萬弟ヲ初發患者トシテ今次ノ流行ハ發生シタモノト考ヘラレル、而シテ此ノ「ペスト」患者ハ前郭旗管内ニテハ本年始メ發生セル「ペスト」患者デアツテ、當時他ノ地域ニハ「ペスト」ノ流行ガ未ダ發生シテ居ナカツタノデ、今次ノ農安ノ「ペスト」流行ハ原發性流行デアルト考ヘルコトガ出來ル。

第1表　流行發生當初ニ於ケル「ペスト」患者表

番號	住　　　所	氏　　　名	性	年齢	轉歸	發病月日	轉歸月日	病　　　名	摘　　　要
1	西大街農安醫院裏	陳萬弟	男	58	死	不詳	6.17	推定「ペスト」	周圍ノ事情ヨリ死後「ペスト」ト判定ス
2	西大街興順東雇人	張　財	男	57	死	6.24	6.27	〃	〃
3	西大街農安醫院	李永芳	男	34	死	6.30	7.2	〃	〃
4	西大街農安醫院裏	陳山頭	男	3	死	7.7	7.9	〃	〃
5	西大街農安醫院雇人	王田氏	女	38	死	7.6	7.10	〃	〃
6	西大街協和園飯店	王連聯	男	24	死	7.9	7.11	〃	〃
7	〃	吳元林	男	48	死	7.7	7.11	腺ペスト	剖檢、「ペスト」菌陽性
8	市大街三號	李于氏	女	32	死	7.13	7.13	〃	〃
9	十字街恒增東雇人	楊秀春	男	32	死	7.8	7.14	〃	〃
10	西門外路南	劉贇鳳	男	54	死	7.12	7.14	〃	〃
11	西大街廣菜永	劉殿榮	男	47	死	6.29	7.2	推定「ペスト」	周圍ノ事情ヨリ死後「ペスト」ト判定ス
12	十字街(西大街路南)	亞延強	男	52	死	7.9	7.10	〃	

偕而次ニ農安ニ於ケル過去ノ「ペスト」流行ニ就テミル記録ニ殘サレテキル範圍ニ於テハ昭和13年度ニ附近ノ部落ニ若干ノ「ペスト」患者ノ發生ヲ見タ他ニハ縣城内ニ「ペスト」患者ノ發生ヲ見タコトハナカツタ、從ツテ今次縣城内ニ「ペスト」患者ノ原發シタノハ病毒ノ越年ニ因ルモノデハナクテ新シク病毒ガ輸入サレタタメデアルト考ヘラレル、併シナガラ其ガ如何ニシテ輸入サレタモノデアルカハ全然不明デアル、勿論縣城附近ノ部落ニハ恒坷子ノ如ク年々「ペスト」患者ノ發生ヲ見ル部落モアルノデ農安縣城附近ノ齧歯類ガ病毒ヲ保有シテキルコトハ想像ニ難クナイガ、果シテ其ガ原因ヲナシテキルモノデアルカ否カハ全然不明デアル。

次ニ流行發生當初ニ於ケル斃鼠ノ狀況ヲ調査セル、6月中旬ニ前記農安醫院附近ノ張財ナルモノノ所有セル穀類庫ヨリ多數ノ斃鼠ガ發見サレタコトガ明カニサレタ、此ノ事實ト前述ノ患者ノ發生狀況ヨリ考察スレバ病毒ハ先ヅ西大街ノ農安醫院附近ニ輸入サレ、其ノ地區ノ鼠族間ニ「ペスト」ノ流行ヲ惹起シ、次テ病毒ガ住居ニ波及シテ「ペスト」患者ノ發生ヲ起スニ至ツタモノト考ヘラレル(第1圖參照)、以上ノ如クニシテ西大街農安醫院附近ニ發生シタ「ペスト」ノ流行ハ氷署ニ其ノ姿勢ヲ強メ、西門外、東街、南街ヘト漸次全街ニ蔓延シ、更ニ附近部落ニ迄傳播サレルニ至ツタモノト思ハレル、而シテ此ノ病毒ノ傳播ハ人ヨリ人ヘノ直接ノ傳播モ考ヘラレルケレドモ、其ノ病型傳播ノ狀況等ヨリ考ヘルト、先ヅ鼠族間ニ「ペスト」ノ流行ガ傳播シ、其ニ因ツテ人ニ「ペスト」ノ流行ガ傳播シタモノト考ヘルノガ安當デアロウ、此ノ事ハ7月下旬大降雨ニ際シテ東門附近ノ「マンホール」ヨリ多數ノ斃鼠ノ發見サレタコトヨリモ略ミ想像スルコトガ出來ル、何ト

514——4

ナレバ此ノ鼠疫ハ下水系統圖(第4圖參照)ヨリ見レバ當時ノ「ペスト患者ノ發生ノ見ラレナカツ
タ東北關ヨリ流レテ來タモノト考ヘラレルモノニシテ、而モ其ノ後、東北關ニ「ペスト患者ノ發
生ヲ見ルニ至ツタコトヨリ考ヘレバ、先ヅ鼠族間ニ「ペスト」ノ流行發生シ、次デ人ペスト」ノ發
生ヲ見ルニ至ツタモノト想像シ得ラレルノデアル。

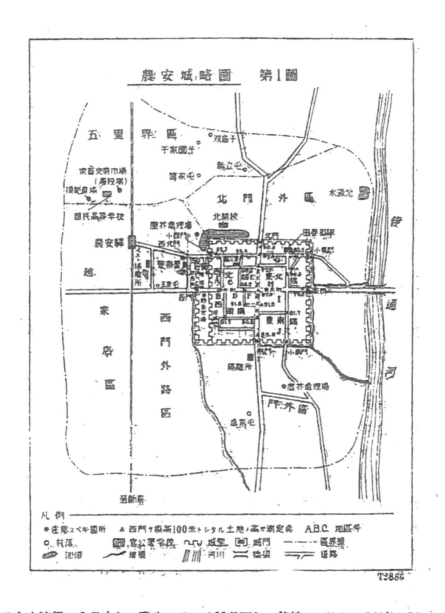

新クシテ今次流行ハ6月中旬ニ發生シテヨリ11月下旬ニ終熄スル迄凡ソ160餘日間ニ亙リ發生
シタ「ペスト患者ノ總數353名ニシテ、其ノ日々ノ發生數ヲ示セバ第2圖ノ如クデアル。此ノ圖ニ
ヨツテ患者發生ノ狀況ヲ概ネ知ルコトガ出來ル(前鼠族調査所ノ調査ニヨル)。

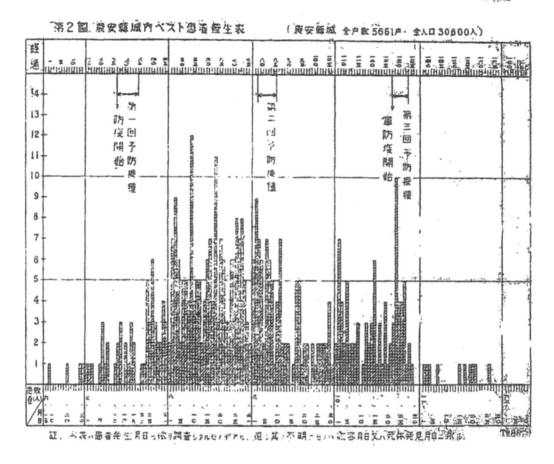

第2圖 農安縣城內ペスト患者發生表　　（農安縣城 全戶數 5661戶・全人口 30800人）

第2章　流行ノ疫學的觀察

第1節　流行ノ季節的消長（吉村氏ノ調査ニヨル）

滿洲ノ「ペスト」常在地域ニ於ケル「ペスト」ノ流行曲線ハ頗ル特異ニシテ毎年其ノ軌ヲ一ニシ、6, 7月ノ候ニ初發シ、漸次增加シツツ9月ニ於テ其ノ頂點ニ達シ、11月酷寒ノ襲來ト共ニ終熄スルニ至リ所謂夏季型ヲ呈スルコトハ既ニ食内、昔日等ノ明ニシタ處デアルガ、今次ノ流行ニ於テモ正ニ其ノ軌ヲ一ニシ、6月中旬流行ノ發生シテヨリ漸次疫勢ヲ高メ、8月及9月ニ於テ最モ患者多發シ、其ヨリ漸次疫勢衰ヘ、11月下旬ニ至ツ全ク終熄シ、其ノ後ハ患者ノ發生ヲ認メナカツタ（第2圖參照）。今月別ノ患者發生數ヲ示セバ第2表ノ如クニシテ其ノ流行ノ季節的消長ガ全滿洲ノ流行ノ年々ノ季節的消長ニ一致シテキルコトヲ知得タ。

斯クノ如キ「ペスト」流行ノ季節的消長ガ氣象ト密接ナ關係ヲ有スルコトハ研究者ノ等シク認ムル處ニシテ、滿洲ノ「ペスト」ノ流行曲線ガ滿洲ペスト」常在地域ノ氣象ト密接ナ關係ヲ有スル

第2表　月別患者發生數

月　次	患者　數（人）
5 月	0
6 〃	4
7 〃	54
8 〃	167
9 〃	98
10 〃	86
11 〃	10
12 〃	0
1 〃	0

514—6

ルコトハ舍内ノ詳細ニ論ジタルモノデアル、卽チ滿洲ノ「ベスト」ハ所謂夏季型ニシテ6月氣溫ノ20°C
內外ニ達スルヤ發生ヲ開始シ、7月ノ酷暑モ之ヲ阻止スルコトナク漸次蔓延シ、9月氣溫ノ15°C
內外ノ時頂點ニ達シ、15°C 以下ノ氣溫ハ其ノ流行ヲ阻止スルモノノ如ク、10月其ノ氣溫7°C內
外ニ及ブヤ漸減シ、11月氣溫零下ニ降ルヤ激減シテ終熄スルニ至ルコトヲ認メ、流行ガ氣溫ト密
接ナル關係ヲ有スルコトヲ明ニシタ。

　溫度及降水量ト「ベスト」流行トノ關係ニ就テハ溫度ハ「ベスト」ノ流行ニ對シテハ何等ノ關聯ナ
キモノノ如ク、「ベスト患者發生曲線ハ之ト無關係ニ相乖離スルヲ認メ、降水量ニ關シテハ日本、
臺灣、香港、ラングーン、カルカツタ、ボンベイ等ニ於テハ其ノ增加ガ「ベスト」發生ヲ抑制スル
ガ如キ現象ヲ認メ得ラレルニ拘ラズ、滿洲ニ於テハ降水量ハ7月雨期ニ入リテ最高ニ達シ、8月
稍ミ降リ、9月ニ入リテ激減スルモ、降水量ノ急激ナ增多モ患者ノ發生ヲ阻害セズ、流行ハ益ミ
猖獗ヲ極メルコトヲ認メテキル。

　今次ノ流行ニ就テ氣象ト「ベスト」發生ノ關係ヲ調査セルニ第3圖ニ示ス如キ成績ヲ得ルコトガ
出來タ。本圖ニ於テハ便宜上氣象諸元ハ各ミ1週間ノ1日平均值(雨量ハ1週間ノ總和)ヲ取リ、
又發生患者數ハ1週間ノ累計ヲ取ツテ「グラフ」ヲ作製シタモノデアル。

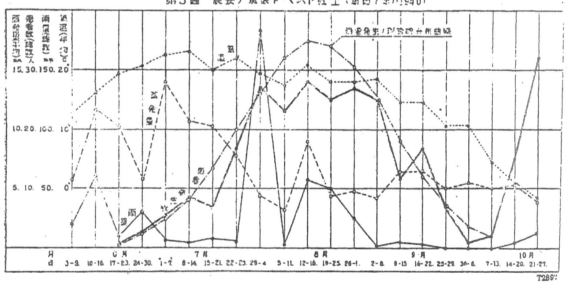

第3圖　農安ノ氣象トベスト發生 (康德7年)(1940)

　氣溫ト患者發生トノ關係、本圖ニ於テ見ル如ク患者發生ハ氣溫ノ上昇(20°C)附近ト共ニ始マ
リ、氣溫ノ低下ト共ニ漸次減少スルノヲ認メルコトガ出來タ。
　蒸發量ト患者發生トノ關係、兩者ノ間ニハ一定ノ關係ヲ認メルコトガ出來ナカツタ。
　雨量ト患者發生トノ關係、兩者ノ間ニハ一定セル關係ヲ認メルコトガ出來ナカツタガ、雨量ノ
增加ガ「ベスト」ノ發生ヲ抑制シナイコトヲ明ニスルコトガ出來タ、之ハ前述ノ舍內ノ成績ニ一
致スルモノデアツタ。滿洲ノ流行ニ限リ斯クノ如ク降雨量ノ影響ガ現レナイノハ滿洲珠ニ內蒙附

553

514—7

近ハ比較的降水量ガ少クテ雨期デモ高々1ケ月150mm或ハ其以下デアツテ、内地ノ雨期ノ1ケ月降水量平均200mm以上デアルノニ比スレバ其ノ降水量ガ少ナイノデ、雨期ト雖モ其ガ「ペスト」ノ發生ニ抑制的ニ働カナイノデアロウト考ヘラレル（吉村氏ニヨル）。

以上ノ如ク「ペスト」ノ發生ガ氣温ト密接ナ関係ガアルノハ氣温ガ「ペスト」ノ發生ニ直接關與スルノデハナクテ、氣温ノ變化ガ嚙歯類及昆蟲類ノ繁殖及生活現象ニ影響スル結果、間接的ニ人「ペスト」ノ流行ニ関係スルモノト考ヘラレル、之ヲ明カニスルニハ「ペスト」關係嚙歯類及昆蟲類ノ生活現象ト氣象トノ關係ヲ明瞭ニスルコトガ必要デアル、卽チ滿洲ノ「ペスト」常在地域ニ於ケル嚙歯類及昆蟲類ノ季節的消長ヲ明カニシ、且其ノ生活現象ト氣象トノ關係ヲ詳細ニ調査スルコトガ必要デアルケレドモ今次流行ニ於テハ其ヲ調査スルコトガ出來ナカツタ。

茲ニ興味深ク思ヘラレル點ハ流行ノ末期ニ再ビ患者多發シタ曲線ヲ示シタコトデアル、之ハ流行ノ末期ニ至リ軍ガ防疫ニ關與シ、隱匿患者ノ摘發ガ嚴重ニナツタタメニ現レタ現象デアツテ、此ノ成蹟ヨリ考ヘテモ滿洲ノ流行地ニ於テ記録サレタ患者ノ發生數並ニ死亡數ハ眞ノ值トハ相當大ナル差ガアルモノト考ヘラレル。

第2節 流行ノ環境衛生學的觀察（吉村氏ノ調査ニヨル）

第1項 農安縣城内各地區ノ特性ト「ペスト」流行トノ關係

農安ニ於ケル「ペスト」ノ發生狀況ヲ地域別ニ觀察スルニ第4圖ノ如クニシテ6月中旬A地區ニ初發シタ「ペスト」ハ次第ニ疫勢ヲ高メ、7月ニ入ルヤA地區ニハ頻々患者ノ發生ヲ見、其ノ大半ハ第二周邊ノ城外地區ニ波及シ、尚一方ニハF地區ニ飛火シテ此處ニ患者ノ多發ヲ見タ、8月ニ入ルヤA、F兩地區ノ流行ハ漸次擴大シ、殊ニA地區ノ流行ハ途ニB地區ニ波及シテ此處ニ患者ノ多發ヲ見、更ニD地區ニ波及スルニ至ツタ、一方F地區ノ流行ハH地區ニ波及シテ此處ニ患者ノ多發ヲ見ルニ至ツタ、9月ニ入ルヤA、B兩地區ノ流行ハ更ニ西方ニ波及シ、F、H兩地區ノ流行ハ更ニE地區及F地區ノ南方地區ニ波及スルニ至リ、10月ニハ更ニG地區ニ波及シテ此處ニ患者ノ多發ヲ認ムルニ至リ、殆ド全縣城内ガ「ペスト」病毒ニヨツテ汚染サレルニ至ツタノデアル、A地區ニ發生シタ流行ガ何故ニ以上述ベタ如キ傳播經路ヲ取ツテ全縣ニ波及スルニ至ツタカヲ玆ニ考察シテミルニ病毒ガ人間ニヨツテ運バレタ場合〔患者ガ自身直接ニ病毒ヲ運搬スル場合ト有關蟲ガ人ノ衣服ニ附着シ或ハ人ノ運搬スル荷物ニ附着シテ運搬サレル場合トガ考ヘラレル〕ト有關鼠ノ移動ニヨツテ運バレタ場合トヲ考ヘルコトガ出來ルデアロウ、而シテ患者ニヨツテ病源ガ運バレタ際ニハ患者ノ發生ハ比較的近親者ニ限ラレテ患者ノ多發ハ認メラレナカツタ従來ノ經驗ニ徵スレバ各地區ニ於ケル患者ノ發生狀況及斃鼠ノ發見狀況ヨリ考ヘルト、A地區ヨリ各地區ヘノ病毒傳播ハ鼠ニヨツテナサレタモノト考ヘラレル、卽チ先ヅ鼠族ノ間ニ前述ノ如キ系統ニテ病毒ノ傳播ガ起リ、其ニ因ツテ人「ペスト」ノ流行ガ前述ノ如キ系統ニテ傳播サレタモノデハナカロウカト考ヘラレル、此ノ事ハ流行ノ末期ニ於テ軍ガ防疫ヲ開始シタ時ニ縣城内ニテ捕獲シタ鼠族及體表寄生昆蟲ニ就テ菌檢索ヲ行ツタ結果、「ドブネズミ」、「マンシユウハツカネズミ」ノ中ニ著

514—8

菌鼠ヲ檢出スルコトガ出來タ成績ヨリモ推論スルコトガ出來ル。

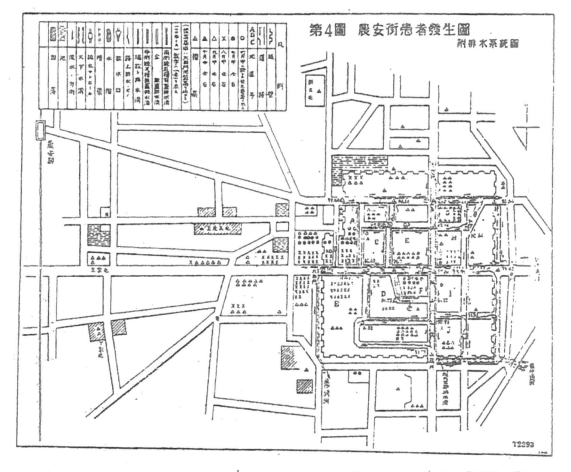

然ラバA地區ニ發生シタ鼠ペスト」ノ流行ガ何故ニ周圍ニ漸次ニ擴大シタ以外ニF地區、H地區、G地區等ニ飛火シタモノデアロウカ、B地區ヘノ波及ニ就テハ鼠ノ習性等ヨリ先ヅ隣接地區ニ波及スルノハ當然デアルト考ヘラレルケレドモF地區、H地區、G地區等ヘノ波及ニ就テハ別ノ考察ガナサレナケレバナラナイノデアロウ、又隣接地區タルC地區或ハD地區ニ何故ニ波及シナカツタノデアロウカ、之ニ就テモ特別ナ考察ガナサレナケレバナラナイデアロウ。

鼠蚤ノ移動及交通ガ下水溝ヲ介シテ行ハレルコトハ想像ニ難クナイノデ先ヅ農安街ノ下水ノ概況ヲ調査セル、第4圖ノ如クニシテ城內ノ各道路ノ兩側ニハ下水溝ガアリ、此等ノ下水溝ハ南門ノ下水溝出口、東門ノ下水溝出口、城壁東側下水溝、城壁西側下水溝等ニ集ツテキル、而シテ城壁外ニ出タ下水ハ東門、南門、城壁ノ西南隅ヨリ夫々一本ノ下水溝トナツテ伊通河ニ注イデキル。

此ノ下水溝ノ狀況ヨリ見ルトA地區トB.F.H.G等ノ各地區ガ特別ナ關係ニ置カレテキルモノトハ考ヘラレナイ、A地區ハ何レノ地區ニモ下水溝ニヨツテハ殆ド同樣ノ條件ニ於テ關係ヅケラレテキルト考ヘルノガ安當デアロウ、然ラバ何故ニB.F.G.H等ノ各地區ニ患者ガ多發シ、C.D.

514番

E.I.J等ノ各地區ニハ散發シタノデアロウカ、若シ各地區ガ平等ニ汚染サレル機會ガアツタト假定スレバ（此ノ假定ハ各地區ガ下水溝ニヨツテA地區ト何レモ同樣ノ條件ニヨツテ結ビ附ケラレテキルコトヨリ考ヘレバ許サルベキ假定デアル）以上ノ如ク地區別ニ患者ノ發生狀況ガ異ツテ現レタコトハ各地區ニ夫々特有ナ「ペスト」流行ノ發生素因ノ强弱ガアルモノト考ヘラレル、此ノ「ペスト」流行ノ發生素因ハ其ノ地區ノ鼠族ノ種類及其ノ數量ト其ニ附着シテヰル蚤ノ種類及其ノ數量ニ直接ノ關係ヲ有シ、又其ノ地區ノ住民ノ文化程度及衛生狀態（生活樣式及生活程度）ニ直接或ハ間接ノ關係ヲ有スルコトハ想像ニ難クナイ。

各地區ノ鼠族及鼠間附着昆蟲ノ種類及其ノ數量ニ就テハ今回ハ何等調査スルコトガ出來ナカツタケレドモ各地區ノ衛生狀態ニ就テハ若干調査スルコトガ出來タノデ各地區ノ住民ノ環境衛生ト「ペスト」發生トノ關係ヲ比較考察シテ、其等ノ間ニ如何ナル關係ガ見出サレルカヲ考察シテミヤウト思フ。勿論此ノ考察ハ前述ノ如キ假定ノ上ニ立ツモノニシテ、自然界ノ現象ニハ人智ノ及ビ得ナイ偶發的事項ノ伴スルコトハ勿論デアルカラ以下述ベル事ガ眞理デアルト主張スルモノデハナイ、唯此ノ種ノ研究ガ比較的少ナイ事實ニ鑑ミテ敢テ茲ニ以下述ベルガ如キ結果ヲ試ミ諸賢ノ批判ヲ乞フモノデアル。

1. 人口密度並ニ家屋密度ト「ペスト」流行トノ關係

各地區ノ人口密度並ニ家屋密度ト患者發生トノ關係ヲ調査セル結果ハ第3表ニ示ス如クニシテ患者發生率ノ高イA,B,F,G,Hノ各地區ハ同時ニ患家ノ發生率モ高イコトヲ認メタ、低クテガラ患者發生率ノ低イC,D,E,I,Jノ各地區トノ間ニハ人口密度及家屋密度ニ於テモ若右差異ノナイコトガ判ツタ、以上ノ成績ヨリ人口密度及家屋密度ト患者發生率トノ間ニハ一定セル關係ハナイモノト考ヘラレル。

第 3 表　人口密度並ニ家屋密度ト患者發生トノ關係（吉村）

地區	人口（人）	家屋數（世帯單位）（戸）	患者數（人）	患家數（戸）	面積（m²）	人口密度「ヘクタール」當リ人口（人）	患者發生率 人口1000人當リノ患者數	家屋密度「ヘクタール」當リ家數（戸）	患家屋數比 1000戸當リノ患家數
○ A	676	144	81	23	58,600	114.0	463	21.3	159
○ B	369	80	26	7	56,300	65.5	704	14.2	87
C	489	94	6	5	90,000	54.3	123	10.5	53
D	697	128	11	9	57,000	122.0	158	22.5	70
E	499	83	7	6	65,000	76.9	140	12.8	72
○ F	182	38	9	7	20,000	91.0	495	19.0	484
○ G	299	100	(13)	(7)	52,000	57.5	(435)	19.2	(205)
○ H	679	153	(16)	(13)	60,000	113.3	(236)	25.5	(85)
I	902	199	(2)	(2)	73,000	123.5	(202)	27.1	(10)
J	987	221	(0)	(0)	94,000	109.9	(0)	23.5	(0)
總計又ハ平均	5,684	1,240	121	79	625,000	90.9	213.9	19.8	63.7

註　1) A,B兩地區ノ成績ハ全部貫測セル結果ナルモ、C〜F地區ノ人口、家屋數ハ各區ノ區長ヨリ申告セシメタルモノニシテ、面積、患者數及患家數ハ實測ニヨルモノナリ、從G〜J區ノ人口、患者數、患家數ハ主トシテ區長ノ申告ニヨルモノニシテ不確實ナリ。
　　2) 患家トハ患者ノ發生セル世帯ヲ意味ス。
　　3) （ ）ヲ附シタルハ調査成績ノ不確實ナルモノヲ示ス。
　　4) ○ヲ附シタルハ流行ノ激シキ地區ヲ示ス。

514—10

2. 職業ノ状況ト「ペスト」流行トノ關係

職業ノ種類ハ「ペスト」發生ニ對シ同様ノ關係ヲ有スルト考ヘラレルモノハ可及的ニ之ヲ纏メ
ル方針ノ下ニ之ヲ次ノ如ク分類シタ。

　　　　労務關係……店員、鍛冶、吏員、苦力、學生

　　　　飲食物關係……飲食商、牛乳商、酒商、穀類商、果實商、農業

　　　　衣類靴關係……呉服商、質屋、靴商、皮革業

　　　　家具建築關係……大工業、材木商、運送業、印刷業、家具商

　　　　雑商關係……雑貨商(「デパート」、小賣商)、薬商、理髮業、煙草商、寫眞業

　　　　無　　職……失業、寡婦、老人、子供

各地區ノ住民ノ職業ヲ上述ノ分類ニ從ツテ調査シタ成績ハ第4表ニ示ス如クニシテ之ト「ペ
スト患者發生ノ状況(第3表)トヲ比較スルニ患者ノ多發セルA.B.F.G.Hノ各地區ニ於テハ
飲食物關係ノ職業ガ他ノ患者散發地區ニ比シテ多イノヲ認メタ、其ノ他ノ職業ニ關シテハ患者
多發地區ト散發地區トノ間ニハ差異ガ認メラレナカツタ、飲食物關係職業ノ多イ地區ニ患者ガ
多發シタノハ斯様ナ地區デハ鼠族ガ多ク棲息シ且住民トノ接觸ガ頻繁ナ為メデハナイカト考ヘ
ラレル。

第4表　　各地區住民職業分布比率(吉村)

地　區	労務關係 (%)	家具建築關係 (%)	衣類靴關係 (%)	飲食物關係 (%)	雑商關係 (%)	無　職 (%)
○ A	25.7	6.3	4.9	19.4	36.8	7.0
○ B	16.3	8.8	12.5	20.0	25.0	17.5
C	27.7	3.2	8.5	13.8	27.7	19.1
D	25.8	5.5	19.5	14.1	23.4	11.7
E	25.3	4.8	14.5	10.8	39.8	4.8
○ F	18.4	0	34.2	5.3	34.2	7.8
○ G	53.0	4.0	11.0	13.0	7.0	12.0
○ H	31.4	5.2	9.8	19.6	26.8	6.6
I	38.2	4.0	4.5	10.6	35.2	7.5
J	39.8	2.4	10.4	13.1	23.1	11.8
平　均	32.7	4.4	10.7	14.4	27.1	10.2

註　1)　○ヲ附シタルハ流行ノ激シキ地區ヲ示ス。

3. 飼育動物ノ状況ト「ペスト」流行トノ關係

各地區ニ就テ飼育動物ノ分布状態ヲ檢査セル成績ハ第5表ニ示ス如クニシテ患者多發地區ノ
一戸當リノ飼育動物類ハ何レモ全市街ノ平均値ヨリモ大ニシテ、飼育動物ノ有無ト「ペスト」發
生トノ間ニハ若干ノ關係ノアルコトヲ思ハセタ。

第5表　各地區ノ飼育動物分布調査（吉村）

地區		大動物				中動物			小動物			總數	密度（一戶當リノ飼育數）
		馬	牛	豚	山羊	兎	犬	猫	雞	家鴨	信鳥		
○	A	17	1	103 (28.8%)	4	0	7 (1.6%)	0	170	124	5 (69.6%)	431 (100%)	2.99
○	B	41	19	59 (33.1%)	0	1	6 (2.2%)	1	137	84	11 (64.7%)	359 (100%)	4.49
	C	31	3	83 (42.8%)	9	0	0 (4.0%)	1	105	34	6 (53.2%)	273 (100%)	2.91
	D	14	3	74 (51.2%)	0	0	0 (3.8%)	0	16	53	9 (45.0%)	176 (100%)	1.38
	E	5	0	16 (31.9%)	0	0	3 (4.6%)	0	35	4	3 (63.5%)	66 (100%)	0.80
○	F	6	0	17 (30.7%)	0	10	(13.3%)	0	19	21	2 (56.0%)	75 (100%)	1.97
○	G	7	0	36 (22.7%)	0	0	10 (6.4%)	2	89	38	7 (70.9%)	189 (100%)	1.89
○	H	28	2	14 (26.4%)	0	0	7 (4.1%)	0	90	21	5 (69.5%)	167 (100%)	1.09
	I	43	1	109 (41.5%)	0	7	3 (3.1%)	1	142	55	7 (55.4%)	368 (100%)	1.85
	J	7	3	43 (23.2%)	0	11	6 (7.9%)	1	114	38	5 (68.9%)	228 (100%)	1.03
平	計均	109	32	554 (33.9%)	4	29	59 (3.9%)	6	917	472	60 (62.2%)	2,332 (100%)	1.88

註　1)　括弧內ノ數値ハ同一地區內ノ動物ノ大、中、小組別ノ比率ヲ示ス。
　　　2)　○印ハ流行ノ激シキ地區ヲ示ス。

4. 家屋ノ構造及方位ト「ペスト」流行トノ關係

　　各地區ノ家屋ヲ其ノ方位並ニ構造別ニ調査セル成績ハ第6表ニ示ス如クニシテ家屋構造ニ就テハ患者多發地區ト患者散發地區トノ間ニハ著明ナ差異ヲ認メルコトガ出來ナカツタ、又方位ニ就テモ兩者ノ間ニ著明ナ差異ヲ認メルコトガ出來ナカツタ。

514—12

第6表　農安　各地區ノ家屋構造及方位(吉村)

地區號	家屋總數	家屋構造別比率				家屋方位別比率			
		土造 1「ヘクタール」當リ戸數	煉瓦造リ	煉瓦土造折中	木造	東向	西向	南向	北向
○ A	144戸	79.9%(17.0戸)	7.6%	2.1%	10.4%	7.6%	18.8%	73.6%	0.0%
○ B	80〃	40.0〃(5.7〃)	38.7〃	2.5〃	18.8〃	16.9〃	12.1〃	36.1〃	34.9〃
C	94〃	36.2〃(3.8〃)	43.6〃	20.2〃	0〃	35.1〃	18.8〃	42.1〃	4.0〃
D	128〃	40.6〃(9.1〃)	56.3〃	3.1〃	0〃	48.9〃	5.3〃	26.2〃	19.6〃
E	83〃	38.6〃(4.9〃)	56.6〃	4.8〃	0〃	20.7〃	10.7〃	48.9〃	20.0〃
○ F	38〃	13.2〃(2.5〃)	86.8〃	0〃	0〃	23.1〃	16.9〃	35.4〃	24.6〃
○ G	100〃	52.0〃(10.0〃)	39.0〃	9.0〃	0〃				
○ H	153〃	41.3〃(10.5〃)	56.2〃	2.6〃	0〃				
I	199〃	48.2〃(13.1〃)	47.2〃	4.5〃	0〃				
J	221〃	74.2〃(17.5〃)	23.5〃	2.3〃	0〃				
總計(平均)	1,240〃	52.0〃(10.3〃)	40.8〃	4.8〃	2.4〃				

備考　但シ土造家屋ノ内ニハ純粹ノ土造ノ外ニハ木造土造ノ折中ノモノヲ合ミ、煉瓦造リノ内ニハ木造煉瓦造リノ折中ノモノヲ含ム、又方位ノ内、東、西、南、北ノ中間ノモノ例ヘバ東南向キノモノハ東又ハ南ノ内ノ多タ片寄レル方向ノ方位中ニ含マシメタリ。

5. 土地ノ高低並ニ下水ノ狀況ト「ベスト」流行トノ關係

　　第1圖及第4圖ニテ明カデアル如ク農安衙ハ其ノ北西ハ一般ニ高ク東南ハ低クナリ城外ニ至ツテ一層低クナツテ伊通河ニ達シテキル土地ノ高低ヲ城内ノ各地區ニ就テ調査シ、之ト流行トノ關係ヲ比較セルニ其ノ間ニ特別ナ關係ヲ認メルコトハ出來ナカツタ、又下水ノ狀況ヲ各地區ニ就テ比較セルニB地區ヲ除イテ一般ニ下水ヲ放流セル地區多ク、之ト「ベスト」流行トノ間ニハ一定ノ關係ヲ認メルコトガ出來ナカツタ。

6. 各地區ノ環境衞生的特性ト「ベスト」流行トノ關係總括

　　患者多發地區ト患者散發地區ニ就テ人口密度、家屋密度、職業ノ狀況、飼育動物、家屋構造及方位土地ノ高低及下水ノ狀況等ヲ調査シ、「ベスト」流行トノ關係ヲ檢査セルニ患者多發地區ハ患者散發地區ニ比シテ飲食物關係ノ職業ヲ營ムモノノ多キ他ニハ環境衞生學的ニハ特別ナ差異ヲ認メルコトガ出來ナカツタ、恐ラク各地區ノ「ベスト」發生素因ハ前述セル如ク其ノ地區ノ鼠族ノ種類及其ノ數量ト其ニ附着シテキル蚤ノ種類及其ノ數量ト最モ密接ナ關係ヲ有スルモノト考ヘラレル、而シテ住民ノ環境衞生學的諸元ハ此ノ鼠族並ニ昆蟲ノ繁殖及生活現象ニ直接影響ヲ與ヘ、之ガ間接ニ人ベスト」ノ流行ニ影響シテ來ルモノト考ヘラレル、從ツテ將來住民ノ環境衞生ト鼠族並ニ昆蟲ノ生活現象トノ關係ヲ詳細ニ研究スルコトガ必要デアツテ、其ノ結果或地區ノ「ベスト」發生素因トイフ問題ハ解決サレルニ至ルモノト考ヘラレル。

　　　第2項　「ベスト患者ト一般住民ノ環境ノ比較

　　「ベスト患者ガ如何ナル居住環境ニ在ルモノヨリ發生スルモノデアルカヲ知ルコトハ極メテ興味深イコトデアルノデ患者發生地區ニ於テ患者發生家屋ト非發生家屋ト」ニ就テ環境衞生學的ノ調査

ヲナシ、患者ト一般住民ノ居住環境トヲ比較セルニ興味アル成績ヲ得タノデ茲ニ報告スル次第デアル。

1. 患者ノ職業ノ状況

　　患者ノ職業ト一般住民ノ職業ノ比率トヲ比較シタ結果ハ第7表ニ示ス如クデアル（但シ調査分類シタノハ世帯主ノ職業ニ援ツタモノデアル）、本表ニテ見ル如ク患者ノ職業ノ比率ヲ一般住民ノ其ニ比較スル飲食物關係及家具建築關係ニ於テ其ノ比率高ク、勞務關係者及衣類關係ニ於テ其ノ比率低イノヲ認メタ、又「ペスト」患者ハ飲食物關係並ニ家具建築關係ノ職業ニ關與シテキル者ニ多ク發生シ、勞務關係及衣類關係ノ職業ニ關與シテキル者ニ比較的少ナイゴトヲ明カニシタ、此ノ飲食物關係業者（致類業者ヲモ含ム）及家具建築業者（運送業者ヲモ含ム）ニ多イ理由ハ鼠ニ接スル機會ガ多イ爲メデアロウト考ヘラレル、之ニ反シテ勞務關係業者（軍人、官吏、會社員ヲ含ム）及衣類靴業者（呉服店、仕立屋等ヲ含ム）ニ少イノハ此等ノ職業ノ者ノ比較的知識程度高クシテ衛生的ナ生活ヲ營ミ、又然ラザル場合ニモ其ノ家屋内比較的清潔ニシテ鼠族ノ侵入跳梁少キ爲ナラント考ヘラル。

第7表　職業ト患者發生（吉村）

項　　目		勞務關係	家具建築關係	衣類靴關係	飲食物關係	職　商	無　職	計
患者	世帯數	9	9	3	26	24	8	79
	比率（%）	12.4±3.5	11.4±3.5	3.8±2.2	32.9±5.2	30.4±5.1	10.1±3.3	100.0
一般住民	世帯數	402	55	133	179	343	128	1,240
	比率（%）	32.7±1.3	4.4±0.6	10.7±0.9	14.4±1.0	27.6±1.3	10.2±0.9	100.0
	比率ノ差（%）	−(21.3)±3.6	+(7.0)±2.2	−6.9±2.3	+(18.5)±5.2	+(2.8±5.2	−(0.1)	
	發生率（%）	2.2±0.7	16.4±4.9	2.3±1.3	14.5±3.1	7.0±1.4	6.3±2.1	6.4±0.7

　　備考　±以下ノ數値ハ標準偏差ヲ示ス、又比率ノ差ニ於テ＋ハ患者ノ方ガ一般住民ヨリモ多イ場合、−ハ患者ノ方ガ一般ヨリモ少キ場合ヲ示ス、（　）ハ有意ノ差ヲ示ス。

2. 家屋ノ構造及方位ノ比較

　　患者發生家屋ト一般家屋ニ就テ構造上ノ比較ヲナセル成績ハ第8表ニ示ス如ク、ニシテ兩者ノ間ニハ差異ヲ認メルコトガ出來ナカツタ、一般ニハ陳舊ナ泥造リノ家屋ニ於テ鼠ニ藏其多ク爲メニ「ペスト」ノ發生多キモノトサレテ居リ、又農安地方ノ土民ノ舊家ヘハヨレバ数十年間「ペスト」ノ發生ヲ見ナイト云フ、然ルニ今次ノ調査成績ニ於テハ家屋ノ構造ト患者發生トノ間ニ差異ヲ認メルコトガ出來ナカツタノハ調査セル民家ガ一様ニ隊舍不潔ナモノデ構造ノ家屋デモ所々ニ鼠穴ヲ散見スル状態デアツテ、構造上ノ防鼠ニ對スル相違ガ年代ニ職關セルコト（孰レモ20年以上ヲ經過セル家屋デアル）ニ故ヘレバ「ペスト」發生ニ對シテ著明ナ差異ヲ生ジナカツタモノデアロウト考ヘラレル。

　　次ニ家屋方位（家屋正面方向）ニ就テ比較セルニ第9表ノ如キ成績ニシテ患家ト一般家屋トノ間ニハ著明ナ差異ヲ認メナカツタ、又各方位ニヨル患家發生率ノ差ヲ認メルコトモ出來テカツタ。

S14—14

第 8 表　家屋構造ト患者發生トノ關係(吉村)
(西北、西南、兩隅ニ於ケル實地調査)

家屋構造	一般家屋		患者家屋		患者發生率(±標準偏差)(％)
	總數	比率(％)	總數	比率(％)	
煉瓦造	33	15	3	10	9.1±5.0
煉瓦土造折中	5	2	2	7	13.2±5.5
土造	137	61	18	60	13.1±2.9
土造、木造折中	10	5	1	3	
木造	30	13	4	13	14.3±5.0
煉瓦木造折中	9	4	2	7	
總計	224	100	30	100	13.4±2.4

第 9 表　家屋方位ト患者發生トノ關係(吉村)

方法	一般家屋		患家		患家發生率(±標準偏差)(％)
	總數	比率(％)	總數	比率(％)	
東	322	26.6	18	26.9	5.59±1.289
西	176	14.5	5	7.5	2.84±1.24
南	536	44.3	40	59.7	7.46±1.14
北	177	14.6	4	6.0	2.26±1.13
總計	1,211	100.0	67	100.0	5.53±0.65

備考　調査家屋ハ第5表ノモノト多少相異セリ。

3. 家屋內環境ノ比較

A. B兩地區ニ於テ患家ト一般民家ニ就テ氣容、窓面積ト床面積ノ比、家屋內紫外線ノ强度、照度、家屋內氣溫及濕度等ヲ調查シタ成績ハ第10表及第11表ノ如クデアル、第10表ニ就テ説明スレバ表中ニ居間ニ就テノ氣容トアルノハ各民家ノ蓋所、便所、倉庫等ヲ除キ、主トシテ居間又ハ寢室トシテ使用セル室ニ就テ測定シタ氣容デアル、又家全體ニ就テノ氣容トハ蓋所、土間(玄關)居間等ヲ含メテ測定シタ氣容デアル、本表ニ見ル如ク氣容及採光窓面積ノ點ニ於テハ患家ト一般民家トノ間ニハ殆ド差異ヲ認メルコトガ出來ナカツタ。

次ニ第11表ニ就テ見ルニ家屋內ノ紫外線ノ强度、照度、外界ト室內ノ氣溫ノ差、外界ト室內ノ比濕度ノ差等ニ就テハ一般民家ト患家トノ間ニハ殆ド差異ガ認メラレナカツタ、唯室內氣溫ノ平均值ガ患家ノ方ガ比較的低クアツタ、而シテ其ノ差ハ居間ノ氣溫ノ差デハナクテ土間ノ氣溫ガ患家ニ於テ低イタメデアツタ、此ノ差ガ何ニヨルカハ明カデナイガ患家ニ於テハ健康隔離サレテ住人ガ僅少トナツテキルノデ炊事ノ爲ノ火氣ガ比較的少ナイタメデアルカモ知レナイ、從ツテ之ト「ペスト」發生トノ間ニ直接ノ因果關係ガアルカ否カハ疑問デアル。

第10表　氣容ト採光窓ノ面積(吉村)

項目	種別	測定戸數	居間ニ就テノ平均値	家屋全體ニ就テノ平均値
1人當リ氣容	患家	29	12.48±1.61m³	26.61±2.50m³
(m³)	一般民家	39	13.72±1.93〃	31.14±3.05〃
採光面積	患家	42	16.1±1.2	16.4±1.1
床面積(%)	一般民家	56	16.3±1.0	16.7±1.0

備考：家屋内間切リニアル窓ハ其ノ面積ノ10%ヲ以テ有効面積ト見做シ、之ヲ外界ニ面セル窓面積ニ算入ス、±ハ平均値ノ標準偏差ヲ示ス。

第11表　室内採光並ニ溫濕度(吉村)

家類別	測定戸數	窓種別	紫外線強度	照度(ルックス)	外界ト室内トノ溫度ノ差	外界ト室内トノ比溫度ノ差
患家	32	居間	2.3±0.2	132.0±25.1	+14.4°C ±0.6	−3.7±1.8%
		土間	2.1±0.2	121.5±24.0	+ 1.5 ±0.7	−0.4±2.0
		平均	2.2±0.1	126.9±17.3	+ 3.0 ±0.5	−2.1±1.1
一般民家	51	居間	2.4±0.2	133.9±20.4	+ 5.0 ±0.6	−2.1±1.3
		土間	2.1±0.2	121.6±18.3	+ 6.3 ±0.6	−0.3±1.4
		平均	2.3±0.1	127.9±13.6	+ 5.7 ±0.4	−1.2±1.1

備考：各測定ハ一戸ニ付代表的ナル居間各ミ一ニ付行ヒ、且時別ハ概ネ10～14時ノ畫間ニシテ室内溫度平均値9.9°C濕度平均値68.5%ナリ、十ハ室内溫濕度高キ事ヲ示シ、－ハ其ノ反對ナリ、±ハ平均値ノ標準偏差ヲ示ス。

4. 民家周圍ノ汚物處理ノ狀況

　　A.B兩地區ニ於テ患家ト一般民家トニ就テ各民家ノ周圍1,000m²中ニ含マレル塵捨場、堆肥ノ數、水溜ノ數、家畜小屋數、便所數等ヲ調査シ、此等ヲ平均シタ結果ハ第12表ニ示ス如クニシテ一般民家ト患家トノ間ニハ差異ヲ認メルコトガ出來ナカツタ。

第12表　周圍1,000m²內ノ汚物處理狀況(吉村)

種別	測定戸數	塵捨場及堆肥數	水溜(ドブ)ノ數	家畜小屋數	便所數
患家	34	1.32±0.27	0.71±0.16	0.97±0.21	0.71±0.14
一般民家	258	1.45±0.10	0.40±0.04	1.27±0.09	0.83±0.06

備考　±以下ノ數値ハ平均値ニ附屬スル標準偏差ナリ。

5. 飼育動物ノ狀況

　　一般民家並ニ患家ノ飼育動物ヲ調査セル成績ハ第18表ニ示ス如クニシテ患家ニ於テハ一般民家ニ比シテ大動物ノ極メテ多イノヲ認メタ、之ハ斯カル大動物ヲ多數飼育スル時ニハ民家ノ周圍ガ不潔トナツテ鼠ノ良キ溫床ヲ提供スルタメ「ペスト」發生ニ關係アルガ如キ成績ヲ得タモノト考ヘラレルケレドモ果シテ斯カル關係ガ他ノ流行地ニ於テモ認メラレルカ否カハ將來ノ問

514—16

探ヲ要スルモノト思ヘラル、従ツテ此ノ成績ヨリミカラ大動物ヲ多数飼育スルコトガ其ノ土地ニ
「ペスト」發生素因ヲ與ヘルモノデアルト判定スルコトハ差控ヘナケレバナラナイデアロウ。

第13表　患家ト一般民家ノ飼育動物ノ比較（吉村）

種別	調戸定数	項　　目	大　動　物	中　動　物	小動物（鳥）	計
患家	79	動物比率(%)	50.4±2.3	1.6±0.6	48.0±2.3	1000.0
		一戸當リ飼育数	2.18	0.07	2.07	4.32±0.45
一般民家	1,240	動物比率(%)	33.9±1.0	3.9±0.4	62.2±1.0	1000.0
		一戸當リ飼育数	0.64	0.08	1.17	1.88±0.11
動物比率ノ差（%）			+16.5±2.5	−2.3±0.7	−14.2±2.5	2.44±0.46

備考：大動物、中動物、小動物ノ内譯ハ第3表ニ同ジ。
十ハ患家ノ飼育ノ多キ場合ヲ示シ、一ハ其ノ反對ナリ。
土以下ハ標準偏差ナリ。

6.「ペスト患者ト一般住民ノ環境衛生ノ比較總括

　　患家ト一般民家トノ環境衛生ヲ比較シタ結果ヲ總括スルニ「ペスト患者ハ職業別ニハ飲食物
關係業者及家具建築關係業者ニ多ク發生シ、又大動物ヲ多ク飼育シテヰル家屋ニ多ク發生シテ
ヰルコトヲ認メタ、其ノ理由ハ恐ラク斯様ナ民家ニ於テハ鼠ノ棲息數多ク、又住民ト鼠ノ接觸
スル機會ガ比較的多イ爲メデアロウト考ヘラレル。

　　其ノ他ノ事項即チ民家周圍ノ汚物處理ノ狀況家屋内ノ物理的環境、家屋ノ構造等ニ就テハ一
般民家ト患家トノ間ハ特別ナ差異ノナイ様ナ成績ガ得ラレタ。

　　併シナガラ常識的ニモ住民ノ密居セル、暗イ濕氣ノ多イ不潔ナ家屋ハ鼠及蚤ノ良キ溫床トナ
リ、從ツテ「ペスト」發生素因ヲ有スルモノト考ヘラレルノデ「ペスト」發生素因ニ就テノ環境衛
生學的研究ハ將來更ニ詳細ニ究明セラルベキ問題デアロウ。

　　　第3項　本　節　小　括

1.　農安縣城内ノ患者多發地區ト患者散發地區ニ就テ人口密度、家屋密度、職業ノ狀況、飼育動
物ノ狀況、家屋ノ構造及方位、土地ノ高低、下水ノ狀況等ヲ調査シテ比較セル結果、患者多發
地區ハ患者散發地區ニ比シテ飲食物關係ノ職業ニ從ムモノノ多イノヲ認メタケレドモ其ノ他ノ
諸元ニ就テハ兩者ノ間ニ著明ナ差異ハ認メラレナカツタ、併シナガラ農安縣ハ一般的ニ觀テ衛
生狀態不良ニシテ鼠及蚤ノ良キ溫床ヲ提供シ、從ツテ一度本縣ニ「ペスト」ノ病毒侵入スル時ハ
忽チ全縣ニ波及シテ大流行ヲ惹起シ得ル條件ヲ具備シテヰルモノト考ヘラレル。

2.　農安縣一般民家ト患家トニ就テ其ノ職業、家屋構造及方位、家屋内氣溫及濕度及採光狀態、
家屋周圍ノ汚物處理ノ狀況、飼育動物ノ狀況等ヲ比較シタ結果、「ペスト患者發生ノ多イノハ飲
食物關係業者並ニ家具建築關係業者ニシテ衣服類關係業者、勞務關係業者ニハ比較的發生ノ少
ナイノヲ認メタ、之ハ住民ト鼠トノ接觸機會ノ多少、家屋内清潔ノ狀況等ニ差ガアル爲メデア

563

ロウト考ヘラレル、又「ペスト患豪ニ於テハ飼育動物特ニ大動物ノ多數デブルコトヲ認メタ
ガ、之モ亦飼育動物多キ爲ニ其ノ居住環境ガ非衛生的トナリ、從ツテ鼠ノ良キ温床トナルヤ否ト
ニ因ルモノト考ヘラレル。其ノ他ノ諸元ニ就テハ兩者ノ間ニ大差ハ認メラレテヰカツタ。

之ヲ要スルニ住民ノ環境衛生學的諸元ハ鼠族及昆蟲ノ繁殖及生活現象ニ直接影響シ、其ガ間
接ニ人ペスト」ノ流行ニ影響シテ來ルモノト考ヘラレル。從ツテ將來ハ住民ノ環境衛生ト鼠族
並ニ昆蟲ノ生理現象トノ關係ヲ詳細ニ研究スルコトガ必要デアロウ。

第2節　流行ノ統計的觀察

今大興安ノ「ペスト」流行ハ第2圖ニ示ス如ク6月18日ニ患者ガ初發シテョリ11月26日ニ終熄ス
ル迄凡ソ163日ノ長キニ及ビ其ノ間ニ發生セル「ペスト患者ハ記録サレタモノ353名デアルケレ
モ其ノ他ニ蔽蔽サレタト考ヘラレルモノモ相當ニアルノデ實際ノ患者數ハ可ナリニ多イモノ推測
ハレル。就レニセヨ全人口 30,800人ニ對シテ約 1.5% 以上ノ罹患率ヲ示スモノデアルガヲ相當ニ
激烈ナ流行デアツタト考ヘラレル。

此ノ間ニ得ラレタ患者ニ關スル統計的ノ資料ハ防疫員ガ防疫診療ノ傍ラ蒐集シタモノデアルカラ
正確ヲ期シ得ナイガ、之モ亦現在ノ防疫機構ニ於テハ止ムヲ得ナイコトデアロウ。

今前郭旗調査所ノ防疫員ニョツテ蒐集サレタ資料ニョツテ統計的觀察ヲ試ミレハ次ノ如クデア
ル。

性別、年齡別患者發生狀況、檢查セル成績ハ第14表ニ示ス如クニシテ各年齡ノ間ニハ太ナル差
異ガ認メラレナカツタガ、男31～40歲、女21～40歲ノ間ノ患者ガ多カザルモ併シナガラ人口ノ年
齡的構成ガ明瞭デナイノデ此ノ成績カラハ罹患率ノ年齡的差異ヲ明ニスルコトハ出來ナカツ
タ。

第14表　性別、年齡別患者發生狀況

性別 年齡(歲)	患者數			患者總數ニ對スル割合		
	男	女	計	男	女	計
1～5	8	14	22	12	18	14
6～10	17	13	30			
11～15	14	14	28	15	16	16
16～20	18	11	29			
21～30	20	31	51	9	20	14
31～40	47	35	82	23	23	23
41～50	27	9	36	13	6	10
51～60	34	12	46	16	8	13
61～70	15	8	23	7	5	6
70歲以上	4	2	6	1	1	1
計	204	149	353	100	100	100

病型、診斷名ガ確實デナイノデ各型ノ出現率ヲ明カニスルコトハ出來デガツタケレモ、公表

514—18

ノ流行ハ腺ペスト」ノ流行ニシテ病型トシテハ腺ペスト」ガ大部分デアリ、其ニ皮膚ペスト」、「ペスト敗血症、肺ペスト」等ガ若干介在シテキタ。

経過日数、之ニ就テモ正確ナ統計資料ヲ得ルコトハ出來ナカツタガ「ペスト」隔離所勤務員ノ調査シタ成績ニ據レバ第15表ノ如クニシテ一般ニ經過日數ノ短イコトガ認メラレタ、之ハ滿人ハ極メテ亟篤ナ症狀ヲ呈シナケレバ發病ト自覺シナイ爲デアロウト考ヘラレル。

第15表　患者ノ經過日數

經過日數	實　數
1　日	113
2　〃	75
3　〃	41
4　〃	24
5　〃	16
6　〃	13
7　〃	4
8　〃	2
9　〃	1
10　〃	3
11　〃	2
12日以上	0
平　均	2.5日

死亡率、今次流行ノ死亡率ハ84.4%（患者353名中死亡者296名）ニシテ、之ハ一般ノ腺ペスト」流行ニ於ケル死亡率ニ類似スル値デアツタ。

以上ノ如ク今次農安ノ「ペスト流行ハ大體從來ノ滿洲ニ於テ經驗サレタ流行ト其ノ流行狀態ヲ一ニシテキテ特異ナ點ハ認メラレナカツタ。

第3章　傳染經路ニ關スル考察

滿洲ノ「ペスト常在地域ニ於ケル「ペスト病毒ノ傳播ニ關シテ倉內ハ人ヨリ人ニ携行セラレテ周圍ニ蔓延スル如ク考ヘ、鼠ペスト」ナキ人ペスト」ノ流行デアロウト考ヘ、原發性流行ヲ起ス傳染源トシテハ鼠科ヨリモ寧ロ內蒙沙漠平原特異ノ「ハタリス」、跳兎等ガヨリ多ク關與スルモノノ如ク考ヘラレルト述ベテキル、此ノ問題ニ關シテハ其ノ後春日ハ流行時ノ「ドブネズミ」、「モウコハツカネズミ」、「セスヂキヌゲネズミ」、「セスヂネズミ」等ヨリ「ペスト菌ヲ分離シ、且鼠體附着ノ「ケオビス鼠蚤ヨリ菌ヲ檢出シ、其ノ成績ヨリ人ペスト」ノ直接ノ原因ハ鼠ペスト」デアロウト述ベテキル、今次流行ニ於テ余等ハ流行ノ末期デハアツタガ有菌鼠（「ドブネズミ」及「アジアハツカネズミ」）ヲ檢出シ、又鼠體ニハ「ケオビス鼠蚤及「アニ ズス鼠蚤ガ多數附着シテキルノヲ認メタ、而シテ流行ノ狀態ヲ環境衞生學的ニ檢査シタ成績ニヨツテモ患者ノ發生ガ鼠族及昆蟲ト密接ナ關係ヲ有スルコトヲ推論スルコトガ出來タ、從ツテ是等ノ成績ヨリ考ヘレバ滿洲ノ「ペスト常在地域ニ於テハ人ペスト」ノ直接ノ傳染源トナルモノハ「ドブネズミ」間ノ流行ニシテ、其ヲ媒介スルノハ「ケオビス鼠蚤ガ主デアリ、「アニ ズス鼠蚤モ亦相當ナ役割ヲシテキルモノデアルト考ヘルノガ妥當デアロウ、而シテ流行ノ季節的消長ニ關與スル要約及病毒ノ越年等ノ問題ニ就テハ更ニ詳細ナ研究ガナサレナケレバ解決サレナイデアロウト考ヘラレル。

総　　括

昭和15年6月中旬ニ發生シ、同年11月下旬ニ終熄シタ農安ノ「ペスト」流行ニ就テ、先ヅ流行ノ發生狀態及流行狀態ニ就テ述ベ、次ニ其ニ就テ疫學的觀察ヲ試ミタ。

今次流行ハ農安縣城ニ原發シタ流行ニシテ鼠ペスト」ニ由來スル人ペスト」ノ流行デアルト考ヘ

ラレルケレドモ其ノ病毒搬入ノ經路ニ就テハ不明デアツタ。

　今次流行ハ6月中旬ニ發生シ、11月下旬ニ終熄スル迄凡ソ160餘日ニ亘リ、其ノ間ニ發生シタ患者ハ記錄サレタノミニテモ353名ニ上リ、全人口ノ約1.5％ニ相當スル數デアツタ。

　今次流行ノ季節的消長ヲ觀察スルニ其ハ滿洲ノ「ペスト」常在地域ニ於ケル年々ノ「ペスト」ノ流行曲線（季節的消長）ト類似シテキテ、氣溫ト密接ナ關係ヲ有スルコトヲ認メタ。

　今次流行ニ於テ盤安縣城内ノ患者多發地區ト患者散發地區ニ就テ環境衛生學的調査ヲナシ、兩者ノ成績ヲ比較シテ觀ルニ患者多發地區ハ患者散發地區ニ比シテ飲食物關係ノ職業ヲ營ムモノノ多イコトヲ認メタケレドモ其ノ他ノ點ニ就テハ特別ナ差異ハ認メラレナカツタ、併シナガラ盤安縣ハ全般的ニ觀テ環境衛生學的ニハ「ペスト流行ノ發生素因ヲ具備シテキルコトヲ認メタ。

　尚患者發生家屋ト一般民家ニ就テ環境衛生學的調査ヲナシ、兩者ノ成績ヲ比較シテ觀ルニ「ペスト患者ノ發生ハ飲食物關係業者並ニ建築關係業者ノ家族ニ多ク、又患家ニハ一般民家ニ比シ家畜特ニ犬動物ノ多數飼育サレテキルノヲ認メタ。

　今次流行ヲ統計的ニ觀察シタ成績ハ大體從來ノ滿洲ノ「ペスト常在地域ニ於ケル流行ノ其ト類似シテキテ特異ナ點ハ認メラレナカツタ。

　最後ニ種々ノ調査成績ヲ綜合シテ考察スレバ今次流行ニ於テハ人ペスト」ノ直接ノ傳染源ハ「ドブネズミ」間ノ病獸デアツタト考ヘラレルコトヲ述ベタ。

文　獻

1) Tsuchia, K. a Li Te Chuan : Jl. Orient. Med., (1929), 10, 33, 11, 85.　　2) 滿鐵衛生課：日本公衆保健協會雜誌、(昭. 3)、4, 143.　　3) 滿鐵衛生課：滿洲醫學雜誌、(昭. 3), 9, 67.　　4) 倉内：滿洲醫學雜誌、(昭. 5), 12, 569.　　5) 倉内：滿洲醫學雜誌、(昭. 5)、12, 671, 827.　　6) 滿鐵衛生課：「ペスト」防疫指針、(康德2年6月)　　7) 安東洪次：日本傳染病學會雜誌、(昭. 5)、4, 411.　　8) 春日：東京醫事雜誌、(昭. 12), 3041、1929.　　9) 明治43, 4年南滿洲「ペスト」流行史　　10) 春日：細菌學雜誌、(昭. 14)、518, 231.　　11) 春日：大陸醫學、(昭. 16,)、1, 38.　　12) 飯村：日本ニ於ケル「ペスト」ノ疫學ニ關スル綜合的研究、內務省衛生局、(昭. 4).　　13) 飯村：日本傳染病學會雜誌、(昭. 3)、3, 724, 797.　　14) 倉岡彦助：臺灣ニ於ケル「ペスト」ノ流行學的研究、臺灣醫學會、(大. 9, 3).　　15) 寺島毅一：大阪醫學會雜誌、(明. 41)、6, 10, 12.

4.2.3　昭和 15 年農安及新京ニ発生セル「ペスト」流行ニ就テ　第 1 編　流行ノ疫学的観察（其ノ 2）新京ノ流行ニ就テ

资料出处：日本国立国会図書館関西館蔵、博士論文。

内容点评：本资料为《陆军军医学校防疫研究报告》第 2 部第 515 号《关于昭和 15 年农安和新京发生的鼠疫流行　第 1 编　鼠疫流行的疫学观察（其 2）关于新京的流行》，1943 年 4 月 12 日提交。

陸軍軍醫學校防疫研究報告
第2部　第515號

昭和15年農安及新京ニ發生セル「ペスト」流行ニ就テ
第1編　流行ノ疫學的觀察（其ノ2）
新京ノ流行ニ就テ

陸軍軍醫學校軍陣防疫學教室（主任　增田大佐）

陸軍軍醫少佐　高　橋　正　彦

第　　2　　部
原　　　　著
分　類
441—2
333—41
受附 昭和 18. 4. 12

515—2

擔任指導　陸軍軍醫少將　石　　井　　四　　郎

緒　　言

　昭和15年9月下旬新京ニ「ベスト」ノ流行發生シタ際ニ患者ノ發生狀況及流行狀態ヲ調査シ、尙流行發生ト季節トノ關係並ニ環境衞生(動物環境、昆蟲環境、居住環境)トノ關係ニ就テ調査シタノデ其等ノ成績ニ就テ報告シ、併セテ感染經路ニ關スル考察ヲ試ミル次第デアル、此等ノ成績ハ防疫業務ヲ實施スル傍ラ得タモノデアリ、而モ人員ノ關係上系統的ナ調査ガ出來ナカツタノデ極メテ不備ナモノデハアルケレドモ、將來ノ此ノ種ノ研究ニ對シ或指針ヲ與ヘルモノト信ジ、玆ニ報告スル次第デアル。

第1章　患者ノ發生狀況及流行狀態

　今次流行ニ於テハ「ベスト」ノ流行デアルト判ル迄ニ流行發生後凡ソ1週間ヲ經過シテ來タノデ發生當初ノ眞相ヲ知ルコトハ極メテ困難デアツタガ、小池中尉等ノ熱心ナ調査ニヨツテ概ネ其ノ全貌ヲ明カニスルコトガ出來タ、今其ニ就テ述ベレバ次ノ如クデアル。

　東三條通44番地田島犬猫病院(院主田島義次)傭人王合(同家三女忠子ノ子守)ハ9月23日朝ヨリ發病シタノデ型24日ニ實父ヲ呼出シ、同人ト共ニ寬城子韓家屯ノ自宅ニ歸ラセ療養ニ努メサセタケレドモ型25日極メテ重篤ナ肺症狀ヲ起シテ死亡シタ、續イテ23日ニハ田島義次三女忠子發病シ、27日ニハ王合ト同室ニ居住シテキタ宋丕德發病シ、28日ニハ同樣王合ト同室ニ居住シテキタ

韓秀臣發病シ、28日ニハ田島義次二女天津子發病シ、執レモ體温高ク且一般症状ガ重篤デアツタ、其ノ間忠子ハ市内醫師（滿○醫院小兒科醫）ノ診療ヲ受ケタ結果流行性感冒ト診斷サレテ治療ヲ受ケテキタガ29日ニ遂ニ死亡シタ、其處デ田島方獸醫井○一夫ハ懇意ノ間柄デアツタ中央通警察署勤務警尉補渡邊太一ニ29日15:00時頃忠子ノ火葬許可願ノ認可ヲ受ケニ來テ、其ノ時上述ノ状況ヲ渡邊ニ知ラセタ、渡邊ハ犬猫病院ニ發生シタ患者ニ對シテ不信ヲ抱イテ居タドコロニ同日19:00時頃ニ犬猫病院ノ隣ニ居住シテキタル中西興吉（太田安次ノ前室ニ居住シテキルモノ）及葛城誠治（太田安次ノ下ノ室ニ居住シテキルモノ）ノ兩名ガ來テ、田島犬猫病院ニ死亡者及患者ノ發生シテキル状況及犬猫病院ノ隣ニ居住シテキタ太田安次ガ9月23日急ニ發病シ、24日滿鐵醫院ニ入院シ、次デ陸軍病院ニ入院シタコトヲ詳細ニ通知シ、調査ノ必要ヲ述ベタ、茲ニ於テ渡邊ハ翌30日登廳スルヤ直チニ上述ノ次第ヲ首都警察廳ノ關係上司ニ報告シタ此ノ報ニ接シタ首都警察廳衛生課デハ市衛生試驗所ニ上述ノ事ヲ通報シ、尙田島家ニ就テ直接調査シタ結果上述ノ次第ヲ明カニスルコトガ出來タ。

一方太田安次ハ9月23日夕刻發病シ、翌24日ニ滿鐵醫院ニ至リ内科長○醫師ノ診療ヲ受ケタ上同院ニ入院シタガ、症状ガ重篤デアツタノデ25日18:00時頃陸軍病院ニ轉入シタ、其ノ後陸軍病院ニ於テハ病名ノ究明ニ努メルト共ニ看護ニ專心シテキタケレドモ29日朝ヨリハ胸内溶融ヲ訴ヘ海沫状ノ血痰ヲ喀出シ、13:00時遂ニ死亡シタ、併シナガラ此ノ時ニ至ルモ病名ノ決定ガ困難デアツタノデ新京醫大ノ山本敎授ノ來援ヲ得テ剖檢シタ結果脾ノ腫脹ヲ認メ肺ニハ肉腫樣硬度ヲ認メタケレドモ一般ニ炎症所見輕度ニシテ、且各臟器ノ塗擦標本ヲ鏡檢シタ結果ニ於テモ病原菌ヲ認メナカツタノデ急性肺炎兼肺臟壞疽ト病名ヲ決定シタ、併シナガラ不審ノ點ガアツタノデ翌9月30日朝市衛生試驗所ニ「肺ペスト」ノ病理所見ヲ問ヒ合ハセ、尙宮城所長ニ太田安次ノ材料ヲ檢鏡シテ貰ヒタイト依頼シタ、宮城所長ハ其ノ時恰モ首都警察廳衛生課ヨリ田島犬猫病院ノ状況ニ關スルノ通報ヲ受ケ、早速調査ニ出カケル所デアツタガ、上述ノ如キ陸軍病院ヨリノ依頼モアツタノデ犬猫病院ニハ醫師ノ心得アル庶務長ヲ派シテ事情ヲ調査スル樣ニシ、所長ハ直チニ陸軍病院ニ至リ太田安次ノ塗擦標本ヲ檢査セルニ咽頭ヨリノ塗擦標本ニ2, 3箇ノ「ペスト菌類似ノ菌ヲ認メタ、併シナガラ之ノミデハ「ペスト」ト斷定シ難キコトヲ述べ、太田安次ノ屍體ヨリ檢査材料ヲ採取スルコトヲ陸軍病院阿部中尉ニ依頼シタ、其ヨリ所長ハ16:00時頃田島犬猫病院ニ至リ療養中ノ患者（宋、韓）ヲ診斷シ、臨牀上「ペスト」ト決定シ、首都警察廳衛生課、市衛生處ト連絡協議ノ結果「ペスト」防疫ヲ開始スルコトニ決シ30日13:00時頃田島犬猫病院一帶ヲ隔離シ、患家附近ノ交通ヲ遮斷シ、此ノ状況ヲ民政部保健司、關東軍司令部等ニ通報シタ。

尙診斷ヲ確定スルタメニ患者（宋、韓）ヨリ血液塗擦標本ヲ作リ衛生試驗所ニ持チ歸リ鏡檢シタケレドモ其ノ標本ヨリハ「ペスト菌ヲ檢出スルコトガ出來ナカツタノデ、解剖ノ準備ヲナシテ田島犬猫病院ニ赴キ、棺内ニ納メラレテキタ忠子ノ屍體ヨリ檢査材料（淋巴腺腫）ヲ採リ、之ニ就テ鏡檢上「ペスト菌ヲ檢出スルコトガ出來タノデ30日23:00時類似ペスト」ト決定シ、防疫態勢ヲ一層强化シタ、即チ犬猫病院附近一帶ノ隔離ヲ更ニ嚴重ニナシ、尙市立千早病院ニ患者收容所ヲ開設

515—4

シテ患者ヲ收容スル準備ヲナサシメルト共ニ濃厚ニ汚染サレテキルト考ヘラレル患者發生家族及
患者ト交通ノアツタ人々ヲ健康隔離スル準備ヲナサシメ、取敢ズ犬猫病院ノ現在患者ヲ收容シ、
尚其ノ附近居住家族ヲ健康隔離シタ、其ヲ終了シタノハ10月1日ノ午前2.00時頃デアツタ。

一方犬猫病院附近居住家族ニ就テ「ペスト」發生ノ有無ヲ調査シタトコロ寶昌ビル居住福田鐵男
ハ9月29日ヨリ發病シ、夕刻軍醫部小泉大尉ノ往診ヲ受ケ、自宅ニテ療養ニ努メテキルケレドモ
症狀極メテ重篤ニシテ、「ペスト」ノ疑濃厚ナルコトヲ知リ、尚本人ノ姉中野砂子ハ同室ニ居住シ
テキタノデアルガ9月25日發病シ、市保健所ニ入院9月28日死亡シ、其ノ病名ハ急性肝臟萎縮症
トサレテキルケレドモ症狀ヨリ考ヘテ「ペスト」ノ疑ノ濃厚デアルコトガ判ツタ、尚寶昌ビル居住
藤田君香ハ9月25日發病シ、共和醫院ノ醫師ノ來診ヲ受ケ、9月27日ニハ長春醫院小兒科德〇醫
師ノ來診ヲ受ケタケレドモ病名不明ニシテ症狀ガ重篤デアルタメニ9月30日滿鐵醫院ニ入院シテ
療養ヲ受ケツツアルコトガ判リ、其ノ妹キヌ子ハ9月26日朝發病シ、同日夕長春醫院ニ到ツテ診
察ヲ受ケタケレドモ碇タル病名不明ニシテ惡性感胃デアロウトノ診斷ノ下ニ治療ヲ受ケテキルウ
チニ9月30日自宅ニテ死亡シテキルコトガ判明シタ。斯樣ナ調査ニヨツテ「ペスト」ノ病毒ガ犬猫
病院附近一帶ニ相當濃厚ニ浸潤シテキル狀況ガ明瞭ニナツタノデ、10月1日在京ノ滿洲國警務機
關及衛生機關、軍關係、滿鐵關係、滿赤關係等相會シテ防疫會議ヲ開キ、防疫本部ヲ編成シ、田
村副市長統監トナツテ防疫業務ノ全般ヲ統べ、市衛生處及市衛生試驗所ガ主體トナツテ愈々本格
的ニ「ペスト」防疫ガ開始サレタ。

而シテ10月1日ニハ上述ノ各般ノ狀況ニ鑑ミテ所謂三角地域ノ交通遮斷ヲ斷行シ、同地域一帶
ノ消毒及鼠族及昆蟲ノ驅除ニ努メタ、併シナガラ當時既ニ病毒ハ三角地域ノ鼠族間ニ相當濃厚ニ
浸潤シテキタ爲(之ハ三角地域内ニテ捕獲セル鼠族ニ就テノ菌檢索ノ結果カラ知ルコトガ出來タ)
其ノ後モ尚10名内外ノ患者ノ被發ヲ認メ、更ニ病毒ハ三角地域ヨリ周圍ニ波及シテ猛威ヲ逞クセ
ントスル勢ヲ示シタケレドモ時機ニ適シタ軍官民協同ノ強力ナ防疫處置ニヨツテ流行ノ蔓延ヲ抑
壓シ、11月13日ニ發生セル「ペスト患者ヲ最終トシテ52日間ニ亙リ28名ノ患者ノ發生ヲ以テ終熄
シタ。

發生シタ「ペスト患者ヲ一覽表ニシテ示セバ第1表ノ如クデアリ、尚其ノ日々ノ發生數ヲ示セ
バ第1圖ノ如クデアル、此等ニヨツテ患者ノ發生狀況及流行狀態ヲ概ネ知ルコトガ出來ル。

515—5

第1表 「ペスト」患者一覧表

番號	發生場所	氏名	性	年齡	人種別	發病月日	轉歸月日	病名	摘要
1	東三條通44田烏方	王　○　合	男	13	滿 死	9.23	9.25	推定「ペスト」	周圍ノ事情ヨリ死後「ペスト」ト判定ス。
2	東三條通42	太田○夫	男	33	日 死	9.23	9.29	「ペスト」敗血症	入院死亡
3	室町4丁目7資昌ビル	蘇○柈○	女	8	日 死	6.25	10.2	腺ペスト」（左鼠蹊腺）	入院死亡
4	〃	蘇○キ○子	女	5	日 死	9.26	9.30	推定「ペスト」	周圍ノ事情ヨリ死後「ペスト」ト判定ス。
5	東三條通44田烏方	田○忠○	女	2	日 死	9.26	9.29	推定「ペスト」	同上
6	〃	宋○徳	男	23	滿 死	9.27	10.1	推定「ペスト」	同上
7	〃	辟○匡	男	25	滿 死	9.28	10.2	腺ペスト」（右鼠蹊腺）	入院死亡
8	〃	田○天○子	女	8	日 死	9.29	10.3	腺ペスト」（右頸腺）	同上
9	室町4丁目7資昌ビル	紹○織○	男	17	日 死	9.29	10.1	腺ペスト」（右鼠蹊腺）	同上
10	東三條通44田烏方	井○和○	男	24	日 死	9.30	10.2	腺ペスト」（右鼠蹊腺）	同上
11	〃	松○正○	男	23	日 死	9.30	10.4	腺ペスト」（左腋高腺）	同上
12	室町4丁目7資昌ビル	高○眞○	女	3	日 死	9.30	10.20	腺ペスト」（頸）	同上
13	室町四丁目5金城アパート	矢○正○	男	21	日 死	10.2	10.7	腺ペスト」（右鼠蹊腺）	同上
14	室町4丁目7大成館	徐○富○	女	12	日 死	10.2	10.4	腺ペスト」（右腋高腺）	同上
15	東三條通44田烏方	宋○山	男	56	滿 死	10.5	10.10	肺ペスト」	隔離中ニ看護患者ノ看護ニ服ス。
16	室町4丁目5金城アパート	俊○愛○	女	17	日 治癒	10.5	10.22	腺ペスト」（左鼠蹊腺）	入院治癒
17	室町4丁目5金城アパート	李○金	男	10	滿 死	10.6	10.8	「ペスト」敗血症	隔離中ニ發病並ニ死亡
18	露月町4丁目滿○肚宅	黄○氏	女	45	滿 死	不明	10.11	「ペスト」敗血症	屍體檢所前時診見
19	入船町2丁目雙盛泰	陳○玉	男	55	滿 死	不明	10.11	腺ペスト」（右鼠蹊腺）	同上
20	室町4丁目5金城アパート	羅○勉	男	27	日 死	10.9	10.11	腺ペスト」（右鼠蹊腺）	隔離中ニ發病
21	〃	崔○源	男	18	滿 死	10.10	10.13	腺ペスト」（左鼠蹊腺）	同上
22	梅ヶ枝町3丁目23	寇○田	男	37	滿 死	不明	16.13	皮膚ペスト」	發生死亡屍後檢所前時發見
23	室町4丁目7大成館	土○○	女	58	日 死	10.11	10.17	「ペスト」敗血症	隔離中ニ發病
24	露月町行路病者	王○東	男	36	滿 治癒	10.12	11.2	眼ペスト」?	入院治療
25	日本橋通75國際ホテル	桃○春	男	31	日 死	10.17	10.22	皮膚ペスト」	入院死亡
26	日本橋通75廣本洋行	宋○林	男	40	滿 死	10.22	10.22	腺ペスト」（右鼠蹊腺）	
27	日本橋通62の1	張○俊	男	46	滿 死	11.8	11.12	「ペスト」敗血症	
28	梅ヶ枝町4丁目14	尹○禎	男	19	滿 死	11.13	11.15	腺ペスト」（右鼠蹊腺）	

515—6

第 1 圖 「ペスト患者日別發生狀況

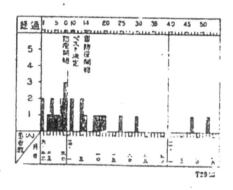

T29

第1章 流行ノ疫學的觀察

第1節 流行ノ季節的消長

滿洲ノ「ベスト」常在地域ニ於テハ「ベスト」ノ流行曲線ハ毎年其ノ規ヲ一ニシ、6,7月ノ候ニ初發シ、漸次增加シツツ9月ニ於テ其ノ頂點ニ達シ、11月嚴寒ノ襲來ト共ニ終熄スル所謂夏季型ヲ呈スルモノニシテ、流行ノ消長ガ季節ニ密接ナ關係ヲ有スルコトハ既ニ倉內、春日等ノ明カニシタ所デアル、昭和15年度ノ「ベスト常在地域ニ於ケル「ベスト」發生狀況ヲ全般的ニ觀察スレバ第2表ニ示ス如クニシテ6月ニ初發シ、漸次疫勢ヲ高メ、9日最高ニ達シ、其ヨリ漸次減少シテ11月ニ終熄シテキル、倘之ヲ部落別ニ觀察スレバ第3表ニ示ス如クニシテ先ヅ始メニ數箇ノ部落ニ流行原發シ、其ヨリ人的及物的ノ交通ニヨッテ流行ガ周圍ニ傳播シ、所謂二次性流行ガ發生シタト思ヘレル部落ガ相當ニアル、而シテ原發性ノ流行モ續發生ノ流行モ略ゝ同樣ノ季節的消長ヲ示シ、8月9月ノ候ニ最高ニ達シ、其ヨリ漸次減少シ、11月ニハ終熄シタコトヲ知ルコトガ出來ル、此ノ「ベスト常在地域ニ於ケル「ベスト」ノ流行狀態ヨリ觀察スル時ハ今次新京ノ「ベスト」ハ常在地域ヨリ何等カノ因子ニヨッテ波及シテ來タモノデ此處ニ原發シタモノデハナイコトガ判ル、此ノ事ハ過去ニ於ケル新京ノ「ベスト」流行史ヲ見テモ白ヲ明カデアル(之ニ就テハ後ニ述ベル)、而シテ常在地域ニ於ケル「ベスト」流行ノ場合ト全ク同樣ノ因子ニヨッテ11月寒氣ノ襲來ト共ニ終熄シタモノデアルト考ヘラレル、倘思者ノ發生ガ比較的少數ニ終ツタコトハ軍官民協同ノ强力ナ防疫ノ效果ニ歸セラルベキモノト考ヘラレル。

第 2 表 月別患者發生數
（昭和15年、前郊旗管內）

月 次	患 者 數
5	0
6	12
7	102
8	349
9	382
10	243
11	21
12	0

515-7

第3表　部落別　月別患者發生狀況

（昭和15年、前郭旗管內ノ一部ヲ示ス）

縣名	屯名	6月	7月	8月	9月	10月	11月	計
殷	段安街	4	53	138	80	68	10	353
	苗家屯		1	24				25
	干家園子			2	10			12
安	山東屯			2	9	8		19
	佩坨子				10	1		11
縣	韓家店				40	33		73
	遲家店					4	1	5
大賚縣	大賚街		2	20	26	6		54
	十八家戶	8	13	1				22
安廣縣	拉々屯		1					1
	陶家行子			20	3			23
	前朗梧樹			14	7			21
長嶺縣	太屯					2		2
	泰和閣			1				
	伐之就屯			3	10			
	七撮屯				1	18	5	24
扶餘縣	茂賢屯		4	9	5			18
	瓦窯屯			3	6			9
	五家站				9	1		10
前郭旗	抬拉吐山		1	4				5
	三圖山			12	9			21
	王府屯			1				1
	新立屯		12	8				20
	六股道		5	4				20
	金山屯			9				9
	茨慈屯				2			2

　　滿洲ニ於ケル「ペスト」ガ上述セル如キ夏季型ヲ取ルノハ專ラ氣溫ニ密接ナ關係ヲ有スルモノニシテ、氣溫ノ推移ガ「ペスト」關係動物並ニ昆蟲ノ繁殖及生活現象ニ直接影響ヲ與ヘ、之ガ間接ニ「ペスト」流行ニ影響ヲ與ヘルコトハ倉內ノ既ニ指摘セル所デアル、今大新京ノ「ペスト」流行ガ前述ノ如キ季節的消長ヲナシ、氣溫ノ推移ト密接ナ關係ヲ示シタコトハ滿洲ノ「ペスト」ノ季節的消長ト全ク同一ノ因子ニヨルモノト考ヘラレル。

　　從ツテ流行ノ消長ハ新京ニ於ケル「ペスト」關係動物及昆蟲ノ季節的消長ト「ペスト」關係動物ノ「ペスト」感受性ノ季節的消長ニ直接ノ關係ヲ有スルモノト考ヘラレルガレドモ、其ニ關スル確實ナ調査成績ナキ爲ニ、此ノ問題ヲ詳細ニ考察シ得ナイコトハ殘念デアル。

515—8

第2節　流行ノ環境衛生學的觀察

新京ヲ第2圖ノ如ク地域別ニ區劃シテ「ペスト患者ノ發生狀況ヲ地域別ニ觀察スルニ第4表ニ示ス如クニシテ三角地域ニ於テ最モ患者多發シ、次デ其ニ隣接スル四角地域及第Ⅰ地域ニ患者發生シ、尙第Ⅲ地域ヨリ2名ノ患者ノ發生シテキルヲ認メル、第Ⅲ地域ヨリ發生シテキル2名ノ患者ノ內ノ1名王振東ハ果シテ「ペスト患者デアルカ否カ疑ハシイモノデアリ、他ノ1名黃〇氏ノ隣ハ田島犬猫病院傭人韓秀臣（9月28日發病10月2日死亡）ノ父韓學淳ノ家ニシテ韓秀臣ガ鼠ト生家ニ出入シタコトハ明カデアルカラ韓秀臣ガ病毒ヲ搬入シ（有菌蚤ヲ衣領ニ附着サセテ運搬スルコトガ考ヘラレル）、其ノ病毒ガ直接ニ有菌蚤ニヨツテ黃氏ニ運搬セラレ、或ハ其ガ鼠族間ニ侵入シ、次デ黃氏ノ發病ニ至ツタモノデハナカロウカト想像サレルノデアルカラ、「ペスト」ノ流行ハ先ヅ三角地域ニ發生シ、其ヨリ周圍ノ四角地域及第Ⅰ地域ニ波及シ、又第Ⅲ地域ニハ前述ノ如キ狀殊ナ事情ニヨツテ傳播サレタモノデハナカロウカト考ヘラレル、此ノ事ハ各地域ニ於ケル日別ノ患者發生狀況ヲ調査シタ第5表ノ成績ヲ見レバ一層明カデアル、卽チ本表ニ於テ見ル如ク三角地域ニ9月23日發生シタ「ペスト」ガ同地域ニテ多數患者ノ積發ヲ起シ、其ヨリ次第ニ四角地域ニ擴ガリ、更ニ第Ⅰ地域ニ傳播シテ行ツタモノト推論スルコトガ出來ル。

第2圖　新京ノ要圖

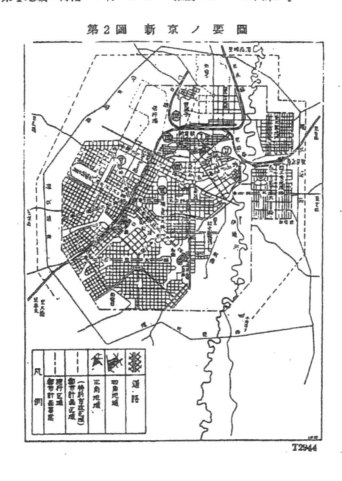

T2944

515—9

第4表　地域別患者發生狀況

地區＼患者	發生數	發生率(%)
三角地域	20	71.8
四角地域	3	10.7
第Ⅰ地域	3	10.7
第Ⅱ地域	0	0
第Ⅲ地域	2	7.1
第Ⅲ地域	0	0
其ノ他	0	0

第5表　地域別ノ日別患者發生狀況

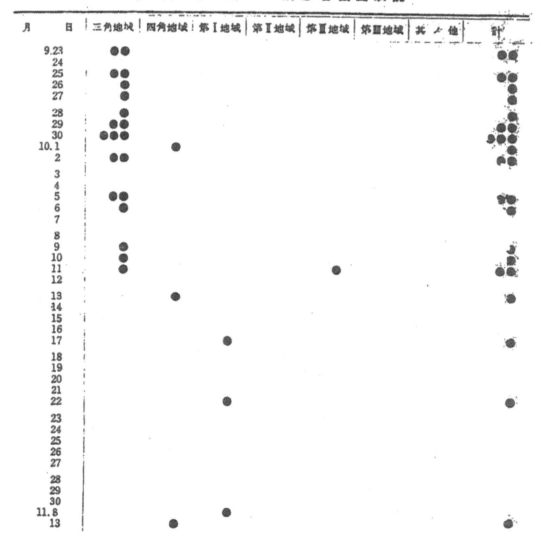

515--10

偕而腺ペスト」流行ノ發生ハ其ノ地域ノ「ペスト」關係動物就中鼠族ノ種類及其ノ數量ト「ペスト」關係昆蟲ノ種類及其ノ數量ニ密接ナ關係ヲ有シ、從ツテ其ノ地域ノ居住環境ニ間接ニ關係シテキルノデ、新京就中三角地域附近ニ於テ此等ノ事項ニ就テ調査シタ成績ヲ述ベテ「ペスト」流行トノ關係ヲ考察スレバ次ノ如クデアル。

第1項　新京ニ於ケル「ペスト」關係動物ノ種類及其ノ數量的觀察（動物環境）附近ノ細菌學的檢査

「ペスト」流行ノ發生セル後10月6日ヨリ11月3日ニ至ル間ニ三角地域ヲ中心トシテ新京市內ニテ捕獲シタ鼠ノ數ハ實ニ92,480頭ノ多キニ及ンダガ其ノ內5,245頭ニ就テ其ノ種類ヲ檢査セル成績ハ第6表ニ示ス如クニシテ「ドブネズミ」ガ極メテ多數ヲ占メテキタ、其ノ後11月4日ヨリ昭和16年1月25日迄ニ新京市內及其ノ附近ニ於テ捕獲シタ鼠ニ就テ其ノ種類ヲ分類セル成績ハ第7表ニ示ス如クデアル、前者ニ於テ「ドブネズミ」ノ極メテ多イノハ家屋內ニテ捕獲シタモノガ大部分デアリ、且菌檢索及蚤檢査ノ必要上「ドブネズミ」ヲ多ク選ンダ爲ニシテ、之ハ新京ニ於ケル鼠族ノ分布濃度ヲ示スモノデハナイ、其ニ比シテ後者ノ成績ハ概ネ新京ニ於ケル鼠族ノ分布濃度ヲ示スモノト考ヘラレル、其ハ昭和12年10月中旬～11月中旬ノ調査成績第8表ト比較對照スレバ自ラ明カデアル、第7表及第8表ニ於テ判ルノ如ク新京ノ人家及其ノ附近ヨリ鼠族ヲ採

第6表　新京市內ニ於テ捕獲セル鼠ノ種類（長花）
（昭15.10.6～15.11.3）

鼠ノ種類	箇體數
ドブネズミ	5,154
マンシウハツカネズミ	57
マンシウセスヂネズミ	8
セスヂキヌゲネズミ	10
ヨシネズミ	15
カヤネズミ	1
計	5,245

第7表　「ペスト菌保有鼠檢索ノタメ新京ニ於テ捕獲セル鼠ノ種類
（昭15.11.4～16.1.25）

鼠ノ種類	箇體數
アジアハツカネズミ	32,557
ドブネズミ	15,531
セスヂネズミ	4,995
セスヂキヌゲネズミ	2,851
ヨシハタネズミ	1,255
タイリクカヤネズミ	54
キヌゲネズミ	1
計	57,244

註　衛生技術廠ノ調査ニヨル。

第8表　新京市ニ於テ捕獲セル鼠ノ種類
（昭12.10.中旬～12.11中旬）

鼠ノ種類	箇體數
アジアハツカネズミ	832
ドブネズミ	281
セスヂネズミ	83
セスヂキヌゲネズミ	39

註　衛生技術廠ノ調査ニヨル。

取スレバ「アヂアハツカネズミ」(「マンシウハツカネズミ」ト同一ノモノナリ)ガ最モ多数ヲ占メ、「ドブネズミ」ガ之ニ次デキル、以上ハ半住家性ノ鼠族ニシテ、満洲ニ於テハ半住家性鼠族トシテハ此ノ2種ガアルダケデアル、其ノ他ノ鼠族トシテハ「セスヂネズミ」、「セスヂキヌゲネズミ」、「ヨシハタネズミ」、「タイリクカヤネズミ」、「キヌゲネズミ」等ガアルガ、是等ハ孰レモ野外性鼠族ニシテ且其ノ数モ極メテ少ナイ。

尚三角地域ト他ノ地域トノ間ニ鼠ノ種類及数量ニ差異ガアツタカ否カハ検査スルコトガ出来ナカツタケレドモ全般ノ成績ヨリ考ヘレバ三角地域ト他ノ地域トノ間ニ特別ナ差異ガアツタモノトハ考ヘラレナイ。

次ニ捕獲セル鼠族ニ對シテ菌検索ヲ行ツタ成績ハ第9表及第10表ニ示ス如クニシテ10月5日～11月6日迄ニハ總数13,735頭ノ中ヨリ63頭ノ有菌鼠ヲ検出シ、11月4日～昭和16年2月3日迄ニハ總数57,224頭ノ中ヨリ5頭ノ有菌鼠ヲ検出シテキル、其ヲ種類別ニ見ルト「ドブネズミ」ニ就テノミ菌ヲ検出シテ居テ其ノ検出率ハ13,664頭中63頭(0.46%)及15,531頭中5頭(0.03%)ニシテ、其ノ他ノ鼠族ヨリハ1頭モ有菌鼠ヲ検出スルコトガ出来ナカツタ、此ノ検査成績ヨリ見レバ今次ノ流行ニ於テハ「ドブネズミ」間ノ病毒ガ人ペスト」ノ直接ノ伝染源トナツタモノト考ヘラレル。

第9表　鼠族ノ菌検索成績（軍搭営）
（昭15.10.5～15.11.6）

鼠　ノ　種　類	検索数	陽性数	陽性率(%)
ド　ブ　ネ　ズ　ミ	13,644	63	0.46
マンシウハツカネズミ	57	0	0
マンシウセスヂネズミ	8	0	0
セスヂキヌゲネズミ	10	0	0
ヨ　シ　ネ　ズ　ミ	15	0	0
カ　ヤ　ネ　ズ　ミ	1	0	0
計	13,735	63	0.45

第10表　鼠族ノ菌検索成績（衛生技術廠搭営）
（昭15.11.4～16.2.3）

鼠　ノ　種　類	検索数	陽性数	陽性率(%)
ド　ブ　ネ　ズ　ミ	15,531	5	0.03
アヂアハツカネズミ	32,557	0	0
セ　ス　ヂ　ネ　ズ　ミ	4,995	0	0
セスヂキヌゲネズミ	2,851	0	0
ヨ　シ　ネ　ズ　ミ	1,255	0	0
カ　ヤ　ネ　ズ　ミ	54	0	0
キ　ヌ　ゲ　ネ　ズ　ミ	1	0	0
計	57,224	5	0.009

515—12

尚此ノ有菌鼠ノ地域別ニ觀察スレバ第11表ニ示ス如クニシテ三角地域ニ於テ其ノ檢出率最モ
高ク、次ニ四角地域、第Ⅰ地域、第Ⅲ地域ノ順序ニシテ概ネ各地域ノ患者發生數ニ併行セル關係
ニアルコトヲ認メタ、尚「ペスト患者ノ發生ヲミナカツタ地域ニ於テハ有菌鼠ノ檢出率ハ極メテ
低クアツタ、此ノ成績ヨリ人ペスト」ノ發生スルタメニハ有菌鼠ノ率ガ或程度以上（此ノ場合ニハ
約0.5デアツタ）ニ昇ルコトノ必要デアルコトガ判ル。

第11表　地域別有菌鼠檢出成績

地區	有菌鼠		檢查數	陽性數	陽性率(%)
三角地域			153	15	9.8
四角地域			442	13	3.0
第Ⅰ地域			2,097	18	0.9
第Ⅱ地域			4,775	5	0.1
第Ⅱ地域			225	1	0.4
第Ⅲ地域			1.450	3	0.2
其ノ他			4,491	8	0.2

次ニ地域別ニ有菌鼠ノ日々ノ檢出成績ヲ示セバ第12表ノ如クニシテ先ヅ三角地域ニ有菌鼠多
ク檢出セラレ、其ヨリ時日ノ經過ト共ニ四角地域、第Ⅰ地域ニ有菌鼠檢出セラレ、遂ニハ全地域
ニ亙リ有菌鼠ノ檢出セラルルニ至ツタコトガ判ル、尚此ノ成績ト第5表ノ成績トヲ比較對照シテ
觀察スル時ハ三角地域ニ於テハ流行ノ當初有菌鼠多ク且患者ノ發生モ多イガ、流行ノ末期有菌鼠
ノ檢出セラレザルニ至ルトトモニ患者ノ發生モ終熄スルニ至ルコトヲ認メルコトガ出來タ、四角
地域及第Ⅰ地域ニ於テハ三角地域ヨリモ遲レテ有菌鼠ガ檢出セラレ、其ニ引續イテ患者ノ發生ス
ルノヲ認メルコトガ出來タ。

有菌鼠ノ檢索ガ全市ニ亙ツテ一樣ニ開始サレナカツタタメニ病毒傳播ノ狀況ハ明カデナイガ第
12表及第5表ノ檢查成績ヨリ考ヘル時ハ「ペスト」ノ病毒ハ先ヅ三角地域ノ鼠族間ニ浸潤シ、其ヨ
リ隣接地區タル四角地域及第Ⅰ地域ニ擴ガツタモノト考ヘルコトガ出來ル。

次ニ鼠族以外ニ「ペスト」ノ傳染源トナル動物ガアルカ否カヲ檢査スル爲ニ病毒ノ最モ濃厚ニ
浸潤セル三角地域ニ於テ捕獲シタ2,3種ノ家畜ニ就テ「ペスト菌ノ檢索ヲ行ヘル成績ハ第13表ニ
示ス如クニシテ犬、猫、「シマリス」、「イタチ」等ニ就テハ「ペスト菌ヲ檢出スルコトガ出來ナ
カツタ、勿論檢査數ガ少イノデ決論ヲ下スコトハ出來ナイガ從來ノ成績カラ考ヘテモ犬、猫等ノ家
畜ハ傳染源トシテノ役割ハナイモノト考ヘラレル、唯猫ニ就テハ「ペスト菌ニ感受性ガアリ、其
ガ傳染源トナツタ例ガ報告サレテキルケレドモ、斯樣ナ例ハ極メテ少イモノデアルト考ヘラレ
ル。

第12表 地域別ノ日別有菌屋検出成績

月日	三角地域 検数	三角地域 陰数	三角地域 陽性件	四角地域 検数	四角地域 陰数	四角地域 陽性件	第Ⅰ地域 検数	第Ⅰ地域 陰数	第Ⅰ地域 陽性件	第Ⅰ地域 検数	第Ⅰ地域 陰数	第Ⅰ地域 陽性件	第Ⅱ地域 検数	第Ⅱ地域 陰数	第Ⅱ地域 陽性件	第Ⅲ地域 検数	第Ⅲ地域 陰数	第Ⅲ地域 陽性件	其ノ他地域 検数	其ノ他地域 陰数	其ノ他地域 陽性件	合計 検数	合計 陰数	合計 陽性件
10.5																								
6																								
7																								
8	16		4	3			16															35		4
9				8			25															35		
10	19		6	9			46		4				1						6			81		10
11	18		1	14			10		3				13						8			63		3
12	8		3	5			22		1				6		3				1			45		4
13	12			14		4	58		1													84		4
14	5			11			27		1										2			45		5
15	7		2	27		4	52		2				5						6			52		2
16	9		1	41			37		1				1						1			82		5
17	10			45		3	51						5						6			103		4
18	9		1	30			60						15						8			126		
19							75															137		
20	5		1	30			59			53		2	2			1			34			130		3
21	3			11			46		1	27			7			8			42			163		2
22	6		1	37			88		1	41		1	15			18			120		1	301		1
23	1			26			58			128			2			53			68			214		
24				5			93						18						130			427		1
25	1		1	12			30			104			9			3			166			325		1
26				2			79			20			6						137			245		
27				20		1	109			74		1	10			59			165			437		1
28	3			3			16			96			3			43			87			251		
29	4			19			131			324						190		1	196		1	864		
30				17			139			500			2			301			170			927		1
31	16			12			213			570			21			104			397		1	1,333		1
11.1				22		1	135			900			3			241			527		1	1,828		2
2				5			61		1	407			4			312		1	239		2	1,028		2
3				5						1,021			25			85			1,166		2	2,487		2
4			1	9		1	185						50			29		1	909		2	1,683		4
5	9						176			510														
6																								
7																								

515—14

第13表　三角地域ニテ捕獲セル家畜ノ菌検索成績

動 物 種 類	捕 獲 場 所	檢 查 数	陽 性 数
犬	三 角 地 域	12	0
猫	〃	2	0
シ　マ　リ　ス	〃	1	0
イ　タ　チ	〃	1	0

第2項　新京ニ於ケル「ペスト」關係昆蟲ノ種類及其ノ數量的觀察(昆蟲環境)
　　　　附其ノ細菌學的檢查

「ペスト」ノ流行發生セル後10月6日～11月3日迄ニ亙ル間ニ三角地帯ヲ中心トシテ新京市内ニテ捕獲セル鼠族ニ附着シテキル蚤ノ種類及其ノ數量ヲ檢查セル成績ハ第14表ニ示ス如クニシテ、尚11月4日～昭和16年2月25日迄ニ新京市内ニテ捕獲セル「ドブネズミ」及「アジアハツカネズミ」ニ附着シテキル蚤ノ種類及其ノ數量ヲ檢查セル成績ハ第15表ニ示ス如クデアル。

第14表　新京産鼠族ヨリ得タル蚤ノ種類(長花)

(昭15. 10. 6～15. 11. 3)

鼠ノ種類 蚤ノ種類	ドブネズミ (5,154)	マンシウハ ツカネズミ (57)	マンシウセ スヂセネズミ (8)	セスヂキヌ ゲネズミ (10)	ヨシネズミ (15)	カヤネズミ (1)
Xenopsylla cheopis	10,533	6	0	2	4	0
Ceratophyllus anisus	2,752	4	0	0	2	0
Ceratophyllus fasciatus	6	0	0	0	0	0
Neopsylla bidentatiformis	5	0	0	1	0	0
Rectofrontia insolita	0	0	0	1	0	0

第15表　新京産鼠族ヨリ得タル蚤ノ種類

(昭15. 11. 4～16. 2. 25)

鼠ノ種類 蚤ノ種類	ドブネズミ (15,527)	アジアハツカネズミ (32,557)
Xenopsylla cheopis	5,342	73
Ceratophyllus anisus	2,198	27
Neopsylla bidentatiformis	56	2
Ceratophyllus fasciatus	30	0
Rectofrontia insolita	3	2
Pulex irritans	3	0
Paradoxopsyllus curvispinus	1	0
Ctenopsyllus segnis	1	0

　　註　衛生技術廠ノ調査ニヨル。

581

本表ニ於テ見ルガ如ク「ドブネズミ」ニハ X. cheopis, C. anisus, C. fasciatus, Neopsylla bidentatiformis, Rectofrontia insolita, Pulex irritans 等ノ蚤ガ附着シテキテ其ノ内 X. cheopis ガ最モ多ク、C. anisus ガ其ノ次ニ位シ、其ノ他ノモノハ極メテ少ナイ。第14表ノ成績ニ於テハ「ドブネズミ」ノ蚤指数ハ2.4ニシテ其ヲ、更ニ鼠別スレバケオピス蚤指数ハ1.9「アニズス蚤指数ハ0.5デアル、然ルニ第15表ノ成績ニ於テハ蚤指数ハ0.49ニシテ其ノ内「ケオピス蚤指数ハ0.34「アニズス蚤指数ハ0.14デアル、斯クノ如ク第15表ノ成績ニ於テ蚤指数ガ低イノハ季節的ノ消長モ考ヘラレルケレドモ（後者ハ及衰期ニ獲得セル鼠族デアツタ為）、之ハ検査材料ガ総テ死鼠體デアツタ為メデアルト考ヘラレル、尚新京ノ平素ニ於ケル鼠ノ蚤ヲ検査セル成績ハ第16表ニ示ス如クニシテ「ドブネズミ」ノ蚤指数ハ5.2ニシテ其ノ内「ケオピス蚤指数ハ2.7「アニズス蚤指数ハ2.5デアリ、其ノ他ノ種類ノ蚤ハ極メテ少ナイ。

大ニ「アジアハツカネズミ」ニハ附着シテキル蚤ノ数ガ極メテ少ナイ、之ハ此ノ鼠ニ附着スル Neopsylla bidentatiformis ガ蹄巣性ガ大デ長ク鼠體ニ止マライイ性ヲ持ツテキルカラデアル。

第16表　新京産鼠族ヨリ得タル蚤ノ種類

（昭12. 10. 10中旬〜昭12. 11. 中旬）

蚤ノ種類 　　　鼠ノ種類	ドブネズミ (129)	アジアハツカネズミ (832)
Xenopsylla cheopis	344	1
Ceratophyllus anisus	319	1
Neopsylla bidentatiformis	4	0
Pulex irritans	1	0

註　衛生技術廠ノ調査ニヨル。

尚蚤ノ種類ノ季節的消長ハ不明デアルケレドモ前述ノ成績ヨリ新京ノ「ドブネズミ」ハ「ペスト」流行ノ發生ニ充分ナ蚤指数ヲ有スルモノト考ヘルコトガ出來ル。

次ニ以上ノ如タニシテ鼠體ヨリ蒐集シタ蚤ニ就テ「ペスト菌ノ検索ヲ行ツタ結果ハ第17表ノ如キ成績ニシテ、X. cheopis 及 C. anisus ヨリ「ペスト菌ヲ検出スルコトガ出來タ、尚其ノ検査成績ヲ日別ニ観察スレバ第18表ノ如キ成績ニシテ患者ノ多發セル頃ハ陽性数多キモ、其ヨリ次第ニ「ペスト菌検出ノ困難ニナルコトガ判ツタ、是等ノ成績ヨリ考察スル時ハ鼠ペスト其ノ媒介ヲ大ニ演揮ルモノハ X. cheopis ガ主デアリ、C. anisus モ亦極メテ大キナ役割ヲ演ジテキルコトガ判ル。

第17表　鼠體附着蚤ノ菌検索成績

蚤ノ種類	検査匹数	検査件数	陽性件数	陽性率 (%)
Xenopsylla cheopis	8,725	1,853	12	0.65
Ceratophyllus anisus	2,334	558	4	0.41
Ceratophyllus fasciatus	4	4	0	0

515—16

第18表　日別有菌蚤検出數

検査月日	検査件數	陽性件數	検査月日	検査件數	陽性件數
10.7	3		22		
8	7	2	23		
9	6	2	24		
10	6	4	25		
11	3	2	26		
12	6	1	27	23	
13	2	1	28	63	
14	5	2	29	173	1
15	6		30	268	
16			31	306	1
17			11.1	398	
18	5		2	400	
19			3	455	
20	1		4	382	
21	1		5	197	

次ニ地域別ニ「ドブネズミ」ニ附着シテキル蚤ノ種類及數量ヲ検査セル成績ハ第19表ニ示ス如ク
ニシテ三角地域ニ於テハ他ノ地域ニ比スレバ「ケオピス蚤指數モ「アニズス蚤指數モ極メテ高ク、
四角地域ニ於テハ「ケオピス蚤指數極メテ高ク「アニズス蚤指數モ比較的高イノヲ認メタ、之ハ三
角地域及四角地域ニ於テハ鼠族間ニ「ペスト」ノ流行ガ激烈デアツタタメニ多クノ斃鼠ヲ出シ、其
ガタメニ捕獲セル鼠體ニ就テハ蚤指數ガ極メテ高ク現レタモノト考ヘラレル、尚有菌蚤ノ検出成
績ヲ地域別ニ觀察スレバ第20表ニ示ス如クニシテ三角地域ニ於テ陽性數ガ最モ多クアツタ、此等
ノ成績ヨリ考ヘテモ三角地域ガ最モ濃厚ニ汚染サレテキタコトガ判ル。

第19表　地域別ノ蚤ノ種類及其ノ數量(「ドブネズミ」ニ就テノ觀察)

地域	検鼠數	Xenopsylla cheopis	Ceratophyllus anisus	Ceratophyllus fasciatus	Neopsylla bidentatiformis	cheopis 指數	anisus 指數
三角地域	147	961	572	2	0	6.5	3.9
四角地域	156	1,135	175	0	1	7.5	1.1
全地域	5,154	10,533	2,752	6	5	1.9	0.5

第20表　地域別ノ有菌蚤數

地區	Xeno. cheopis	Cerato. anisus	計
三角地域	8	2	10
四角地域	1	0	1
第Ⅰ地域	1	0	1
第Ⅱ地域	0	0	0
第Ⅲ地域	1	1	2
第Ⅳ地域	0	0	0
其ノ他	1	1	2

尚流行發生前ニ於ケル各地域ノ蚤ノ種類及數量ニ差異ガアツタカ否カハ不明デアルケレドモ全般ノ成績ヨリ考ヘテ其程大キナ差ガアツタモノトハ考ヘラレナイ、然ルニ三角地域ガ「ペスト」ニ最モ濃厚ニ汚染サレタノヘ「ペスト」ノ病毒ガ先ヅ此ノ三角地域ニ搬入サレタタメデアロウト推論スルコトガ出來ル。

大ニ人及家畜動物ニ附着シテキル蚤ノ種類及數量ヲ檢査セル成績ハ第21表ニ示ス如クナリチ、是等ノ蚤ヨリハ菌ヲ檢出スルコトガ出來ナカツタガ、鼠體ニ最モ多數附着シテテ而モ最モ有菌蚤トナリ易イ X. cheopis ガ人及犬、猫等ニ附着シテキルコトハ X. cheopis ガ直接ニ鼠ヘ「ペスト」ヲ人ニ傳搔シ、又犬、猫等ニヨツテ X. cheopis ガ運搬サレテ間接ニ人ヘノ傳搔ガ起リ得ルコトヲ想像スルコトガ出來タ、斯ク考ヘル時ハ犬、猫等ハ X. cheopis ヲ運搬スル意味ニ於テ人ペスト」ノ發生ニ或役割ヲ滴ズルモノデアルト云ヘル。

第21表　人及家畜ニ附着シテキル蚤ノ種類

蚤　ノ　種　類	人　（2）	犬　（12）	猫　（1）	シマリス（1）
Xenopsylla cheopis	2	3	1	0
Pulex irritans	2	53	0	0
Ctenocephalides canis	0	217	0	0
Ctenocephalides felis	0	0	25	0

第3項　患者發生地域及患者發生家屋ノ環境衛生學的觀察（居住環境）

（吉村氏ノ調査ニヨル）

1. 患者發生地域ノ環境衛生學的觀察

「ペスト」流行ノ發生ガ其ノ地域ノ環境衛生學的條件ニヨツテ左右サレルコトハ想像ニ難クナイ、依ツテ今次大流行ノ發生地タル三角地域トノ間ニ環境衛生學的ニ觀テ差異ガアルカ否カヲ調査シタ其ノ結果新京ノ環境衛生ヘ之ヲ新市街舊市街ニ區別シテ觀察スル時ハ其ノ間ニ相當ナ差異ノアルコトヲ認メタ、卽チ新市街及舊市街ノ內ニ適當ナ調査地區ヲ夫々數ケ所選定シ、各調査地區ニ就テ調査區域全面積、敷地面積、建築面積、建築延面積、室數、密數、諸室面積、便所數、世帯數、居住人員等ヲ調査シテ其ノ成績ヨリ居住環境ヲ考察セル新市街ノ居住環境ハ敷地比較的高燥ニシテ居住樣式ノ或部面ヘ別トシテ一般ニ都市ノ居住環境上問題トナル所ヘナチイケレドモ、之ニ反シテ舊市街ノ日滿混合居住地域竝ニ滿系居住地域ヘ其ノ敷地低儀ナル爲濕氣多ク、其ノ居住密度モ頗ル大デアル、而モ此等密集居住地域ノ家屋ハ地割整理ノ不徹底ナルガ爲ニ道路ノ走行或ヘ隣接家屋ノ狀態ニ拘束サレテ其ノ方位ノ全ク考慮サレテキナイモノガ多ク、從ツテ四季ヲ通ジテ西北西ノ烈風ノ多イ新京地方ノ風ヲ正面ニ受ケテ其ノ惡影響ニ災セシメルモノ多ク而モ樹木ニ惠マレナイタメニ冬季ニ於ケル寒風ノミナラズ春秋二季ノ黃塵ヤ砂麈ヲ防グコトモ殆ド考ヘラレテキナイ狀態デアル、又縱ヘ方位ニ好適ナ家屋デアツテモ隣接家屋其ノ他ニ遮ラレテ日光ノ射入殆ドナキ住居ノ多數存スルコトハ保健防疫上注意ニ値スルコトト考ヘ

515--18

ラレル、又舊市街ノ内デモ滿系居住地域ハ其ノ敷地ガ低濕ナルニ加ヘテ汚物ノ處理ガ殆ド顧ラレテキナイ状態デアル。

之ヲ要スルニ舊市街ニ於ケル居住環境ハ敷地低濕ニシテ、而モ家屋ノ建築ニ當ツテ床或ハ天井ニ防濕防塵工事ノ施サレテキナイモノガ多ク、更ニ日光ト通風ニ惠マレナイノニ加ヘテ日系ニアリテハ布圑類、疊等ノ發塵性ノ用具ガアリ、滿系ニアリテハ汚物ノ處理殆ド顧ラレズ、入浴洗濯ノ習慣ナキタメ孰レモ其ノ居住環境ハ鼠族及昆蟲ノ好適ナ培養溫床トナルコトハ想像ニ難クナイ。

次ニ各地區ノ生活環境ノ内物理環境及空氣環境ヲ檢査セルニ大體之モ新市街ト舊市街ニ區別シテ觀察スルト兩者ノ間ニ差異ヲ認メルコトガ出來タ、即チ舊市街ハ新市街ニ比シテ市内ノ商業中心街ヲナシ、人、車馬ノ交通輻輳シ、人口ノ密度モ極メテ大デアリ（１ヘクタール」當リ190～878人）、而モ此ノ地域ニハ生活水平低ク衛生狀態ノ極メテ低劣ナ滿人ガ多數雜居シテ居リ、又空中塵埃並、汚物塵埃並モ新市街ニ比シテ一般ニ多クアリ、紫外線強度ハ低クアツタ、併シナガラ溫濕度ニハ大差ナク、又風速ニ就テモ特有ナ現象ハ認メラレナカツタ。

次ニ新市街及舊市街ニ居住スル日本人ノミニ就テ傳染病發生ノ狀況ヲ比較スルニ第22表ノ如クニシテ、先ヅ本表ニ就テ消化器傳染病ニ就テ比較スルニ新舊兩地域ニ於テハ其ノ統計ニ於テモ内譯ニ於テモ差異ヲ認メナカツタ、經氣道傳染病ニ就テハ其ノ統計ニ於テハ兩地域ノ間ニ差異ガナカツタケレドモ其ノ内譯ニ就テ觀ルトキハ新市街ニ於テハ猩紅熱多ク、舊市街ニ於テハ痘瘡ガ多カツタ、猩紅熱ノ新市街ニ多イノハ本地域ニハ舊市街ヨリモ子供ノ多イト云フ特殊ナ事情ニ基クモノト考ヘラレル、舊市街ニ痘瘡ノ多イノハ其ノ環境衛生學的ノ條件ノ不良ナコトガ重要ナ原因ヲナシテヰルモノト思ハレル、次ニ經皮傳染病ニ就テ比較スルニ其ノ統計ニ於テモ内譯ニ於テモ孰レモ舊市街ノ方ガ新市街ヨリ多クアツタ、此ノ原因ハ新舊市街ノ環境衛生學的條件ノ差異ニ因ルモノト考ヘラレル、此處ニ經皮傳染病トシテ舉ゲタモノハ主トシテ蚤、蝨等ノ昆蟲ニヨツテ媒介サレル疾病デアルカラ此ノ發生並ニ傳播ハ其ノ地域ノ環境衛生學的條件ニ支配サレルコトガ極メテ大デアル理デアル、從ツテ新舊市街ノ傳染病發生率ノ差ガ特ニ此ノ經皮傳染病ニ於テ著明ニ現レタノハ當然ト云フベキデアロウ、斯クノ如ク舊市街ハ環境衛生學的ニ觀察シテモ經皮傳染病ノ發生素因ヲ有スル地域デアルト云フコトガ出來ル。

尚三角地域ハ舊市街ニ含マレル地域ニシテ、環境衛生學的ニ觀察シテ此ノ地域ニノミ特異ナ點ハ認メラレナカツタノデ此處ニ流行ガ發生シタノハ結局此ノ地域ニ直接病毒ガ移入サレタ爲ニシテ、此處ニ搬入サレタ病毒ハ其ノ傳播ニ有利ナ素因ヲ有スル此ノ地域ニ於テ流行ノ發生ヲ惹起スルニ至ツタモノト考ヘラレル、而シテ三角地域ニ比較的限局シタノハ此ノ地域ガ廣キ道路ニヨツテ隔離狀態ニサレテキタ爲ト考ヘラレル。

第22表　新京市舊新市街市街日本人ノ傳染病發生主要ノ比較（昭和15年1月〜同年10月）

地區別	人口	消化器傳染病				呼吸器傳染病			其他傳染病			總計
		コレラ	赤痢	腸チフス	パラチフス	猩紅熱	ヂフテリヤ	流行性脳脊髄膜炎	新發疹チフス	ペスト	比較皮膚病	
舊市街（中央通四近辺）計	71,331人	0.14±0.14	49.2±2.62	24.1±1.84	27.2±1.95	7.2±1.0	3.2±0.66	2.10±0.54	1.12±0.39	0		121.4±1.29
罹病區分別　小計			73.5±3.16			44.7±2.50			3.22±0.67			
新市街（櫻和天神若）計	56,167人	0.53±0.31	52.0±3.03	19.4±1.85	33.8±2.45	8.0±1.19	1.6±0.53	4.6±0.9	0.36±0.25	0		120.4±4.58
罹病區分別　小計			71.9±3.46			48.1±2.92			0.36±0.25			
新舊市街各傳染病別比較		−0.39±0.33	−2.8±4.0	+4.7±2.61	−6.6±3.13	−0.8±1.56	+5.6±1.13	−1.4±1.12	+2.1±0.76	+0.76±0.46	0	+1.0±6.08
罹病區分別比較			+1.6±4.69			−3.4±3.74			+2.86±0.71			

註
1) 罹生率ハ人口10,000人ニ對スル罹病數
2) ±以下ノ數値ハ標準偏差
3) 罹生率ノ差ハ低キ恐市街ノ方ガ大ナルトキハ−、新市街ノ方ガ大ナルトキハ＋ニテ示ス。

2.「ペスト患者ト一般住民ノ環境衛生ノ比較

　前述セル如ク舊市街ハ経皮傳染病發生ニ對シテ良好ナル條件ヲ提供シテキルノデ其處ニ撒入サレタ「ペスト」ノ病毒ガ其處ニ流行ヲ惹起スルニ至ッタコトハ想像ニ難クナイガ、以上ノ如クニシテ三角地域一帯ニ病毒ガ一様ニ浸潤シタト思ハレルニ拘ラズ、第3圖ニ示ス如ク或家屋ニ居住スル者ニ於テノミ「ペスト患者ノ發生シタノハ何故デアロウカ、其ニ就テハ遅遅的事項ヲ見逃スコトハ出來ナカッタレドモ患家ト一般民家トノ間ニ環境衛生學的差異ガアルカ否カヲ檢査スルコトヲ極メテ意義深セモノトシテ考ヘラレ、ソシテ其ニ就テ檢査シタ成績ヲ述べレバ次ノ如クデアル。

　先ヅ患者ノ初發シタト考ヘラレル犬猫病院ハ不潔ナ動物小屋ヲ有シ且犬、猫、牛、鷄等ノ出入多ク、鼠族及昆蟲ニ對シテ良好ナ温床ヲ提供シテキタコトハ想像ニ難クナイ、又同一家屋内ニ非衛生的ニ幾人ノ雑居シテキタコトモ流行ノ發生ニ對シテ良好ナ條件ヲ提供シテキタモノト考ヘラレル。

　尚三角地域内ノ他ノ患者發生家屋ハ總テ「アパート」ニシテ多數ノ家族ガ集團的生活ヲ營ミ、且人口密度モ極メテ高ク、從ッテ人ノ出入交通頻繁ニシテ一般ニ不潔ニシテ

515—20

リ易ク、又畳敷ニテ布團ヲ用ヒル生活ノ爲塵埃多クシテ昆蟲發生ノ溫床ヲ提供シ、一方世帶數多キ爲ニ食物殘渣等多ク且汚物處理ノ不良ナタメニ鼠族ニ恰好ナル棲息所ヲ提供シ、尙家屋ノ構造上室內ノ照度低ク、紫外線强度低ク且換氣不良ノタメニ濕度高キ等ノ不良ナ環境ト相待ツテ、斯クノ如キ家屋ニ患者ガ多發シタモノデブロウト考ヘラレル。

第3圖 「ペスト」患者發生要圖

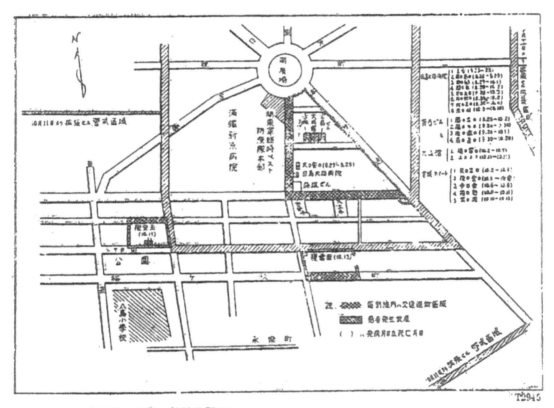

第3節 流行ノ統計的觀察

今次新京ニ發生シタ流行ハ腺ペスト」ノ流行ニシテ先ヅ鼠族間ニ「ペスト」ノ流行發生シ、其ニ原因シテ人ペスト」ノ流行ヲ惹起シタモノト考ヘラレル。

今茲ニ人ペスト」ノ流行ニ關シテ統計的觀察ヲ試ムレバ夫ノ如クデアル。

今次ノ流行ハ三角地域ヲ中心トシテ9月23日ニ突發的ニ發生シ、其ノ地域ニハ患者ノ多發ヲ見タケレドモ適切ナ防疫處置ト季節ノ影響ニヨリ周圍ニ蔓延スルコトナク、比較的遠カニ終熄ノ經過ヲ辿ツタモノニシテ患者發生ノ狀況ハ第1圖ニ示ス如クデアル、流行期間ハ9月23日ヨリ11月13日ニ至ル52日間ニシテ其ノ間ニ發出セル患者ハ總數28人デアル。

人種別、性別、年齡別罹患狀況、三角地域內ニ發生セル「ペスト患者ヲ人種的ニ觀察スレバ第23表ノ如キ成績ニシテ滿人ハ日本人ニ比シテ稍ミ罹患率高キモ之ハ「ペスト菌ニ對スル抵抗性ノ人種ニヨル差異ニ因ルモノデハナクテ滿人ノ居住環境ガ不良デアル爲ニ感染機會ニ遭遇スル頻

度ガ高イノニ因ルモノト考ヘラレル、次ニ「ペスト患者ヲ性別、年齢別ニ観察シタ成績ハ第24表ニ示ス如クニシテ、絶對數ニ就テ見レバ男ガ多ク、年齢ニ於テハ30歳以下ガ多イ様ナ成績デアル透ケレドモ、人口構成ノ明瞭ナ三角地域ニ就テ性別ノ罹患率ヲ見レバ第25表ノ如クニシテ男女ノ間ニハ殆ド差異ヲ認メナカツタ、然ルニ之ヲ15歳以下ト16歳以上ニ區別シテ見ルト第26表ノ如キ成績ニシテ男ニ於テハ大人ト子供トノ間ニ殆ド差ガ認メラレナカツタケレドモ女ニ於テハ子供ニ於テ罹患率ノ高イノヲ認メタ。

第23表　人種別患者發生數

人　　　　種	總　員（人）	患者數（人）	罹患率（%）
日　　本　　人	536	13	2.42
朝　　鮮　　人	81	0	0
滿　　　　人	128	6	4.69
外　人（白人）	10	0	0

第24表　性別、年齡別患者發生數

年　齡（歳）	男	女	計
1～5	0	3	3
6～10	1	2	3
11～15	1	1	2
16～20	3	1	4
21～30	6	0	6
31～40	4	0	4
41～50	2	1	3
51～60	2	1	3
61歳以上	0	0	0
計	19	9	28

第25表　性別罹患率（三角地域ニ於ケル）

性別	總　員	患　者　數	患者發生率（%）
男	414	12	2.6
女	341	8	2.8
計	755	20	2.6

第26表　年齡別罹患率（三角地域ニ於ケル）

性別	大　人（16歳以上）			小　人（15歳以下）		
	總　員	患者數	患者發生率（%）	總　員	患者數	患者發生率（%）
男	347	10	2.9	67	2	2.9
女	245	2	0.8	96	6	6.3

515—22

此ノ性別、年齢別ノ罹患率ハ感染機會ト「ペスト菌ニ對スル抵抗性ノ差異ノ二ツノ條件ニ關係シテキルノデ、女ノ子供ニ於テ罹患率ノ高カツタノハ感染機會ガ多カツタ爲デアルカ或ハ體質上「ペスト菌ニ對スル抵抗ガ弱イ爲デアルカ不明デアル。

　病　　型　　「ペスト患者ヲ病型別ニ觀察シタ成績ハ、第27表ニ表ス如クニシテ腺ペスト」ガ最モ多ク、次ニ「ペスト敗血症ガ多イ、此ノ成績ヲ見ルト今次ノ流行ハ從來ノ腺ペスト」流行ニ於ケル各病型ノ出現率ニ比シテ「ペスト敗血症型ノ多イノガ特徴トシテキル樣デアル、15例ノ腺ペスト患者ヲ原發腺腫別ニ見レバ、第28表ノ如キ成績ニシテ鼠蹊腺ガ最モ多ク、腋窩腺及頸腺ガ之ニ次デアル、此ノ成績ハ從來ノ流行ニ於ケル統計的數値ニ類似スルモノデアル。

第27表　患者ノ病型		
區分 / 病型	實　數	%
腺ペスト」	15	62.5
肺ペスト」	1	4.2
眼ペスト」	1 ?	4.2
皮膚ペスト」	2	8.3
「ペスト敗血症	5	20.8
計	24	100.0

第28表　淋巴腺ノ罹患狀況			
區分 / 淋巴腺		實　數	%
鼠蹊腺	右	8	
	左	3	73.4
	計	11	
腋窩腺	右	1	
	左	1	13.3
	計	2	
頸　腺	右	2	
	左	0	13.3
	計	2	

第29表　患者ノ經過日數	
經過日數(日)	實　數
1	1
2	7
3	2
4	6
5	3
6	2
7	1
19	(1)
平	3.6日

　經過日數　　「ペスト患者ノ發病ヨリ死亡迄ノ經過日數ヲ觀察セル成績ハ第29表ニ示ス如クニシテ2〜4日ノ間ニ死亡スルモノ極メテ多ク7日ヲテ殆ド總テ死亡スルヲ認メタ、19日間生存シタノハ極メテ珍ラシイ臨床的經過ヲ取ツタ症例デアル、今此ノ例外的ナ症例ヲ除イタモノニ就テ平均生存日數ヲ計算スレバ3.6日ニシテ從來ノ腺ペスト」流行ニ於ケル平均生存日數ヨリ極メテ短イコトガ判ル。

　死亡率　　今次流行ニ於テ隔離病舍ニ收容サレタ患者ハ8名ニシテ其ノ內治癒シタモノハ2名デアル、併シナガラ治癒ト判定サレタ2名ハ「ペスト症ナルカ否カ疑ノ存シタモノデアルカラ之ヲ除外スレバ死亡率ハ100%トナル、之ハ從來ノ腺ペスト」ノ流行ニ比シテ極メテ高イ死亡率デアル。

　偕而腺ペスト」ノ流行ニ於テハ上述ノ各項ニ就テ得ル數値ハ(1)感染機會（之ハ環境衛生學ノ條件ニヨツテ左右サレルコトガ多イモノデアル）(2)流行菌ノ毒力ノ強弱(3)大衆ノ保有スル免疫ノ程度（先天性免疫及後天性免疫）等ニヨツテ左右サレルモノト考ヘラレル、即チ流行ノ發生狀況及其ノ經過ハ主トシテ環境衛生學的條件ニヨツテ支配セラレ、性別、年齢別ノ罹患率モ之ニヨツテ

支配サレルトコロガ大デアルト考ヘラレル。其ニ反シテ性別、年齢別ノ發病率，病型（臨床的所見），發病ヨリ死亡迄ノ經過日數，罹患者ノ死亡率等ハ主トシテ流行菌ノ毒力及大衆ノ保有スル免疫ノ程度ニ支配サレルモノト考ヘラレル。

今次流行ガ從來ノ「腺ペスト」ノ流行ニ比シテ「ペスト敗血症型ノ出現率高ク，死亡迄ノ經過日數短ク，且死亡率ノ高イノヲ特徴トシタノハ毒力强キ「ペスト菌」ガ「ペスト」ニ對スル免疫ヲ保有シテヰナイ大衆ノ間ニ侵入シテ流行ヲ起シタ爲デアルト考ヘラレル。此ノ事ハ毒力ノ强キ「ペスト菌ガ免疫ヲ保有セザル抵抗性弱キモノニ對シテハ敗血症型ヲ呈シ、免疫ヲ保有スルモノニ對シテハ皮膚ペスト」或ハ輕症腺ペスト」ヲ起シ、疾病ノ經過日數長クシテ治癒ノ經過ヲ辿ルモノノ多イコト及毒力ノ弱イ菌ガ免疫ヲ有セザルモノニ對シテハ皮膚ペスト」或ハ輕症腺ペスト」ヲ起シ得ルモ、免疫ヲ有スルモノニ對シテハ殆ド發症ノ起シ得ナイコトヨリモ推論スルコトガ出來ル。猶此ノ事ハ今次流行ノ發生經路ヲ考察シテモ自ラ明カデアル、即チ今次ノ流行ハ農安ノ「ペスト」流行ヨリ波及シテ來タモノト考ヘラレルノデ侵入シテ來タ病毒ガ數代ニ亘リ人體ヲ通過シ、毒力ヲ增强セラレテキタコトハ想像ニ難クナイ、其ハ新京ノ流行時ニ分離シタ人由來株、鼠由來株、蚤由來株等ガ總テ强キ毒力ヲ保有シテキタコトヨリモ推論スルコトガ出來ル、一方新京ノ大衆ガ「ペスト」ニ對スル免疫ヲ保有シテヰナカツタコトハ其マデニ「ペスト・ワクチン」ノ接種ヲ受ケテヰナカツタコト及過去ニ於テ相當長イ期間新京ニ於テハ「ペスト」ノ流行ガナカツタコトヨリ推論スルコトガ出來ル。

上述ノ如キ考察ヨリ今次ノ流行ハ毒力强キ菌ガ免疫ナキ大衆ノ中ニ流行ヲ惹起シタ場合ニ見ラレル流行ノ型式デアロウト考ヘラレル。

併シナガラ流行ノ型式ヲ上述ノ如キ觀點ヨリ觀察シテ斯クノ如ク考察スルコトガ妥當デアルカ否カハ將來更ニ多數ノ流行ニ就テ詳細ニ檢探サレタ上デナケレバ判定スルコトガ困難デアル。

第3章　感染經路ニ關スル考察
第1節　病毒搬入經路ニ關スル考察

今次ノ流行ニ於テ病毒ガ如何ニシテ搬入セラレタルカニ就テ種々ノ點ニ就テ調査シタガ、竟ニ其ヲ明カニスルコトガ出來ナカツタノハ遺憾デアツタ。

今故ニ病毒搬入ノ經路ニ關シテ考ヘ得ベキ場合ヲ考察シテ述ベレバ次ノ如クデアル。

I. 傳染源ニ關スル考察

今次ノ人ペスト」ノ流行ヲ鼠ペスト」ノ流行ヲ先驅トシテヰルモノデアルカ否カニ就テハ次ノ諸點ヨリ鼠ペスト」ガ先行シ、其ニ引續イテ人ペスト」ノ流行ガ發生シタモノト推論スルコトガ出來ル。

1) 患者發病前10日間ノ行動ヲ調査シ、特ニ初發患者ト目セラルル王合及太田○次ニ就テ發病前ノ行動（自身病毒ヲ取扱ヒタルコトノ有無、「ペスト」流行地域ヘ出入ノ有無、病毒ニ接近セル人（「ペスト」流行地域ト交通ノアル人、「ペスト菌ヲ取扱フ研究機關ニ關係ヲ有スル人ト

515—24

ノ交通ノ有無)ヲ詳細ニ調査シ、同時ニ患者ノ家族及患者ト密接ナ關係ヲ有スル者ニ就テ同樣ノ調査ヲシタケレドモ何等確思ヲ肯定シ得ル樣ナ關係ヲ見出スコトハ出來ナカツタ、即チ患者ハ孰レモ各家庭ニ於テ感染機會ヲ意識スルコトナク罹患發病シタモノデアツテ病毒ヲ直接患者ヨリ受ケタモノデモナク、或ハ不良分子ニヨツテ直接謀略的行爲ヲ受ケタモノデモナカツタ、斯クノ如ク不知不識ノ間ニ家庭ニ於テ罹患シ、「腺ペスト」ヲ發症シ、而モ其ノ屍體ニ就テ多數ノ蚤ノ刺螫跡ヲ認メタコトハ蚤ニヨツテ病毒ヲ受ケタモノデアルコトヲ示スモノニシテ、尚各患者ノ發生狀況ヲ見ルニ相互ニハ交通關係ナクシテ而モ發病月日ヲ同ジクシテヰルコトハ「鼠ペスト」ノ流行ガ先行シテヰテ、其ヨリ蚤ヲ介シテ「人ペスト」ノ流行ガ發生シタコトヲ暗示スルモノト云フコトガ出來ル。

2) 患者發生前ニ於ケル患者發生地域(三角地域)及其ノ附近ノ斃鼠ノ狀況ヲ調査セルニ第30表ノ如キ成績ニシテ三角地域ニ於テハ斃鼠ノ多カツタコトハ確實デアルカラ此ノ事ヨリモ「人ペスト」ノ流行ニ先行シテ「鼠ペスト」ノ流行ガアツタコトヲ想像スルコトガ出來ル。

第30表 「人ペスト」發生前ノ三角地域內ニ於ケル斃鼠ノ調査成績(長花)

發見月日	發 見 場 所	斃鼠數	發 見 者
9.17	東三條通(犬猫病院附近) 森喬華宅ノ裏	4	佐 藤 城
20	同 上 鳩坂アパート5號宅內	1	高松チトセ
20	同 上 盃 所	1	同 上
20	同 上 (犬猫病院附近) 森晴夫宅ノ門附近	1	森 晴 夫
22	室町4丁目 東京庵(そば屋)倉庫中	2	土 屋 ヨ レ
22	同上家ノ前ノ道路上ニテヒヨロヒヨロセル鼠ヲ發見	1	同 上
22	室町4丁目(大成館裏)假田宅玄關外	1	假田ハルエ
22	同 上 玄關內	2	同 上
9.17～9.22	計	13	

3) 流行發生後患者發生地域ニテ捕獲セル鼠ニ就テ菌檢索ヲ行ツタ結果多數ノ有菌鼠ヲ檢出シ、又其ニ附着シテキタ蚤(X. cheopis 及 C. anisus)ヨリ菌ヲ檢出シタコト及其ノ檢出率ガ概ネ患者ノ發生率ニ併行セル關係ニアツタコトハ「人ペスト」ガ「鼠ペスト」ニ由來スルコトヲ物語ル有力ナ事實デアル。

4) 今次ノ流行ガ「腺ペスト」ノ流行デアツタコトモ「鼠ペスト」ニ由來セル「人ペスト」ノ流行デアルコトヲ示スモノデアル。

Ⅱ. 流行發生地域ニ關スル考察

「ペスト」ノ病毒ガ一番最初ニ何處ニ搬入サレタモノデアルカニ就テハ次ノ諸點ヨリ所謂三角地域ニ最初ニ搬入サレタモノデアルト推論スルコトガ出來ル。

1) 流行發生前ニ三角地域ニ斃鼠ガ非常ニ多ク發見サレタコト(第30表參照)

515-425

2）患者ノ發生狀況ヲ見ルニ三角地域ニ初發シ、而モ同地域ニ相當多發セル後ニ周圍ノ地域ニ若干ノ患者ノ發生ヲ認メルニ至ツタコト。

3）流行發生後三角地域ヲ中心トシテ附近一帶ヨリ捕獲セル鼠ニ就テ菌檢索ヲ行ヘルニ最初ハ三角地域ノ鼠ニ菌ノ檢出率高ク次第ニ其ノ周圍ノ地域ヨリ捕獲セル鼠ニモ菌ヲ檢出スルニ至ツタコト。

又鼠體ニ附着シテキル蚤ノ數量的觀察及菌檢索ノ成績ヨリモ先ヅ三角地域ニ鼠ペスト」ノ流行發生シ、次デ其ガ周圍ノ地域ニ傳播シタコトヲ推論シ得タコト。

4）環境衛生學的ニ觀察スル時ハ新市街ト舊市街トノ間ニハ比較的著明ナ差異ガ認メラレ、舊市街ハ經皮傳染病ニ對シ流行發生ノ素因ヲ有スルコトヲ認メ得タケレドモ三角地域ガ特ニ其ノ發生素因ヲ多ク有スルモノトハ考ヘラレナカツタ、從ツテ三角地域ニ流行ノ發生シタノハ病毒ガ先ヅ第一ニ此ノ地域ニ搬入サレタ爲デアルトスルノガ妥當デアルト考ヘラレタコト。

上述セル處ヨリ病毒ハ最初三角地域ニ搬入サレタモノデアルト考ヘルノガ妥當デアルケレドモ三角地域內ノ何處ニ搬入サレタモノデアロウカ、此ノ事ニ關シテハ次ノ點ヨリ考察スルニ田島犬猫病院ニ先ヅ最初ニ搬入サレタモノデアロウト推論スルコトガ出來ル。

1）田島犬猫病院ニ於テ初發患者ノ發生シタコト及同家族ヨリ多數ノ患者ガ續々ト發生シ同家屋ガ病毒ニヨツテ極メテ濃厚ニ汚染サレテキタコトガ想像シ得ラレルコト。

2）同家ヨリ捕獲セル鼠及附着昆蟲ノ菌檢出率ノ高カツタコト。

3）同家ハ人ノ出入多ク、又家畜ノ出入ノ多カツタコト、特ニ農安方面ヨリ診療ヲ爲ニ牛馬ノ出入スルモノノアツタコト。

以上ノ點ヨリ田島犬猫病院ニ先ヅ病毒ガ搬入サレタモノト考ヘラレルケレドモ、之ハ推論デアツテ、或ハ三角地域ノ他ノ部分ニ搬入サレタ病毒ガ鼠ペスト」ノ發生ニ好適ナ素因ヲ有ツテキル犬猫病院ニ於テ鼠ペスト」ノ流行ヲ發生シタモノデアルカモ知レナイ。

孰レニセヨ「ペスト」ノ病毒ガ先ヅ三角地域ニ搬入サレタコトハ確實デ、其ノ內容ヲ種々ノ點カラ考ヘテ田島犬猫病院ニ先ヅ病毒ガ搬入サレタモノデハナカロウカト考ヘラレル。

Ⅲ．病毒搬入時期ニ關スル考察

三角地域ニ鼠ペスト」ノ流行ヲ惹起シタ病毒ノ搬入セラレタ時期ニ關シテハ全ク不明デアルト云フヨリ他ハナイガ次ニ述ベルコトヨリ考察スレバ8月下旬デアロウト推論スルコトヲ得ル。

文獻ニヨルト鼠ペスト」ノ流行ハ人ペスト」ノ流行ニ先行スルコト約2週間前後ヲ以テ成サレテキル、從ツテ三角地域ニ於テハ9月10日前後ニ鼠ペスト」ノ流行ガ發生シタモノト考ヘラレル、又人ペスト」ノ流行ノ發生前ニ於ケル斃鼠ノ發見狀況カラ考ヘテモ9月10日前後ニ鼠族間ニ「ペスト」ノ流行ガ發生シタモノト考ヘラレル。

然ラバ其ノ鼠ペスト」ノ流行ヲ惹起シタ病毒ハ何時頃ニ三角地域ノ鼠族間ニ搬入サレタモノ

515—26

デアロウカ、此ノ事ニ關シテハ病毒ガ有菌蚤ニヨツテ運バレタカ或ハ有菌鼠ニヨツテ運バレタ
カニヨツテ若干ノ差異ガ生ズルノデアル、又其ノ有菌蚤或ハ有菌鼠ノ數ニヨツテ左右サレルノ
デアツテ一時ニ多數ノ有菌鼠或ハ有菌蚤ガ搬入サレレバ速カニ流行ヲ發生シ得ルケレドモ極メ
テ少數ノ有菌蚤或ハ有菌鼠ニヨル時ハ鼠族間ニ「ペスト」ノ流行ヲ發生スル迄ニハ相當ノ期間ヲ
要スルコトハ想像ニ難クナイ。

　　若シ1匹ノ有菌蚤ニヨツテ病毒ガ運搬サレ、其ガ三角地域内ノ一頭ノ鼠ニ附着シタトスレバ
其ノ鼠ガ發症シテ敗血症ヲ起シテ斃死スル迄ニハ少クトモ3～7日ヲ必要トスル、其ノ鼠體ニ附
着シテキタ蚤ノ數ガ3デアルトスレバ（之ハ新京ニ於ケル蚤指數ノ調査成績ヨリ知ルコトガ出
來ル）、其ガ有菌蚤トナツテ次ノ3頭ニ附着スルコトニナル、蚤ハ鼠ガ斃死シナケレバ他ノ鼠體
ニ移ラナイ、又「ペスト菌ヲ吸引シタ蚤ガ感染能力ヲ有スル爲ニハ胃内ニ吸ヘタ「ペスト菌ガ
其處デ増殖スルコトガ必要デアルカラ少クトモ2～3日ヲ必要トスル、從ツテ其ノ地域ノ鼠ノ蚤
指數ヲ3トスレバ1匹ノ有菌蚤ガ其ノ地域ニ搬入サレテ直チニ1頭ノ鼠ニ附着スル時ハ約1週間
後ニ3匹ノ有菌蚤ガ出來ル、其ガ各々1頭宛ノ鼠ニ附着シテ其ヲ發症サセルトスレバ始メカラ
約2週間後ニハ3²ニ9匹ノ有菌蚤ガ出來ル、從ツテ次ニハ9頭ノ有菌鼠ヲ發生セシメ得ルコトニ
ナル、斯クテ有菌鼠ハ等比級數的ニ増加シテ鼠族間ニ「ペスト」ノ流行ガ發生スルモノト考ヘラ
レル。

　　次ニ鼠族間ニ幾％ノ有菌鼠ガ發生シ、其ノ有菌鼠ト其ノ地域ニ居住スル住民トノ比ガ如何ナ
ル割合ニナツタ時ニ人ペスト」ノ流行ガ發生スルモノデアルカハ就テハ今ノトコロ不明デアル
ケレドモ上述セル鼠ペスト」流行ノ發生要約及其ガ人ペスト」ノ發生ヲ惹起スルニ至ル要約ハ其
ノ地域ノ環境衞生學的條件ニヨツテ支配サレルノデ場合場合ニヨツテ異ツテ來ルモノデアロウ
ト考ヘラレル、ノミナラズ其ニハ偶發的事項ノ關興スルコトガ多イノデ其等ノ現象ノ間ニ一定
ノ時期的關係ヲ推論スルコトハ殆ド不可能デアロウト考ヘラレル。

　　今次ノ流行ニ於テモ病毒搬入ノ時期ガ何時頃デアツタカハ全ク不明デアルト云ハザルヲ得
ナイガ以上述ベタ所ヨリ推論スレバ鼠族間ノ「ペスト」ノ流行ガ相當強クナリ、其ガ人ペスト」ノ
流行ヲ起スニ足ル迄ニナツタノハ人ペスト」ノ發生状態ヨリ考ヘルト9月中旬頃ト思ヘルノ
デ、若シ「ペスト病毒ガ㐱數ノ有菌蚤或ハ有菌鼠ニヨツテ此ノ地域ニ搬入サレタモノトスレバ
其ヨリモ2週間～3週間前ト考ヘラレルノデ其ノ時期ハ8月下旬デアロウト推論シ得ラレルノ
デアル。併シナガラ之ハ大シテ深イ根據ノアル推論デナイコトハ前述セルトコロヨリ明カデア
ル。

Ⅲ. 病毒搬入經路ニ關スル考察

　　病毒ガ如何ニシテ三角地域ニ搬入セラレタモノデアルカニ就テハ謀略ノ目的ニテ人工的ニ搬
入サレタ場合ト自然的ニ何等故爲ナク搬入サレタ場合トヲ考ヘルコトガ出來ル。

謀略ニ依ル搬入ニ關スル考察

　　時局柄謀略的行爲ヲ否定スルコトハ出來ナイノデ次ノ諸點ニ就テ調査シ、以テ謀略ヲ肯定シ

得ル資料ヲ獲得セント努メタケレドモ、其ヲ肯定シ得ル成績ハ得ラレナカツタ。

1) 流行發生ノ直前ニ於ケル新京來往ノ外人ニ關スル調査ヲシタケレドモ特別ニ疑ハシイ點ハ認メラレナカツタ。

2) 新京市內ニ居住スル要注意者ノ動向ヲ調査シタケレドモ特別ニ疑ノ存スル點ハナカツタ。

3) 容疑者ヲ訊問シタケレドモ疑問ノ點ハナカツタ。

4) 容疑物件ノ蒐集ニ努メタケレドモ特別ナモノハ得ラレナカツタ。

5) 新京市內ノ「ペスト菌ヲ取扱ツテヰル研究機關關係者ノ狀況ヲ調査シタケレドモ疑ハシイ點ハ認メラレナカツタ。

6) 新京市內ノ細菌用具ノ販賣者ニ就テ其ノ販賣狀況ヲ調査シタケレドモ購買者ノ狀況ニハ疑ハシイ點ハ認メラレナカツタ。

7) 田島犬猫病院ト外人トノ關係ヲ調査セルニ詳細ハ不明デアルケレドモ、獨逸及伊太利公使館員ニテ犬ノ診療ヲ受ケタモノノアル他ニハ出入者ナク、謀略的行爲ヲ肯定シ得ル資料ハ得ラレナカツタ。

8) 田島犬猫病院ニ於ケル受診家畜ノ狀況ヲ調査シタ結果此ノ受診家畜ヲ介シテ謀略ヲ行ツタノデハナイカト思ハレル點ハ見當ラナカツタ。

自然發生ニ關スル考察

上述セル如ク謀略的行爲ハ否定スルコトガ出來タノデ次ニ自然發生トシテ其ノ病毒搬入ノ經路ニ就テ考察スル必要ガアル。而シテ自然發生トスレバ其ノ病毒ハ次ノ諸點ヨリ考察シテ「ペスト常在地域特ニ農安ヨリ搬入サレタモノデアルト推論スルコトガ出來ル。

1) 昭和15年ノ「ペスト常在地域ニ於ケル流行ノ發生狀態ヲ見ルニ第3表ニ示ス如クニシテ6月中旬農安縣城內ニ初發シタ流行ハ大第ニ疫勢ヲ高メ、農安縣城內ニ猛烈ナ流行ヲ起シタバカリデナク遂ニハ周圍ノ部落ニ傳播シテ流行ハ終熄ノ傾向ナキ狀態デアツタ、而シテ新京ト農安ハ僅カニ62kmヲ隔テルノミデアツテ其ノ間ハ一望ノ田野ニシテ其ノ間ニ農村小部落ガ介在シテヰル狀況デアルカラ此ノ地理的狀況カラ考ヘテモ病毒ガ新京ニ侵入シ得ルコトガ考ヘラレタ。

2) 農安縣城內ニ發生セル「ペスト流行ノ新京ヘノ侵入ヲ防禦スルタメニ兩者ノ間ニ介在スル長春縣ヲ障壁トスル如ク防疫態勢ハ整ヘラレテキタケレドモ其ノ狀況ヲ見ルニ7月15日ニハ新京—農安間ノ重要道路ニハ「ペスト」防疫監視哨ヲ設ケテ人ノ交通ヲ監視スルト共ニ豫防接種ヲ行ツテキタケレドモ、其ノ業務ハ僅カニ檢診及豫防接種ヲ實施スルニ過ギナクテ交通ヲ禁止シタノデハナカツタノデ「ペスト」病毒ノ侵入スル機會ハアツタモノト思ハレル、殊ニ夜暗ヲ利用シ、或ハ他ノ道路ヨリ新京市內ニ潜入スルモノガ多タ、是等ヲ防止スルコトハ困難デアツタ、其處デ9月7日以後ハ之ヲ撤退シタ爲ニ其ノ後ハ殆ド自由ニ交通ガ行ハレテキタ、從ツテ其ノ間ニ病毒侵入ノ機會ノ極メテ多カツタコトハ想像ニ難クナイトコロデアル。

515—28

3) 新京ト農安ノ人的及物的ノ交通ノ状況、上述セル如ク新京ト農安トノ間ニハ人ノ交通ハ自
由ニ行ハレテキタ、殊ニ農安ハ新京ト経済的ニ頗ル緊密ナ関係ニアルノデ其ノ間ニハ人的及
物的ノ来往ガ頻繁デアルバカリデナク農安ノ重要商店ハ殆ド新京大商店ノ支店デアル爲ニ今
次流行ノ發生ニ際シ「ペスト患者ヲ出シタ農安ノ支店ヨリ使用人ガ逃亡シテ來京シテ來タコ
トハ確實デアル、又農安ト新京トハ鐵道ニヨツテモ自由ニ人的及物的ノ交通ガ行ハレテキ
タ、殊ニ自動車、牛車、馬車或ハ馬ニヨツテ荷物ガ農安ヨリ新京ニ運搬サレテキタコトハ確
實デアル、從ツテ是等ノ手段ニヨツテ病毒ノ搬入ガ行ハレタコトハ容易ニ考ヘ得ラレルトコ
ロデアル。

4) 新京ニ於ケル過去ノ「ペスト」流行ノ状況、新京ニ於テハ明治44年北満ヲ席巻セル肺ペスト」
ノ流行時ニ満鐵附屬地ニ105人ノ肺ペスト」ノ發生ガ記録サレテヰル、其ノ後康徳元年10月ニ
農安方面ヨリ來京シタ「トラツク」ノ運轉手（日本人）ガ満鐵新京醫院ニ入院死亡シテ臉ペス
ド」ト決定サレタ、康徳6年2月ニハ市内ノ某研究所ニテ實驗室感染ニヨル肺ペスト患者發
生シ、其ノ患者ヨリ自宅感染ニヨツテ1名ノ肺ペスト患者ヲ出シタコトガ記録サレテヰル、
併シナガラ是等ノ患者ノ感染經路ハ明瞭ニシテ新京ニ病毒ガ固定シテキテ、其カラ發生シタ
モノデナイコトハ確實デアル、此ノ成績ヨリ考ヘテモ今次流行ノ病毒ガ他ヨリ搬入サレタモ
ノデアルコトハ明カデアル。

5) 「ペスト菌ヲ取扱フ研究調査機關ト保者ノ状況、新京市内ニテペスト菌ヲ取扱ヒ且其ヲ保
有シテヰルノハ衛生技術廠及市衛生試驗所ノ2ヶ所ニシテ、同所ヨリ試驗動物ノ逃亡或ハ従
業員ニヨツテ有菌蚤ノ搬出サレルコトガ考ヘラレルノデ施設及従業員ノ勤務状況ヲ調査シ、
尚家族ノ衛生状態ヲ調査シタケレドモ特記スベキ事ナク、又此等従業員ニシテ田島犬猫病院
附近ニ居住シテヰルモノモナク、載ハ同醫院關係者ト密接ナ交通ノアルモノモナカツタ。
　以上ノ諸點ヨリ考察スレバ今次流行ノ病毒ハ農安流行地ヨリ搬入サレタモノデアルトスル
ノガ妥當デアルト考ヘラレル。

Ⅴ　農安流行地ヨリ三角地域ヘノ病毒搬入經路ニ關スル考察
　病毒ノ搬入經路ニ就テハ患者ニヨル場合ト有菌鼠ニヨル場合ト有菌蚤ニヨル場合トガ考ヘラ
レルノデ是等ノ事項ニ就テハ考察スレバ次ノ如クデアル。

1)　患者ニヨル病毒ノ搬入
　満州ニ於テハ病毒ガ患者ニヨツテ搬入サレルコトガ屡々アルノデ此ノ點ヲ考慮シテ三角地域
ヲ中心トシテ其ノ周圍ノ地域ニ於ケル8月1日以降9月中旬ニ至ル間ノ死亡者及行路病死者
ノ死亡原因ヲ調査セルモ疑ハシイモノハ見當ラナカツタ、従ツテ患者ニヨル病毒ノ搬入ハ否
定スルコトガ出來ル。

2)　有菌鼠ニヨル病毒ノ搬入
　有菌鼠ガ自發的ニ移動シテ農安ヨリ三角地域ヘ病毒ヲ搬入シタトイフコトモ考ヘラレルケ
レドモ、斯様ナ大距離ノ移動ハ殆ド起リ得ナイモノト考ヘラレル、従ツテ有菌鼠ニ依ツテ病

蚤ガ搬入サレタトスレバ其ガ貨物ト共ニ搬入サレタ場合ガ考ヘラレル、此ノ事ハ洮安ヨリ新京トノ間ニハ鉄道ニヨルベカリデナク自動車、馬車、牛車等ニヨル荷物ノ運搬ガ頻繁ニ行ハレテキタノデ此ノ荷物ニ紛レ込ンダ有菌鼠ガ三角地域ニ搬入サレタト云フコトガ考ヘラレルナレドモ洮安ヨリ輸送サレタ荷物ガ特ニ多ク三角地域ニ搬入サレタト云フコトハナク従ツテ若シ斯様ナ手段ニテ病蚤ガ搬入サレタモノトスレバ他ノ地域ニ於テモ同様ニ流行ガ發生シ得ル理デアルケレドモ特ニ三角地域ニ流行ガ發生シタノハ他ノ原因ニヨルモノデアルコトヲ示スモノ考ヘラレル、併シナガラ三角地域ニ運搬サレタ荷物ニ偶々有菌鼠ガ紛レ込ンデヰテ、其ガ其處ニ流行ヲ起シタト云フ遇發的ナコトガアツタカ否カヘ否定スルコトハ出來ナイ。

3） 有菌蚤ニヨル病蚤ノ搬入

先ヅ第一ニ有菌蚤ガ人（患者及健康者）ノ衣類ニ附着シテ運搬サレルコトガ考ヘラレルガ、此ノ事ニ關シテハ三角地域ノ住民ガ洮安流行地ニ行キ有菌蚤ヲ附着シテ歸ツタコトガアルカ否カ、又洮安方面ヨリ其ノ衣服ニ有菌蚤ヲ附着シテ三角地域ニ來タ人ガアルカ否カ、或ハ三角地域ノ人ガ洮安方面ト交通アル人ト接觸シテ其ノ人ニ附着シテキタ有菌蚤ヲ自分ニ附着サセルヤウナ機會ガアツタカ否カ、其ノ他種々ノ場合ヲ考察シテ調査シナケレバナラナイデアルガ實際問題トシテ其ハ殆ド不可能ニ近イコトガアル、併シナガラ若シ斯様ナ手段ニテ有菌蚤ガ運搬サレ、其ガ「ペスト」ノ流行ヲ惹起シタモノトスレバ三角地域以外ニ於テモ流行ガ起リ得タ筈デアル、然ルニ三角地域ニ限局シテ發生シタノハ他ノ原因ニヨルモノデアルト考ヘルノガ安當デアラウ、併シナガラ一方ニハ以上述ベタ様ナ手段ニ依ツ遇發的ニ三角地域ニ流行ガ發生シタコトモ考ヘラレナイコトデナイ。

次ニ有菌蚤ガ鼠體ニ附着シテ搬入サレルコトガ考ヘラレル、此ノ事ニ關シテハ有菌鼠ニヨル搬入ノ場合ト同様ニ考ヘラレル。

次ニ有菌蚤ガ荷物ニ附着シテ搬入サレルコトガ考ヘラレル、之ハ衣類、家具等ガ運搬サレル時ニハ歴々起リ得ルコトト考ヘラレル、而モ洮安ト新京トノ間ニハ前述ノ如ク荷物ノ交通ハ常ニ行ハレテキタノデカラ最モ起リ得ル経路デアルト思ハレルケレドモ此ノ實際ニヨツテ特ニ三角地域ニ流行ノ發生スル根據ハ認メラレナイ。從ツテ若シ此ノ手段ニヨツテ三角地域ニノミ流行ガ發生シタモノトスレバ其ハ全ク偶發的ノコトニ因ツタモノデアルト云ウヨリ外ハナイ。

次ニ考ヘラレルコトハ有菌蚤ガ田島犬猫病院ニ受診ニ來タ家畜ニヨツテ搬入サレタカ否カノ問題デアル、此ノ事ニ關シテハ8月1日以降同病院ニ受診ニ來タ犬、猫、牛馬等ノ病歴ヲ調査シタケレドモ資料ガ散逸シテヰタ爲ニ明カニスルコトガ出來ナカツタ、聞ク所ニヨルト犬、猫ハ主トシテ新京市外ノモノニシテ遠ク「ペスト」潜在地區ヨリ受診ニ來タモノハナイ様デアル、又洮安方面ニ狩獵ニ出タ犬ガ受診ニ來タカ否カヲ稽査セシガ斯カル例ハ見當ラナカツタケレドモ流行地ニ侵入セル形跡ナク且其ノ時期モ病蚤搬入時期ニ一致シテ居ナイノ等頗

515—30

ヲ置クコトハ出來ナカツタ、尚牛、馬等ハ現金拂ニテ受診ニ來テ居タ爲ニ受診簿ノ如キモノナク、該畜獸ノ所有者ハ明確デナイケレドモ聞ク所ニヨルト農安方面ヨリモ相當ニ來テ居タコトハ確實デアル、牛、馬等ガ蚤ヲ自體ニ附着シテ運搬スルコトハ少ナイケレドモ是等ノ牛馬ニ乘セラレテ來タ荷物或ハ其ノ裝具等ニ蚤ガ附着シテ運搬サレルコトハ屢ミアルコトト考ヘラレル、從ツテ農安方面ヨリ受診ニ來タ牛、馬ノ荷物ニ附着シテ來タ有菌蚤ガ犬猫病院ニテ診療ヲ受ケテヰル間ニ其處ニ落チテ其ガ犬猫病院ノ鼠ノ間ニ侵入シ、鼠族及昆蟲ノ溫床タル此處ニ先ヅ鼠ペスト」ノ流行ヲ惹起シ、次デ人ペスト」ノ發生ヲ起シタモノト考ヘルコトガ出來ル、患者ノ發生狀況カラ考ヘテモ此ノ方法ガ起リ得ル公算ノ最モ大デアツタモノト思ハレル。

以上述ベタ如ク病毒ガ三角地域ニ搬入サレタ經路ニ關シテハ積極的ニ之ヲ證明スルコトハ出來ナカツタケレドモ上述ノ如クイロイロノ點ヨリ考察シテミルト田島犬猫病院ニ農安ヨリ受診ニ來タ牛或ハ馬ノ荷物ニ有菌蚤ガ附着シテ來テ其ガ犬猫病院ニ落チテ其處ニ鼠ペスト」ノ流行ヲ惹起シ、次デ人ペスト」ノ流行ヲ惹起シタモノデアルト考ヘルノガ最モ安當デアルト思ハレル。

4) 小 括

農安流行地ヨリ三角地域ヘノ病毒搬入經路ニ關シテハ農安ト交通ノアツタ人ノ衣類ニ附着シテキタ有菌蚤ガ偶然ニ三角地域ニ搬入サレタ場合モ考ヘラレ、又荷物ニ附着シテキタ有菌蚤ガ偶然ニ三角地域ニ搬入サレタ場合モ考ヘラレルケレドモ、上述セルトコロヨリ考察スレバ「ペスト」ノ病毒ガ農安ノ流行地ヨリ先ヅ三角地域ノ鼠族間ニ運搬サレ、其處ニ鼠ペスト」ノ流行ヲ惹起シ、次デ人ペスト」ノ流行ヲ惹起シタモノデアルコトハ確實ニシテ、而モ其ノ病毒ハ有菌蚤ニヨツテ運搬サレタモノト考ヘラレル、而シテ其ノ方法ハ田島犬猫病院ニ農安方面ヨリ受診ニ來タ牛、馬等ノ荷物ニ附着シテ運搬サレタモノデアロウト考ヘルノガ最モ安當デアロウ。

第2節 病毒傳播經路ニ關スル考察

第1節ニ於テ述ベタコトヨリ今次流行ニ於テハ「ペスト」ノ病毒ガ先ヅ鼠ペスト」ノ流行ヲ起シ、次デ人ペスト」ノ流行ヲ起シタモノト考ヘルコトガ出來ル、從ツテ患者ノ發生狀況ヲ觀テモ患者相互ノ間ニハ交通關係ナク全ク、無關係ニ發生シ、人ヨリ人ヘノ傳染ハ特殊ノ例ヲ除イタ他ニハ考ヘラレナイ。

而シテ人ペスト」ノ直接ノ傳染源ハ有菌ノ「ドブネズミ」デアルコトハ明カデアリ、之ヲ人ニ傳播シタモノハ X. cheopis 及 C. anisus デアルコトハ菌檢索ノ成績(第17表)及流行地域ノ塵埃ノ中ニ X. cheopis ヲ見出シタコト第32表及吸著試驗ニヨツテ居室ニ是等ノ蚤ノ游離シテヰルコトヲ證明シタコト第31表及人ニ X. cheopis 附着シテヰルコトヲ見出シタコト(第21表)等ヨリ推論シ得ラレル、即チ是等ノ成績ヨリ考察スレバ X. cheopis ガ有菌鼠體ニ附着シテ吸血シタ後其

515→31

ノ鼠ガ乾死スルト蚤ガ鼠體ヨリ遊離シテ、機會ガアルト人ヲ刺螫シ、其ニヨツテ人ニ「ペスト」ヲ
發症セシメルモノデアルト考ヘラレル、尚患者ノ發生シタ家屋ヲ環境衛生學的ニ觀察セル成績ヨ
リ其ノ家屋ガ鼠族ノ出入容易ニシテ且蚤ノ繁殖ニ好適ナ條件ヲ備ヘテヰルコトヲ認メタノデ此ノ
事ヨリモ鼠族ガ傳染源デアツテ其ヲ傳播シタモノハ蚤デアツタコトヲ想像スルコトガ出來タ。

第31表　患者發生家屋及一般民家ノ屋内遊離蚤ノ種類（長花）

試驗月日	試驗代施場所	放證動物		蚤 著 蚤 數			
		海豚	白鼠	Xeno. cheopis	Cera. anisus	Pulex irritans	計
10.2～10.12	三角地域（患者發生家屋）	28	6	25	1	0	26
10.7～10.14	三角地域	108	34	2	0	0	2
10.14～10.15	有病鼠發見家屋内	27	36	0	0	0	0
10.2～10.10	異常ナキ一般ノ家屋内	29	2	1	0	1	2
	計	192	78	28	1	1	30

第32表　塵埃内ノ遊離蚤ノ種類（長花）

檢查月日	檢查場所	檢查材料	檢 查 成 績		
			Xeno. cheopis	Cera. anisus	計
10.8	三角地域	家屋内外ノ塵埃	0	0	0
10.9	三角地域	衣類（メリヤスズボン）	6	10	16
10.13	新京市内	大掃除時ノ塵	3	2	5
10.21	列車中	塵埃	0	0	0

總　括

昭和15年9月下旬新京ニ發生セル「ペスト」ノ流行ニ就テ先ヅ患者ノ發生狀況及流行狀態ヲ述
ベ、大ニ其ニ就テ疫學的觀察ヲ試ミタ。

今次流行ハ其ノ病毒ガ「ペスト」流行地タル農安方面ヨリ先ヅ三角地域内ノ鼠族間ニ搬入セラ
レ、其處ニ鼠ペスト」ノ流行ヲ起シ、次デ人ペスト」ノ流行ヲ惹起シタモノト考ヘラレルケレドモ其ノ
病毒搬入ノ經路ハ不明デアツタ。

今次流行ハ9月23日ニ發生シ、11月13日ニ終熄スル迄凡ソ52日ニ亙リ、其ノ間ニ28名ノ患者ノ
發生ヲ見タ。患者多發地區（三角地域）ニ於テハ患者發生ハ住民ノ約2.6％ニ昇ツタ。

今次流行ハ滿洲ノ「ペスト」常在地域ニ於ケル年々ノ流行ト同樣ニ11月寒氣ノ襲來ト共ニ終熄シ
タ。

今次流行ニ於テ流行ノ發生ト環境衛生ノ關係ニ就テ先ヅ新京ノ動物環境特ニ鼠族ノ種類ト其ノ
數量的關係ヲ調查シ、併セテ細菌學的檢查ヲ行ツタ結果「ドブネズミ」間ノ病毒ガ人ペスト」ノ直
接ノ傳染源デアルコトヲ推論スルコトガ出來タ。

515—32

次ニ昆蟲環境特ニ鼠體ニ附着セル蚤ノ種類及其ノ數量的關係ヲ調査シ、併セテ細菌學的檢査ヲ行フ結果、鼠ペスト」ヲ人ニ傳播スルモノハ「ケオピス鼠蚤及「アニズス鼠蚤デアルコトヲ推論スルコトガ出來タ、尚人虱ガ病毒ヲ人ヨリ人ヘ直接ニ傳播スルノデハナイカト考ヘラレル成績ヲ得タ。

尚居住環境ト「ペスト患者發生ノ關係ヲ調査シタ結果、「ペスト患者ハ鼠族及昆蟲ノ好適ナ培養温床トナル樣ナ居住環境ニ發生スルコトヲ認メタ。

次ニ統計的觀察ヲ試ミタ結果、今次流行ハ從來ノ腺ペスト」ノ流行ニ比シテ「ペスト敗血症型ノ出現率高ク、死亡迄ノ經過日數短ク、且死亡率ノ高イノヲ特徵トシテキルコトヲ認メタ。

今次流行ノ病毒搬入經路ハ不明デアツタガ、種々ノ點ヨリ考察シテミルニ、農安方面ヨリ田島犬猫病院(三角地域內ニアル)ニ受診ニ來タ牛、馬ノ荷物ニ附着シテ運搬サレタ有菌蚤ガ同病院ノ鼠族間ニ侵入シテ流行ヲ惹起シ、大テ三角地域ノ鼠ペスト」ノ流行ヲ起シ、其ガ人ペスト」ノ直接ノ傳染源トナツタモノト考ヘラレル、而シテ住民間ノ病毒ノ傳播ハ人ヨリ人ニ直接行ヘタモノデハナクテ、「ドブネズミ」間ニ傳播サレタ病毒ヨリ「ケオピス鼠蚤及「アニズス鼠蚤ヲ介シテ行ヘレタモノト考ヘラレル。

文　　献

1) Dieudonne, A. & Otto, R. : "Handbuch der Pathogenen Microorganismen," (1928), III. aufl., 4, 179.　2) 倉內：滿洲醫學雜誌、(昭. 5)、12, 569. 671. 827.　3) 安東：日本傳染病學會雜誌、(昭. 5)、4, 411,　4) 春日：東京醫事新誌、(昭. 12)；3,041 1,929. 5) 鶴見，其ノ他：日新醫學、第11年、2, (昭. 3).　6) 春日：細菌學雜誌、(昭. 14), 518, 231.　7) 春日，其ノ他：大陸醫學、(昭. 16), 1, 38.　8) 阿部：大陸醫學、(昭. 16), 1, 3.　9) 飯村：日本ニ於ケル「ペスト」ノ疫學ニ關スル綜合的研究、內務省衛生局、(昭. 4,6). 10) 倉岡：臺灣ニ於ケル「ペスト」ノ流行學的研究、臺灣醫學會、(大. 9.3)

4.2.4 昭和 15 年農安及新京ニ発生セル「ペスト」流行ニ就テ 第 2 編 流行ノ臨床的観察 附「ペスト」血清殺菌反応ニ就テ

资料出处： 日本国立国会図書館関西館蔵、博士論文。

内容点评： 本资料为《陆军军医学校防疫研究报告》第 2 部第 525 号《关于昭和 15 年农安和新京发生的鼠疫流行 第 2 编 流行的临床观察》，附《关于鼠疫血清的杀菌反应》，1943 年 4 月 12 日提交。

陸軍軍醫學校防疫研究報告
第2部　第525號

昭和15年農安及新京ニ發生セル「ベスト」流行ニ就テ
第2編　流行ノ臨床的觀察
附　「ベスト血清殺菌反應ニ就テ

陸軍軍醫學校軍陣防疫學敎室（主任 增田大佐）
陸軍軍醫少佐　高　橋　正　彦

第　　　2　　　部		
原　　　　　著		
分　類		
	441—6	
	332—41	
受附　昭和 18. 4. 12		

525-2

増任指導　陸軍軍醫少將　石　井　四　郎

目　次

緒　言

　今次新京ノ流行ニ於テハ發生シタ「ペスト」患者ハ28名デアツタガ、其ノ内ニハ死殿ニテ發見サレ解剖ノ結果「ペスト症ト決定サレタモノ及死體埋葬後ニ周圍ノ部棺ヨリ「ペスト症ト推定サレタモノモアツテ、隔離病舍ニ收容シ臨床症狀ヲ觀察シ得タモノハ18例ニ過ギナカツタ、而モ是等ノ症例モ比較的早キ經過ヲ取ツテ死亡シタ爲ニ充分ナ臨床的觀察ヲナシ得ナカツタ。

　尙農安ニ於テハ17名ノ患者ニ就テ其ノ臨床症狀ヲ觀察スルコトガ出來タケレドモ設備ノ全クナイ急設ノ隔離病舍ニ於テノ檢査デアツタノデ充分ナモノデハナカツタ。

　併シナガラ「ペスト」ハ多ク警探及檢査ノ設備ノナイ僻陬ノ地ニ發生スルノデ一般ニ詳細ナ臨床的觀察ハ極メテ困難デアル、從ツテ其ニ關スル報告モ比較的少イ樣デアル、余等ノ檢査シタ成

545—3

縱モ杜撰ナモノデハアルガ何等カノ參考ニナルテアラウト考ヘテ茲ニ報告スル次第デアル。

第1章 臨床檢査ヲナセル患者ニ就テ

今次新京ノ流行ニ於テ發生セル患者ハ第1表ニ示ス如クニシテ之ニ依ツテ患者ノ發生狀況ヲ概ネ知ルコトガ出來ル、此ノ内隔離病舍ニ收容シテ其ノ臨床症狀ヲ觀察シ得タモノハ18例ニシテ其ノ内5例ハ同一家族或ハ附近ニ「ペスト患者ガ發生シタ爲ニ健康隔離者トシテ別棟ニ收容サレテキタモノノ中ヨリ收容中ニ發症シタモノデアル、併シナガラ是等ノ患者ハ收容後短キモ2日、長キモ6日ニシテ發病シテキルノデ其ノ周圍ノ關係及「ペスト」ノ潛伏期間ヨリ考察スルニ孰レモ收容サレル前ニ感染ヲ受ケタモノト考ヘラレ、院内感染トハ認メラレナイモノデアル。

尙收容患者ノ内カラハ僅カニ2例ノ治癒者ヲ出シタノミデアルガ此ノ2例ハ臨床症狀ハ「ペスト」ノ疑ガ濃厚デアツタケレドモ「ペスト菌ヲ檢出シ得ナカツタモノデアル、尙是等ノ患者ニ就テハ血清反應其ノ他ノ檢査ヲ若干ハ賦ミタケレドモ充分ノ檢査ヲスル機會ガナクテ「ペスト症ナルカ否カヲ決定シ得ナカツタコトハ殘念デアル。

以上揭ゲタ例ノ他ニモ臨床上「ペスト症ヲ疑ヘルニ拘ラズ、菌ヲ檢出シ得ズシテ治癒ノ經過ヲ辿ツタ爲ニ「ペスト症ナルカ否カノ判定ニ苦シンダモノガ數例アツタ、是等ノ症例ハ孰レモ不明熱性疾患トシテ治癒シタモノデアルガ此等ガ輕症ナ「ペスト症デアツタカ或ハ他ノ疾病デアツタカニ就テ徹底的ニ檢査ヲスル機會ノナカツタコトハ殘念デアル、一般ニ「ペスト症ノ菌ノ檢索ハ比較的容易デアルトサレテキル、成程死亡スル樣ナ重篤ニシテ著明ナ所見ヲ呈ネルモノデハ腺腫ヨリノ菌ノ檢出ハ比較的容易デアルケレドモ治癒ノ經過ヲ辿ル樣ナ輕症ナ「ペスト症ニ於テハ腺腫ヨリノ菌ノ檢出ハ相當ニ困難デアル、而モ斯樣ナ症例ガ果シテ「ペスト症デアルヤ否カハ從來ノ血淸診斷ガ「ペスト患者ニ於テモ僅カニ50％内外陽性ニ現レルニ過ギナイモノデアルノヲ忘レテモ診斷ハ困難デアル。

然ルニ流行時ニハ熱發ト淋巴腺腫ヲ主徵トシテ臨床上「ペスト」ニ一致シ、而モ他ノ疾病ヲ考ヘラレナイ症例ガ相當ニ存スルモノデ、是等ノ内ニハ菌ノ檢出ガ陰性デアル爲ニ不明疾患トシテ經過スルモノガ多イノデアル、斯樣ナ症例ガ果シテ「ペスト症ナルカ否カノ確實ナ診斷法ガ發見セラレナイ限リ流行時ニ「ペスト患者ヲ取扱ツタ人ノ頭ニハ何時マデモ割切レナイモノガ殘ルコトト思ハレル、余等ハ今次此ノ問題ニ就テ究明スルトコロガアツタノデ之ニ就テハ本編附錄トシテ別ニ述ベル考ヘデアル。

603

525—4

第1表　新京ニ於ケル「ペスト患者ノ一覽表

番號	氏名	性別	年齡	人種	病名	轉歸	發病 月日	歸 月日	經過 (日)	摘要
1	王○合	男	13	滿	推定ペスト」	死	9.23	9.25	2	周圍ノ事情ヨリ死後「ペスト」ト判定ス
2	太田○次	男	33	日	「ペスト敗血症	死	9.23	9.29	6	入院死亡
3	藤○君○	女	8	日	左鼠蹊腺ペスト」	死	9.25	10.2	7	入院死亡
4	藤○キ○子	女	5	日	推定ペスト」	死	9.26	9.30	4	周圍ノ事情ヨリ死後「ペスト」ト判定ス
5	田○忠○	女	2	日	推定ペスト」	死	9.26	9.29	3	〃
6	宋○德	男	23	滿	推定ペスト」	死	9.27	10.1	4	
7	秤○臣	男	25	滿	右鼠蹊腺ペスト」	死	9.28	10.2	4	入院死亡
8	山○天○子	女	8	日	右頸腺ペスト」	死	9.29	10.3	4	〃
9	隔○鐵○	男	17	日	右鼠蹊腺ペスト」	死	9.29	10.1	2	〃
10	井○和○	男	24	日	右鼠蹊腺ペスト」	死	9.30	10.2	2	〃
11	松○正○	男	23	日	左腋窩腺ペスト」	死	9.30	10.4	4	〃
12	高○愼○	女	3	日	頸腺ペスト」	死	9.30	10.20	20	〃
13	矢○正○	男	21	日	右鼠蹊腺ペスト」	死	10.2	10.4	2	〃
14	德○富○	女	12	日	右腋窩腺ペスト」	死	10.2	10.7	5	〃
15	宋○山	男	56	滿	肺ペスト」	死	10.5	10.10	5	隔離中ニ資料患者ノ看護ニ服ス
16	後○愛○	女	17	日	右鼠蹊腺ペスト」?	治癒	10.5	10.22	17	入院治癒
17	李○金	男	10	滿	「ペスト敗血症	死	10.6	10.8	2	隔離中ニ資料
18	黃○氏	女	45	滿	「ペスト敗血症	死	不明	10.11	不明	發生死亡 屍體解剖時發見
19	陳○玉	男	55	滿	右鼠蹊腺ペスト」	死	不明	10.11	不明	
20	隔○勉	男	27	日	右鼠蹊腺ペスト」	死	10.9	10.11	2	隔離中ニ發病
21	牟○源	男	18	滿	左鼠蹊腺ペスト」	死	10.10	10.13	3	〃
22	蘇○田	男	37	滿	皮膚ペスト」	死	不明	10.13	不明	發生死亡 屍體解剖時發見
23	上○ヨ○	女	58	日	「ペスト敗血症	死	10.11	10.17	6	隔離中ニ發病
24	王○東	男	36	滿	右眼ペスト」?	治癒	10.12	11.2	20	入院治癒
25	枳○秦○	男	31	日	皮膚ペスト」	死	10.17	10.22	5	入院死亡
26	宋○林	男	40	滿	右鼠蹊ペスト」	死	10.22	10.22	1	
27	張○俊	男	46	滿	「ペスト敗血症	死	11.8	11.12	4	
28	尹○槐	男	19	滿	右鼠蹊腺ペスト」	死	11.13	11.15	2	

農安ニ於テ余等ガ取扱ツタ「ペスト患者ハ第2表ニ示ス如クニシテ、此ノ内ノ大部分ハ屍體ニテ發見サレ解剖ノ結果「ペスト症ト決定サレタモノデアリ、臨床觀察ノ出來タノハ僅カニ17例デアツタ、前モ是等ハ重篤ノ症狀ヲ呈シタ後ニ始メテ收容サレテ來タモノデアルカラ詳細ナ檢査ヲシテキル暇ナク、死ノ轉歸ヲ取ルモノガ多カツタ、此ノ表ニヨツテ明カデアル如ク滿洲ノ「ペスト常在地域デハ民度ノ低イ爲ニ「ペスト流行時ニ患者ハ隱蔽セラレ、死亡スルモ屆出ヅルコトナク蔽葬サレル場合ガ多イノデ記錄ニ現レタ數字ノミヨリ「ペスト常在地域ニ於ケル流行ノ眞相ヲ知ルコトハ困難デアツテ、「ペスト」ノ病型或ハ經過日數等ハ殆ド頼リニナラナイコトガ判ル。

尚斯様ナ状態デアルカラ「ペスト」ノ防疫ハ極メテ困難デアツテ、斯様ナ點ニモ「ペスト」常在地域ノ「ペスト」ヲ撲滅シ得ナイ惱ガアル様ニ考ヘラレル。

第2表　農安ニ於ケル「ペスト」患者ノ一覧表

番號	氏　　　名	性別	年齢	病　　　名	輸歸	發病月日	轉歸月日	經過	摘　要
1	張　格　子	女	48	皮膚ペスト」	死	不明	10.21	不明	發生死亡
2	王牟氏太生	女	35	皮膚ペスト」	〃	〃	10.21	〃	〃
3	李趙氏	女	35	右腋窩腺ペスト」	〃	〃	10.21	〃	〃
4	仲永	男	6	皮膚ペスト」	〃	〃	10.21	〃	〃
5	李永	男	50	左鼠蹊腺ペスト」	〃	〃	10.21	〃	〃
6	李胖子	女	3	皮膚ペスト」	〃	〃	10.21	〃	〃
7	仲新生	男	5	「ペスト」敗血症	〃	〃	10.21	〃	〃
8	李甲英	女	72	扁桃腺ペスト」	〃	〃	10.22	〃	〃
9	弟氏	女	18	「ペスト」敗血症	〃	〃	10.22	〃	〃
10	朗	女	51	「ペスト」敗血症	〃	〃	10.22	〃	〃
11	買廷林	男	40	右鼠蹊腺ペスト」	〃	〃	10.22	〃	〃
12	王興氏子	男	35	右鼠蹊腺ペスト」	〃	〃	10.23	〃	〃
13	李九	女	30	「ペスト」敗血症	〃	〃	10.23	〃	〃
14	艱白	女	8	右鼠蹊腺ペスト」	〃	〃	10.23	〃	〃
15	趙	子	29	「ペスト」敗血症	〃	〃	10.23	〃	〃
16	夏金	女	32	左腋窩腺ペスト」	〃	〃	10.24	〃	〃
17	劉興氏	男	33	右鼠蹊腺ペスト」	〃	〃	10.24	〃	〃
18	陳李堅	男	3	右鼠蹊腺ペスト」	〃	〃	10.25	〃	〃
19	高	男	78	肺ペスト」	〃	〃	10.26	〃	〃
20	林氏	女	22	右鼠蹊腺ペスト」	〃	〃	10.27	〃	〃
21	張比	子	10	右鼠蹊腺ペスト」	〃	〃	10.28	〃	〃
22	初盛景	男	6	左腋窩腺ペスト」	〃	〃	11.2	〃	〃
23	劉甫氏	男	63	皮膚ペスト」	〃	〃	11.3	〃	〃
24	姜小	女	30	右腋窩腺ペスト」	〃	〃	11.4	〃	入院
25	高	女	13	「ペスト」敗血症		10.21	10.22	1日	
26	宇財	男	51	右鼠蹊腺ペスト」	〃	10.23	10.24	1日	〃
27	王旺興牟子	男	45	左鼠蹊腺ペスト」	〃	10.22	11.9	18日	〃
28	趙永	男	31	右鼠蹊腺ペスト」	〃	10.23	10.24	1日	〃
29	陳傳	女	63	「ペスト」敗血症	〃	10.23	10.25	2日	〃
30	鳥其永芳	女	31	右鼠蹊腺ペスト」	〃	10.24	10.26	2日	〃
31	傳孫氏子	女	52	右鼠蹊腺ペスト」	〃	10.25	10.26	1日	〃
32	張香英	女	6	右腋窩腺ペスト」	〃	10.25	10.27	2日	〃
33	張子三氏	女	15	右鼠蹊腺ペスト」	治癒	10.25	11.2	8日	〃
34	陳氏	女	8	肺ペスト」	死	10.26	10.26	1日以內	〃
35	董劉	女	62	肺ペスト」	〃	10.26	10.27	1日	〃
36	孫奇	男	28	右鼠蹊腺ペスト」	〃	10.27	11.1	6日	〃
37	周國富子	男	36	左腋腺窩ペスト」	〃	10.27	10.29	2日	〃
38	親孫玉珍	女	38	右鎖骨上窩ペスト」	〃	10.28	10.29	1日	〃
39	陳玉氏名	女	12	皮膚ペスト」	〃	10.29	10.29	1日以內	〃
40	沁幕	女	53	右鼠蹊腺ペスト」	〃	10.30	10.31	1日	〃
41	王	男	60	「ペスト」敗血症	〃	10.30	11.6	7日	〃

第2章　統計的觀察

第1節　性別、年齡別患者發生狀況

新京及農安ノ患者ニ就テ性及年齡ノ明カナモノニ就テ性別、年齡別ニ患者發生ノ狀況ヲ檢査セ第3表ノ如キ成績ヲ得タ、農安ノ成績ハ前郭旗ペスト調査所ノ調査ニヨツタモノデアル。

525－6

第3表　性別、年齢別患者發生狀況

年齢　　性別	新　京			農　安		
	男	女	計	男	女	計
1 ～ 5歳	0	3	3	8	14	22
6 ～ 10	1	2	3	17	13	30
11 ～ 15	1	1	2	14	14	28
16 ～ 20	3	1	4	18	11	29
21 ～ 30	6	0	6	20	31	51
31 ～ 40	4	0	4	47	35	82
41 ～ 50	2	1	3	27	9	36
51 ～ 60	2	1	3	34	12	46
61歳以上	0	0	0	19	10	29
合　計	19	9	28	204	149	353

　本表ニ於テ見ルガ如ク患者數ニ於テハ男ノ方ガ女ヨリモ多イケレドモ之ハ性別ノ人口ノ構成ヲ知ラ
ナケレバ其ノ罹患率ノ差ヲ論ズルコトハ出來ナイ、又年齢別ニ見ルト各年齢ニ於テ孰レモ患者ノ
發生ヲ認メ、發生數ニ於テハ 1～40歳ノ間ニハ大ナル差異ガナイケレドモ41歳以上ニ於テハ其ノ
數ノ少ナイノヲ認メタ、併シナガラ年齢別ノ人口構成ヲ知ラナケレバ此ノ成績ヨリ「ペスト罹患
率ノ年齢的差異ヲ論ズルコトハ出來ナイ。

第2節　病型別觀察成績

　「ペスト患者ノ病型ヲ決定スルコトハ臨床所見ノミニヨツテハ困難ナコトガ屢ミアルノデ今回
余等ハ臨床所見、病理解剖所見及各臟器ニ就テノ菌檢索成績等ヲ綜合判定シテ病名ヲ決定シタ、
從ツテ其ノ病型ハ臨床家ノ判定シタモノト若干相違スルモノガアルト思ハレルケレドモ上述ノ理
由ニヨリ余等ガ最モ正確ナ診斷ヲナシテキルモノト信ジテキル。

　新京及農安ノ「ペスト患者ニ就テ各病型ノ出現率ヲ觀察スレバ第4表ノ如クニシテ腺ペスト」

第4表　病型出現率

病型　　數及%	新　京		農　安	
	實　數	%	實　數	%
腺 ペ ス ト	15	62.5	24	58.6
肺 ペ ス ト	1	4.2	3	7.3
眼 ペ ス ト	1	4.2	0	0.
皮膚 ペ ス ト	2	8.3	6	14.6
「ペスト敗血症」	5	20.8	8	19.5
計	24	100.0	41	100.0

最モ多ク、患者ノ大部分ヲ
占メ、次ニ「ペスト敗血症、
皮膚ペスト」、肺ペスト」ノ
順序デアルノヲ認メタ、此
ノ成績ハ印度或ハ蓋湾ノ腺
ペスト流行ニ於ケル各病型
ノ出現率ニ比較スレバ「ペ
スト敗血症ノ出現率ノ極メ
テ高イコトヲ認メルコトガ

出來ル、此ノ成績ハ孰レモ滿洲ノ「ペスト常在地域ニ於ケル「ペスト」流行ノ末期ニ於テ觀察サ
レタ成績デアルガ、流行ノ末期ニナリ寒氣ノ襲來スルト共ニ「ペスト敗血症型ノ出現率ノ高イコ
トハ滿洲ニ於テ過去ニ（明治43～44年、大正9～10年）肺ペスト」ノ大流行ガ冬季ニ發生シタ

525—7

トト考ヘ合ハセル時ハ極メテ興味深ク思ハレル。

　次ニ腺ペスト患者ニ就テ一次性ニ犯サレタ部位ニヨツテ淋巴腺別ニ分類スレバ第5表ノ如クニシテ鼠蹊腺（股腺ヲ含ム）最モ多ク其ノ大半ヲ占メ、次ニ腋窩腺及頸腺ノ順位ニナツテキル、此ノ成績ハ日本或ハ印度ニ於ケル分類ノ成績ト大體類似セルモノデアル。

第5表　淋巴腺ノ罹患状況

淋巴腺 \ 地區	實數及%	新　京		農　安	
		實数	%	實数	%
鼠蹊腺（股腺ヲ含ム）	右	8		14	
	左	3	73.4	2	66.7
	計	(11)		(16)	
腋窩腺	右	1		3	
	左	1	13.3	3	25.0
	計	(2)		(6)	
頸腺	右	2		2	
	左	0	13.3	0	8.3
	計	(2)		(2)	

　尚茲ニ興味深キコトハ鼠蹊腺ニ於テハ右側ニ来ルモノガ左側ニ比シテ極メテ多イコトデアル、鼠蹊腺ペスト」ハ下肢及下腹部ヨリ菌ノ侵入スル場合ニ發症スルモノデアルカラ此ノ成績ヨリ考ヘルト右下肢或ハ下腹部ガ特ニ蚤ニ刺螫セラレ易イコトヲ示スモノデ、之ハ膝位時ノ姿勢ニヨルモノデアルカ或ハ下肢ガ特ニ蚤ノ附着シ吸血スルニ適スル素因ヲ有シテキルノニヨルモノデアルカハ興味深イ問題デアル。

第3節　經過日數及死亡率

経過日数　新京ノ「ペスト患者ニ就テ發病ヨリ死亡迄ノ經過日數ヲ検査セル成績ハ第6表ニ示ス如クニシテ第3病日乃至第5病日ノ間ニ死亡スル者極メテ多ク、遅クモ第7病日乃至第8病日ニ死亡スルヲ認メタ、尚20日ノ經過ヲ取ツタモノハ稀有ナ1例デアツタ、此ノ成績ヨリ見ルトキハ満洲ニ於テハ「ペスト患者ハ概ネ1週間以内ニ死ノ轉歸ヲ取ルモノニシテ、然ラザルモノハ治癒ニ赴クモノト考ヘラレル。

　農安ノ「ペスト患者ハ重篤ニナツテヨリ收容サレルモノガ多ク斯カルモノニ就テハ發病月日等モ明瞭ヲ缺クモノガ多カツタノデ正確ナ經過日數ヲ知ルコトハ困難デアツタ。

　死亡　新京ニ於テハ患者28例ノ内治癒セルモノハ僅カニ2例デアツタノデ其ノ死亡率ハ92.8%ニナル、併シナガラ前述セル如ク此ノ2例ハ菌検出ノ出来ナカツタ症例デアルカラ果シテ「ペスト症

第6表　經過日數

病　日	實　数
第1病日	
第2病日	1?
第3病日	7
第4病日	2
第5病日	6
第6病日	3
第7病日	2
第8病日	1
第20病日	1

525—8

デアツタカ否カノ判定ニ苦シムモノデアル、従テ此ノ2例ヲ除外スレバ死亡率ハ100%トナリ、従来ノ腺ペスト流行ニ見ザル高イ死亡率デアツタ。

農安ニ於テハ發生患者353例ニシテ其ノ内死亡セルモノハ298例デアツタノデ其ノ死亡率ハ84.4%デアツタ、併シナガラ農安ニ於テハ密葬サレタモノモ相當アルト考ヘラレルノデ死亡率ハモツト高イモノデハナイカト思ハレル、余等ガ隔離病舎ニ收容シタ患者ニ就テハ17例中1例ノ治癒者ヲ見タノミデアルカラ此ノ成績ヨリ考ヘテモ死亡ハ相當ニ高カツタモノト思ハレル、而シテ之ハ敗血症型ガ多イ爲デアロウト考ヘラレル。

第3章　臨床症狀觀察成績（主トシテ新京ノ「ペスト患者ニ就テ觀察シタ成績ヲ述ベル）

第1節　感染經路

新京ノ「ペスト患者ニ就テ觀察スルニ腺ペスト」、「ペスト敗血症、皮膚ペスト」等ノ患者ハ皮膚ヨリ病毒ノ侵入ヲ受ケタモノニシテ、其ハ有菌蚤ノ刺螫ニヨツタモノト考ヘラレタ、此ノ事ハ患者ノ皮膚ニ就テ蚤ニ刺螫サレタ跡ヲ検査シタ成績ヨリモ推論スルコトガ出來タ。

肺ペスト患者ハ腺ペスト患者ヲ看護シテキル間ニ罹患シタモノデ其ノ腺ペスト」患者ガ末期ニハ著明ナ二次性肺ペスト」ノ症狀ヲ呈シテキタコトヨリ飛沫傳染デアルコトガ明カデアル。

第2節　潜伏期

各患者ニ就テハ感染機會ガ不明デアツタノデ潜伏期ヲ明カニシ得タモノハ1例モナカツタ。

第3節　前驅症狀

特別ナ前驅症狀ヲ現スモノハ少ナカツタガ時ニ前驅症狀トシテ經微ナ全身違和、全身懈怠、食慾不振、齲骨痛、頭痛ヲ認メルモノガアツタ、一般ニ何トナク元氣ノナイ顔貌ヲ呈スル様ニ思ハレタ（隔離中ニ發病セルモノニ就テノ觀察ニヨル）。

第4節　一般症狀

發病　多クハ突然ニ悪寒ヲ以テ發熱シ、尚戰慄ヲ作フモノモアツタ、同時ニ眩暈、頭痛、嘔吐ヲ訴ヘ、經過ト共ニ無欲狀ヲ呈スルモノト苦悶、不安、恐怖ノ狀ヲ呈スルモノトガアツタ。

體温　體温ハ急激ニ上昇スルヲ常トシタ、最高温ニ就テ觀ルニ40℃以上ノモノ6例、40℃～39℃ノモノ10例、39℃以下ノモノハ2例デアツタ、熱型ハ弛張型ノモノガ比較的少ナク稽留型ト思ハレルモノガ多カツタ、併シナガラ稽留型ノモノデモ高低ノ差ガ割合ニ大デアツタ。

心臟及血管ノ症狀　發病後極メテ速カニ且高度ニ心機障礙ヲ惹起シ、脈搏ハ初期ヨリ頻數トナリ、小兒ニ於テハ150以上、成人ニ於テハ140前後ノモノガ多カツタ、初期ニハ充實シ、且重複脈性ヲ呈スルケレドモ次第ニ張力減弱シ、微弱且不正トナリ、末期ニハ算定不能ニ陷ルモノガ多カツタ。

心音ハ弱ク且不純トナリ屢々第一音ヲ聽取スルコトノ出來ナイモノガアツタ、尚心尖及第2肋間ニ於テ往々收縮性ノ雜音ノ聞カレルモノガアツタ、此ノ心臟及血管ノ所見ハ他ノ傳染病ニ比シ

608

525—9

テ極メテ犯サレル程度ガ高イ爲ニ「ベスト症ヲ診断スル上ニ大キナ手懸リトナルモノト考ヘラレル。

全身症状　　發病ノ當初ヨリ一般ニ全身症状ガ亜篤デアツテ、一見シテ亜症疾病ニ罹患シテキルコトヲ思ハセタ、卽チ全身倦怠、全身違和甚ダシク且ツ激烈ナ頭痛、眩暈、嘔氣、嘔吐ヲ伴ツタ。

顔　貌　　無速無力ノ状ヲ呈シ眼球陷没、結膜充血、眼眸固定シテ眼ニ力ナク、イカニモ重症疾病ニ犯サレテキルトイフ様ナ顔貌ヲ呈スルモノガ多カツタ、顔ハ初メハ潮紅シテ欝血状デアツタガ後ニハ蒼白トナツタ。

神經症状　　常ニ認メラレタモノハ頭痛及眩暈ニシテ此等ノ症状ハ劇烈ニシテ患者ノ最モ苦痛トスルトコロデアツタ、殊ニ頭痛ハ極メテ劇烈デアル爲ニ愿モ診斷ノ手懸リトナツタ、尚眩暈ガ強イノデ歩行サセルトヨロヨロト歩イタ、此ノ歩行蹣跚モ「ベスト症診斷ノ手懸リトナリ得タモノト考ヘラレル。

末期ニ於テハ神經症状ハ二ツノ型ヲ取ツテ現レタ、其ノ一ツハ興奮状態ヨリ發揚状態ヲ呈スルモノデアリ、他ノ一ツハ沈欝状態ヲ呈スルモノデアツタ、以上ノ他ニ言語ノ遲滯ヲ起スモノ或ハ言語ノ重舌性トナルモノガアツタ。

消化器系統ノ症状　　舌ハ乾燥シ、始メハ白苔ヲ被ルモ1日～2日ニシテ舌尖、舌緣或ハ正中線部ノ苔消失シ、該部ノ乳嘴ノ腫脹、潮紅スルノガ認メラレタ、咽頭ハ發赤シ、扁桃腺ノ腫脹充血スルモノガ多カツタガ僞膜或ハ潰瘍ヲ形成スルモノハナカツタ。

食慾ハ不足ニシテ煩渇ヲ訴ヘルモノガ多カツタ、又初期ニハ嘔氣、嘔吐ヲ訴ヘルモノガ多カツタ、便ハ秘結スル傾向ガ認メラレタ。

肝臓、脾臓ノ腫大ヲ觸知シタモノハナカツタ。

第5節　固有症状

腺ベスト」

「ベスト菌ノ侵入セル局所ニ水疱、膿疱ヲ認メルモノハナカツタ、又淋巴管炎ヲ認メルモノモナカツタ、淋巴腺炎ハ前述ノ如ク鼠蹊腺（股腺ヲ含ム）ニ多ク且右側ニ著シク多キコトヲ認メタ、次ニ位スルモノハ腋窩腺及頸腺デアツタ、腺腫ハ1個乃至數個ニシテ其ノ大サハ小豆大ヨリ鷄那大ニ至ルイロイロノ大サノモノガアツタガ一般ニ腺腫ノ小サイ症例ガ比較的多イ樣ニ思ハレタ、卽チ初診時ニハ腺腫ガ辛ウジテ觸知シ得ル程度ニシテ壓痛ニヨツテ始メテ之ヲ認メル様ナ症例ガ多カツタ、尚腺腫ハ經過ト共ニ比較的速カニ大キクナリ、自發痛ヲ訴ヘ、僅カノ壓迫ニヨツテ激烈ナ疼痛ヲ訴ヘタ。

腺腫ノ硬度ハ常ニ硬固ニシテ弾力性ヲ帶ビルノヲ特徴トシタ、此ノ性状ト壓痛ノ極メテ激烈ナコトガ「ベスト腺腫ヲ診断スル上ノ手懸リトナル様ニ思ハレタ、尚腺腫部位ノ表面ノ皮膚ニ炎症所見ヲ認メタ症例ハ僅カデアツタ。

新京ノ腺ベスト」ガ斯クノ如ク定型的ナ腺ベスト」ノ所見ヲ呈セズニ輕度ノ腺腫ヲ認メタノミ

525—10

ニテ比較的速カニ死ノ轉歸ヲ取ツタノハ感染菌ノ毒力ガ强大デアツタ爲デハナイガト考ヘラレ
ル。

原發性腺腫ヨリ轉位性ニ續發性腺腫ヲ生ジテキルモノガ比較的多ク見ラレタガ、續發性腺腫モ
極メテ小サイモノガ多カツタ、尚末期ニ至ツテハ總テ敗血症ヲ起シテ死亡シタケレドモ特ニ二次
性ペスト肺炎ノ症狀ガ比較的早ク且著明ニ現レタ症例ガ多ク見ラレタ。

「肺ペスト」

末期ニ二次性肺ペスト」ノ症狀ヲ起シタ腺ペスト患者ヲ看護シテキタモノガ罹患シタ症例ニシ
テ飛沫傳染ニヨルコトハ確實デアル、肺ペスト」ハ胸痛、咳嗽、血痰等ノ肺症狀ヲ表ハスモノデ
アルガ、初期ニ於テハ呼吸困難、胸痛等ノ症狀輕度ニシテ僅カニ體溫ノ上昇ヲ認メルニ過ギナカ
ツタ、然ルニ經過ニツレテ極メテ速カニ一般症狀頓篤トナリ、激烈ナ肺症狀ヲ現シ、速カニ死ノ
轉歸ヲ取ルノヲ特徵トシタ、喀痰ハ始メハ唾液ヲ多ク含ミ、氣泡ヲ有スル濁キ痰デアツタケレド
モ次第ニ濃ク粘液狀ニナリ、發熱後10數時間ニシテ泡沫ヲ含ム純血液ニ變ジタ、其ノ中ニハ培下
純培發ノ樣ニ多數ノ「ペスト菌ガ認メラレタ、末期ニナルト胸痛强ク、咳嗽發作多クナリ、一般
症狀增惡シ、呼吸困難ヲ訴へ、床上ニ伸吟シ或ハ轉々反側シテ悲慘ナ狀ヲ呈シテ死亡シタ。

「皮膚ペスト」

右臂部ニ定型的ナ「ペスト疵ヲ發生シタ患者ニ就テ觀察スルニ其ノ部位ニ2箇ノ蚤ノ刺螫痕ヲ
認メルコトガ出來タノデ、其ノ部位ヨリ病毒ガ侵入シタモノト思ハレル、初メハ其ノ部位ニ小指
頭大ノ硬結ヲ觸知シ、炎皮發赤シテ暗赤色ヲ呈シ、壓痛著明デアツタガ、硬結次第ニ大キクナリ、
周圍ノ發赤、浸潤モ甚ダシクナリ、中心部壞死ニ陷リ、遂ニ破開シテ膿樣分泌物ヲ排出シ、潰瘍
ヲ形成シタ、潰瘍低面ハ稍々黑色ヲ帶ビ知覺ナク、壓痛ハ認メラレナカツタ、潰瘍ノ周圍ニハ水
疱ガ多數發生シタ、自發痛ハ比較的弱カツタ、尚潰瘍周圍ノ發生浸潤ハ著ルシク擴大シ、此ノ浸
潤部ヨリ淋巴管炎ヲ起シ、次デ右鼠蹊腺ノ「ペスト性淋巴腺炎ヲ起シ、遂ニ敗血症ニテ死亡シタ。

「ペスト敗血症

表在性ノ淋巴腺炎ヲ認メルコトナク、又特別ナ肺炎症狀ヲ呈スルコトナク急激ナ發熱ヲ以テ始
マリ、全身症狀重篤ニシテ意識混濁シ、速カニ心臟ノ衰弱ヲ來タシテ死亡シタ症例ニシテ是等ノ
症例ハ皮膚或ハ粘膜ヨリ病毒ノ侵入ヲ受ケタモノデアルガ病毒ノ毒力强ク且個體ノ抵抗性ガ弱カ
ツタ爲ニ感染菌ガ淋巴腺ニ止マルコトナク速カニ血液中ニ入ツテ此處ニテ旺盛ニ增殖シ、所謂一
次性ノ敗血症ヲ起シタモノデアルト考ヘラレル。

「眼ペスト」

此處ニ眼ペスト」トシテ揭ゲル症例ハ右眼ノ急性結膜炎ヲ認メ、膿樣分泌物ヲ多量ニ排出シ、
且顳部淋巴腺ノ腫脹及壓痛ヲ認メタノデ眼ペスト」ヲ疑ツタノデアルガ比較的ノ輕症ニテ治癒スル
ニ至ツタモノデアル、細菌學的檢查デハ始メ眼分泌物中ニ鏡檢上「ペスト菌ニ類似セル桿菌ヲ認
メタノデアルガ培養試驗デハ雜菌混入ノ爲ニ菌ヲ分離スルコトガ出來ナカツタ、尚此ノ患者ニ就
テハ其ノ後血淸學的檢查ヲスル機會ガナカツタ爲ニ果シテ「ペスト症デアツタカ否カノ判定ニ苦

525—11

シムノデアルケレドモ、熱型及症狀ノ經過ヨリミレバ、之ハ眼ペスト」デハナカツタモノト考ヘ
ラレル、當時菌檢索ニ動物試驗ヲ行ハナカツタ爲ニ菌檢索ノ方法ニ不十分ナ點ガアツテ結局「ペ
スト症デアツタカ否カノ決定ヲナシ得ナカツタコトヲ考ヘルト、眼分泌物ノ如キ雜菌混入多キ材
料ニ就テ菌檢索ヲ行フ時ニハ必ズ動物試驗ヲ用ヒナケレバナラナイコトヲ痛感スルモノデアル。

　　　第6節　血液像檢查成績

　新京及農安ノ「ペスト患者ニ就テ血液像ヲ檢查シタ成績ハ第7表ニ示ス如クニシテ檢查例數少
ナキ爲ニ此ノ成績ヲ以テ「ペスト症ノ血液像ヲ云々スルコトハ困難デアルケレドモ本表ニ於テ見
ル如ク「ペスト患者ハ病症ノ如何ヲ問ハズ大部分ニ於テ白血球增多症ヲ認メタ、併シナガラ其ノ
程度ハ比較的低ク、多クハ1萬箇～1萬5千箇ノ間ニアル樣デアル、倚症例ニヨツテハ白血球ノ
增加ノ著明ナモノ、或ハ白血球數ノ移動ナキモノ、或ハ反ツテ減少スルモノモアル樣デアルケレ
ドモ斯様ナ症例ハ寧ロ例外的ナモノト考ヘラレル。

　白血球像ヲ檢スルニ中性暗好細胞ノ增加著明ニシテ80～90％ヲ占メ、其ノ內特ニ桿狀核ノモノ
多ク、又幼弱型ノ出現スル場合多ク、之ニ反シテ分葉核ノモノハ減少シ、所謂左方移行ノ型ヲ現
ルコトガ出來タ。

　淋巴球ハ發病ト同時ニ減少著明ニシテ10％以下ニナルコト多ク、豫後ノ不良ノモノニ於テ特ニ
此ノ淋巴球ノ減少ガ著明ニ認メラレタ。

　斯クノ如ク左行　行ノ型ヲ取リ而モ淋巴球ノ著明ナ減少ヲ伴フコトガ「ペスト症ノ血液像ノ特
徵ノ樣ニ考ヘラレタ。

　「エオヂン暗好細胞ハ減少或ハ消失シテ認メラレナイモノガ大部分デアツタ。

　大單核及移行型ハ大ナル變化ハ見ラレナカツタガ一般ニハ減少ノ傾向ヲ示スヤウニ思ヘタ。

　鹽基性暗好細胞ニハ大ナル變化ハ見ラレナカツタ、又多クノ場合ニ於テ「プラスマ細胞ノ出現
ガ認メラレタ。

　上述セル如キ白血球像ハ發病ノ極メテ初期ニ出現シ、殊ニ發病ノ初期ニハ白血球數ハ6,000～
8,000ノ正常ノ值ヲ保ツテオルニ拘ラズ、白血球像ハ前述セル如キ左方移行ノ型ヲ取リ、淋巴球
ノ減少ヲ來タシ、特徵アル像ヲ呈スルモノガ多イノデ此ノ白血球像ノ檢查ハ「ペスト症ヲ診斷ス
ル上ニ手懸リトナルモノト考ヘラレル。

　赤血球ニハ著明ナ變化ハ認メラレナイケレドモ「ポエキロチトーゼ」、「アニソチトーゼ」、「ポ
リクロマジー」等ノ變化ヲ來ス場合ガオリ、又嗜性顆粒、空胞、チレー氏封入體ヲ認メルモノ
ガ多カツタ。

　赤血球沈降速度ハ發病ノ初期ヨリ中等度ニ促進スルモノガ多カツタ。

611

525—12

第 7 表　「ペスト患者

地區	番號	氏	名	性	年齡	病　名	轉歸經過	病日(日)	白血球數	B
農	1	王○興		男	45	腺ペスト」	死(18)	16 17 22	13,100	
	2	萬○城		男	28	腺ペスト」	死(6)	6	13,500	
	3	宇　財		男	51	腺ペスト」	死(2)	2	29,800	
	4	陣○氏		女	63	「ペスト敗血症	死(3)	2 3	12,000	1
	5	魏○子		女	38	腺ペスト」	死(2)	2		
安	6	盤○子		女	15	腺ペスト」	治癒(9)	7		1
	7	課○奇		男	36	腺ペスト」	死(3)	3	14,000	1
	8	趙○年		男	31	腺ペスト」	死(2)	2		
	9	湯○氏		女	53	腺ペスト」	死(2)	2		1
	10	遲○子		女	36	腺ペスト」	治癒	不明	13,000	1
	11	于○氏		女	33	腺ペスト」	治癒	不明	10,000	1
	1	田○天○		女	8	腺ペスト」	死(5)	5		
	2	松○正○		男	23	腺ペスト」	死(5)	5		
新	3	德○宮○		女	12	腺ペスト」	死(6)	6	12,255	
	4	高○眞○		女	3	腺ペスト」	死(21)	21	4,741	
	5	宋○林		男	40	腺ペスト」	死(2)	2	37,800	
京	6	宗○山		男	56	肺ペスト」	死(6)	5		
	7	梶○春○		男	31	皮膚ペスト」	死(6)	7	9,800	1
	8	後○愛○		女	17	腺ペスト」？	治癒(18)	不明	10,274	

第7節　檢尿成績

農安ノ「ペスト患者ニ就テ檢査セル成績ハ第8表ニ示ス如クニシテ「ペスト患者ハ尿量減少シ、其ノ比重ハ高ク、反應ハ酸性ニシテ中ニハ少量ノ蛋白ヲ出スモノガアツタ、「ヂアゾ反應ハ陽性ナ場合モアツタガ糖、「インヂカン」、「アセトン」等ハ陰性デアツタ、之ニ反シテ「ウロビリン」、「ウロビリノーゲン」、「ワイス」等ノ反應ハ陽性ニ出ル場合ガ多カツタ、之ハ「ペスト症ニテハ肝臟機能ヲ犯サレル場合ガ多イ爲デアルト考ヘラレル。

次ニ春日ハ「ペスト患者ノ尿中ニ「ペスト菌ノ Envelope ガ排出セラレルコトヲ沈降反應ニヨツテ證明シ、之ニヨツテ「ペスト症ノ診斷ガ可能デアルコトヲ述ベテヰル。

今回余等ガ檢査セル成績ニ於テモ患者尿ヲ抗原トシテ Envelope 免疫血清ヲ以テ沈降反應ヲ行フ時ニハ陽性ニ現レルノヲ認メタケレドモ、其ノ陽性出現ハ不定デアツタ、從ツテ此ノ反應ヲ「ペスト症ノ診斷ニ用ヒ様トスル場合ニハ極メテ慎重ニヤラナケレバナラナイモノト考ヘラレル。

525—13

ノ血液検査成績

E.	N				L.	M.	Pl.	備考
	J.	St.	Seg.	計				
	3	32	52		6	5	2	
	4	39	48		7	2	1	
	1	50	33		12	3	1	核崩壊セルモノ多シ。
	4	21	41		19	11	1	
	2	25	31		8	34		
	2	45	38		6	2	7	
		15	66		12	5	1	
	3	34	36		25	10	2	原形質青色染色不均等 毒性顆粒(卅)、空胞(卅)
		25	51		17	6		毒性顆粒(卅)
	5	59	28		4	2	1	デリー氏封入體(卄) 毒性顆粒(卅)、核崩壊
	10	42	16		11	20	1	
	11	52	15		10	8	3	毒性顆粒(卅)、核崩壊
		15	66	1	12	5	1	
	5	59	28		4	2	1	毒性顆粒(卅)
	3	47	20		28	1	1	
	1	23	56		18	2		
		32	28		35	4	1	
		37	26		37			
	3	31	47.5		11.5	7		
		32	46		14	8		
		12	61		20	6		
		24	34		37	5		

第8節 血清反應檢査成績

検査方法

凝集反應 患者ノ血清ヲ型ノ如クシテ採取シ、其ヲ遞減稀釋法ニヨツテ生理食塩水ヲ以テ倍數的ニ稀釋シ、共ノ0.5cc宛ニ「ペスト菌(No.1株)ノ普通寒天37℃ 45時間培養菌ヲ1cc 1mgノ生理食塩水菌浮游液ヲ抗原トシテ共ノ0.5cc宛ヲ加ヘ、良ク振盪混和シタ後37℃ノ孵卵器ニ入レテ作用サセ、凡ソ20時間ノ後取出シテ直チニ反應ノ出現ヲ検査シタ、肉眼ニテ検査シ沈應ノ陽性ナルモノヲ十トシ、陰性ナルモノヲ一トシ、變ハシキモノヲ土トシタ。

沈降反應 沈降反應ノ検査方法ハ Uhlenhuth 氏重疊法ニヨリ、抗原ハペスト菌(No.1株)ノ普通寒天37℃ 45時間培養菌ヲ以テ1cc 1.0mgノ生理食塩水菌浮游液ヲ作リ、20分間煮沸浸出シ、強力遠心沈降シタル上清ヲ採ツテ用ヒタ、即チ患者血清ノ原液ニ上述ノ如キ抗原ヲ生理食塩水ニテ倍數的ニ稀釋シテ重疊シ、室温ニ放置シテ30分後ニ重疊面ニ現レル白色輪環ノ程度ニヨリ、共ノ成績ノ記載ハ白色輪環ノ明瞭ニ認メラレルモノヲ十トシ、不明瞭ナモノヲ土トシ、全然現レナイモノヲ一トシタ。

613

525—14

第 8 表　曇安「ペスト

番號	氏　　名	性	年齢	病　名	轉歸	檢査 月日	病日	性	色調
1	王旺興	男	45	腺ペスト」	死(9/XI)	28/X	7	陰性	淡黄色
						29/〃	8	〃	褐色
						30/〃	9	〃	褐黄色
						31/〃	10	〃	〃
2	萬國斌	男	28	腺ペスト」	死(1/XI)	28/X	3	〃	淡黄色
						29/〃	4	〃	黄色
						30/〃	5	〃	褐黄色
						31/〃	6	〃	〃
3	張英子	女	15	腺ペスト」	治癒	29/X	4	〃	ベラ色
						30/〃	5	〃	褐黄色
						31/〃	6	〃	〃
4	潯嘉奇	男	36	腺ペスト」	死(29X)	28/X	2	〃	淡黄色
5	遲王氏	女	36	腺ペスト」 ?	治癒	28/X	不明	〃	乳褐色
						29/〃	〃	〃	乳黄色
						30/〃	〃	〃	淡褐色
						31/〃	〃	〃	淡黄色
6	于王氏	女	33	腺ペスト」 ?	治癒	28/X	〃	〃	黄色
						29/〃	〃	〃	乳黄色
						30/〃	〃	〃	淡黄色
						31/〃	〃	〃	褐黄色

補體結合反應　抗原ハ「ペスト菌（No.1株）ノ普通寒天37°C 45時間培養菌ノ1cc 5mgノ生理食鹽水浮游液ヲ作リ、其ヲ20分間煮沸溶出セル後、强力遠心沈降シタ上清ヲ抗原トシテ用ヒタ。其ノ使用量ハ自家防止ヲナサザル最大量ノ $\frac{1}{2}$ ヲ用ヒタ。

補體ハ數頭ノ健康海猽ヨリ採血シテ集メタ新鮮ナ血清ニシテ、最少溶血價ノ2倍量ヲ使用シタ。

溶血素ハ緬羊ノ血球ヲ以テ處置セル家兎免疫血清ニシテ1,800倍ノ溶血價ヲ有スルモノヲ用ヒ、最少溶血價ノ3倍量ヲ使用シタ。

血球浮游液ハ新シク採取シタ脱纖維素緬羊血液ヲ生理食鹽水ヲ以テ3回洗滌シ、之ヲ5%ノ割合ニ生理食鹽水ニ浮游サセタモノヲ用ヒタ。

患者血清ハ56°C 30分ニテ非働性ニシタモノヲ用ヒタ。

實驗方法ハ血清稀釋法ニヨリ0.5cc System ニ據リ法ノ如ク行ツタ。

檢査成績

新京及曇安ヲ「ペスト患者ニ就テ血清ヲ採取シ、其ニ就テ凝集反應、沈降反應、補體結合反應等ヲ檢査セル成績ハ第9表ニ示ス如クニシテ凝集反應ニ就テハ患者20例中陽性ニ現レタモノハ11例ニシテ、此ノ反應ハ發病ノ初期ニハ出現シナイケレドモ發病後2週間〜3週間後ニ出現シ、次第ニ其ノ凝集價ハ高クナリ、1ケ月位ニテ最高ニ達シ、其ヨリ相當長期間ニ亘リ陽性ニ出現スル様デアル、併シナガラ凝集反應ノ陰性ナモノモ相當ニアリ、陽性ニ出現スルノハ患者ノ50%內外デアルト考ヘラレル、而モ凝集價ハ一般ニ低ク血清稀釋10倍〜160倍ノ間ニ在リ、40倍附近ノ

625—15

患者ノ検尿成績

清濁	比重	蛋白	糖	デアゾ	インデカン	アセトン	ウロビリン	ウロビリノーゲン	ワイス	ベスト尿沈降反應
透明	1.022	−	−	−	弱+	−	+	+	−	+
混濁	1.022	+	−	+	−	−	±	+	±	−
稍ㇰ混濁	1.026	−	−	−	−	−	±	+	+	−
混濁	1.024	−	−	−	−	−	±	卌	+	−
透明	1.023	+	−	+	−	−	+	−	−	+
″	1.021	+	−	−	−	−	+	弱+	−	+
″	1.026	±	−	−	−	−	−	+	+	+
混濁	1.028	−	−	+	−	−	±	卌	+	−
透明	1.024	+	−	−	−	−	−	−	+	+
″	1.026	−	−	−	−	−	−	+	+	−
混濁	1.026	±	−	−	−	−	±	卌	+	−
透明	1.021	−	−	−	−	−	−	±	−	−
混濁	1.035	−	弱+	−	−	−	−	−	−	−
″	1.026	+	+	−	−	−	−	−	−	−
稍ㇰ透明	1.024	−	−	−	−	−	−	−	−	−
透明	1.022	−	−	−	−	−	−	−	±	−
混濁	1.021	−	−	−	−	−	−	−	−	−
″	1.022	−	−	−	−	−	−	−	−	−
透明	1.026	−	−	−	−	−	−	−	−	−
混濁	1.024	−	−	−	−	−	−	−	−	−

モノガ多カツタ。

沈降反應ハ20例中陽性ニ現レタモノハ12例ニシテ、沈降反應價ハ抗原稀釋ニテ1倍～8倍ノ間ニ在リ、其ノ出現ノ時期及陽性率等モ大體凝集反應ニ類似シ、之ト併行セル關係ニアルノヲ認メタ。

補體結合反應ハ20例中陽性ニ現レタモノハ11例ニシテ、其ノ反應價ハ血清稀釋ニテ5倍～80倍ノ間ニ在リ、其ノ出現ノ時期及陽性率ハ大體沈降反應ト類似シ、且之ト併行セル關係ニアルモノヲ認メタ。

以上述ベタ血清反應ガ「ペスト症ニ對シテ特異性ガ高イモノデアルカ否カヲ檢査スル爲ニ發熱、腺腫等ノ症狀ヲ有スル爲ニ「ペスト症ノ疑ヲ以テ隔離病舎ニ收容サレタモノ39人及家族或ハ近隣ニ「ペスト患者ガ發生シタ爲ニ健康隔離者トシテ收容サレタモノ379人、計418人ニ就キ上述セル如キ血清反應ヲ檢査セルニ、凝集反應ノ陽性ニ現レタモノハ2人（0.48%）、沈降反應ノ陽性ニ現レタモノハ3人（0.72%）、補體結合反應ノ陽性ニ現レタモノハ1人（0.24%）デアツタ。此等ノ血清反應ノ陽性ニ現レタモノハ「ペスト・ワクチン」ヲ接種シテキル者デアルカ、此ニヨツテ陽性ニ現レタモノデアルト考ヘラレルノデ此ノ成績ヨリ「ペスト患者ノ凝集反應」沈降反應及補體結合反應ノ特異性ハ極メテ高イモノデアルト云ヘル、從ツテ上述ノ血清反應ガ陽性ニ現レタモノハ「ペストワクチン」ノ接種ニヨルモノヲ除ケバ「ペスト症デアルト推定シテ殆其ヘナイモノデアルト考ヘラレル、唯是等ノ血清反應ノ陽性出現率ス低イコトガ診斷上ノ價値ヲ減ズルモノデアル。

25—16

第 9 表　「ペスト患者

地區	番號	氏 名	性	年齡	病 名	轉歸	病日	10	20	40	80	160	320	640	K
新	1	宋○山	男	56	肺ペスト」	死	4	—	—	—	—	—	—	—	—
京	2	高○眞○	女	3	腺ペスト」	〃	12	—	—	—	—	—	—	—	—
	1	王○興	男	45	腺ペスト」	死	12	—	—	—	—	—	—	—	—
	2	裴○子	女	15	〃	治癒	8	—	—	—	—	—	—	—	—
	3	王○氏	女	35	〃	〃	87	+	+	+	—	—	—	—	—
農	4	于○海	男	17	〃	〃	59	+	+	+	+	—	—	—	—
	5	杜○氏	女	50	〃	〃	49	+	+	+	—	—	—	—	—
	6	齊○氏	女	55	〃	〃	44	+	+	+	+	+	—	—	—
	7	李○氏	女	26	〃	〃	43	+	+	+	±	—	—	—	—
	8	李○柱	男	6	〃	〃	43	+	+	+	±	—	—	—	—
	9	孫○氏	女	26	〃	〃	41	—	—	—	—	—	—	—	—
	10	孫○德	男	54	〃	〃	26	—	—	—	—	—	—	—	—
	11	李○男	男	5	〃	〃	24	+	±	—	—	—	—	—	—
	12	軍○氏	女	42	〃	〃	19	±	±	—	—	—	—	—	—
	13	張○林	女	15	〃	〃	18	+	+	±	—	—	—	—	—
	14	張○珍	女	17	〃	〃	18	±	±	—	—	—	—	—	—
安	15	宋○洲	男	35	〃	〃	17	—	—	—	—	—	—	—	—
	16	李○連	女	14	〃	〃	13	—	—	—	—	—	—	—	—
	17	王○香	男	15	〃	〃	23	±	—	—	—	—	—	—	—
	18	吳○林	男	36	皮膚ペスト」	〃	54	—	—	—	—	—	—	—	—

尚本表ニ於テ見ル如ク「ペスト患者ヨリ採取セル血清ノ「ペスト菌ニ對スル殺菌反應ハ共ノ陽性率極メテ高ク、而モ發病ノ初期ヨリ陽性ニ出現スルノヲ認メタ、此ノ殺菌反應ガ「ペスト症ノ診斷上相當ニ價値ノアルコトハ此ノ反應ノ特異性ニ就テ檢査シタ結果ヨリモ確メルコトガ出來タノデ此ノ事ニ就テハ本編ノ附錄トシテ別ニ報告スル考ヘデアル。

第9節　皮膚反應檢査成績

「ペスト患者ニ就テ「アレルギー性皮膚反應ノ檢査ヲ試ミタ成績ハ第9表ニ示ス如クニシテ本反應ハ免疫抗體ノ産生ト略ミ併行シテ陽性ニ出現スルノヲ認メ、且「ペスト患者ニ於テハ100%陽性ニ出現スルノヲ認メタノデ此ノ反應ノ意義ニ關シテハ別ニ報告スル。

第4章　「ペスト」治癒者ニ就テノ觀察

新京ニ於テ「ペスト」治癒者ト判定サレタモノハ2例ニシテ、共ノ1例ハ右鼠蹊腺ペスト」ト診斷サレタ後○愛○デアリ、他ノ1例ハ眼ペスト」ト診斷サレタ王○東デアル。

後○愛○患者ハ「ペスト患者ノ多發シタ金城アパート」ニ居住シテキテ10月5日ニ發熱シ、右股腺雀卵大ニ腫脹シ、壓痛ヲ認メタノデ「ペスト」ノ疑ヲモツテ收容サレタモノデアル。入院後

ノ 血 清 反 應 檢 査 成 績

	沈	降	反		應			補	體	結	合	反		應		殺菌反應	皮膚反應
1	2	4	8	16	32	64	K	5	10	20	40	80	160	320	K		
−	−	−	−	−	−	−	−	L	L	L	L	L	L	L	L	+	
−	−	−	−	−	−	−	−	L	L	L	L	L	L	L	L	+	
−	−	−	−	−	−	−	−	L	L	L	L	L	L	L	L	+	十
−	−	−	−	−	−	−	−	L	L	L	L	L	L	L	L	+	廿
+	+	+	−	−	−	−	−	H	fH	k	L	L	L	L	L	+	卅
+	+	+	−	−	−	−	−	H	fH	k	sp	L	L	L	L	+	卅
+	−	−	−	−	−	−	−	fH	k	sp	L	L	L	L	L	+	卅
+	+	+	+	−	−	−	−	H	fH	K	k	sp	L	L	L	+	卅
+	+	−	−	−	−	−	−	fH	k	sp	L	L	L	L	L	+	卅
+	−	−	−	−	−	−	−	K	k	L	L	L	L	L	L	+	卅
+	−	−	−	−	−	−	−	H	k	sp	L	L	L	L	L	+	十
−	−	−	−	−	−	−	−	fL	L	L	L	L	L	L	L	−	十
+	+	−	−	−	−	−	−	fH	K	sp	L	L	L	L	L	+	卅
+	−	−	−	−	−	−	−	k	L	L	L	L	L	L	L	+	卅
+	−	−	−	−	−	−	−	k	L	L	L	L	L	L	L	+	卅
+	−	−	−	−	−	−	−	K	sp	L	L	L	L	L	L	+	卅
−	−	−	−	−	−	−	−	L	L	L	L	L	L	L	L	+	卅
−	−	−	−	−	−	−	−	L	L	L	L	L	L	L	L	+	卅
−	−	−	−	−	−	−	−	L	L	L	L	L	L	L	L	+	卅
+	−	−	−	−	−	−	−	L	L	L	L	L	L	L	L	+	卅

ハ39℃前後ノ發熱ヲ4日間程持續シ、熱型ハ弛張型ニシテ、心臟及血管系ノ所見モ著シクナク、一般症狀モ比較的良好ニシテ治癒ノ經過ヲ辿ツタモノデアル。

此ノ患者ニ就テハ數回ニ亙リ腺腫穿刺液、喀痰、血液等ニ就テ菌檢索ヲ行ツタケレドモ常ニ陰性デアツタ、尚股腺ノ1部ヲ摘出シテ之ヲ病理組織學的ニ檢査シタ結果デハ特殊性淋巴性肉芽腫ノ像ヲ呈シテキタモノデアル、從ツテ此ノ患者ガ「ペスト症デアツタカ否カハ判定ニ苦シム所デアルケレドモ、患者ノ處女デアツタコト、股腺ノミガ犯サレテキタコト等ヨリ考ヘレバ特殊性淋巴性肉芽腫ト考ヘルヨリハ寧ロ輕症ナル「ペスト症ト考ヘル方ガ妥當デアルト思ハレル、又病理組織學的ニハ淋巴性肉芽腫ノ像ヲ呈シテキタト云フケレドモ腺ペスト」ニ於テモ慢性ノ經過ヲ取ツテ治癒シタ症例ニ於テハ淋巴腺ニ網狀織內被細胞ノ著明ナ增殖ヲ認メルコトハ屢々アルコトヲ考ヘナケレバナラナイ、

尚此ノ患者ニ就テ詳細ニ血淸反應及皮膚反應ヲ檢査スルコトガ出來ナカツタノデ、此ノ方面ヨリノ診斷ノ資料ヲ得ラレナカツタコトハ殘念デアツタケレドモ、此ノ患者血淸ヲ以テ「ペスト菌ニ對スル殺菌反應ヲ檢査セル成績ニ於テハ明カニ陽性デアルコトヲ認メタ。

以上ノ諸檢査ノ成績ヲ綜合シテ考ヘル時ハ此ノ患者ハ輕症ナル腺ペスト症デアツタト判定スル

525—18

ノガ最モ安當ト思ハレル、併シナガラ此デモ尚割切レナイモノノ残ルコトヲ考ヘルト更ニ詳細ニ特異性肉芽腫トシテ診断（例ヘバフライ氏反應）或ハ「ペスト症トシテノ診断ヲシテ置ケバヨカツタト後悔サレル。

　王○東患者ハ眼ペスト」ト診断サレタモノデアルガ、之ガ果シテ「ペスト症デアツタカ否カノ制定ハ検査ノ不備ナ爲ニナシ得ナカツタコトハ既ニ述ベタ所デアル、併シナガラ諸検査ノ成績ヨリ考ヘルト之ハ急性結膜炎ニ眼瞼ノ膿瘍ヲ合併シタモノデアツタト考ヘラレル。

第10表　治癒患者體温表

　農安ノ「ペスト患者ニ就テ余等ガ經驗シタ治癒例ハ腺ペスト患者唯1例デアツタ、即チ張○子患者（女、15歳）ハ右鼠蹊腺鷄卵大ニ腫脹、壓痛著明ニシテ定型的ノ腺ペスト」ノ所見ヲ呈シ、且腺瘍穿刺液ヨリ「ペスト菌ヲ検出シタモノデアルガ、此ノ患者ハ體温比較的低ク、心臓及血管系ノ所見モ良好ニシテ第11病日ニハ平熱ニ快復シ、治癒ノ經過ヲ遡ツタモノデアル。（第10表）

　次ニ今次農安ノ流行ニ於テ治癒者トシテ記録サレタモノ55人ニ就テ病型、性別年齡別治癒率、治癒迄ノ經過日數等ヲ観察セル成績ハ次ノ如クデアル。

　病型・治癒セルモノノ病型ハ腺ペスト」及皮膚ペスト」ニシテ殊ニ皮膚ペスト」ニハ比較的輕症ニシテ治癒セルモノガ多イ様デアル。

　性別、年齡別治癒率　治癒者55人ヲ性別、年齡別ニ観察スレバ第11表ノ如クニシテ性別ニハ大ナ

ル差異ナク、又患者ノ治癒率ニ於テモ男女ノ間ニハ差ガ認メラレナカツタ（第12表）。年齡別ニ見ルト41歳以上ニ於テハ治癒者ガ少ナク、又年齡別ニ患者ノ治癒率ヲ見テモ41歳以上ニ於テハ極メテ低ク、1歳〜10歳及21歳〜40歳ノ間ハ大差ナク、11〜20歳ノ患者ニ於テ治癒率最モ良好デアルノヲ認メタ（第11表）。斯様ニ治癒率ニ年齡的差異ノ認メラレルコトハ或程度年齡別ノ「ペスト菌ニ對スル抵抗性ノ差異ヲ現スモノト

第11表　治癒者ノ性別、年齡別観察成績

年齡(歳)	患者數	治癒者數			治癒率(%)
		男	女	計	
1〜5	22	1	3	4	18.2
6〜10	30	4	0	4	13.3
11〜15	28	6	4	10	35.7
16〜20	29	5	4	9	31.0
21〜30	51	4	5	9	17.6
31〜40	82	5	7	12	14.6
41〜50	36	3	0	3	8.4
51〜60	46	2	2	4	8.7
61以上	29	0	0	0	0
計	353	30	25	55	15.6

第12表　性別ノ治癒率

性別	患者數	治癒者數	治癒率（%）
男	204	30	14.7
女	149	25	16.7

第13表
治癒迄ノ經過日數

經過	件數
第1週	0
2	4
3	2
4	3
5	4
6	7
7	9
8	7
9	7
10	5
11	4
12	0
(13)	(1)
(14)	(1)
(21)	(1)
平均	6.8週

將ヘラレル、而シテ21歳～40歳ニ於テ治癒率ノ低イノハ期様ナ年齢ニ在ルモノハ社會生活上活動ヲ除儀ナクセラレ、其ガ爲ニ豫後ヲ不良ニスル爲デハナカロウカト將ベラレタ。

治癒迄ノ經過日數、退院ノ日ヲ以テ治癒トスレバ「ペスト」患者ノ發病ヨリ治癒迄ノ經過日數ハ第13表ニ示ス如クニシテ、早キハ2週間ニテ治癒シ、遲キモノハ11週間ヲ要シ、平均6.8週間デアル。

總括

新京及農安ノ流行ニ於テ發生セル「ペスト」患者ノ臨床所見ヲ觀察シ、併セテ血液像及血清反應ヲ檢査シタ成績ヲ總括シテ述ベレバ次ノ如クデアル。

1　今次流行ニ於ケル患者ニ就テ統計的觀察ヲナシ、性別、年齡別患者發生狀況、病型別患者發生狀況、發病ヨリ死亡迄ノ經過日數及死亡率ヲ檢査セルニ特別ナ點ハ認メラレナカッタガ、印度或ハ蓋爾ノ腺ペスト」流行ニ於ケル各病型之出現率ニ比較スレバ「ペスト敗血症ノ出現率ハ極メテ高ク、且患者ノ發病ヨリ死亡迄ノ經過日數短ク、死亡率ノ高イノヲ認メタ、此ノ傾向ハ新京ノ流行ニ於テ特ニ著明ニ認メラレタ。

2　患者ノ一般症狀及同病型ヲ固有症狀ニ就テ觀察セルニ特別ナ點ハ認メラレナカッタ。

3　患者ノ血液像ヲ檢査セルニ白血球增多症ヲ認メ、中性嗜好細胞ノ增加著明ニシテ、而モ桿狀核ノモノ多ク、幼若型出現シ、分葉核ノモノハ減少シ所謂左方ヘ移行ノ型ヲ取リ、同淋巴球ハ發病ト同時ニ著シク減少スルノヲ認メタ。

4　患者ノ尿ヲ檢査セルニ尿症減少シテ、小量ノ蛋白ヲ證明シ、又「ウロビリン」及「ウロビリノーゲン反應ノ陽性ニ現レルモノガ多カッタ。

患者尿ヲ抗原トシテ「ペスト免疫血清ニ對スル沈降反應ヲ檢査セルニ其ノ成績ハ不定デアツタ。

5　患者血清ニ就テ「ペスト菌ニ對スル凝集反應、沈降反應、補體結合反應ヲ檢査セルニ患者20例中凝集反應ノ陽性ニ現レルモノハ11例、沈降反應ノ陽性ニ現レルモノハ12例ニシテ、補體結合反應ノ陽性ニ現レルキノハ11例デアツタ。

6　「ペスト患者血清ノ「ペスト菌ニ對スル殺菌反應ハ總テ陽性ニ現レ、又「アレルギー性皮膚反應モ總テノ「ペスト患者ニ於テ陽性ニ現レルノヲ認メタ、是等ノ成績ニ就テハ別ニ報告スル。

7　「ペスト治癒者ニ就テ病型別治癒率」性別、年齡別治癒率、治癒迄ノ經過日數等ヲ觀察セルニ治癒者ハ皮膚ペスト」及腺ペスト」ノ患者ニ多ク、性別ニハ大差ナキモ、年齡別ニハ11歳～20歳

'25—20

ノ患者ニ於テ治癒率ノ大デアルノヲ認メ、尚治癒迄ノ經過日數ハ平均6.8週デアルコトヲ認メタ。

文　獻

1) Dieudonne, A. & Otto, R.: "Handbuch der pathogenen Microorganismon,"(1928), Ⅲ. aufl., 4, 179.　2) 倉內：滿洲醫學雜誌、(昭.5), 12, 569.　3) Tsuchia, K. a. Li Te chuan：Jl. Orient. Med., (1929), 10, 32., 11, 85.　4) 安東：日本傳染病學會雜誌、(昭.5), 4, 411.　5) 安部：大陸醫學、(昭.16), 1, 17.　6) 飯村：日本傳染病學會雜誌、(昭.3), 3, 724, 797.　7) 飯村：日本ニ於ケル「ペスト」ノ疫學ニ關スル綜合的研究、內務省衛生局、(昭.4. 6).　8) 倉岡：臺灣ニ於ケル「ペスト」ノ流行病學的研究、臺灣醫學會、(大.9.3).　9) 春日：細菌學雜誌、(昭.12), 493, 121. 10) Tsuchia K. & Li Te chuan：Jl. Orient. Med., (1929), 11, 85.　11) 寺島毅一：大阪醫學會雜誌、(明.41), 9, 1012.

525－21

附　「ペスト血清殺菌反應ニ就テ

緒　言

一般ニハ「ペスト症ノ診斷ハ臨床的所見及菌檢索ニヨツテナサレテヰルケレドモ、患者ノ中ニハ其等ニヨル診斷ガ困難ナ場合ガアル、斯様ナ時ニハ「チフス性疾患ノ場合ト同様ニ血清診斷ノ方法ガ用ヒラレテヰル。而シテ一般ニ用ヒラレテヰルモノハ患者血清ニ就ノ凝集反應及補體結合反應ニシテ、凝集反應ニ就テハ Zabolony[1] ハ此ノ反應ハ第 7 病日頃ヨリ出現シ其ノ凝集價ハ第 3 週頃ニ最高ニ達スルケレドモ「ペスト患者ノ内ニハ陽性ニ現レナイモノモ相當ニアルノデ腸チフス」ニ於ケル Widal 反應ノ様ナ診斷的價値ハナイト述ベテヰル。Schtschastny モ凝集反應ハ第10病日頃ヨリ出現スルモノモアルケレドモ、多クハ20～30病日ニ至ツテ始メテ出現シ、而モ其ノ凝集價ハ 5～80倍ニシテ就中10～40倍ノモノガ最モ多ク、而モ其ノ陽性率ハ50%內外デアルト報告シテヰル。補體結合反應ニ就テハ、Schtschastny[21] ハ患者ノ約半數（53%）ニ於テ陽性ニ出現スルノヲ認メ、特ニ重症例ニ於テ證明セラレルノヲ認メタケレドモ、7週病日以前ニハ殆ンド出現シナイノデ診斷的價値ハ少ナイト述ベテヰル。Moses[8] ハ第9病日ニ採取セル患者血清ニ就テ補體結合反應ヲ檢査セルニ38例中25例ニ於テ陽性ニ現レルノヲ認メタ。Jaltnin[10] 及 Simard[5] ハ補體結合反應ガ「ペスト患者ニ於テノミ特異性ニ陽性ニ現レ、僞陽性反應ヲ呈スルコトノナイノヲ認メ、本反應陽性ノ意義ノ大デアルコトヲ述ベテヰル、Dickie[6] モ亦之ヲ承認シテヰル。

以上ノ他 Weinstein[7] ハ Wright ノ方法ニ從ツテ「ペスト患者ニ就テ「オプソニン」ヲ檢査シ、其ガ診斷的價値ノアルコトヲ認メ、尼子[8] ハ「ペスト患者ニ就テ皮膚反應及眼反應ヲ檢査シタ結果、其ノ陽性率ハ50%內外ニ過ギナイ爲ニ診斷的價値ハ少ナイモノデアルト述ベテヰル。

一方 Row[9] ハ1902年ニ「ペスト患者及恢復者ノ血清ガ特異性ニ「ペスト菌ヲ殺菌スルコトヲ認

525-122

メ、此ノ検査ガ「ペスト症ノ診断ニ用ヒ得ラレルコトヲ述ベテキル、此ノ検査方法ハ「ペスト患者血清ノ一滴ニ「ペスト菌ノ生理食塩水菌浮游液ノ一滴ヲ混ジ、其ヨリ懸滴標本ヲ作リ、其ヲ室温ニ於テ 24 時間作用セシメタ後ニ菌滴ノ附着シテキル蓋板ヲ其ノ儘乾燥シ、「アルコール」及「エーテル」等分液ニテ固定シ、其ヲ染色シテ菌ノ形態ヲ観察スル方法デアル、患者血清ヲ以テセル時ニハ菌ガ膨脹シテ次第ニ殺滅サレル状態ヲ見ルコトガ出来、之ニ反シテ健康血清ヲ以テセル時ニハ菌ハ速カニ増殖シテ菌塊ヲ作リ、或ハ短連鎖ヲ作ルノヲ認メルコトガ出來タ。

余ハ試験管内検査方法ニヨツテ「ペスト患者血清ノ「ペスト菌（普通寒天 37℃ 45時間培養菌）ニ對スル殺菌作用ヲ検査セル 100% 陽性ニ現レルノヲ認メ、而モ偽陽性反應ト思ハレルモノナク、従ツテ「ペスト症ノ診断上極メテ有効デアルト考ヘラレル成績ヲ得タノデ茲ニ報告シテ諸賢ノ批判ヲ乞フ次第デアル。

第1章 検査方法

血清分離 被験者ノ正中静脈ヨリ約 2cc ノ血液ヲ採取シ、其ヲ中試験管ニ入レ、斜メニシテ室温ニ放置シ、約2時間ニテ血液ノ凝固スルヲ待チテ之ヲ氷室ニ入レ、血清ヲ折出セシメテ、翌日之ヲ無菌的ニ分離シテ直チニ使用ニ供シタ。

検査術式、前述ノ如クニシテ無菌的ニ分離シタ血清ヲ非働性ニスルコトナク働性ノ儘 0.5cc 小試験管ニ取ズ、其ニ「ペスト菌（No. 1 株即テ Otten, "Tjiwidej"[10] 株）ノ普通寒天 37℃ 45時間培養菌ヲ以テ 1cc 10⁻⁴mg ノ生理食塩水菌浮游液ヲ作リ、其ノ 0.5cc ヲ加ヘテ良ク混合セル直後ニ其ノ 0.1cc ノ有スル生菌数ヲ計算シ、次ニ之ヲ 37℃ ノ孵卵器内ニ於テ作用サセテ 4時間後及24時間後ニ其ノ 0.1cc ノ有スル生菌数ヲ計算シ、其ノ値ヲ比較シ、被験血清ガ「ペスト菌ニ對スル殺菌作用ガアルカ否カヲ検査シタ、對照トシテハ血清ノ代リニ普通ブイヨン」ヲ用ヒ、其ノ中ニ於ケル菌数ヲ計算シテ其ノ値ト比較スル如クシタ。

生菌数ヲ計算スル方法ハ混合液ノ 0.1cc 宛ヲ精確ニ 2枚ノ遠藤平板ニ取ツテ、其ヲコンラーヂ棒ニテ丁寧ニ平板全面ニ塗布シ、其ヲ 37℃ ニテ 45時間培養シ、平板面ニ発生セル聚落数ヲ計算シテ 2枚ノ値ヲ平均シ、其ヲ 0.1cc ノ有スル生菌数トシタ。

第2章 検査成績

第1節 「ペスト患者ニ就テノ検査成績

今次農安及新京ノ「ペスト」流行ニ於テ「ペスト患者ニ就テ其ノ血清ヲ採取シ、其ノ働性血清ノ「ペスト菌ニ對スル殺菌作用（爾後之ヲ「ペスト血清殺菌反應ト稱ス）ヲ検査セル成績ハ第1表ニ示ス如クニシテ「ペスト菌ハ健康人血清及普通フイヨン」ノ中ニテハ著シク増殖スルニ拘ラズ、患者ノ血清ノ中ニテハ速カニ死滅スルノヲ認メタ、之ハ患者血清ガ「ペスト菌ニ對シテ殺菌作用ヲ有スル為デアルト考ヘラレル、而シテ此ノ殺菌作用ハ発病ノ極メテ初期ニ既ニ陽性ニ現レ、其ヨリ相当ニ長イ期間保存サレルノヲ認メタ、此ノ殺菌作用ハ患者ニヨリ其ノ証明ニ認メラレル

525—23

モノト然ラザルモノトガアツタ、斯様ニ共ノ殺菌作用ノ強サニ差異ガアルノハ臨床症状ノ重輕及
發病ヨリノ經過日數等ト密接ナ關係ガアルモノト考ヘラレルガ、症例ガ少ナクタ且同一症例ニ就テ
經過的ニ檢査スル機會ガナカツタノデ共ノ間ノ事情ヲ明カニスルコトガ出來ナカツタケレドモ、
重症ナモノ程者明ニ認メラレ、又發病ヨリノ經過日數ガ餘リ長クナルト弱クナル様ニ思ハレタ。
斯クノ如ク共ノ血清ニ「ペスト菌ニ對スル殺菌作用ノ認メラレルモノヲ血清殺菌反應陽性トシ
タ、而シテ成績ノ判定ハ對照トシテ用ヒタ普通ブイヨン」ニ於ケル生菌數ニ比シテ被驗血清ニ於
ケル生菌數ガ少ナイ場合ニハ之ヲ陽性トシタ、斯クノ如ク成績ヲ判定スル時ニハ「ペスト患者ニ
於テハ血清殺菌反應ハ100%陽性ニ出現スルノヲ認メタ。

第1表　「ペスト患者ノ血清殺菌反應檢査成績

番號	氏　名	性	年齡	科　名	轉歸	病日	菌　數		
							0時	4時	24時
1	宋○山	男	56	肺ペスト	死	4		0	0
2	高○眞○	女	3	腺ペスト	〃	12		0	0
3	王○魁	男	45	〃	〃	12		150	0
4	氣○子	女	15	〃	治癒	8		0	0
5	王○子	女	35	〃	〃	87		24	0
6	于○海	男	17	〃	〃	59		0	0
7	杜○氏	女	59	〃	〃	49		12	0
8	郭○氏	女	55	〃	〃	44		0	0
9	李○子	女	26	〃	〃	43		0	0
10	李○桂	男	6	〃	〃	43		25	0
11	孫○氏	女	26	〃	〃	47		250	0
12	孫○德	男	54	〃	〃	26		750	1500
13	李○男	男	5	〃	〃	24		100	0
14	軍○氏	女	42	〃	〃	19		50	0
15	駁○林	女	15	〃	〃	18		750	0
16	亞○季	女	17	〃	〃	18		150	0
17	宋○洲	男	35	〃	〃	17		50	0
18	李○迢	女	14	〃	〃	13		150	0
19	王○香	男	15	〃	〃	23		250	0
20	吳○林	男	36	皮膚ペスト	〃	54		750	1250
對照	健康人血清						1150	1250	∞
	普通ブイヨン						1250	1250	∞

525—24

第 2 表
健常者ノ「ペスト血清殺菌反應檢査成績

番號	氏　名	性	年齡	菌　數		
				0 時	4 時	24時
1	略　ス	男	26		1250	∞
2	〃	男	38		1350	∞
3	〃	男	42		1450	∞
4	〃	男	36		1150	∞
5	〃	女	18		1350	∞
6	〃	女	28		1250	∞
7	〃	女	32		1450	∞
8	〃	男	64		1150	∞
9	〃	女	15		1350	∞
10	〃	男	22		1420	∞
11	〃	女	26		1150	∞
12	〃	女	27		1250	∞
13	〃	男	34		1350	∞
14	〃	男	38		1250	∞
15	〃	女	28		1250	∞
對照	普通ブイヨン			1050	1150	∞

第 2 節　健常者ニ就テノ　檢査成績

「ペスト血清殺菌反應ハ1種ノ免疫反應デアルト考ヘラレルケレドモ或ハ健常者ニ於テモ非特異性ニ現レル場合ガアルカモ知レナイト考ヘラレタノデ既往ニ「ペスト・ワクチン」ヲ接種シタコトノナイ全ク「ペスト」ニ關係ノナイ健康者ト「ペスト・インムノーゲン」ヲ接種シタコトノアル健常者ニ就テ檢査シタ。

1　「ペスト・ワクチン」ヲ接種セルコトナキ健常者ニ就テノ檢査成績

「ペスト・ワクチン」ヲ接種セルコトノナイ全ク「ペスト」ニ無關係ナ健常者163名ニ就テ「ペスト血清殺菌反應ヲ檢査セル成績ハ第2表（表ハ1部ノ成績ノミヲ示ス）ニ示ス如クニシテ、

斯カル健常者ノ血清ハ「ペスト菌ニ對シテ全然殺菌作用ヲ認メズ、對照タル普通ブイヨン」中ニ於ケルト同樣ニ「ペスト菌ノ增殖ハ著明デアツタ。即チ此ノ成績ヨリ「ペスト・ワクチン」ヲ接種セルコトナキ健常者ニ於テハ「ペスト」ノ血清殺菌反應ハ陰性デアルト云フコトガ出來ル。

2　「ペスト・ワクチン」ヲ接種セル健常者ニ就テノ檢査成績

新京及農安ノ「ペスト」流行時ニ「ペスト・インムノーゲン」ヲ1回乃至2回接種セル健常者247名ニ就テ「ペスト血清殺菌反應ヲ檢査セルニ3名ニ於テ陽性ニ現レルノヲ認メタ（第3表）。檢査セル此ノ血清ハ「ペスト・ワクチン」接種後幾日位經過シタ後ニ採取シタモノデアルカ不明デアル爲ニ「ペスト・ワクチン」接種ト血清殺菌反應ノ陽性出現トガ如何ナル關係ニアルカヲ知

第 3 表　「ペスト・ワクチン」接種者ノ

番號	氏　名	性	年齡	豫　防　注　射			檢査月日	殺菌反應（時）			凝　集　反					
								0	4	24	10	20	40	80	160	320
1	略	男	35	中10/7	中10/9	26/X	2/XI		950	1250	+	±	±	−	−	−
2	〃	女	20	〃	〃	〃	〃		24	0	+	+	±	−	±	−
3	〃	男	24	〃	〃	〃	〃		1150	1250	−	−	−	−	−	−
對照	普通ブイヨン						〃	1250	1350	∞						

525—25

ルコトガ出来ナカツタケレドモ此ノ血清殺菌反應ノ陽性ニ現レタ3名ノ内2名ハ凝集反應及沈降反應ガ陽性デアリ、其ノ内ノ1名ハ補體結合反應モ陽性デアツタノデ確實ニ「ペスト・ワクチン」ノ接種ニヨツテ血清中ノ免疫抗體ノ産生サレタモノデアリ、従ツテ此ノ血清殺菌反應モ陽性ニ現レタモノデアルト考ヘラレル、他ノ1例ハ血清中ニ免疫抗體ノ産生ハ認メラレナカツタモノデアルガ上述ノ「ペスト・ワクチン」ヲ接種セルコトナキ健常者ニ於テハ總テ陰性デアツタコト及本例ノ「アレルギー性皮膚反應ガ陽性デアツタコトヨリ考ヘルト之モ「ペスト・ワクチン」ノ接種ニヨリ免疫抗體ガ産生サレタ爲デアルト考ヘラレル。

3　小　括

「ペスト血清殺菌反應ハ「ペスト・ワクチン」ヲ接種セルモノニ於テノ極メテ小數例ニ於テ陽性ニ現レルモノガアツタケレドモ、「ペスト」ニ關係ナキ健常者ニ於テハ總テ陰性デアツタ、此ノ成績ヨリ考ヘルト非特異性ノ陽性反應ハ殆ド無イモノト考ヘラレル。

第3節　「ペスト容疑患者ニ就テノ檢査成績

新京及農安ノ「ペスト」流行時ニ發熱、腺腫等ノ所見ガアツタ爲ニ「ペスト容疑患者トシテ隔離病舎ニ收容サレタ有熱患者26名ニ就テ「ペスト」ノ血清殺菌反應ヲ檢査セル成績ハ第4表ニ示ス如クニシテ陽性ニ現レタモノハ4名デアツタ、其ノ他ノモノハ陰性ニシテ其ノ内ノ1名王□來ハ眼ペスト」ト判定サレタノデアルケレドモ此ノ患者ハ菌ノ檢出陰性ニシテ且臨床的所見ヨリモ眼ペスト」デナクテ急性結膜炎ニ眼瞼腺腫ヲ併發シタモノト考ヘタ方ガ安當デアルコトハ既ニ述ベタ所デアルガ、此ノ患者ニ就テ「ペスト血清殺菌反應ガ陰性デアツタコトハ本病ガ「ペスト症デナカツタコトヲ裏書キスルモノデアルト考ヘラレル、其ノ他ノ陰性者ハ流行時ニ發熱ヲ認メタノデ「ペスト容疑患者トサレタモノガ多ク、孰レモ比較的速カニ解熱シ、臨床上モ「ペスト症デアル點モナク、夫レ急性氣管支炎或ハ感冒等ニ診斷サレタモノデアル。

共處デ「ペスト血清殺菌反應ガ陽性ニ現レタ患者ガ果シテ「ペスト症デアツタカ否カヲ檢探スル必要ガ生ジテ來ルノデ、兹ニ是等ノ臨床所見ニ就テ述ベレバ次ノ如クデアル。

「ペスト血清殺菌反應檢査成績

庫		沈	降	反	應			補	體	結	合	反	應		皮膚反應	ペスト菌検索
640	K	1	2	4	8	16	32	K	5	10	20	40	80	160	K	
－	－	＋	－	－	－	－	－	L	L	L	L	L	L	L	﹢	土
－	－	＋	＋	－	－	－	－	K	卯	L	L	L	L	L	﹢	－
－	－	＋	－	－	－	－	－	L	L	L	L	L	L	L	﹢	

525-26

第4表 「ペスト容疑患者ニ就テノ「ペスト血清殺菌反應検査成績

番號	氏 名	性	年齡	臨床所見	轉歸	病日	殺菌反應 0時	4時	24時	摘 要
1	後○愛○	女	17	發熱，淋巴腺腫脹「腺ペスト」？	治癒	5 21	0 0		∞ ∞	
2	王 徳○	男	36	（眼ペスト」？）	〃	2 14	950 1250	0 0		
3	柳○良○	女	4	發熱，鼠蹊腺腫脹（腺ペスト」？）	〃	12 26	400 0	0 0		
4	平井正元	男	21	發熱，鼠蹊腺腫脹（腺ペスト」？）	〃	6 12 23	100 0 250	0 0 0		
5	藤田加代	女	42	發熱，腺腫（腺ペスト」？）	〃	3 20	250 650	0 0		
6	青○清○	〃	25	發熱，腺腫	〃	4	950		∞	結核性疾患
7	佐○ヂ○	〃	19	發 熱	〃	8	1050		∞	急性氣管支炎
8	嚴○茂○	男		發熱、咳嗽、胸痛	〃	2	1150		∞	腸チフス」
9	何○綿○	男	17	發 熱	〃	1	950		∞	
10	飾○笠	男		發 熱	〃	2	1250		∞	急性咽頭炎
11	陳 ○○	男		發 熱	〃	2	950		∞	感 冒
12	宋 ○○	男		發 熱	〃	2	1050		∞	〃
13	溫 ○○	女		發 熱	〃	2	1150		∞	〃
14	木府○義	男	20	發 熱	〃	7	950		∞	急性氣管支炎
15	柳原○郎	男	31	發熱，腺腫	〃	2	850		∞	
16	韓○麗	男		發 熱	〃	4	950		∞	
17	石川○	男		發 熱	〃	4	1250		∞	感 冒
18	屠 ○	男		發 熱	〃	2	950		∞	〃
19	王○田	男		發 熱	〃	2	1050		∞	〃
20	張○興	男		發 熱	〃	2	1150		∞	
21	揭○雅	男	38	發 熱	〃	10	1250		∞	急性氣管支炎
22	高○妹	男	10	發熱，腺腫	〃	8	1250		∞	急性氣管支炎
23	漂○輝	男	14	〃	〃	5	1050		∞	
24	蔡○五	男	6	〃	〃	6	1250		∞	急性氣管支炎
25	劉○有	男	15	〃	〃	5	1350		∞	
26	閔○泉	女	9	發 熱	〃	4	1250		∞	

1. 後○愛○ 此ノ患者ハ右股腺ペスト」ニ診斷サレテ治癒シタモノデ、此ノ患者ガ果シテ「ペスト症デアツタカ否カノ判定ハ検査ノ不備ナタメニ出來ナカツタコトハ既ニ述ベタ處デアル。今此ノ患者ノ體温表ヲ示セバ第5表ノ如クニシテ、斯樣ナ發熱經過ト股腺ノ腫脹及壓痛ノ臨床所見トヲ考ヘ合ハセル時ハ輕症ナル腺ペスト」ト診斷スルノガ妥當デハナカロウカト思ハレル症例デアル。而モ此ノ患者ニ於テ「ペスト血清殺菌反應ガ陽性ニ現レタコトハ極メテ興味深ク考ヘラレル。

第 5 表

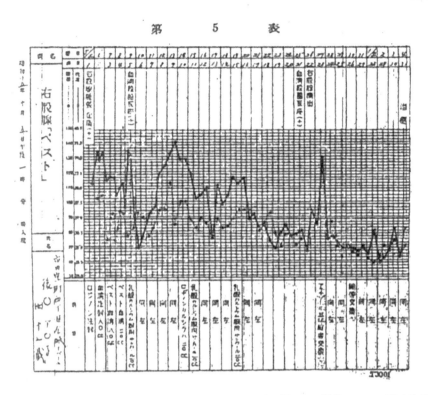

2 柳〇良〇 此ノ患者ハ「ペスト患者ノ多発シタ資昌ビル内ニ居住シテキタモノデ10月末頃夜発熱シ、右頸腺ノ腫脹ヲ著明ニ認メタルトモ疼痛少ク、且腺腫穿刺液ニ就テハ再三菌検索ヲ行ツタサレドモ「ペスト菌ノ検出ハ陰性デアツタ。尚患者ノ體温表ヲ示セバ第6表ノ如クニシテ此ノ臨床所見ヨリ考ヘル時ハ此ノ患者ハ腺ペスト症トスルノガ妥当デハナカロウカト思ハレル。而シテ此ノ患者ニ於テモ「ペスト血清殺菌反應ハ陽性ニ現レタ。

3 平〇正〇 此ノ患者ハ「ペスト患者ノ多発セシ資昌ビル内ニ居住シテキタモノデ、発熱及右鼠蹊腺ノ腫脹及疼痛ヲ主徴トシ、第7表ニ示スガ如キ発熱ノ経過ニテ治癒シタモノデアル。腺腫穿刺液、血液、喀痰等ニ就テ菌検索ヲ行ツタケレドモ「ペスト菌ハ陰性デアツタ、此ノ患者ニ於テモ「ペスト血清殺菌反應ハ陽性ニ現レタ。

以上ノ所見ヨリ此ノ患者ハ輕症ナル「ペスト」デアツタモノト考ヘラレル。

第 6 表

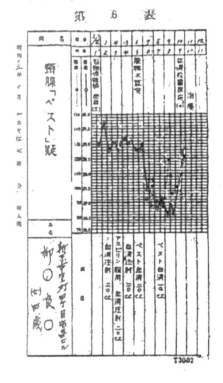

525—28

4　藤〇加〇　此ノ患者ハ「ペスト患者ノ多發シタ寶鷄ビル内ニ居住シテキタモノデ、健旋隔離サレテキル間ニ發熱シ、右鼠蹊腺ノ腫脹ヲ認メ、第8表ニ示ス如キ發熱ノ經過ニテ治癒シタモノデアル。此ノ患者ニ於テハ腺腫穿刺液、血液、喀痰ノ菌檢索ノ結果ハ陰性デアツタケレドモ「ペスト血清殺菌反應ハ陽性ニ現レタ。

以上述ベタ如ク是等ノ患者ニ就テ檢査セルニ「ペスト血清殺菌反應ガ總テ陽性ニ現レタコトハ極メテ興味深イコトニシテ、「ペスト血清殺菌反應ガ健康者ニ於テハ非特異性陽性反應ヲ示スモノ少ドナク、而モ「ペスト患者ニ於テハ100%陽性ニ此現スル成績ヨリ考ヘルト以上揭ゲタ症例ハ總テ輕症ナル「ペスト症ト診斷スルノガ安當デアルト思ハレル、尚是等ノ症例ガ臨床所見モ極メテ「ペスト」ニ類似セルモノデアルコトハ益ヶ斯ク診斷スルコトノ安當デアルコトヲ物語ルモノト云フコトガ出來ル。

流行時ニハ斯樣ナ症例ニ屢々遭遇スルモノデアルカラ斯カル症例ガ果シテ輕症ペスト」ト云ヘルモノデアルガドウカヲ臨床的檢査、細菌學的檢査及血清學的檢査ニヨツテ判定スルニ努メルコトヲ望ムト共ニ併セテ「ペスト血清殺菌反應ヲ檢査シテ、此ノ反應ガ特異性ニシテ斯樣ナ輕症ペスト」ノ診斷ニ役立ツモノデアルカ否カヲ檢探シテ戴キタイト念願スルモノデアル。

第3章　總括及考察

結言ニ於テ述ベタ如ク「ペスト症ノ血清診斷ニハ凝集反應及補體結合反應ガ用ヒラレテキルケレドモ、是等ノ血清反應ハ發症後2週～3週ニシテ漸ク陽性ニ現レ、而モ其ノ陽性率ハ50%内外ニ過ギナイノデ、北ノ診斷的價値ハ極メテ低イモノデアル、然ルニ「ペスト流行時ニハ臨床所見ニ於テハ「ペスト」ヲ疑ヘルニ拘ラズ、菌檢出ノ陰性ナ患者ガ相當ニアリ、其ノ診斷ニ苦シムモノデアル、余ハ此ノ點ニ就テ「ペスト症ノ血清診斷法ノ再檢探ヲシタクシデアルガ茲ニ其ノ結果ヲ總括シテ述ベレバ次ノ如クデアル。

第　7　表　鼠蹊腺「ペスト」疑

第　8　表　鼠蹊腺「ペスト」疑

525-42

今次ノ新京及鼠安ノ「ペスト」流行ニ於テ「ペスト」患者ヨリ其ノ血清ヲ分離シ、其ノ働性血清ノ「ペスト菌ニ對スル殺菌作用（「ペスト」血清殺菌反應ト假稱ス）ヲ檢査セルニ「ペスト」患者血清ハ總テ「ペスト」菌ニ對シテ作用ヲ有スルコトヲ認メタ。

其處デ健常者163名ニ就テ此ノ「ペスト」血清殺菌反應ヲ檢査セルニ1例ニ於ヲモ陽性ヲ現ハレルモノヲ認メナカツタ、然ルニ「ペスト・ワクチン」ヲ接種セルモノニ於テハ247名中3例ニ於テ陽性ニ現ハルノヲ認メタ。

以上ノ成績ヨリ考察スレバ上述セル「ペスト」患者血清ノ「ペスト菌ニ對スル殺菌作用（「ペスト」血清殺菌反應）ハ特異性ノモノニシテ、1種ノ免疫反應デアルト考ヘラレルケレドモ、其ノ本態ニ就テハ今回ハ究明スル暇ガナカツタノデ將來之ヲ明カニスル考ヘデアル。

此ノ血清反應ハ「ペスト」患者ニ於テハ100%陽性ニ現レ、而モ發病ノ極メテ初期（第1病日）ヨリ既ニ陽性ニ現ハレルモノニシテ、「ペスト・ワクチン」ヲ接種セルモノニ於テハ陽性ニ現ハルモノモアルガ、其ノ陽性率ハ極メテ低イノヲ認メタ。

次ニ「ペスト」流行時ニ臨床所見ガ「ペスト」患者ニ類似シテキタ爲ニ「ペスト」輕疑患者トシテ蒐容サレタ26名ニ就テ其ノ血清ノ「ペスト」血清殺菌反應ヲ檢査セルニ大部分ノモノニ於テハ陰性デアツタガ、1部ノモノニ於テハ陽性ニ現ハレルノヲ認メタ、陰性ノモノハ比較的速カニ解熱シ、臨床上ニモ「ペスト」症ヲ疑フ點ナク、天々急性氣管支炎或ハ感冒ト診斷セラレタモノデアリ、之ニ反シ陽性ノモノハ其ノ臨床所見ハ極メテ「ペスト」症ニ類似セルモノデアツタ、是等ノ患者ニ就テモ菌檢索ノ結果ハ陰性デアツタケレドモ、周圍ノ事情特ニ其ノ發生狀況ヨリモ「ペスト」症ト考ヘラレルモノデアツタ、此ノ成績ヨリ考察スレバ「ペスト」血清殺菌反應ハ菌檢出ノ困難ナ輕症ペスト症ノ診斷ニ用ヒラレル樣ニ考ヘラレル、併シナガラ此ノ血清反應ガ果シテ特異性ニ十テ他ノ諸疾患ニ於テハ全然陽性ニ現レルコトノナイモノデアルカ否カニ就テハ更ニ檢探ヲ要スルモノト考ヘラレル。

結　言

余ハ「ペスト」血清殺菌反應ヲ檢査セル結果、此ノ反應ハ「ペスト」患者ニ特異性ニシテ、而モ發病ノ極メテ初期ヨリ100%陽性ニ出現スルノデ診斷的價値ノ大デアルコトヲ認メタ。

文　獻

1) Zabolotony : Dtsch. med. Wochschr., (1897), 23, 392.　2) Schtschastny : Die Pest in Odessa, 1910, St. Petersburg, (1912).　3) Moses ; Mem. Inst. Oswaldo Cruz, 1, quot. by Dieudonné & Otto, (1909).　4) Jaltrain, E. : C. R. acad. Sci., Paris, (1920), 171, 413.　5) Simard : Bull. Off. Internat. Hyg. Public., (1921), 13, 984.　6) Dickie, W. M. : Proc. Conf. State & Prev. Health auth. North America, 30, quot. Trop. Dis. Buel, (1926), 25, 314.　7) Weinstein : Westn. obsohtsch. Hygieni, st.

525—30

Petersburg, (1909).   8) Amako, T. : Zbl. Bakt, I. Orig., (1909), 51, 674.

9) Row, R. : Brit. med. Jl., (1902), II, 1895., (1903), I, 1076.   10) Otten, L. : Gen. Tijdschr. v. Ned.-Indië, (1934), 74, 2948.   11) Tsuchia, K. & Li Te Chuan : Jl. Orient. Med., (1929), 11, 85.

4.2.5 昭和15年農安及新京ニ発生セル「ペスト」流行ニ就テ 第3編 流行ニ於ケル菌検索成績

資料出処：日本国立国会図書館関西館蔵、博士論文。

内容点评：本资料为《陆军军医学校防疫研究报告》第2部第526号《关于昭和15年农安和新京发生的鼠疫流行 第3编 流行中病菌的检索成绩》，1943年4月12日提交。

陸軍軍醫學校防疫研究報告
第2部　第526號

昭和15年農安及新京ニ發生セル「ペスト」流行ニ就テ

第3編　流行ニ於ケル菌檢索成績

陸軍軍醫學校軍陣防疫學教室（主任　增田大佐）

陸軍軍醫少佐　高　橋　正　彦

第　2　部
原　　著
分　類
441—1
378—41
受附 昭和 18. 4. 12

526—2

増任指導　陸軍軍醫少將　石　　井　　四　　郎

緒　言

昭和15年9月下旬新京ニ「ペスト」ノ流行發生セル際ニ余等ハ菌檢索業務ヲ命ゼラレ、新京及農安ニ於テ患者及死亡者ニ就テ菌檢索ヲ行ヒ、併セテ流行地域ニテ捕獲シタ鼠及其ノ附着昆蟲ニ就テ菌檢索ヲ行ツタ結果、患者及屍體ヨリ71株、鼠ヨリ29株、蚤ヨリ9株、虱ヨリ1株計110株ノ「ペスト菌株ヲ分離スルコトガ出來タノデ其ノ檢索成績ニ就テ報告スル。

第1章　菌檢索方法ノ概要

「ペスト菌ノ檢索ハ鏡檢試驗、培養試驗及動物試驗ノ方法ニ據ツタ、尚參考ノタメニ屍器熱沈降反應試驗ヲ行ツタ場合モアル、今是等ノ檢査方法ノ概要ニ就テ述ベレバ次ノ如クデアル。

1、鏡　檢　試　驗

可檢材料ヲ直接物體板ニ塗擦シ、「アルコール」、「エーテル」等分液ニテ10分間固定セル後マンソン氏液ニテ約10分間染色シ、油浸裝置ニテ丁寧ニ鏡檢シ、標木中ニ短桿菌ニシテ兩端濃染シ、「ペスト菌特有ノ形態ヲ備ヘタ菌ヲ見出シタ時ハ鏡檢試驗成績陽性トシタ。

同所要ニ應ジ視野ニ現レル菌數ニヨツテ數視野ニ1箇アルモノヲ十、1視野ニ1～10箇ノモノヲ卄、1視野ニ11～100箇アルモノヲ卅、其以上アルモノヲ卌トシテ記載シタ。

2、培　養　試　驗

可檢材料ヲ直接遠藤平板ニ塗擦シ、之ヲ37℃ニテ45時間培養セル後ニ「ペスト菌ノ定型的集

落ヲ發生シ、尚共ニ就テ20倍稀釋「ペスト菌免疫家兎血清ヲ以テ擬定凝集ヲ行ヒ、共ガ陽性ニシテ前モ鏡檢ノ結果前述ノ如キ形態ヲ有スル菌ヲ見出シタ時ハ培養試驗成績陽性トシタ。

　増菌試驗　　可檢材料ヲ普通ブイヨン」ニ入レ、17℃位ノ溫度ニテ3日～5日間培養シ、共ノ培養液ニ就テ平板培養ヲ行ヒ「ペスト菌ノ聚落ガ發生スルカ否カヲ檢査シタ、此ノ方法ニヨル時ハ可檢材料中ニ含マレル菌ガ極メテ微量ナ時デモ菌ヲ檢出スルコトガ出來タ、尚此ノ方法ニヨツテ菌ヲ檢出シタ時モ培養試驗陽性ト記載シタ。

3、動物試驗

　體重凡ソ250g內外ノ海猥3頭ヲ1群トシテ、共ニ對シ可檢材料ノ所要量ヲ右股部皮下ニ注射シ、尚所要ニ應ジ海猥ノ腹部ヲ抜毛シ、「メス」ニテ僅カニ出血スル程度ニ傷ヲツケ、共ノ部分ニ可檢材料ヲ可及的大量ニ擦入シタ、斯クシテ後海猥ノ斃死スルノヲ待ツテ之ヲ解剖シ、病變ヲ觀察セル際ニ特有ナ病變ヲ呈シ、且淋巴腺、肝臟、腎臟、心血等ヨリ鏡檢上及培養上前述ノ如キ菌ヲ檢出シタ時ハ動物試驗成績陽性トシタ。

　可檢材料ニ雜菌ノ混入シテキナイモノハ皮下接種法ニヨリ、雜菌ノ混入シテキルト思ハレルモノハ經皮接種法ニヨツタ。

4、臟器熱沈降反應試驗

　被驗體ノ脾臟及肝臟ノ各一片ヲ滅菌シャーレ」ニ採リ、其ニ2.0ccノ生理的食鹽水ヲ加ヘテ乳劑トナシ、其ヲ100℃ 20分振盪シテ共ノ遠沈上清液ヲ取リ、之ヲ抗原トシテ「ペスト菌免疫血清（Envelope抗體ヲ含有スル血清ヲ使用ス）ニ重疊シテ輪環法ニヨリ沈降反應ヲ檢査シタ、檢査成績ハ室温放温30分後ニ白色輪環ノ明瞭ニ認メラレルモノヲ十、異ハシネモノヲ士、其ノ現レタイモノヲ一トシタ。

　而シテ「ペスト」ノ制定ハ可檢材料ニ就テ上述ノ各試驗ヲ行ヒ共等ノ檢査成績ヲ綜合シテ行ツタ、斯クノ如クシテ可檢材料ヨリ分離培養シ得タ「ペスト菌ハ110株デアツタ。

第2章　屍體ニ就テノ菌檢索成績

第1節　檢索材料

「ペスト患者トシテ隔離所ニ收容サレテ後ニ死亡セルモノハ勿論、其ノ他不明ノ疾患ニテ死亡セル行路病者ノ屍體ニ就テ「ペスト菌ノ檢索ヲ行ツタ、檢索セルモノハ新京ニ於テ76體、農安ニ於テ48體デアツタ。

第2節　檢索方法

　屍體ノ全身解剖ヲ行ヒ、淋巴腺、各內臟器及所要ノ箇所ニ就テ菌檢索ヲ行ツタ、檢索方法ハ鏡檢試驗及培養試驗ニ據リ、尚必要ニ應ジテ動物試驗及臟器熱沈降反應試驗ヲ行ツタ。

第3節　檢索成績

　屍體124體ニ就テ鏡檢試驗、培養試驗、動物試驗及臟器熱沈降反應試驗ニヨツテ菌檢索ヲ行ツタ結果、「ペスト」ニ因ル斃死ト決定シ得タモノハ58體デアツタ。

526—4

今「ペスト」ノ病型ニヨツテ分類シ、屍體ノ各臓器ニ就テノ菌檢出成績ヲ示セバ次ノ如クデアル。

即チ第1表ハ腺ペスト」ニテ死亡セルモノノ各臓器ニ於ル菌ノ檢出成績ヲ示スモノデ、各臓器ヨリ菌ヲ檢出シ、狹レモ敗血症ニテ死亡セルコトヲ明カニスルコトガ出來タ。第2表ハ皮膚ペスト」ニテ死亡セルモノニ就テノ菌檢索成績ニシテ、此ノ場合ニモ敗血症ニテ死亡シテキルコトガ明カデアル。第3表ハ肺ペスト」ニテ死亡セルモノニ就テノ菌檢索成績ニシテ肺臓ニ於テ特ニ多數ノ菌ヲ檢出スルコトヲ特徴トシテキルヤウデアル、第4表ハ「ペスト敗血症ニテ死亡セルモノニ就テノ菌檢索成績ニシテ淋巴腺ヨリモ塚ロ脾臓、即臓等ニ多數ノ菌ヲ檢出スルモノヲ特徴トシテキル様デアル。

第3章 患者ニ就テノ菌檢索成積

第1節 檢索材料

新京及農安ニ於テ臨床上「ペスト」トシテ隔離病舍ニ收容サレタ患者ニ就テ淋巴腺腫穿刺液、血液（正中靜脈ヨリ採取）、略痰（或ハ咽頭粘液）及皮膚病竈ノ濃汁等ニ就テ菌檢索ヲ行ツタ。

第2節 檢索方法

淋巴腺腫ヲ觸知セルモノハ腺腫ノアル局所ノ皮膚ヲ豫メ酒精ニテ消拭シテ消毒シタ後滅菌シタ注射器ニ生理的食鹽水ノ小量（0.2cc）ヲ入レ、其ヲ腺腫內ニ注入シタ後ニ內容ヲ洗ヒ出ス如クシテ組織液ヲ吸收シテ、其ノ穿刺液ニ就テ先ヅ培養試驗（增菌試驗ヲモ含ム）、動物試驗ヲ行ヒ、尚殘ツタ材料ニ就テ鏡檢試驗ヲ行ツタ。

血液ハ患者ノ正中靜脈ヨリ約2cc採取シ、共ニ就テ先ヅ培養試驗（增菌試驗ヲ含ム）、動物試驗（腹腔內注射或ハ皮下注射ニヨル方法）ヲ行ヒ、殘ツタ材料ニ就テ鏡檢試驗ヲ行ツタ。

略痰ハ患者ノ略出シタモノヲ滅菌シヤーレ」ニ取リ、共ニ就テ鏡檢試驗ヲ行ヒ、尚培養試驗ヲ行ツタ後其ヲ生理食鹽水ニテ乳劑トナシテ動物試驗（經皮接種ニヨル方法）ヲ行ツタ、略痰ヲ得ラレナイモノハ咽頭粘液ヲ採取シテ同樣ノ檢査ヲ行ツタ。

皮膚患部即チ「ペスト膿疱、瘡、疣、膿疱性發疹等ヨリハ注射器ヲ以テ可及的深部ヨリ內容液ヲ採取シ、共ニ就テ培養試驗及鏡檢試驗ヲ行ツタ後ニ其ヲ生理的食鹽水ニテ乳劑トナシテ動物試驗（雜菌混入ノ有無ニヨツテ時ニ皮下接種法ヲ用ヒ、時ニ經皮接種法ヲ用ヒタ）ヲ行ツタ。

第3節 檢索成績

上述ノ如キ方法ニヨツテ「ペスト患者ヨリ菌ヲ檢出セル成績ハ第5表ニ示ス如クニシテ、新京ニ於テハ7人ノ患者ニ就テ生前ニ菌ヲ檢出シ、農安ニ於テハ9人ノ患者ヨリ菌ヲ檢出シ得タ、一般ニ「ペスト患者ヨリ菌ノ檢出ハ必ズシモ容易デナク且經過ガ早イノデ生前ニ菌ヲ檢出シテ「ペスト」ト決定スルコトハ比較的困難デアル。

腺腫穿刺液デハ比較的菌ノ檢出ハ容易デアルケレドモ略痰ノ中ニハ形態上「ペスト菌ニ類似スル桿菌ガ認メラレルノデ培養試驗及動物試驗ヲシナケレバ「ペスト菌ト決定スルコトハ比來ナ

第1表　腺ペストニ依ル死亡者ニ就テノ剖検業成績

収集地	番號	氏名	性別	年齢	剖檢所見	罹病 經過(日)	皮膚				腹				殿				胸				皮				淋巴腺 反應陽 ビ培養試驗	
							區域	族	肌	心血	脾	肝	腎	其他	局	腎	肝	脾	心血	肌	肌	腎	肝	脾	心血	的
新	1	劉田 仕春	♀	8	右鼠蹊腺ペスト	7																				
	2	田鳥天津子	♂	3	右頭腺 "	3																				
	3	神田 秀	♂	25	右鼠蹊腺 "	4																				
	4	關田 正光	♂	17	"	2																				
	5	矢松 正玉	♂	21	"	2																				
	6	宋原 正玉	♂	23	左肺炎腺ペスト	4																				
安	7	焙本市貫子	♀	12	右頭高腺 "	5																				
	8	關 貫	♂	27	右鼠蹊腺 "	2																				
	9	陳 湖	♂	55	左鼠蹊腺 "	18																				
	10	李 郭	♀	2	敗血 "	3																				
	11	高松 殷砂子	♀	3	右鼠蹊腺 "	20																				
	12	宋 原 林	♂	44	右鼠蹊腺 "	1																				
青	13	宇 財	♂	51	右鼠蹊腺ペスト																					
	14	趙陳 午子	♀	31	"																					
	15	陳張 兵子	♂	52	"	不明																				
	16	周青 芳子	♀	31	"																					
	17	張 永	♂	6	右鼠蹊腺 "																					
	18	陳 英	♂	36	左肺高腺ペスト																					
	19	魏徐 子	♀	48	右敗血ナ上 "																					
	20	諸李 子	♂	53	腐腺 "																					
	21	寅 國 子	♂	28	右鼠蹊腺 "																					
	22	李 健 兵	♂	35	右肺高腺 "																					
安	23	李 玉	♀	50	左鼠蹊腺ペスト																					
	24	李 甲 子	♂	72	肩 垢腺 "																					
	25	賈 蒸林子	♂	40	右鼠蹊腺 "																					
	26	王 子	♀	25	右鼠蹊腺 "																					
	27	藏 藏	♂	8	右鼠蹊腺 "																					
安	28	星 金 子	♀	32	左鼠蹊腺ペスト																					
	29	謝 藏 兵	♂	33	右鼠蹊腺 "																					
	30	陳 氏	♂	8	"																					
	31	林 比	♂	22	"																					
	32	孟 忠 子	♀	10	左鼠蹊高腺 "																					
	33	初 耀	♂	6	"																					
	34	安 焦 氏	♂	30	右鼠蹊腺 "																					

註　陰性成績 數視野ニ對1個　＋
　1視野ニ對1～10個　卅
　〃　 11～100個　卅
　〃　 100個以上　卌

第2表 皮膚ペスト」死亡者ニ就テノ直接索成績

諸生地	番号	氏名	性別	年齢	剖検所見	諮温(日)	脳	咽頭	血	扁桃	脾	肺	腸	心血	肝	腎	局	其他	脳	脾	熱比赚反應	動物試驗
新京	1	钱田崈夫	男	31	皮膚ペスト	5		++	#	++	#	#	#	++	#	#	#	不明	+	+	+	+
	2	蘇盤	男	37	〃	不明	-	+		+	+	-	+	-	#	#	逃入ノ	不	+	+	-	
戚	3	王恶王	女	12	〃	〃		++	#	+	#	+	-	+	-	#		+	明→	+	+	
	4	柱牛	女	48	〃	〃		+		#		-	-	+	#					+	-	
	5	恶仲	男	35	〃	〃	-	#	+	+		+	+	+	+	#			+	+	+	
	6	永許	女	3	〃	〃	+	+		+	#		+		-		-		+	-	+	
	7	大子	男	63	〃	〃	-			-			+		-				+		-	
安	8	喜事			〃	〃																-

第3表 肺ペスト」死亡者ニ就テノ直接索成績

諸生地	番号	氏名	性別	年齢	剖造所見	諮温(日)	脳	咽頭	血	扁桃	脾	肺	腸	心血	肝	腎	局	其他	脾	脳	熱比赚反應	動物試驗
新京	1	雪山	男	66	肺ペスト	5	-	#	-	#	#	-	-	#	+	+					+	+
戚	2	滕三	女	8	〃	不明															+	+
	3	淫氏	女	62	〃	〃		#		#	#			#		+					-	+
安	4	西恶二	男	73	〃	6								+							-	

第4表 「ペスト」敗血症死亡者ニ就テノ直接索成績

諸生地	番号	氏名	性別	年齢	剖造所見	諮温(日)	脳	咽頭	血	扁桃	脾	肺	腸	心血	肝	腎	局	其他	脾	脳	熱比赚反應	動物試驗
新京	1	大田崈夫	男	33	「ペスト敗血症	6	#	#	#	#		#	-	#	+	+			+	+		+
京	2	李德金	女	10	〃	2	+	+	+	+	#	+		#	#	+				#		-
	3	賀濒	男	45	〃	不明	+	+	+	+	+	-	#	#	+	+			#	#	-	#
	4	土恶二	女	58	〃	6																
戚	5	新恶	男	5	〃	不明	#	#	#	#	#	#	-	#	#	#			#	#	+	+
	6	李真氏	女	18	〃	〃	+	+	+	+	+	+	+	+	+	+			+	#	#	#
	7	徐稻氏	男	51	〃	〃	-	-	#	-	#	+	#	#	+	+	+		+	#	#	#
	8	因恶氏	女	30	〃	〃	+	+	+	+	+	+	+	#	+	+	+	[	+		-	#
	9	白顒氏	男	29	〃	〃	+	+	#	+	#	+	+	#	+	+			+	#		+
	10	高拉	女	13	〃	〃	#	#		-	#	+	+	#	-	+		[	+	#	+	++
安	11	陳小俵氏	男	68±	〃	〃	+	#	+	#	#	+	+	#	+	+			+	+		+

第5表 「ペスト」患者ニ飲ラレタ菌ノ畜接案成績

第6表「ペスト」容疑患者ニ就テノ菌検査成績

発生地	番号	氏名	性別	年齢	病名	転帰	検査月日	病日(日)	鏡検成績 腺	鏡検成績 尿	鏡検成績 喀痰	鏡検成績 流血	鏡検成績 眼分泌	培養成績 腺	培養成績 尿	培養成績 喀痰	培養成績 流血	培養成績 眼分泌	摘要
新京	1	徐○愛○	女	17	左鼠蹊腺ペスト」?	治癒	7/X	3	—	—				—	—				17/X、20/〃、22/〃、23/〃、25/〃ニ検査セルモ菌陰性。
							8/〃	4	—	—	—	—		—	—	—	—		
							10/〃	6	—	—	—	—		—	—	—	—		
	2	王振東	男	36	眼ペスト」?	治癒	13/〃	2					+?					—	鏡検上両眼膿染セル短桿菌ヲ検出セルモ、之ガ「ペスト菌ナリシヤ否ヤノ判定ハ動物試験ヲ行ハザリシタメニ困難ナリ。
							14/〃	3					+?					—	
							15/〃	4					—					—	
							16/〃	5					—					—	
	3	柳原良子	女	4	頸腺ペスト」?	治癒	7/〃	7	(頸) —	—	—	—		(頸) —	—	—	—		発熱腺腫等ノ臨床所見ハ「ペスト症ヲ呈シタリ。
							9/〃	9	—	—	—	—		—	—	—	—		
	4	平井正○	男	21	鼠蹊腺ペスト」?	治癒	8/〃	5	—		—	—		—		—	—		同上
							10/〃	7	—		—	—		—		—	—		

528ページ

イ、又血液中ニ「ペスト菌ガ證明サレルノハ死亡スル直前デアル様ニ思ハレル。

尚鏡檢ニテ菌ヲ認メ得ナイ様ナ微量ナ菌ヲ含ンデヰル材料デモ培養試験ニヨル特殊ニ増菌培養ヲ行フ時ニハ比較的容易ニ菌ヲ檢出スルコトガ出來タ。

次ニ急激ナ發熱及壓痛アル淋巴腺腫ヲ有シ臨床上「ペスト」ヲ疑ヘル患者ニ就テ菌檢索ヲ行ツタ成績ハ第6表ニ示ス如クニシテ、淋巴腺穿刺液、喀痰、流血、眼分泌物等ニ就テ菌檢索ヲ行ツタケレドモ盬ニ菌ヲ檢出スルコトガ出來ナカツタ、從ツテ是等ノ患者ガ眞性ノ「ペスト症」デアツタカ否カハ決定スルコトガ出來ナカツタケレドモ臨床上ハ至々「ペスト症ト考ヘ得ヒ此モ此デアツタ。

「ペスト」流行時ニハ斯樣ナ患者ガ相當ニ存シ、「ペスト菌ノ檢出ガ陰性デアル爲ニ不明ノ熱性疾患トシテ弾ラレテヰルモノト考ヘラレル。

一般ニ死ノ轉歸ヲ取ルモノニ於テハ菌ノ檢出ハ可能デアルゲレドモ、治癒スルモノニ於テハ菌ノ檢出ガ極メテ困難デアルノデ、斯カルモノニ於テハ「ペスト症ヲ決定ガ困難ニナル場合ガ多イ、斯樣ナ患者ハ血清反應其ノ他ノ手段ニヨツテ「ペスト」ト決定セラルベキモノト考ヘラレルケレドモ、現在使用セラレテキル血清反應ハ「ペスト患者ニ於テハ約50％内外陽性ニ出現スルニ過ギナイノデ、之ニ依ル診斷ハ必ズシモ容易デナイ狀態デアル。

次ニ農安ニ於テ喉ペスト」ニ罹患セルモ治療ニヨツテ一般症状良好トナリ、臨床上テハ治癒ト判定サレタ「ペスト」恢復患者16人ニ就テ血液、淋巴腺腫穿刺液、喀痰流涙、皮膚病竈ノ膿汁等ニ就テ鏡檢試驗、培養試驗（増菌試驗ヲモ含ム）ニヨツテ1週間ニ隔ニテ2回乃至8回菌檢索ヲ行ツタケレドモ一例ニ於カモ菌ヲ檢出スルコトガ出來ナカツタ、此ノ成績ヨリ「ペスト患者ニ於テハ恢復後長ク菌ヲ保有シテヰルモノハナイ様ニ思ハレル、此ノ事ハ「ペスト」ノ豫防上重要ナコトデアルト考ヘラレル。

第4章 近接健常者ニ就テノ菌檢索成績
第1節 檢 索 材 料

新京及農安ノ流行發生地域ノ住民ニ就テ健康菌保有者ヲ檢出スル目的ヲ以テ淋巴腺穿刺液、喀痰、血液、尿等ニ就テ菌檢索ヲ行ツタ。

第2節 檢 索 方 法

鼠蹊腺或ハ股腺ヲ觸知シ得ルモノハ其ノ穿刺液ヲ採取シ、先ヅ其ノ一滴ヲ遠藤平板ニ培養シ、殘リハ普通ブイヨン」ニ増菌シテ檢出ヲ試ミタ、喀痰ハ一部ヲ以テ塗擦標本ヲ作リ、殘リハ遠藤平板ニ培養シ、血液ハ正中靜脈ヨリ約3cc採取シ、其ノ一滴ヲ遠藤平板ニ培養シ、約0.5ccヲ普通ブイヨン」ニ増菌シ、殘リハ血淸ヲ分離シテ血淸反應ノ檢査ニ使用シタ、尿ハ新鮮ナモノヲ取リ一滴ヲ遠藤平板ニ培養シ、約2ccヲ普通ブイヨン」ニ増菌シテ菌ノ檢出ヲ試ミタ。

第3節 檢 索 成 績

1、流行時ニ發熱ガアツタ爲ニ「ペスト症ヲ疑ハレテ隔離病舎ニ收容サレタ86人ニ就テ其ノ間

526--6

ヲ隔ニテ2回菌検索ヲ行ツタケレドモ一例ニ就テモ菌ヲ検出スルコトガ出来ナカツタ。

2、同一家族内ニ「ペスト患者ガ發生シタ爲ニ隔離收容サレタ健常者168人ニ就テ1ヶ間々隔テ2回ニ亘リ上述セル如ク菌検索ヲ行ツタケレドモ菌ヲ検出スルコトガ出来ナカツタ。

3、農安縣城内住民ニ就テ「ペスト皮膚反應ヲ行ヒ、其ノ陽性者250人ニ就テ淋巴腺ノ腫張セルモノガアルカ否カヲ検査シ、其ノ内淋巴腺腫ヲ觸知セルモノ96人ニ就テ前述ノ如クニシテ菌検索ヲ行ツタケレドモ1例ニ就テモ菌ヲ検出スルコトガ出来ナカツタ。

4、流行地域住民ノ健常者215人ニ就テ前述ノ如クニシテ菌検索ヲ行ツタケレドモ1例ニ就テモ菌ヲ検出スルコトガ出来ナカツタ。

以上ノ如ク流行地ニ於テ患者ト近接セル健常者555人ニ就テ淋巴腺腫穿刺液、咯痰、血液、尿等ニ就テ菌検索ヲ行ツタ結果1例ニ就テモ菌ヲ検出スルコトガ出来ナカツタ、即チ「ペスト菌ノ健康菌保有症ヲ見出スコトガ出来ナカツタ。

文獻ニ就テ見ルニ Loger, Tanon, Uriarte, Durand, Boston 等ハ「ペスト患者ノ發生シタ周圍ノ人々ニ就テ「ペスト菌ノ検索ヲ行ツタ結果、僅カニ腫眠セル腺腫ヨリ「ペスト菌ヲ検出シ得タコトヲ報ジ、尚斯ガル腺腫ハ疼痛ヲ伴ハナイコトガ多ク且菌保有者ハ何等一般症状ヲ呈シナイモノガ多イ爲ニ其ノ検出ノ困難デアルコトヲ述べ、Nikanorov ハ全ク健康ニ見エル人ノ血液中ヨリ「ペスト菌ヲ證明シ、斯カルモノガ傳染源トナル危險ノ大デアルコトヲ述べテキル、其ノ他 Christie ハ15日間ニ11人ニ「ペスト」ヲ感染セシメタ一健康婦人ニ就テ報告シ、Zlntogoroff 等ハ肺ペスト患者ノ看護人21人ノ咽頭液ヨリ1例ニ於テ「ペスト菌ヲ検出シ、Wulien-Teh ハ滿洲ニ於ケル肺ペスト」ノ流行時ニ咯痰中ニ「ペスト菌ヲ排出セル2例ニ健康菌保有症ヲ報告シ、Gotschlich 等ハ「ペスト恢復者ニシテ2～3ケ月ニ亘リ全然一般症状ヲ認メナイノニ其ノ咯痰中ニ「ペスト菌ヲ排出シタ例ヲ報告シテキル、斯クノ如ク「ペスト菌保有者ニ就テハ若干ノ報告ハアルケレドモ、其ノ検出陽性數ハ他ノ急性傳染病ノ場合ニ比シテ極メテ少イ様デアル、余ノ検査成績カラ考ヘテモ「ペスト」ニ於テハ健康菌保有症ハ疫學上問題ニナル程多ク存在スルモノトハ思ハレナイ。

第5章　「ペスト」關係動物ニ就テノ菌検索成績

第1節　検索材料

新京ニ於テハ流行ノ發生シタ地域ヲ中心トシテ捕獲シタ齧歯類ヲ主トシ、其ノ他ニ患家ニ飼育サレテキタ犬、猫等ニ就テ菌検索ヲ行ヒ、農安ニ於テハ市内ニテ捕獲シタ鼠族ニ就テ菌検索ヲ行ツタ。

第2節　検索方法

鼠ハ全身解剖ノ上其ノ病變ヲ検査シ、次ニ頸腺、鼠蹊腺、肺臟、肝臟、心血等ニ就テ鏡検試驗及培養試驗ヲ行ヒ、尚所要ニ應ジ脾臟　肝臟ニ就テ臟器熱沈降反應ヲ行ツタ、其ノ他2、3ノモノニ就テハ動物試驗ヲ行ツタ。

尚有菌鼠ノ決定ニハ動物試驗マデ行フコトガ必要デアルケレドモ檢査數ガ極メテ多イ爲ニ一々ニ就テ共ヲ行フコトハ困難デアツタ。其處デ鏡檢及培養ニ於テ菌ヲ檢出シタモノヲ以テ陽性トシタ。尚培養試驗モ實施中ニ雜菌ノ混入ガアツテ檢査成績ノ判定ノ困難ナ場合ガアツタガ其ノ時ハ止ムナク鏡檢ノ成績ノミデ陽性ト決定シタモノモアル。

第3節 檢 索 成 績

以上ノ如クニシテ檢査セル成績ハ第7表ニ示ス如クニシテ、新京ニ於テハ「ドブネツミ」13,644頭中ヨリ63頭ノ有菌鼠ヲ檢出シ、農安ニ於テハ「ドブネズミ」325頭ヨリ9頭ノ有菌鼠ヲ「ハツカネズミ」24頭ヨリ1頭ノ有菌鼠ヲ檢出スルコトガ出來タ。

第7表 「ペスト」關係動物ニ就テノ菌檢索成績

地域	動 物 種 類	檢査頭數	陽性頭數	陽性率(%)
新	ド ブ ネ ズ ミ	13,644	63	0.46
	マンシウハツカネズミ	57	0	0
	マンシウセスヂネズミ	8	0	0
	セスヂキヌゲネズミ	10	0	0
	ヨ シ ネ ズ ミ	15	0	0
	カ ヤ ネ ズ ミ	1	0	0
	ミ マ リ ス	1	0	0
	イ タ チ	4	0	0
	野 兎	211	0	0
	シ ベ リ ア 貂	1	0	0
京	犬	12	0	0
	貓	2	0	0
	馬	5	0	0
農安	ド ブ ネ ズ ミ	325	9	2.8
	ハ ツ カ ネ ズ ミ	24	1	4.2

尚新京ノ有菌鼠ヲ地域別及生死別ニ觀察シタ成績ハ第8表ニ示ス如クニシテ地域別ニハ思者ノ多發シタ三角地域ニ於テ檢出率高ク、斃鼠ト捕獲セル鼠ニ就テ比較スレバ有菌鼠ノ檢出率ハ斃鼠ニ於テ高イノヲ認メタ。

此ノ檢査成績ヨリ人ペスト」ノ直接ノ傳染源ハ「ドブネズミ」ノ間ノ「ペスト流行デアルコト」ヲ想像スルコトガ出來タ。

526—8

第8表 地域別、生死別ノ有菌鼠検出成績

地域	生死別		検査数	有菌鼠数	有菌鼠率(%)
三角地帯	捕鼠		119	10	8.4
	斃鼠		34	5	14.7
		計	153	13	9.8
四角地帯	捕鼠		418	11	2.4
	斃鼠		24	2	8.3
		計	442	13	3.0
第I地域	捕鼠		2,017	18	0.9
	斃鼠		80	0	0
		計	2,097	18	0.9
第II地域	捕鼠		4,679	5	0.1
	斃鼠		96	0	0
		計	4,775	5	0.1
第III地域	捕鼠		207	1	0.5
	斃鼠		18	0	0
		計	225	1	0.4
第IV地域	捕鼠		1,295	3	0.2
	斃鼠		155	0	0
		計	1,450	3	0.2
其ノ他地域	捕鼠		4,535	8	0.2
	斃鼠		56	0	0
		計	4,591	8	0.2
合計	捕鼠		13,272	56	0.42
	斃鼠		463	7	1.51
		計	13,735	63	0.45

次ニ有菌鼠ト決定サレタ「ドブネズミ」ニ就テノ各臓器ノ検査成績ヲ示スト第9表ノ如クニシテ、多クノモノニ於テハ臓器ニ病變ヲ認メ、鏡検上及培養試験上菌ヲ検出スルコトガ出来タ、又臓器熱沈降反應モ陽性ニ現レタ、然ルニ一方ニハ鏡検試験デハ陽性デアルニ拘ラズ培養試験デハ菌ヲ検出シ得ズ且臓器熱沈降反應ノ陰性デアルモノガ相當ニ見ラレタ、之ハ有菌鼠デハナカツタモノデアロウト考ヘラレル、足此ノ問題ハ動物試験ヲ併セ行フコトニヨツテ或程度解決シ得ラレタコトデアロウト思ハレルケレドモ検査数ガ大デアツタ爲ニ其ガ出来ナカツタコトハ残念デアツタ。

尚茲ニ興味深ク思ハレルノハ剖検上デハ全然病變ノ認メラレナカツタニ拘ラズ鏡検及培養ニテ菌ノ検出サレタモノガアツタコトデアル。斯様ナ鼠ハ所謂慢性ペスト」ニテ経過シ、保菌鼠トナツテ病源ヲ越年サセルモノデハナカロウカト考ヘラレル。斯様ナ鼠ヲ生存セシメテ置イテ相當長期間観察スレバ果シテ慢性ペスト」トナルカ否カノ問題モ解決サレルニ至ツタモノト考ヘラレルガ當時ハ検査数ガ多カツタ爲ニ其モ不可能デアツタ。

643

第9表　有　菌　鼠　一　覧　表

番號	探月探日	鼠番號	生死別	鼠種類	肝 検 所 見						脾 検 試 験						塊 菱 試 験						常化反応	
					頸	右鼠	左鼠	脾	肝	肺	頸	右鼠	左鼠	脾	肝	肺	心	頸	右鼠	左鼠	脾	肝	肺	心血	脾	肝
1	9/X	8	死	ドブネズミ	+	+	±	+	+	+		+		惜	+	+			+		惜	+	+		±
2	〃	10	〃	〃	±	廿	±	+	+	+		惜		廿	廿	+			惜		惜惜	廿	+		惜
3	〃	13	捕	〃			+	+	+	+			+	惜	惜	+	+			+	惜惜	+	+	+	−
4	〃	14	〃	〃	+	−	−	+	+	+	+			惜	廿	+	+				惜	+	+	+	惜
5	10/〃	76	死	〃	−	−	−	±	±	+		廿		惜	廿	廿			廿		廿	廿	廿		
6	〃	77	捕	〃	−					+		−				−	−		廿		−	−		
7	〃	78	〃	〃	−	+	+	+	+	+		惜		廿	+			惜		廿	+	+		
8	〃	82	不明	〃	−	+	+	+	+	+		+	+	+	+			廿	+	+	+		
9	〃	84	捕	〃	−	+	+	+	+		−		+	+	−		−	−				
10	〃	88	〃	〃	−	+	+	+	+	+		−	+	+	+		−	−		−		
11	〃	92	〃	〃	−	+	+	+	+	−		+	廿	+	+		−	−		−		
12	〃	97	〃	〃	−	+	+	+	+	+		+	廿	+			−				
13	〃	125	〃	〃	−	+	+	+	+			+	+		+			+	+		
14	〃	150	〃	〃	−	+	+	+	+	+	−		+	+			+	+		
15	11/〃	153	〃	〃				+	+			+	+							±
16	〃	157	〃	〃	−	+	+	+	+	−		+	+							−
17	〃	183	〃	〃			+	+	+	+		+	+						
18	12/〃	259	〃	〃		+	+	+	+	−	+	+	惜	+			+	惜	惜	廿	+
19	〃	240	〃	〃	−	+	+	+	+	+	−		+	+	廿		+	惜	+	惜	+
20	〃	320	〃	〃	−	+	+	+	廿				廿			−	+	廿		+
21	〃	294	〃	〃		+	+	+	+	+			−	−					
22	13/〃	343	死	〃	+	+	+	+	+	+		+	惜	廿	+			廿	廿	廿	廿	廿
23	〃	331	捕	〃	+	廿	廿	廿	廿	廿		+	惜	惜			−	+			±
24	〃	286	〃	〃	−	+	+	+	+	−		−	+	−			−	+	−	−	+
25	〃	385	〃	〃		+	+	−	+	+		−	−	−		惜	−	−	−	+
26	14/〃	364	死	〃	−	+	+	+	−		+	惜	廿	+		−		惜	+
27	〃	375	捕	〃	−	+	廿	廿	廿	+	+	惜	廿	廿		−	−	−	+
28	〃	381	〃	〃	−	+	+	−	−	−		惜	+					+
29	〃	382	〃	〃	−	廿	廿	+	廿	廿		−	+	廿	惜		−	−	上	
30	〃	409	〃	〃	−	−	−	+	+	+		−	+		−		
31	15/〃	490	〃	〃	+	+	+	+	+	廿	廿	惜	+		−		+
32	〃	482	死	〃	+	+	+	+	+	+	+	惜	+	+		−		+
33	11/〃	550	〃	〃	±	+	+	+	+	惜	惜	惜	+	+	−			+
34	〃	612	〃	〃	−	−	−	−	−	−		惜	惜	惜	+	−		
35	〃	611	〃	〃	−	−	−	−	−		+	惜	惜	+		+	
36	〃	675	〃	〃	−	+	+	+	+	+		−	−	−		−		+	+
37	〃	688	〃	〃	−	+	+	+	+	+		−	−	−		−	−	+	+
38	16/〃	668	〃	〃	−	+	+	+	−	−		+	惜	惜	+		惜	+	惜	+
39	〃	690	〃	〃	−	−	+	+	−		+	惜	+	−		+	+	廿	+
40	〃	682	〃	〃	−	−	+	+	−	+		惜	+	惜	+		惜	+	廿	廿	廿
41	〃	703	死	〃	惜	惜	惜	廿	廿	+		惜	惜	+	+		廿	+	廿	±	+
42	21/〃	1,098	捕	〃	−	+	+	+	+	+		+	惜	+	+		−	−	−	
43	〃	1,091	〃	〃	−	−	+	+	+	+		−	+	+	+		−	−	−	
44	〃	1,157	〃	〃	−	−	−	+	+	+		−	+	+	+		−	−	−	
45	22/〃	1,211	〃	〃	−	−	+	+	−		廿	+	+	廿	+		−	+	−
46	〃	1,483	〃	〃	−	廿	+	廿	−		惜	+	+	−		惜	廿	廿	+
47	22/〃	1,748	〃	〃	−	+	惜	廿	−	+		+	廿	廿		−	+	廿	廿	+
48	23/〃	2,835	〃	〃	−	+	惜	惜	廿	+		+	惜	廿	廿		廿	惜	廿	廿
49	23/〃	3,777	〃	〃	−	+	+	+	−		惜	惜	+		−	−	−
50	23/〃	3,983	〃	〃	−	−	−	−	+		−	+		廿	廿	廿	廿
51	23/〃	5,515	神	〃	−	+	−	−	+		廿	+	+	+		−	−	−
52	24/〃	6,605	〃	〃	−	−	廿	−	+		+	惜	+	+		−	−	+
53	21/〃	7,886	〃	〃	−	−	+	−	+		+	惜	+	−		−	+	
54	7/XI	11,355	〃	〃	−	−	+	−	−		廿	惜	+	惜		−	−	−
55	〃	14,463	〃	〃	−	+	+	+	±		+	惜	+	+		−	−	−
56	〃	17,117	神	〃	−	−	+	−	−		−	惜	惜	惜		−	−	−
57	〃	33,000	〃	〃	−	−	+	−	−		−	惜	廿	惜		−
58	〃	34,008	〃	〃	−	−	廿	−	−		−	+	+	廿			−
59	〃	11,026	〃	〃	−	−	−	−	−		−	+	+	廿	
60	〃	22,299	〃	〃	−	−	−	−	−		−	+	+	廿	
61	〃	19,694	〃	〃	−	−	−	−	−		−	惜	廿	+	
62	〃	22,203	〃	〃	−	−	−	−	−		−	惜	廿	+	
63	〃	35,230	〃	ドブネズミ	−	+	−	−		−	惜	+	+	

次ニ有菌鼠ニ就テ検索方法別ニ陽性率ヲ検査スレバ第10表ニ示ス如クニシテ剖検所見ノ陽性率最モ高ク、次ニ鏡検試験ノ陽性率高シ、是等ニ比シテ培養試験ノ陽性率ハ可ナリ低カツタ、是等ノ検索方法ノ内デ最モ信頼シ得ル方法ハ培養試験デアルケレドモ此ノ方法ニヨル検索成績ニヨルトキハ有菌鼠ノ検出数ハ極メテ少ナクナル、尚動物試験ニヨレバヨリ正確ニ有菌鼠ヲ検出シ得テ而モ其ノ検出率ハ培養試験ニヨルヨリモ高クナリ、真ノ有菌鼠数ヲ知リ得タコトト思ハ

第10表 検索方法別ノ陽性率

検査方法	検査数	陽性数	陽性率(%)
剖 検	63	58	92.0
鏡 検	63	54	85.7
培 養	61	26	42.6
熱沈反應	45	20	44.4

レルケレドモ多数ニ就テ一々動物試験ヲスルコトハ實際問題トシテ困難デアルノデ、多数ノモノニ就テノ検索ハ矢張リ鏡検及培養ノ試験ニヨル他ハナイト思ハレル。

次ニ臓器熱沈降反應ガ果シテ特異性デアルカ否カノ問題ニ就テ観察スルニ春日ハ此ノ問題ニ就テ詳細ニ研究シタ結果抗 Envelope P 血清ハ「ペスト」感染動物臓器浸出液ト特異性ニ沈降反應ヲ起スノヲ認メ、此ノ方法ニヨツテ有菌鼠ノ検出ノ可能デアルコトヲ述ベタ、今回余等ハ氏ノ研究シタ成績ニ據ツテ特異性沈降反應ノミヲ示スト考ヘラレル診断血清ヲ用ヒテ臓器熱沈降反應ヲ行ツタノデアルガ、検査成績ヲ見ルト鏡検及培養共ニ陰性デアルニ拘ラズ此ノ反應ノ陽性ニ現ルルモノガアツタ、即チ明カニ低陽性反應ト思ハレルモノガアツタノデ此ノ反應ノ特異性ニ就テハ再検討スル必要ガアルト思ハレル、尚更ニ考ヘナケレバナラナイコトハ此ノ沈降反應ニ於テハ抗原ノ濃度ガ問題トナルコトデアル、即チ菌ノ上清液ヲ用ヒテ試験スル場合ニ於テモ其ノ菌量ガ微量ニ過ギル時ハ陽性ニ現レナイモノデアル、從ツテ有菌鼠ノ臓器ニ於ケル菌ノ分布濃度ニヨツテ成績ガ變ルモノデ、共ノ菌数ガ少イ時ニハ陰性ニ現レルノデハナカロウカト考ヘラレル、從ツテ是等ノ問題ヲ検討シテ果シテ此ノ方法ガ有菌鼠ノ検出ニ使用シ得ルカ否カガ検討サレナケレバナラナイデアラウ。

次ニ各臓器別ニ陽性数ヲ観察スレバ第11表ニ示ス如クニシテ鏡検及培養試験ハ孰レモ脾臓ニ於テ最モ陽性数多ク次ニ肝臓、次ニ淋巴腺ノ順序デアルケレドモ共ノ間ニハ大ナル差ハ認メラレナカツタ、之ハ有菌鼠ガ殆ド総テ全身感染ヲ起シテキルコトヲ示スモノデアルト考ヘラレル。

第11表 有菌鼠ノ臓器別陽性数

臓器 検査方法		剖検	鏡検	培養
淋巴腺	頸	8	2	0
	右鼠	39	14	9
	左鼠	43	31	13
	計	43	33	15
脾臓		43	45	21
肝臓		31	36	18
肺臓		31	37	18
心血			6	1

第6章 「ペスト」關係昆虫ニ就テノ菌検索成績

第5節 検索材料

新京及農安ニ於テ蒐集シタ生鼠及斃鼠ヨリ採取シタ「ケオピス」鼠蚤、「アニズス」鼠蚤、「ヨーロツパ」鼠蚤、人蚤、犬蚤、猫蚤、「ダニ」及「ペスト」患者或ハ患者ニ近接モル健康者ヨリ採取シタ人蚤及患者發生家屋ヨリ採取シタ南京蟲ニ就テ菌検索ヲ行ツタ。

526—10

第2節 検索方法

一定地域ヨリ蒐集シタ鼠體ニ附着シテキル蚤ヲ採取シ、其ヲ種類別ニ分類シ、1〜300匹位ノ間ノ適當ノ數ヲ1群トシテ検査シタ、卽チ1群トセル蚤ヲ豫メ滅菌シタ乳鉢ニ取リ普通ブイヨン」1.5ccヲ加ヘテ良ク磨潰シ、其ノ0.5cc宛ヲ3頭ノ海猽ノ右股部皮下ニ注射シテ動物試驗ヲ行ヒ、尙共ノ一部ヲ遠藤平板ニ移植シテ培養試驗ヲナシ、尙共ノ一部ニテ鏡檢標本ヲ作リ鏡檢試驗ヲ行ツタ、併シナガラ検査數ノ極メテ多イ時ニハ止ムナク動物試驗ヲ行ハナカツタ場合モアル。

第3節 検索成績

検査セル成績ハ第12表ニ示ス如クニシテ農安ノ材料ニ就テハ菌ヲ検出シ得ナカツタケレドモ新京ノ材料ニ就テハ「ケオビス鼠蚤ノ検査件數1,853ノ內陽性件數12ニシテ、「アニズス鼠蚤ノ検査件數558ノ內陽性件數ハ4デアツタ、「ヨーロツパ鼠蚤、人蚤、犬蚤、猫蚤、南京蟲、「ダニ」等ニ就テハ検査數モ少ナク陽性ナルモノモナカツタガ、人蝨ニ就テハ1例ニ於テ菌ヲ検出スルコトガ出來タ。

第12表 「ペスト關係昆蟲ニ就テノ菌検索成績

地域	昆 蟲 種 類	検査匹數	検査件數	陽性件數	陽 性 率 (%)
新	ケ オ ビ ス 鼠蚤	8,725	1,853	12	0.65
	ア ニ ズ ス 〃	2,334	558	4	0.41
	ヨ ー ロ ツ パ 〃	4	4	0	0
	人 蚤	3	2	0	0
	犬 蚤	91	3	0	0
	猫 蚤	3	1	0	0
京	蝨	6	4	1	25.0
	南 京 蟲	1	1	0	0
	ダ ニ	48	21	0	0
農	ケ オ ビ ス 鼠蚤	421	66	0	0
	ア キ ズ ス 〃	138	31	0	0
	ヨ ー ロ ツ パ 〃	3	3	0	0
	犬 蚤	36	0	0	0
安	猫 蚤	3	0	0	0
長春縣	ケ オ ビ ス 鼠蚤	35	20	0	0
	ア ニ ズ ス 〃	13	9	0	0

以上ノ成績ヨリ鼠ヨリ人ヘ病毒ヲ傳播スルモノハ「ケオビス鼠蚤及「アニズス鼠蚤デアリ、特ニ「ケオビス鼠蚤ガ大キナ役割ヲシテキルモノト考ヘラレル、尙患者ニ附着シテキタ蝨ニ菌ヲ検出スルコトガ出來タコトハ人ヨリ人ヘノ病毒ノ傳播ガ蝨ヲ介シテ起リ得ルコトヲ示ス成績デアルト云フコトガ出來ル。

次ニ菌検出ノ陽性デアルモノニ就テ検索方法別ニ其ノ成績ヲ觀察スレバ第13表ニ示ス如クニシテ動物試驗ニ於テ最モ検出數ガ多カツタ、鏡檢試驗ト培養試驗トハ陽性數ガ略〻同樣デアツタケ

596—11

レ……ヲ過常試験デハ雑菌ノ混入スルコト多ク菌ノ検出ハ可ナリ困難デアンタ、……口此ノ際ニハ純
粋以験ニヨル方ガ検出率ガ高イノデハナイカト考ヘラレタ、戦レ……ロ鼠等ノ如キモノカラ菌ヲ検
出スルニハ動物試験ニヨルノガ最モ良好デアルト思ハレル。

第13表 検索方法別ノ陽性件数

番 號	採取月日	件 歡 番 號	蚤 ノ 種 類	純培試驗	增菌試驗	動物試驗
1	7/X	蚤 1 號	ケオピス (10匹)	—	—	+
2	〃/〃	〃 2 〃	〃 (10〃)	—	—	+
3	〃/〃	〃 3 〃	〃 (1〃)	—	—	+
4	〃/〃	〃 7 〃	アーズス (10〃)	—	—	+
5	〃/〃	〃 5 〃	ケオピス (105〃)	+	+	+
6	〃/〃	〃 20 〃	〃 (53〃)	+	+	+
7	〃/〃	〃 21 〃	〃 (36〃)	+	+	+
8	〃/〃	〃 22 〃	〃 (1〃)	+	+	+
9	〃/〃	〃 6 〃	〃 (103〃)	+	+	+
10	〃/〃	〃 8 〃	アーズス (51〃)	+	+	+
11	〃/〃	〃 10 〃	ケオピス (47〃)	—	—	+
12	〃/〃	〃 11 〃	〃 (248〃)	—	—	+
13	〃/〃	〃 12 〃	〃 (21〃)	—	—	+
14	〃/〃	〃 13 〃	アーズス (24〃)	—	—	+
15	〃/〃	〃 30 〃	〃 (5〃)	+	—	+
16	〃/〃	〃 35 〃	ケオピス (1〃)	+	—	+
17	〃/〃	鼠 1 〃	衣 虱 (1〃)	—	—	+

結 語

今次流行ニ於テ患者及死亡者ニ就テ菌検索ヲ行ヒ、併セテ流行地域ニヲ捕獲シタ鼠族其其ノ附
着且盎ニ就テ菌検索ヲ行ツタ結果次ノ如キ成績ヲ得タ。

1、民間124檢ニ就テ菌検索ヲ行ツタ結果58檢ニ於テ「ペスト」菌ヲ検出シ、直各病関別ニ各臓器ニ
於ケル菌ノ検出率ヲ観察シタ結果「ペスト患者ハ敗血症ニテ死亡シテキル……ノ証明…………ヲ……
トガ思索タ。

2、「ペスト患者ニ就テ生前ニ淋巴腺穿刺液、喀痰（咽頭粘液ヲ含ム）、血液等ニ就テ菌検索ヲ行
ツタ結果「ペスト菌ヲ検出シ得タモノハ16人ニシテ、一般ニ「ペスト患者ヨリノ菌ノ検出ハ必
ズシモ容易デアタ、且疾病ノ經過ガ速カデアルノデ生前ニ菌ヲ検出シテ「ペスト」ヲ決定スル
コトハ比較的明瞭デアルコトヲ認メタ。

3、従来上治癒ト判定サレタ「ペスト恢復患者16人ニ就テ血液、淋巴腺穿刺液、喀痰、尿、皮膚
利□ノ膿汁等ト就テ菌検索ヲ行ツタ結果、一例ニ於テモ菌ヲ検出スルコトガ出来ナカツタ、此
ノ成績ヨリ「ペスト患者ニ於テハ恢復後長期ニ亘リ菌ヲ保有シテキルモノハナイ様ニ考ヘラレ
タ。

647

526—12

4、「ベスト容疑患者トシテ収容サレタモノ86人、同一家族内ニ「ベスト患者発生セルタメニ隔離サレタ健常者168人、農安縣城内流行地區ノ住民ニ就テ「ベスト」皮膚反應ヲ檢査シ、北ノ陽性ニ現レタモノ96人、北ノ他流行地區ノ住民215人、計565人ニ就テ淋巴腺穿刺液、喀痰、血液、尿等ニ就テ菌檢索ヲ行ツタ結果一例ニ於テモ菌ヲ檢出スルコトガ出來ナカツタ、即チ今次流行ニ於テハ「ベスト菌ノ健康菌保有者ヲ見出スコトハ出來ナカツタ。

5、流行地區ニ於テ捕獲セル鼠族ニ就テ菌檢索ヲ行ツタ結果、新京ニ於テハ「ドブネズミ」13,644頭中ヨリ63頭ノ有菌鼠ヲ檢出シ、農安ニ於テハ「ドブネズミ」325頭中ヨリ9頭ノ有菌鼠ヲ、「マンシウハツカネズミ」24頭ヨリハ1頭ノ有菌鼠ヲ檢出スルコトガ出來タ。

6、鼠體ニ附着シテヰタ蚤及患者或ハ患者ニ近接セル健康者ニ附着シテヰタ人蚤ニ就テ菌檢索ヲ行ツタ結果「ケオピス鼠蚤ハ檢査件數1,853ノ内陽性件數12、「アニズス鼠蚤ハ檢査件數558ノ内陽性件數4ニシテ、其ノ他ノ蚤ヨリハ菌ノ檢出ハ出來ナカツタ。
人蚤ニ就テハ一例ニ於テ菌ヲ檢出スルコトガ出來タ。

文　獻

1）倉内：滿洲醫學雜誌，（昭5）、12，671，827　　2）春日：細菌學報誌，昭14）、518，231　3）倉内、其ノ他：細菌學雜誌，（昭12）、493，121　　4）春日、其ノ他：大陸醫學，（昭16）、1，36　　　5）Leger, M. & Baury, A：C. R. acad. Sci., Paris, (1922), 175, 734　　6）Leger, M. & Baury, A：Bull. Soc. Path. exot., (1923), 16, 54

7）Tanon, L. & Cambessedes：Rev. Méd. Hyg. trop., (1923), 15, 65　　8）Uriarte, L：C. R. Soc. Biol., Paris, (1924), 91, 1089.　　9）Durand, P. & Conseil, E.：Arch. Inst. Pasteur, Tunis, (1927), 15, 93　　10）Nikanorov, S. M.：Seuchenbekämpfung der Infektionskrankheiten, (1927), 4, 140　　11）Christie：Jl. trop. Med. Hyg., (1911), 14, 147　　2）Zlatogoroff & Padlewski：Zur Bakteriologie der Lungenpest, Moskau, (1912)　　13）Wu lien-Teh：Manch. Plague prev. Serv. Rep., (1928), 5, 1　14）Gotschlich, E.　Zschr. Hyg., (1890), 32, 402　　15）阿部：大陸醫學，（昭16），1，3

4.2.6 昭和 15 年農安及新京ニ発生セル「ペスト」流行ニ就テ 第 4 編 流行ニ於テ分離セル「ペスト」菌ニ就テ

資料出处：日本国立国会図書館関西館蔵、博士論文。

内容点评：本资料为《陆军军医学校防疫研究报告》第 2 部第 537 号《关于昭和 15 年农安和新京发生的鼠疫流行 第 4 编 关于流行中鼠疫病菌的分离》，1943 年 4 月 12 日提交。

陸軍軍醫學校防疫研究報告
第2部　第537號

昭和15年農安及新京ニ發生セル「ペスト」流行ニ就テ

第4編　流行ニ於テ分離セル「ペスト菌ニ就テ

陸軍軍醫學校軍陣防疫學教室（主任　增田大佐）

陸軍軍醫少佐　高　橋　正　彦

第　　2　　部
原　　　　著
分類 　　441—1 　　330—41
受附　昭和 18. 4. 12

537—2

擔任指導　陸軍軍醫少將　石　井　四　郎

緒　　言

「ペスト菌ノ生物學的並ニ血淸學的性狀ニ關シテハ多數ノ研究業績ガ發表サレテキルノデ今更寧新シク述ベル必要ヲ認メナイケレドモ同一流行ニ於テ由來ヲ異ニシテ分離サレタ「ペスト菌株ガ同一性狀ヲ有スルモノデアルカ否カヲ知ルコトハ興味アルコトデアルト考ヘ、今次流行ニ於テ余等ガ患者、屍體、鼠、蚤、虱等ヨリ分離シタ「ペスト菌株110株ニ就テ一般ノ生物學的並ニ血淸學的性狀ヲ檢査シタノデ其ノ成績ニ就テ述ベル。

第1章　供試菌株ノ由來ニ就テ

供試セル菌株ハ余等ガ今次流行ニ於テ患者、屍體、鼠、蚤、虱等ニ就テ菌檢索ヲ行ツタ時ニ分離シタモノデ患者及屍體由來ノモノ71株、鼠由來ノモノ29株、蚤由來ノモノ9株、虱由來ノモノ1株計110株デアル、今其ヲ表ヲ以テ示セバ第1～5表ニ示ス如クニシテ、第1表ニ示スノハ昭和15年ノ前郭族調査所管內ニ於ケル原發流行地ニテ流行發生ノ當初ニ分離サレタ菌株ニシテ同調査所ヨリ分與ヲ受ケタモノデアル、第2表ニ示スノハ農安縣城ノ流行ニ於テ余等ガ「ペスト患者及

537—3

屍體ヨリ分離シタ菌株デアル、第3表ニ示スノハ新京ノ流行ニ於テ余等ガ「ペスト患者及屍體ヨリ分離シタ菌株デアル、第4表ニ示スノハ新京及農安ノ流行ニ於テ余等ガ流行地域ノ鼠ヨリ分離シタ菌株デアル、第5表ニ示スノハ新京ノ流行ニ於テ余等ガ蚤及虱ヨリ分離シタ菌株デアル、第6表ニ示スノハ對照トシテ使用シテ兼室保存ノ菌株デアル。

第1表　昭和15年前郭族調査所管內流行ニ於テ分離セル「ペスト菌株

番號	發生地	分離月日	氏名（患者）	性	年齡	科名	經過（日）	轉局	分離部位	普通寒天界面發育ノ況	粘稠性	大	小	S	R	大・小
1	大查縣 十八家戶	2/7	何忍子	女	9	腺ペスト	2	死	屍腺	卅	卅	＋	＋	＋	－	＋
2		19/7	何殿方	男	38	〃	4	〃	〃	卅	卄	＋	＋	＋	－	＋
3		14/7	譚德山	男	53	〃	1	治	生腺	卅	卅	＋	＋	＋	－	＋
4	大查縣城內	4/8	梁篤	男	72	〃	2	死	屍肝	卅	卅	－	＋	＋	－	＋
5		7/8	李劉氏	女	28	〃	5	〃	脾	卅	卅	＋	＋	＋	－	卄
6		7/8	蚤鐵且	男	6	〃	4	〃	〃	卅	卅	＋	＋	＋	－	＋
7		11/8	費丁桂	男	12	〃	1	〃	〃	卅	卅	＋	＋	＋	－	＋
8		8/9	郎德仁	男	57	〃	1	〃	〃	卅	卅	＋	＋	＋	－	卅
9		12/9	于馬氏	男	24	〃	不明	〃	肺	卅	卅	－	＋	＋	－	
10		24/9	王齊山	男	54	〃	〃	〃	腺	卅	卅	＋	＋	＋	－	
11	乾安縣城內	12/9	劉夢群	男	42	〃	6	〃	肺	卅	卅	－	＋	＋	－	卅
12	玉宇井	21/9	泠蒙子	男	7	〃	4	〃	腺	卅	卅	－	＋	＋	－	＋
13	民宇井	10/10	蔣泰香	女	13	〃	2	〃	肝	卅	卅	＋	＋	＋	－	＋
14	知宇井	12/10	曹林氏	女	52	〃	2	〃	〃	＋	卅	＋	＋	＋	－	＋
15	朱爾勒	20/9	尚寛氏	女	49	〃	1	〃	喉	卅	卅	－	＋	＋	－	卅
16	小土城子	24/9	石顥	男	57	〃	1	〃	〃	卅	卅	－	＋	＋	－	＋
17	雙鳳山	7/10	鑾達元	男	30	〃	7	〃	肺	卅	卅	－	＋	＋	－	卅
18	前郭族	11/10	馬小鹹	女	6	〃	2	〃	腎	卅	卅	＋	＋	＋	－	＋
19	新朋	18/10	孟陶氏	女	50	〃	7	〃	肺	卅	卅	＋	＋	＋	－	＋
20	扶餘縣 五家站	28/9	裴楷	男	57	〃	1	〃	肝	卅	卅	－	＋	＋	－	＋

　　註　　分離部位ノ屍腺ハ屍體ノ淋巴腺ヨリ分離セルコトヲ、生腺ハ生前ニ淋巴腺ヨリ分離セルコトヲ示ス、以下同様

537—4

第 2 表、昭和15年曇安縣域内流行ニ於テ分離セル「ペスト菌株

番號	分離月日	氏名(患者)			性	年齡	病名	經過(日)	轉歸	分離部位	普通寒天斜面		遠藤寒天平板上ノ集落				
											發育ノ況	皮膜粘稠性	大	小	S	R	最大小
21	11/7	呉	元	林	男	48	腺ペスト	4	死	屍 脾	╫	╫	+	+	+		╫
22	21/10	仲	永	太	男	6	皮膚ペスト	不明	ⅱ	ⅱ 腺	+	+	+	+	+		╫
23	ⅱ	仲	新	生	男	5	ペスト散血症	ⅱ	ⅱ	ⅱ 心血	╫	╫		+	+		╫
24	ⅱ	王	阜	氏	女	35	皮膚ペスト	ⅱ	ⅱ	ⅱ 腺	╫	╫		+	+		╫
25	ⅱ	李	畔	子	女	3	ⅱ	ⅱ	ⅱ	ⅱ 肝	╫	╫		+	+		+
26	ⅱ	李	永	生	男	50	腺ペスト	ⅱ	ⅱ	ⅱ 脾	╫	╫		+	+		╫
27	ⅱ	張	橋	子	女	48	皮膚ペスト	ⅱ	ⅱ	ⅱ 脾	╫	╫		+	+		+
28	22/10	李	鳳	英	女	18	ペスト散血症	ⅱ	ⅱ	ⅱ 脾	╫	╫		+	+		╫
29	ⅱ	高	小	娘	女	13	ⅱ	1	ⅱ	ⅱ 脾	╫	╫		+	+		╫
30	ⅱ	姜	朝	氏	女	51	ⅱ	不明	ⅱ	ⅱ 肝	╫	╫		+	￭		╫
31	ⅱ	李		甲	女	72	腺ペスト	ⅱ	ⅱ	ⅱ 肺	╫	╫		+	+		╫
32	ⅱ	買	頤	延	男	40	ⅱ	ⅱ	ⅱ	ⅱ 脾	╫	╫		+	+		╫
33	23/10	王	興	林	男	35	ⅱ	ⅱ	ⅱ	ⅱ 脾	╫	╫		+	+		╫
34	ⅱ	李		氏	女	30	ペスト散血症	ⅱ	ⅱ	ⅱ 腺	╫	╫	+	+	+		╫
35	ⅱ	强	九	子	女	8	腺ペスト	ⅱ	ⅱ	ⅱ 脾	╫	╫		+	+		╫
36	ⅱ	趙	白	氏	女	29	ペスト散血症	ⅱ	ⅱ	ⅱ 脾	╫	╫		+	+		╫
37	24/10	王	旺	興	男	45	腺ペスト	18	ⅱ	生 腺	╫	╫		+	+		╫
38	ⅱ	趙	永	年	男	31	ⅱ	不明	ⅱ	屍 脾	╫	╫		+	+		╫
39	ⅱ	字		財	男	51	ⅱ	2	ⅱ	ⅱ 心血	╫	╫		+	+		+
40	ⅱ	劉	興	臨	男	33	ⅱ	不明	ⅱ	ⅱ 脾	╫	╫		+	+		+
41	25/10	陳	傳	氏	女	63	ペスト散血症	2	ⅱ	ⅱ 脾	╫	╫		+	+		╫
42	ⅱ	張	英	子	女	15	腺ペスト		治	生 腺	╫	╫		+	+		╫
43	26/10	陳		三	女	8	肺ペスト	1	ⅱ	屍 脾	╫	╫	+	+	+		╫
44	ⅱ	傅	孫	子	女	52	腺ペスト	1	ⅱ	ⅱ 腺	╫	╫		+	+		╫
45	ⅱ	馬英	永	芳	女	31	ⅱ	2	ⅱ	ⅱ	+	+		+	+		╫
46	ⅱ	萬	國	斌	男	28	ⅱ	6	生	ⅱ	╫	╫		+	+		╫
47	27/10	盧		氏	女	62	肺ペスト	1	ⅱ	屍 脾	╫	╫		+	+		╫
48	ⅱ	張	香	子	女	6	腺ペスト	2	ⅱ	ⅱ 腺	╫	╫		+	+		╫
49	ⅱ			ⅱ	ⅱ	ⅱ	ⅱ	ⅱ	ⅱ	ⅱ 淋	╫	╫		+	+		╫
50	ⅱ	林		氏	女	22	ⅱ	不明	ⅱ	ⅱ 脾	╫	╫		+	+		╫
51	ⅱ	張	坨	子	男	10	ⅱ	ⅱ	ⅱ	ⅱ 脾	+	+		+	+		╫
52	1/10	福 ○ 綠	○		男	17		2	死	ⅱ 脾	╫	╫		+	+		+
53	2/10	蒋	秀	臣	男	25	ⅱ	4	ⅱ	ⅱ 心血	╫	╫		+	+		+
54	ⅱ	藤田	君	香	女	8	ⅱ	7	ⅱ	ⅱ	╫	╫		+	+		╫
55	3/10	田 島	天洋	子	女	8	ⅱ	4	ⅱ	ⅱ	╫	╫		+	+		╫
56	4/10	松 ○ 正	夫		男	23	ⅱ	4	ⅱ	ⅱ	╫	╫		+	+		╫
57	ⅱ	矢 野 ○	光		男	21	ⅱ	2	ⅱ	ⅱ 脾	╫	╫		+	+		╫
58	7/10	德 本 富 ○	子		女	12	ⅱ	5	ⅱ	ⅱ 心血	╫	╫		+	+		╫
59	8/10	李	德	金	男	10	ペスト散血症	2	ⅱ	ⅱ 脾	╫	╫		+	+		╫
60	ⅱ		ⅱ		男		ⅱ	ⅱ	ⅱ	生 流血	╫	╫		+	+		╫

537—5

第 3 表　昭和15年新京流行ニ於テ分離セル「ペスト菌株

番號	分離月日	氏名（患者）	性	年齡	病名	經過（日）	轉歸	分離部位	普通寒天發育ノ状況	表面粘稠性	大	小	S	R	染色大小
61	10/10	宋苷山	男	56	肺ペスト	5	死	屍脾	++	++	+	+	+		|||
62	11/10	陳賣玉	男	55	腺ペスト		〃	〃	〃	++	++	+	+	+	++
63	〃	黄黑氏	女	45	ペスト敗血症	不明	〃	〃	腺	++	++		+	+	++
64	〃	蕳良勉	男	27	腺ペスト	2	〃	〃	肝	++	++		+	+	++
65	13/10	筝德源	男	18	〃	3	〃	〃	腺	++			+	+	++
66	17/10	土屋〇シ	女	58	ペスト敗血症	6	〃	〃	肺	++	++		+	+	++
67	20/10	高松眞〇子	女	3	腺ペスト	20	〃	〃	心血	++	—		+	+	++
68	9/10	〃	〃	〃	〃		〃	生	腺	++	—		+	+	++
69	22/10	桃〇黍〇	男	31	皮膚ペスト	5	〃	屍	腺	++	++	+	+	+	++
70	12/11	張孝俊	男	46	ペスト敗血症	4	〃	〃	〃	++	++	+	+	+	++
71	15/10	尹叚橃	男	19	腺ペスト	2	〃	〃	〃	++	++	+	+	+	++

537—6

第4表 昭和15年新京及農安流行ニ於テ分離セル鼠由來「ベスト菌株

區別	番號	分離月日	鼠	番號	鼠種類	探取塲所	生死	分離部位	普通寒天斜面 頭育ノ況	粘稠性	遺瘻寒天平板上ノ集落 大	小	S	R	叠大ノ小
新	72	³/₁₀	鼠	1號	ドブネズミ	不　　明	斃	脾	⧺	⧺	+	+	+		⧻
	73	⁵/₁₀	〃	8號	〃	三角地帯	〃	〃	⧺	⧺	+	+	+		⧻
	74	¹⁰/₁₀	〃	76號	〃	〃	〃	〃	⧺	⧺	+	+	+		⧻
	75	¹³/₁₀	〃	343號	〃	〃	〃	〃	⧺	⧺	+	+	+		⧻
	76	〃		〃	〃	〃	〃	腺	⧺	⧺	+	+	+		⧻
	77	⁵/₁₀	〃	13號	〃	〃	拘	脾	⧺	⧺	+	+	+		⧻
	78	¹⁰/₁₀	〃	77號	〃	〃	〃	〃	⧺	⧺	+	+	+		⧻
	79	〃	〃	78號	〃	〃	〃	〃	⧺	⧺	+	+	+		⧻
	80	〃	〃	82號	〃	不　　明	〃	〃	⧺	⧺	+	+	+		⧻
	81	〃	〃	150號	〃	三角地帯	〃	〃	⧺	⧺		+	+’		+
	82	¹²/₁₀	〃	240號	〃	露月町	〃	〃	⧺	⧺		+	+		⧻
	83	〃	〃	259號	〃	三角地帯	〃	〃	⧺	⧺		+	+		⧻
	84	〃	〃	〃	〃	〃	〃	腺	⧺	⧺		+	+		⧻
	85	〃	〃	〃	〃	〃	〃	心血	⧺	⧺	+	+			⧻
	86	〃	〃	294號	〃	東二條通	〃	脾	⧺	⧺		+	+		⧻
京	87	〃	〃	320號	〃	八島通	〃	〃	⧺	⧺	+	+	+		⧻
	88	¹³/₁₀	〃	286號	〃	東二條通	〃	〃	⧺	⧺		+	+		⧻
	89	〃	〃	385號	〃	三角地帯	〃	〃	⧺	⧺		+	+		⧻
	90	¹⁷/₁₀	〃	688號	〃	四角地帯	〃	〃	⧺	⧺		+	+		+
	91	¹⁸/₁₀	〃	658號	〃	〃	〃	〃	⧺	⧺		+	+		⧻
	92	〃		〃	〃	〃	〃	腺	⧺	⧺		+	+		⧻
	93	〃	〃	682號	〃	三角地帯	〃	脾	⧺	⧺		+	+		⧺
	94	〃		〃	〃	〃	〃	腺	⧺	⧺		+	+		⧺
	95	〃	〃	690號	〃	四角地帯	〃	脾	⧺	⧺		+	+		+
	96	²⁵/₁₀	〃	3,983號	〃	散步關	〃	〃	⧺	⧺		+	+		⧻
	97	⁴/₁₀	〃	25,230號	〃	四角地帯	〃	〃	⧺	⧺		+	+		⧻
農	98	²⁶/₁₀	鼠	136號	ハツカネズミ	農安城門外甬關	斃	脾	⧺	⧺	+	+	+		⧻
	99	〃		〃	〃	〃	〃	腺	⧺	⧺	+	+	+		⧻
安	100	²⁷/₁₀	鼠	155號	ドブネズミ	山儒屯	〃	〃	⧺	⧺	+	+	+		⧻

537一

第5表　昭和15年新京流行ニ於テ分離セル蚤由来及鼠由来「ペスト」菌株

區別	番號	分離月日	蚤番號	蚤ノ種類	蚤ノ採捕場所	普通寒天斜面 發育ノ狀況	粘稠性	遠藤寒天平板上ノ集落 大	小	S	R	最大小
蚤	101	10/10	蚤5號	ケオピス(105匹)	三角地帯	++	++		+	++		++
	102	11/10	〃6號	〃(103〃)	〃	++	++		+	+		++
	103	12/10	〃10號	〃(47〃)	四角地帯	++	++		+	+		++
	104	13/10	〃11號	〃(262〃)	第一地區	++	++		+	+	+	++
	105	14/20	〃12號	〃(22〃)	三角地帯及第三地區	++	++		+	++		++
	106	9/10	〃7號	アニ-ズス(10〃)	三角地帯	++	++		+	++		++
	107	10/10	〃8號	〃(51〃)	四角地帯	++	++		+	++		++
	108	14/19	〃13號	〃(10〃)	三角地帯	++	++		+	++		++
鼠	109	13/10	〃9號	〃(10〃)	四角地帯	++	++		+	+		++
	110	13/10	鼠1號	衣鼠(1〃)	李德金ニ附着シアタリセノ	++	++		+	+		++

第6表　對照トシテ使用セル棄室保存「ペスト菌株」

番號	菌株名	由来	分離年月日	普通寒天斜面 發育ノ狀況	粘稠性	遠藤寒天平板上ノ集落 大	小	S	R	毒力 最大小	毒力	グリセ分解
111	No. 1	Otten ノ "Tjiwidej" 株	1929	++	++	+	+	+		++	弱	-
112	No. 2	Giroard ノ "E.V." 株	1926	++	++	+	+	+		++	少	-
113	No. 7	「ペスト患者本校保存次水株	?	++	++	+	+	+		++	少	-
114	No. 1004	腺ペスト患者、満洲ニテ分離	昭8	++	++	+	+	+		++	强	-
115	No. 105	腺ペスト患者、満洲ニテ分離	昭13	++	++	+	+	+		++	少	+
116	No. 6	腺ペスト患者、満洲ニテ分離	昭8	++	++	+	+	+		++	少	+

是等ノ表ニ於テ明カデアル如ク供試セル菌株ハ満洲ニ於ケル同一年度ノ流行ニ於テ流行發生地ヲ異ニシ且流行ノ時期(初期、中期、末期)ヲ異ニシテ「ペスト患者及屍體ヨリ分離サレタモノニシテ、同一個體ニ於テ生前ニ分離サレタモノ及死後ニ分離サレタモノガアリ、又分離局所ヲ異ニスルモノガアル、其ノ他同一流行地ノ鼠族ヨリ分離サレタモノ及其ニ附着シテ来タ蚤ヨリ分離サレタモノ或ハ患者ニ附着シテ来タ蚤ヨリ分離サレタモノガアル。

是等110株ノ「ペスト菌」ノ生物學的並ニ血清學的性狀ヲ檢査セルニ殆ド總テガ同樣ノ性狀ヲ示シタケレドモ唯其ノ内ノ1株(高〇眞〇子患者ヨリ分離シタ菌株デアル)ノミガ37℃ニテ培養スルモ粘稠性ヲ缺キ他ト一見シテ異ナル性狀ヲ示シタノデ之ニ就テハ別ニ報告シタ(「ペスト菌ノ非粘稠性變異ニ關スル研究)

第2章　供試菌株ノ生物學的性狀
第1節　形態並ニ運動

供試セル流行株ハ對照タル保存株ト同樣ニ兩端濃染セル兩端鈍圓ノ短桿菌ニシテ、保存株ニ比シテ梢ミ其ノ大イサ大ニシテ且其ノ形ハ短キ太キ感ガアツタ、「グラム」陰性ニシテ鞭毛及芽胞ヲ

537—8.

有セズ、懸滴標本ニヨツテ運動ヲ検査スルニ孰レノ菌株ニ就テモ固有運動ハ認メラレナカツタ。

第2節 培養性状

1. 普通寒天斜面培養性状　普通寒天斜面ニ37°Cニテ培養シ、其ノ發育性状ヲ検査スルニ24時間ニテハ薄キ菌苔ヲ作リ、45時間ニテハ相當厚キ菌苔トナリ、半透明灰白色ニシテ表面濕潤シ、光澤ナク、白金耳ヲ以テ菌苔ノ粘稠性ヲ検査スルニ粘稠性強ク糸ヲ引クノヲ認メタ、20°C以下ノ培養温度ニ於テハ菌苔ハ粘稠性ヲ缺除シテキタ、菌株ニヨル差異ハ殆ド認メラレナカツタ。

2. 普通ブイヨン培養性状　普通ブイヨン」ニ一白金耳量ヲ移植シテ37°Cニ於テ培養スルニ24時間後ニハ培養液價カ混濁シ、管底ニ僅カニ沈澱ヲ生ジ、48時間後ニハ培養液ノ混濁ハ著明ニナルモ、微細顆粒状菌塊ノ浮游スルヲ認メズ、管底ノ沈澱ハ次第ニ多クナリ、更ニ時間ヲ經過スル時ハ液面ノ管壁ニ沿フテ菌膜様ノモノヲ生ジ、其ヨリ鐘乳状ニ菌塊ノ沈降スルノガ見ラレタ、菌株ニヨツテ混濁ノ強イモノ或ハ管底ノ沈澱ノ多イモノガアツタ、尚25°C以下ノ温度ニテ培養スル時ハ培養液ハ比較的清澄ニシテ全體ニ微細顆粒状ノ菌塊ノ多数ニ浮游スルノヲ認メ且管底ノ沈澱ノ多イノヲ認メタ。

第2節 聚落ノ性状

1. 普通寒天平板上ノ聚落　普通寒天平板ニ一白金耳量ヲ移植シ、37°Cニテ培養シ、孤立セル聚落ヲ作ラセテ詳細ニ観察スルニ24時間ニテハ「ルウペ」ニテ僅カニ認メ得ル露滴状ノ小サナ聚落ニシテ48時間ニテハ聚落ハ次第ニ大キナリ、圓形ニシテ隆起シ、恰モ饅頭型ヲ呈シ、灰白色ニシテ表面ハ比較的平滑ナルモ光澤ナク透過光線ニテハ半透明ニシテ稍ミ青味ガカレル青白色ヲ呈シテキタ、尚聚落ノ周圍ニハ透明ニシテ鋸曲状ヲ呈スル輪量ガ認メラレタ、又菌株ニヨツテ大、小ノ聚落ヲ混在スルモノガ多カツタ、而シテ聚落ノ性状モ菌株ニヨツテ若干ノ差異ガ認メラレ、表面ノ比較的平滑ナモノガアリ、又比較的扁平ナモノ或ハ隆起セルモノガアリ、又輪暈ノ大キサモ其ノ程度ハ様々ニシテ極メテ廣ク且厚キモノヨリ殆ド認メラレザルニ至ル種々ノ階段ガアツタ、是等ノ性状ノ差異ハ培養條件ニヨツテ容易ニ變化シ、其ノ間ニ一定ノ關係ヲ認メルコトハ出来ナカツタ。

2. 遠藤寒天平板上ノ聚落　普通寒天平板ニ於ケルヨリ發育良好ニシテ48時間後ニハ圓形ニシテ隆起セル聚落ヲ形成シ、其ノ表面ハ光澤ナキモ普通寒天平板上ノ其ニ比シテ極メテ平滑デアツタ、透過光線ニテハ半透明ニシテ培地ノ色ヲ取ツテ薄桃色ヲ呈シテキタ、尚聚落ニヨツテ「フクシン」ノ赤色ノ極メテ著明ニ現レテキルモノカラ殆ド「フクシン」ノ赤色ノ現レテキナイモノニ至ル種々ノ階段ガアツタ、又菌株ニヨツテ大、小ノ聚落ヲ混ズルモノガアツタ、聚落ノ周圍ノ輪暈モ菌株ニヨツテ大、小様々ノ像ヲ呈シテキタ（第1~6表参照）

657

537—9

第4節　「インドール反應

普通ブイヨン」及「ペプトン水＝各菌株ノ一白金耳量ヲ移植シテ37°C＝テ培養シ、5日目及10日目＝「インドール」産生ノ有無ヲ検査シタ、「インドール反應ノ検査ハ北里、ザルコスキー氏法及エールリツヒ氏法＝ヨツタ、其ノ結果各菌株ハ執レモ「インドール反應陰性デアツタ。

第5節　含水炭素分解試驗

各種糖(純粋ナモノヲ選定使用ス)ヲ1％ノ割合＝加ヘタ「ペプトン水(pH7.2)＝各菌株ノ一白金耳ヲ移植シテ37°Cノ孵卵器內＝置キ2週間＝亘リ其ノ糖分解能ヲ検査セル成績ハ第7表＝示ス如クニシテ各菌株ノ間＝ハ糖分解性ノ差異ヲ認メルコトハ出來ナカツタ、而シテ流行株ハ總ネ3～4日＝テ「グリセリン」ヲ分解シタノデ倉內ノ所謂α型菌デアルコトガ判ツタ。

第7表　糖　分　解　試

區別	株糖	グリセリン	グルコーゼ	キシロ―ゼ	マルト―ゼ	マンニット	マンノ―ゼ	サリシン	ガラクトーゼ	アラビノーゼ	レヱブローゼ	デキストリン	トレハローゼ	サツカローゼ	アドニット	ラムノ―ゼ	ラクト―ゼ	イヌリン	ズルチット	ラフイノーゼ	グリコーゲン	イノジツト
流行株	1～110	+3~4	+1	+2	+1	+2	+2	+2	+2	+2	+1	+1	+1	—	—	—	—	—	—	—	+	—
保存株	111～114	—	+1	+2	+1	+2	+2	+2	+2	+2	+1	+1	+1	—	—	—	—	—	—	—	+	—
保存株	115～116	+3~4	+1	+2	+1	+2	+2	+2	+2	+2	+1	+1	+1	—	—	—	—	—	—	—	+	—

註　＋＝ハ2日目＝能分解陽性＝現レシコトヲ示ス。

第6節　働性血淸ノ有スル「アレキシン」＝對スル抵抗試驗

1. 海狽働性血淸ヲ以テセル試驗

検査方法　新鮮ナ海狽働性血淸0.5cc＝被検菌株ノ普通寒天37°C45時間培養菌ヲ以テ1cc10⁻⁴mgノ生理的食鹽水菌浮游液ヲ作リ、其ノ0.5ccヲ加ヘ、混合セルモノヲ37°Cノ孵卵器內＝於テ作用セシメ、直後、4時間後、24時間後ニ其ノ0.1ccノ有スル生菌數ヲ計算シテ「アレキシン作用＝對スル抵抗ノ有無ヲ検査シタ、菌數ノ計算ハ血淸ト菌液ヲ混合セルモノヲ0.1cc抱遠藤平板2枚＝取リ、其ヲコンラーヂ棒＝テ平等＝塗布セル後37°C＝テ45時間培養シ、發生セル聚落ノ數ヲ計算シテ2枚ノ遠藤平板ノ値ヲ平均シ、其ヲ0.1ccノ有スル生菌數トシタ。

検査成績　流行株ハ保存株ト同樣＝總テ海狽ノ血淸「アレキシン作用＝對シテ抵抗性ヲ有シ、其ノ中＝テ盛＝增殖スルノヲ認メタ、其ノ検査成績ノ一部ヲ示セベ第8表ノ如クデアル。

537—10

第8表　海猽「アレキシン」ニ對スル抵抗試驗

區別	菌株	血清成績		菌　　　　　數		
			0　時	4　時	2 4 時
流行株	5	M 1		860	∞
		〃 2		840	∞
		對	720	780	∞
	25	M 1		860	∞
		〃 2		820	∞
		對	730	760	∞
	75	M 1		780	∞
		〃 2		760	∞
		對	690	680	∞
	103	M 1		940	∞
		〃 2		880	∞
		〃	840	820	∞
保存菌	No. 1	M 1		730	∞
		〃 2		860	∞
		對	720	760	∞

註　1)　數字ハ菌數ヲ示ス。
　　2)　對照ハ血清ノ代リ=「ゾイヨン」ヲ以テセル成績ヲ示ス。

2. 家兎働性血清ヲ以テセル試驗

　　海猽血清ニ於ケル場合ト同樣ニシテ新鮮ナ家兎働性血清ノ「アレキシン作用ニ對スル抵抗ヲ
檢査セルニ流行株ハ保存株ト同樣ニ總テ之ニ對シテ抵抗性ヲ有スルコトヲ認メタ、其ノ檢査成
績ノ一部ヲ示セバ第9表ノ如クデアル。

第9表　感兎「アレキシジ」ニ對スル抵抗試験

區別	菌株	血清	成績 0 時	4 時	2 4 時
流行株	5	K 1		780	∞
		〃 2		760	∞
		對	680	640	∞
	25	K 1		880	∞
		〃 2		840	∞
		對	780	820	∞
	75	K 1		780	∞
		〃 2		820	∞
		對	730	750	∞
	103	K 1		820	∞
		〃 2		860	∞
		對	680	720	∞
保存株	No. 1	K 1		860	∞
		〃 2		830	∞
		對	740	760	∞

第7節　毒力試験

實驗方法　　體重250g前後ノ海猏ヲ使用シ、被檢菌株ノ普通寒天37°C 45時間培養菌ヲ以テ生理的食鹽水菌浮游液ヲ作リ、各遞減量ノ0.5cc宛ヲ各ミ 3頭ヲ1組トセル海猏ノ右大腿部皮下ニ注射シ、16日間觀察シ斃死セルモノハ剖檢及臓器培養試驗ヲナシ、「ペスト菌ニヨル斃死ナルカ否カヲ判定シ、「ペスト菌以外ニヨル斃死ハ生殘セルモノト見做シタ。

實驗成績　　流行株ノ中ヨリ人由來ノモノ、鼠由來ノモノ、蚤由來ノモノ、蝨由來ノモノヲ適當ニ抽出シテ海猏ニ對スル毒力ヲ檢査セルニ第10表ノ如キ成績ヲ得タ、即チ人由來ノ内流行發生初期ニ分離シタモノガ流行末期ニ分離シタモノニ比シテ若干菩毒力ノ弱イ感ガアツタ、併シナガラ其ノ著シイ差デハナカツタ、種々ノ點ヨリ考察シテ流行初期ノ菌ノ毒力ハ末期ノモノニ比シテ弱イモノト考ヘラレルケレドモ、之ハ人ペスト」發生以前ニ鼠族ヨリ菌ヲ分離シ、其ニ就テ檢査スルコトニヨツテ確メラレルモノト思ハレル、人體ヲ1回デモ通過スレバ「ペスト菌ノ毒力ハ低ニ上昇スルモノデアルカラ余等ノ檢査セル此ノ成績ニ於テ見ル如ク流行發生初期ニ人體ヨリ分離セル菌株デモ强キ毒力ヲ保有シテヰルノハ當然ノコトト思ハレル。

537—12

第10表　海猽ニ對スル毒力試驗

區別	由來	菌株	菌量(mg) 10⁻³	10⁻⁴	10⁻⁵	10⁻⁶	10⁻⁷	10⁻⁸
流行株	人	1	³/₃	³/₃	³/₃	²/₃	¹/₃	⁰/₃
		11	〃	⁴/₃	〃	〃	⁰/₃	〃
		19	〃	³/₃	〃	³/₃	²/₃	〃
		20	〃	〃	〃	〃	⁰/₃	〃
		21	〃	〃	²/₃	²/₃	¹/₃	〃
		30	〃	〃	³/₃	³/₃	²/₃	¹/₃
		35	〃	〃	〃	〃	〃	⁰/₃
		52	〃	〃	〃	²/₃	〃	〃
		55	〃	〃	〃	³/₃	³/₃	¹/₃
		60	〃	〃	²/₃	〃	²/₃	〃
		65	〃	〃	³/₃	〃	¹/₃	⁰/₃
		69		〃	〃	〃	²/₃	¹/₃
		71		〃	〃	〃	³/₃	⁰/₃
	鼠	72	³/₃	³/₃	³/₃	³/₃	¹/₃	¹/₃
		73			〃	〃	〃	〃
		80			〃	〃	²/₃	〃
		85			〃	〃	³/₃	〃
		92	³/₃	³/₃	〃	²/₃	¹/₃	〃
		94		〃	〃	³/₃	²/₃	〃
		95			〃	〃	²/₃	〃
		97		〃	〃	²/₃	²/₃	〃
		98		〃	〃	³/₃	¹/₃	〃
		100		〃	〃	〃	³/₃	〃
	蚤	101		³/₃	³/₃	³/₃	²/₃	¹/₃
		105		〃	〃	²/₃	〃	0
		106		〃	〃	³/₃	〃	⁰/₃
	虱	110		³/₃	³/₃	³/₃	²/₃	¹/₃
保存株	人	No.1004		³/₃	³/₃	²/₃	²/₃	⁰/₃
		No.105		〃	〃	〃	¹/₃	〃

註　分母ハ試驗頭數、分子ハ「ペスト」ニヨル斃死數ヲ示ス。

斯レニセヨ菌ノ毒力ガ流行間ニ如何ナル消長ヲ示スカヲ知ルコトハ流行ノ發生、終熄ニ對スル考察ヲスル上ニ極メテ重要ナ要素ヲナスモノデアルカラ此ノ問題ノ可及的速カニ究明セラレルコトヲ望ムモノデアル。

次ニ同一流行ニ於テ鼠ヨリ分離セルモノ（斃鼠ヨリ分離セルモノト生鼠ヨリ分離セルモノガアリ、又淋巴腺ヨリ分離セルモノト肝臟、脾臟、肺臟ヨリ分離セルモノガアル）及其ニ附着シテキタ蚤（「ケオピス鼠蚤及「アニズス鼠蚤）ヨリ分離セルモノ及患者ニ附着シテキタ人虱ヨリ分離セルモノハ總テ殆ド同樣ノ強イ毒力ヲ保有シテキタ、此ノ成績ヨリ感染源ガ鼠族デアリ且其ヲ傳播ス

ルモノガ蚤(「ケオピス鼠蚤及「アニズス鼠蚤)デアルコトガ明カデアル。尚人鼠ガ人ヨリ人ヘノ傳
播ニ大キナ役割ヲ演ジテキルコトモ想像ニ難クナイ。

次ニ故ニ興味强キコトハ流行ノ末期ニ鼠ヨリ分離シタ菌株ガ總テ强キ毒力ヲ保有スルコトデア
ル、而モ是等ノ鼠ノ內ニハ生存シテキタモノガ多イコトヨリ考ヘルト此等ノ鼠族ガ所謂慢性ペス
ト」ニナツテ病毒ヲ越年スルノデハナイカト考ヘラレル、而シテ慢性ペスト」ノ現レルノハ流行
ノ末期ニ「ペスト菌ノ毒力ガ低下スル爲デハナクテ、鼠族ガ流行期間中ニ潜伏性感染ヲ起シ、其ニ
ヨツテ免疫ヲ獲得スル爲デハナカロウカト考ヘラレル、是等ノ問題ハ流行地ニテ捕獲セル鼠ヲ長
期ニ亙リ飼育シテ然ル後ニ剖檢シテ尙臟器ヨリ菌ヲ檢出シ得レバ明カニナシ得ルモノデアロウ、
尚慢性ペスト」鼠ノ出現ハ鼠ガ免疫ヲ獲得セルニ因ルカ否カヘ流行初期ト流行末期ニ捕獲セル鼠
族ニ就テ「ペスト菌感染ニ對スル抵抗ヲ檢査スレバ明カニナシ得ルモノデアロウ、今回ハ防疫業
務ニ追ハレテ是等ノ問題ヲ研究スル暇ガナカツタノデ是等ノ點ニ就テハ將來ノ研究ヲ期待スル次
第デアル。

第3章　供試菌株ノ血清學的性狀
第1節　抗原性ニ就テ
1. 被凝集性檢査成績

供試菌株ヲ以テ菌液ヲ調製シ、其ヲ以テNo.1株免疫家兎血清ニ對スル被凝集性ヲ檢査シタ。

檢査方法

免疫血清　No.1株ノ普通寒天37°C45時間培養菌ノ一定量ヲ生理的食鹽水ニ浮游サセ、
60°C30分ニテ殺菌シタモノヲ抗原トシテ2.5mg, 2.5mg, 5mg, 10mg, 10mgノ各菌量ヲ
夫々5日間隔ニテ家兎ノ耳靜脈內ニ接種シ、最後ノ注射ヨリ10日目ニ至採血シテ血清ヲ分離
シ、其ヲ非働性トシタモノヲ使用シタ。

菌液ノ調製　1%フオルマリン」加生理的食鹽水ヲ以テ供試菌株ノ普通寒天37°C45時間
培養菌ノ1cc 1mgノ菌浮游液ヲ作ツテ使用シタ。

檢査術式　遞減稀釋法ニヨツテ生理的食鹽水ヲ以テ培數稀釋セル免疫血清0.5cc宛ニ上記
ノ菌液ヲ0.5cc宛加ヘ、良ク振盪混和シタ後37°Cノ孵卵器內ニ於テ作用サセ、凡ソ20時間後
ニ取出シテ直チニ成績ヲ檢査シタ、肉眼的ニ檢査セル成績ハ其ノ程度ニヨツテ××、××、
×及册、册、+(×ハ雲絮狀凝集、十ハ顆粒狀凝集ヲ表ハスモノトス)トシテ記載シ、「ア、キ
ノスコープ」ニヨル檢査成績ハ册、册、十トシタ

檢査成績

檢査セル成績ハ第11表ニ示ス如クニシテ菌株ニヨツテ若干ノ差異ハ認メラレタガ血清稀釋
160倍乃至640倍迄雲絮狀ノ凝集反應ヲ起シ、珠ニ320倍迄凝集反應ヲ起スモノガ多カツタ、人由
來株、鼠由來株、蚤由來株ノ間ニハ差異ナク、又保存株トノ間ニモ差異ハ認メラレナカツタ、唯
67株、68株ハ顆粒狀ノ凝集ヲ起シタガ之ハ非粘稠性變異菌デアツテ、之ニ就テハ別ニ報告ス

537—14

第11表 被檢菌性檢查成績(其ノ1)

區別	菌株＼血清稀釋	No.105株 免疫家兔血清								
		20	40	80	160	320	640	1,280	2,560	K
人	1	×××	××	××	×	⊥	—	—	—	—
	2	×××	××	×	×	⊥	⊥	—	—	—
	3	×××	××	××	×		⊥	—	—	—
	4	×××	××	××	××	+	⊥	—	—	—
	5	×××	×××	××	××	×	⊥	—	—	—
	6	×××	××	××	××	×		—	—	—
	7	×××	×××	××	××	×	⊥	—	—	—
	8	×××	××	××	××	×	⊥	—	—	—
	9	×××	×××	××	××	×	⊥	—	—	—
	10	×××	××	××	××	×	⊥	—	—	—
	11	×××	××	××	××	×	⊥	—	—	—
	12	×××	×××	××	××	×	⊥	—	—	—
	13	×××	×××	××	××	×	⊥	—	—	—
	14	×××	××	××	××	×	⊤	—	—	—
	15	×××	××	××	××	×	⊥	—	—	—
	16	×××	××	××	××	×	⊥	—	—	—
	17	×××	×××	××	××	×	⊥	—	—	—
申	18	×××	××	××	××	×	⊥	—	—	—
	19	×××	××	××	×	⊥	—	—	—	—
	20	×××	×××	××	××		⊥	—	—	—
	21	×××	××	××	××	×	⊥	—	—	—
	22	×××	××	××	××	×	⊥	—	—	—
	23	×××	×××	××	××	×	⊥	—	—	—
	24	×××	××	××	××	××	×	⊥	—	—
	25	×××	×××	××	×	⊥		⊥	—	—
	26	×××	××	××	××	×	⊥	—	—	—
	27	×××	××	××	××	×	⊥	—	—	—
	28	×××	××	××	××	×	⊥	—	—	—
	29	×××	××	××	××	×	⊥	—	—	—
	30	×××	××	××	××	×	⊥	—	—	—
黍	31	×××	××	××	××	×	⊥	—	—	—
	32	×××	××	××	××	×	⊥	—	—	—
	33	×××	××	××	××	×	⊥	—	—	—
	34	×××	××	××	×	⊥	—	—	—	—
	35	×××	××	××	×	⊥	—	—	—	—
	36	×××	××	××	×	⊥	—	—	—	—
	37	×××	×××	××	××	⊥	⊥	—	—	—
	38	×××	×××	××	××	××	×	+	⊤	—
	39	×××	××	××	××	×	+	⊤	—	—
	40	×××	××	××	××	×	⊥	—	—	—

第11表　被沼集性检查成绩（其/2）

區別	血清稀釋 血清型株	No.105 株兔疫家兎血清								
		20	40	80	160	320	640	1,280	1,250	K
人	41	×××	××	××	××	×	±	—	—	—
	42	×××	××	××	××	×	±	—	—	—
	43	×××	××	××	××	×	±	—	—	—
	44	×××	××	××	×	±	±	—	—	—
	45	×××	××	××	×	±	—	—	—	—
	46	×××	××	××	×	±	—	—	—	—
	47	×××	××	××	×	±	—	—	—	—
	48	×××	××	××	×	±	—	—	—	—
	49	×××	×××	××	××	×	±	—	—	—
	50	×××	×××	××	××	×	±	—	—	—
由	51	×××	××	××	××	×	±	—	—	±
	52	×××	××	××	××	×	±	—	—	±
	53	×××	××	××	××	±	—	—	—	±
	54	×××	×××	××	××	×	±	—	—	±
	55	×××	××	××	×	±	—	—	—	±
	56	×××	××	××	×	±	—	—	±	±
	57	×××	××	××	×	±	—	—	±	±
	58	×××	×××	××	××	×	±	—	±	±
	59	×××	××	××	×	±	—	—	±	±
	60	×××	××	××	×	±	—	—	±	±
來	61	×××	×××	××	××	×	±	—	±	±
	62	×××	×××	××	××	×	±	±	±	±
	63	×××	×××	××	××	×	±	—	±	±
	64	×××	××	××	××	×	±	—	±	±
	65	×××	××	××	××	±	±	—	±	±
	66	×××	××	××	×	±	—	—	—	±
	67	++	+	+	+	±	±	±	±	±
	68	++	+	+	+	±	±	±	±	±
	69	×××	××	××	××	×	±	—	±	±
	70	×××	××	××	×	×	±	—	±	±
	71	×××	××	××	×	±	±	—	±	±
鼠	72	×××	××	××	×	±	—	—	—	—
	73	×××	××	×	×	±	—	—	—	—
	74	×××	×××	××	××	××	—	—	—	—
	75	×××	××	××	××	×	±	—	—	—
由	76	×××	××	××	×	±	—	—	—	—
	77	×××	××	××	×	±	—	—	—	—
	78	×××	××	××	×	±	±	—	—	—
來	79	×××	××	××	×	±	—	±	—	—
	80	×××	××	××	××	×	—	—	—	—

'537—16

第11表　菌凝集性検査成績（其ノ3）

區別	菌株	No.105 株兔疫家兎血清								
	血清稀釋	20	40	80	130	820	640	1,280	2,560	K
鼠	81	×××	××	××	××	×	十	—	—	—
	82	×××	××	××	×	十	—	—	—	—
	83	×××	××	××	×	十	—	—	—	—
	84	×××	××	××·	××	十	—	—	—	—
	85	×××	××	××	×	十	—	—	—	—
	86	×××	×××	××	××	×	十	—	—	—
	87	×××	××	××	×	十	—	—	—	—
	88	×××	××	××	×	十	—	—	—	—
由	89	×××	×××	××	××	×	十	—	—	—
	90	×××	××	××	××	×	十	—	—	—
	91	×××	××	××	×	十	—	—	—	—
	92	×××	××	××	×	十	—	—	—	—
	93	×××	×××	××	××	×	十	—	—	—
	94	×××	××	××	××	十	—	—	—	—
	95	×××	×××	××	××	十	—	—	—	—
来	96	×××	××	××	×	十	—	—	—	—
	97	×××	××	××	×	十	—	—	—	—
	98	×××	××	××	×	×	十	—	十	—
	99	×××	××	××	×	×	—	—	—	—
	100	×××	××	××	×	十	—	—	—	—
蚤	101	×××	××	××	×	十	—	—	—	—
	102	×××	××	××	×	十	—	—	—	—
	103	×××	××	××	×	×	十	—	—	—
	104	×××	××	××	×	十	—	—	—	—
	105	×××	××	××	×	十	—	—	—	—
由	106	×××	××	××	×	十	—	—	—	—
	107	×××	×××	××	××	××	×	十	—	—
来	108	×××	××	××	×	×	十	—	—	—
	109	×××	××	××	××	×	十	—	—	—
	110	×××	××	××	×	—	—	—	—	—
對	111	×××	××	××	×	十	—	—	—	—
	112	×××	××	××	×	十	—	—	—	—
	113	×××	××	××	×	×	十	—	—	—
	114	×××	××	××	××	×	十	—	—	—
照	115	×××	××	××	×	×	十	—	—	—
	116	×××	××	××	×	十	—	—	—	—

註　×××……凝集菌塊ノ沈降シテ上清ノ澄明ナモノ。

　　×× ……×××ト×ノ中間ニ位スルモノ。

　　× ………肉眼的ニ見得ル凝集菌塊ノ浮游スルモノ。

537－17

2. 沈降原性検査成績

　供試菌株ヲ以テ抗原ヲ作リ、其ヲ以テNo.1株免疫家兎血清ニ對スル沈降反應ヲ検査シタ。

　検査方法　　検査方法ハUhlenhuth氏ノ重畳法ニヨリ抗原ハ供試菌株ノ普通寒天37°C45時間培養菌ヲ以テ1cc1.0mgノ生理的食塩水菌液ヲ作リ、之ヲ20分間煮沸シ、強力遠心沈降シタ上清ヲ取ツテ用ヒ、斯クシテ調製セル抗原ヲ生理的食塩水ヲ以テ倍数稀釋ヲナシ、其ヲ前述ノ家兎免疫血清ニ重畳シテ検査シタ、成績ノ判定ハ30分間室温ニ放置セル後ノ重畳面ニ現ハレル白色輪環ノ程度ニヨツテ行ヒ白色輪環ノ明瞭ニ認メラレルモノヲ＋トシ、不明瞭ナモノヲ±トシ、全然現ハレナイモノヲ－トシタ。

検査成績

　検査セル成績ハ第12表ニ示ス如クニシテ菌株ニヨツテ若干ノ差異ハ認メラレタケレドモ抗原稀釋4〜32倍ニ於テ陽性ニ現レ、抗原稀釋16倍陽性ノモノガ最モ多カツタ、而シテ被凝集性ト同様ニ人由來株、鼠由來株、蚤由來株ノ間ニハ差異ナク、又保存株下ノ間ニモ差異ハ認メラレナカツタ、尚67株、68株ハ僅カニ抗原ノ原液ノミニテ沈降反應ノ陽性ニ現ルルヲ認メタ。

666

537—18

第12表　沈降原性検査成績（其ノ1）

区別	抗原稀釋／菌株	No. 105 株免疫家兎血清							
		1	2	4	8	16	32	64	K
人	1	+	+	+	+	+	+	−	−
	2	+	+	+	+	+	+	−	−
	3	+	+	+	+	±	−	−	−
	4	+	+	+	+	±	−	−	−
	5	+	+	+	+	+	−	−	−
	6	+	+	+	±	−	−	−	−
	7	+	+	+	±	−	−	−	−
	8	+	+	+	+	−	−	−	−
	9	+	+	+	+	+	±	−	−
	10	+	+	+	+	+	+	−	−
	11	+	+	+	+	+	+	−	−
	12	+	+	+	+	+	+	−	−
	13	+	+	+	+	−	−	−	−
	14	+	+	+	−	−	−	−	−
	15	+	+	+	−	−	−	−	−
	16	+	+	+	+	−	−	−	−
由	17	+	+	+	+	+	+	−	−
	18	+	+	+	+	+	−	−	−
	19	+	+	+	+	−	−	−	−
	20	+	+	+	+	±	±	−	−
	21	+	+	+	+	+	+	−	−
	22	+	+	+	+	+	+	−	−
	23	+	+	+	+	+	−	−	−
	24	+	+	+	+	+	−	−	−
	25	+	+	+	+	+	+	−	−
	26	+	+	+	+	−	−	−	−
	27	+	+	+	+	−	−	−	−
	28	+	+	+	+	+	−	−	−
	29	+	+	+	+	+	∓	−	−
	30	+	+	+	+	+	−	−	−
来	31	+	+	+	+	−	−	−	−
	32	+	+	+	+	+	+	−	−
	33	+	+	+	+	+	+	−	−
	34	+	+	+	+	+	+	−	−
	35	+	+	+	+	+	+	−	−
	36	+	+	+	+	−	−	−	−
	37	+	+	+	+	+	−	−	−
	38	+	+	+	+	−	−	−	−
	36	+	+	+	+	+			
	40	+	+	+	+	+			

第12表　沈降原性検査成績(其ノ2)

区別	菌株	1	2	4	8	16	32	64	K
人	41	+	+	+	+	−	−	−	−
	42	+	+	+	+	+	+	−	−
	43	+	+	+	+	+	+	−	−
	44	+	+	+	+	+	−	−	−
	45	+	+	+	+	+	−	−	−
	46	+	+	+	+	+	−	−	−
	47	+	+	+	+	+	−	−	−
	48	+	+	+	+	+	+	−	−
	49	+	+	+	+	+	−	−	−
	50	+	+	+	+	+	−	−	−
由	51	+	+	+	+	−	−	−	−
	52	+	+	+	+	−	−	−	−
	53	+	+	+	+	−	−	−	−
	54	+	+	+	+	−	−	−	−
	55	+	+	+	+	+	−	−	−
	56	+	+	+	+	−	−	−	−
	57	+	+	+	+	−	−	−	±
	58	+	+	+	+	−	−	−	−
	59	+	+	+	+	+	−	−	−
	60	+	+	+	+	+	−	−	−
来	61	+	+	+	+	+	−	−	−
	62	+	+	+	+	+	−	−	−
	63	+	+	+	+	·	−	−	−
	64	+	+	+	+	−	+	−	−
	65	+	+	+	+	−	−	−	−
	66	+	+	+	+	+	−	−	−
	67	+	±	−	−	−	−	−	−
	68	+	±	−	−	−	−	−	−
	69	+	+	+	+	+	−	−	−
	70	+	+	+	+	+	−	−	−
	71	+	+	+	+	+	−	−	−
鼠	72	+	+	+	+	+	−	−	−
	73	+	+	+	+	+	−	−	−
	74	+	+	+	+	+	+	−	−
由	75	+	+	+	+	+	−	−	−
	76	+	+	+	+	+	−	−	−
	77	+	+	+	+	+	−	−	−
来	78	+	+	+	+	+	−	−	−
	79	+	+	+	+	+	−	−	−
	80	+	+	+	+	+	−	−	−

537—20

第12表 沈降原性検査成績（其ノ3）

區別	抗原稀釋/菌株	No.105 株免疫家兔血清							
		1	2	4	8	16	32	64	K
尿由來	81	+	+	+	+	+	−	−	−
	82	+	+	+	+	+	−	−	−
	83	+	+	+	+	+	−	−	−
	84	+	+	+	+	+	−	−	−
	85	+	+	+	+	−	−	−	−
	86	+	+	+	+	±	−	−	−
	87	+	+	+	+	−	−	−	−
	88	+	+	+	+	−	−	−	−
	89	+	+	+	+	−	−	−	−
	90	+	+	+	+	+	−	−	−
	91	+	+	+	+	−	−	−	−
	92	+	+	+	+	−	−	−	−
	93	+	+	+	+	−	−	−	−
	94	+	+	+	+	−	−	−	−
	95	+	+	+	+	±	−	−	−
	96	+	+	+	+	±	−	−	−
	97	+	+	+	+	+	−	−	−
	98	+	+	+	+	−	−	−	−
	99	+	+	+	+	−	−	−	−
	100	+	+	+	+	−	−	−	−
炭山來	101	+	+	+	+	+	−	−	−
	102	+	+	+	+	+	−	−	−
	103	+	+	+	+	−	−	−	−
	104	+	+	+	+	−	−	−	−
	105	+	+	+	−	−	−	−	−
	106	+	+	+	±	−	−	−	−
	107	+	+	+	+	−	−	−	−
	108	+	+	+	+	−	−	−	−
	109	+	+	+	+	−	−	−	−
	110	+	+	+	+	+	−	−	−
對照	111	+	+	+	+	−	−	−	−
	112	+	+	+	+	+	−	−	−
	113	+	+	+	+	+	−	−	−
	114	+	+	+	+	−	−	−	−
	115	+	+	+	+	+	−	−	−
	116	+	+	+	+	+	−	−	−

註　＋………白色輪環ノ明瞭ナルモノ。
　　±………　〃　　ノ不明瞭ナルモノ。
　　－………　〃　　ノ全然認メラレナイモノ。

3. 補體結合原性檢査成績

供試菌株ヲ以テ抗原ヲ作リ、其ヲ以テNo. 1株免疫家兎血清ニ對スル補體結合反應ヲ檢査ゞ
タ。

檢査方法

抗原調製　　生理的食鹽水ヲ以テ供試菌株ノ普通寒天37°C 45時間培養菌ノ1cc 5mgノ菌
浮游液ヲ作リ、20分間煮沸シ、強力遠心沈降シタ上清ヲ抗原トシ、其ノ使用量ハ自家防止ヲオ
サザル最大量ノ $\frac{1}{2}$ トシタ。

補　體　　数頭ノ健康海猂ヨリ採血シテ築メタ新鮮ナ血清ニシテ最少溶血價ノ2倍量ヲ使
用シタ。

免疫血清　　No. 1株ヲ以テ免疫セル家兎血清ニシテ前述ノ凝集反應及沈降反應ニ使用シ
タモノト同一ノモノニシテ之ヲ56°30分ニテ非働性トナシテ使用シタ。

血球液　　新ニ採取シタ脱纖維素緬羊血液ヲ生理的食鹽水ヲ以テ3回洗滌シ、之ヲ5%ノ
割合ニ生理的食鹽水ニ浮游サセタモノデアル。

實驗方法　　免疫血清稀釋ノ方法ニ從ヒ0.5cc Systemニ據リ法ノ如ク行ツタ。

檢査成績

檢査セル成績ハ第13表ニ示ス如クニシテ菌株ニヨツテ若干ノ差異ハアルケレドモ血清稀釋
40～160倍迄完全溶血ヲ防止シ、80倍迄之ヲ防止スル菌株ノ最モ多イノヲ認メタ、而シテ被
凝集性及沈降原性ト同様ニ補體結合反應ノ抗原性ハ人由來株、鼠由來株、蚤由來株ノ間ニ差
異ナク、又對照株トノ間ニモ差異ハ認メラレナカツタ、尚被凝集性、沈降原性及補體結合反
應ノ抗原性ノ間ニハ孰レモ併行セル關係ヲ認メルコトガ出來ナカツタ。

537—22

第13表 補體結合原性検査成績(其ノ1)

区別	菌株	No.105 株 免疫家兎血清									
		5	10	20	40	80	160	320	640	1280	K
人	1	H	H	H	H	H	fH	k	SP	L	L
	2	H	H	H	H	H	K	k	L	L	L
	3	H	H	H	H	K	k	SP	L	L	L
	4	H	H	H	H	H	fH	K	k	L	L
	5	H	H	H	H	K	k	SP	L	L	L
	6	H	H	H	H	H	fH	k	SP	L	L
	7	H	H	H	H	H	fH	k	SP	L	L
	8	H	H	H	H	H	k	SP	L	L	L
	9	H	H	H	H	H	K	k	SP	L	L
	10	H	H	H	H	fH	K	k	SP	L	L
	11	H	H	H	H	H	fH	K	k	L	L
	12	H	H	H	H	H	fH	k	SP	L	L
	13	H	H	H	H	K	K	k	SP	L	L
	14	H	H	H	H	H	fH	k	SP	L	L
	15	H	H	H	H	H	K	SP	L	L	L
	16	H	H	H	H	H	fH	k	SP	L	L
	17	H	H	H	H	fH	K	k	SP	L	L
	18	H	H	H	H	fH	K	k	SP	L	L
由	19	H	H	H	H	K	k	SP	L	L	L
	20	H	H	H	H	H	k	SP	L	L	L
	21	H	H	H	H	K	k	SP	L	L	L
	22	H	H	H	H	H	K	k	SP	L	L
	23	H	H	H	H	K	k	SP	L	L	L
	24	H	H	H	H	K	k	SP	L	L	L
	25	H	H	H	H	K	k	SP	L	L	L
	26	H	H	H	H	fH	K	SP	L	L	L
	27	H	H	H	H	H	K	k	SP	L	L
	28	H	H	H	H	H	fH	k	SP	L	L
	29	H	H	H	H	H	fH	k	SP	L	L
	30	H	H	H	H	H	fH	k	SP	L	L
來	31	H	H	H	H	fH	K	k	L	L	L
	32	H	H	H	H	fH	k	SP	L	L	L
	33	H	H	H	H	K	k	SP	L	L	L
	34	H	H	H	H	H	H	K	k	SP	L
	35	H	H	H	H	H	H	k	SP	L	L
	36	H	H	H	H	H	H	K	k	SP	L
	37	H	H	H	fH	K	k	SP	L	L	L
	38	H	H	H	H	K	k	SP	L	L	L
	29	H	H	H	H	H	fH	k	SP	L	L
	40	H	H	H	H	H	H	K	k	SP	L

第13表　補體結合原性檢査成績（其ノ2）

區別	菌株	No.105 株免疫家兔血清									
	血清稀釋	5	10	20	40	80	160	320	640	1280	K
人	41	H	H	H	fH	K	k	SP	L	L	L
	42	H	H	H	H	H	fH	K	k	SP	L
	43	H	H	H	fH	K	k	SP	L	L	L
	44	H	H	H	H	K	k	SP	L	L	L
	45	H	H	H	H	H	K	k	SP	L	L
	46	H	H	H	H	H	k	k	SP	L	L
	47	H	H	H	H	H	K	SP	SP	L	L
	48	H	H	H	H	H	fH	k	SP	L	L
	49	H	H	H	H	H	K	k	SP	L	L
	50	H	H	H	H	fH	K	k	SP	L	L
中	51	H	H	H	H	H	K	k	SP	L	L
	52	H	H	H	H	H	K	k	SP	L	L
	53	H	H	H	H	H	fH	k	SP	L	L
	54	H	H	H	H	H	K	k	SP	L	L
	55	H	H	H	H	H	K	k	SP	L	L
	56	H	H	H	H	H	K	k	SP	L	L
	57	H	H	H	H	H	fH	K	k	SP	L
	58	H	H	H	H	H	k	k	SP	L	L
	59	H	H	H	H	H	K	SP	SP	L	L
	60	H	H	H	H	H	fH	K	SP	L	L
来	61	H	H	H	H	H	K	k	SP	L	L
	62	H	H	H	H	H	K	k	SP	L	L
	63	H	H	H	H	H	K	k	SP	L	L
	64	H	H	H	H	H	fH	K	k	SP	L
	65	H	H	H	H	H	fH	k	SP	L	L
	66	H	H	H	H	H	K	k	SP	L	L
	67	H	H	H	fH	K	k	SP	L	L	L
	68	H	H	H	fH	k	k	SP	L	L	L
	69	H	H	H	H	H	fH	K	SP	L	L
	70	H	H	H	H	H	H	K	k	SP	L
	71	H	H	H	H	H	K	k	SP	L	L
鼠	72	H	H	H	H	K	k	SP	L	L	L
	73	H	H	H	H	K	k	SP	L	L	L
	74	H	H	H	H	K	k	SP	L	L	L
由	75	H	H	H	H	K	k	SP	L	L	L
	76	H	H	H	H	H	K	k	SP	L	L
	77	H	H	H	H	K	k	SP	L	L	L
来	78	H	H	H	H	K	k	SP	L	L	L
	79	H	H	H	H	K	k	SP	L	L	L
	80	H	H	H	H	H	K	k	SP	L	L

537—24

第13表 補體結合原性検査成績（其ノ3）

区別	値株	No.105 株兎疫家兎血清									
		5	10	20	40	80	160	320	630	1280	K
鼠 血 来	81	H	H	H	H	H	K	k	SP	L	L
	82	H	H	H	H	H	k	k	SP	L	L
	83	H	H	H	H	H	K	k	SP	L	L
	84	H	H	H	H	H	H	K	k	SP	L
	85	H	H	H	H	fH	K	k	SP	L	L
	86	H	H	H	H	H	K	k	SP	L	L
	87	H	H	H	H	H	K	k	SP	L	L
	88	H	H	H	H	K	k	SP	L	L	L
	89	H	H	H	H	K	k	SP	L	L	L
	90	H	H	H	H	K	k	SP	L	L	L
	91	H	H	H	H	fH	K	k	SP	L	L
	92	H	H	H	H	fH	K	k	SP	L	L
	93	H	H	H	H	K	k	SP	L	L	L
	94	H	H	H	H	K	k	k	L	L	L
	95	H	H	H	H	fH	k	k	SP	L	L
	96	H	H	H	H	H	K	k	SP	L	L
	97	H	H	H	H	H	fH	K	k	SP	L
	98	H	H	H	H	H	fH	K	k	L	L
	99	H	H	H	H	K	k	SP	L	L	L
	100	H	H	H	H	K	k	SP	L	L	L
歪 血 来	101	H	H	H	H	K	k	SP	L	L	L
	102	H	H	H	H	fH	K	k	SP	L	L
	103	H	H	H	H	fH	K	k	SP	L	L
	104	H	H	H	H	H	K	k	SP	L	L
	105	H	H	H	H	K	k	SP	L	L	L
	106	H	H	H	H	fH	K	k	SP	L	L
	107	H	H	H	H	fH	k	k	SP	L	L
	108	H	H	H	H	K	k	SP	L	L	L
	109	H	H	H	H	fH	K	SP	L	L	L
	110	H	H	H	H	H	H	K	k	SP	
対 照	111	H	H	H	H	H	K	k	SP	L	L
	112	H	H	H	H	H	fH	k	SP	L	L
	113	H	H	H	H	H	K	k	SP	L	L
	114	H	H	H	H	H	fH	K	SP	L	L
	115	H	H	H	H	fH	K	k	SP	L	L
	116	H	H	H	H	H	K	k	SP	L	L

胜 H………完全溶血防止
fH………痕跡溶血
K、k…不完全溶血
SP………痕跡溶血防止
L………完全溶血

　　　　第2節　免疫抗體產生能ニ就テ

　人由來株，鼠由來株，蚤由來株，虱由來株ヨリ適當ナ菌株10株ヲ選定シ、其ト對照株タルNo.
1株No.105株ノ各ミヲ以テ家兎ヲ免疫シ、免疫抗體ノ產生能ニ差異ガアルカ否カヲ檢查シタ。
實驗方法

　　免疫抗原ノ調製、被檢菌株ノ普通寒天37°C 45時間培養菌ノ一定量ヲ生理的食鹽水ニ浮游サ
セ、60°C 30分ニテ殺菌セルモノヲ以テ免疫抗原トシタ。

　　免疫方法　　前述ノ免疫抗原ノ2.5mg, 2.5mg, 5mg, 10mg, 10mgノ各菌量ヲ夫々5日目每
ニ體重3kg內外ノ家兎ノ耳靜脈內ニ接種シ、最後ノ注射ヨリ10日目ニ探血シテ血液ヲ分離シ
其ノ免疫血液內ニ凝集素、沈降素補體結合抗體等ノ免疫抗體ガ如何ナル程度ニ產生セラレテヰ
ルカヲ檢查シタ。

1.　凝集素產生能檢查成績

　　前述ノ如クニシテ免疫セル家兎血清ノ中ニ產生セラレタ凝集素ヲNo.1株、No.105株、1
株、52株、80株、101株等ヨリ調製セル菌液ヲ以テ檢查シタ（檢查方法ハ被凝集性ヲ檢查セル
方法ト同樣デアル）、檢查セル成績ハ第14表ニ示ス如クニシテ各菌株ノ間ニハ差異ヲ認メナカ
ツタ、即チ孰レノ菌株ヲ以テ免疫セル家兎血清ニテモ血清稀釋160～320倍迄凝集反應ノ陽性
ニ現レルノヲ認メタ、而モ凝集ハ孰レモ霊絮狀ニ現レタ。

2.　沈降素產生能檢查成績

　　前述ノ如クニシテ免疫セル家兎血清ノ中ニ產生サレタ沈降素ヲNo.1株、No.105株、1株、
52株、80株、101株等ヨリ調製シタ抗原ヲ以テ檢查シタ（檢查方法ハ沈降原性ヲ檢查シタ方法
ニ從ツタ）、檢查セル成績ハ第15表ニ示ス如クニシテ 各菌株ノ間ニハ殆ド差異ヲ認メナカツ
タ、即チ孰レノ菌株ヲ以テ免疫セル家兎血清ニテモ抗原稀釋16～32倍迄沈降反應ノ陽性ニ現
レルノヲ認メタ。

3.　補體結合抗體產生能檢查成績

　　前述ノ如クニシテ免疫セル家兎血清ノ中ニ產生サレタ補體結合抗體ヲNo.1株、No.105株、
1株、52株、80株、101株等ヨリ調製シタ抗原ヲ以テ檢查シタ（檢查方法ハ補體結合原性ヲ檢
查シタ方法ニ從ツタ）、檢查セル成績ハ第16表ニ示ス如クニシテ 各菌株ノ間ニ 殆ド差異ヲ
認メナカツタ、即チ孰レノ菌株ヲ以テ免疫セル家兎血清ニテモ血清稀釋80～160倍迄完全溶
血ヲ防止シタ。

537—26

第14表 菜薹产座生能检查成绩

第15表 沈降聚产生能检查成绩

537—28

第16表 補體結合抗體產生能檢查成績

抗原菌株：對照（保存株）— 血清稀釋：No. 1

免疫菌株		5	10	20	40	80	160	320	640	1280	K
人由來	1	H	H	H	H	H	K	k	SP	L	L
	24	H	H	H	H	H	k	SP	L	L	L
	52	H	H	H	H	H	fH	k	SP	L	L
	68	H	H	H	H	H	K	K	SP	L	L
鼠由來	80	H	H	H	H	H	K	k	SP	L	L
	65	H	H	H	H	H	H	k	SP	L	L
	100	H	H	H	H	H	fH	K	SP	SP	L
蚤由來	101	H	H	H	H	H	H	k	SP	L	L
	100	H	H	H	H	H	fH	K	k	SP	L
虱由來	110	H	H	H	H	H	H	k	SP	L	L
對照	No. 1	H	H	H	H	H	K	k	SP	L	L
	No.105	H	H	H	H	H	fH	K	SP	L	L

抗原菌株：對照（保存株）— 血清稀釋：No. 105

免疫菌株		5	10	20	40	80	160	320	649	1280	K
人由來	1	H	H	H	H	H	K	k	SP	L	L
	24	H	H	H	H	H	fH	k	SP	L	L
	52	H	H	H	H	H	H	k	SP	L	L
	68	H	H	H	H	H	H	k	SP	L	L
鼠由來	80	H	H	H	H	H	K	k	SP	L	L
	65	H	H	H	H	H	K	k	k	L	L
	100	H	H	H	H	H	fH	K	SP	L	L
蚤由來	101	H	H	H	H	H	H	K	k	SP	L
	100	H	H	H	H	H	K	k	SP	L	L
虱由來	110	H	H	H	H	fH	K	k	SP	L	L
對照	No. 1	H	H	H	H	fH	K	k	SP	L	L
	No.105	H	H	H	H	H	K	SP	SP	L	L

抗原菌株：人由來株 — 血清稀釋：1

免疫菌株		5	10	20	40	80	160	320	640	1280	K
人由來	1	H	H	H	H	K	SP	L	L	L	L
	24	H	H	H	H	K	k	SP	L	L	L
	52	H	H	H	H	fH	k	SP	L	L	L
	68	H	H	H	H	fH	K	SP	L	L	L
鼠由來	80	H	H	H	H	fH	k	k	SP	L	L
	65	H	H	H	H	K	k	SP	L	L	L
	100	H	H	H	H	fH	K	k	L	L	L
蚤由來	101	H	H	H	H	H	K	k	SP	L	L
	100	H	H	H	H	fH	K	k	SP	L	L
虱由來	110	H	H	H	H	K	K	SP	L	L	L
對照	No. 1	H	H	H	H	H	K	k	SP	L	L
	No.105	H	H	H	H	K	k	SP	L	L	L

抗原菌株：人由來株 — 血清稀釋：52

免疫菌株		5	10	20	40	80	160	320	640	1280	K
人由來	1	H	H	H	H	fH	k	k	SP	L	L
	24	H	H	H	H	H	K	k	SP	L	L
	52	H	H	H	H	H	K	k	SP	L	L
	69	H	H	H	H	H	fH	k	L	L	L
鼠由來	80	H	H	H	H	H	K	k	SP	L	L
	65	H	H	H	H	H	fH	k	SP	L	L
	100	H	H	H	H	H	K	k	SP	L	L
蚤由來	101	H	H	H	H	H	K	k	L	L	L
	100	H	H	H	H	H	fH	K	k	SP	L
虱由來	110	H	H	H	H	H	fH	k	SP	L	L
對照	No. 1	H	H	H	H	H	K	SP	L	L	L
	No.105	H	H	H	H	H	H	k	SP	L	L

抗原菌株：鼠由來株 — 血清稀釋：80

免疫菌株		5	10	20	40	80	160	320	640	1280	K
人由來	1	H	H	H	H	H	fH	k	SP	L	L
	24	H	H	H	H	H	K	k	SP	L	L
	52	H	H	H	H	H	K	k	SP	L	L
	69	H	H	H	H	H	k	SP	SP	L	L
鼠由來	80	H	H	H	H	H	fH	k	SP	L	L
	65	H	H	H	H	H	K	k	SP	L	L
	100	H	H	H	H	fH	K	k	k	L	L
蚤由來	101	H	H	H	H	H	K	SP	L	L	L
	100	H	H	H	H	H	fH	k	SP	L	L
虱由來	110	H	H	H	H	H	fH	k	SP	L	L
對照	No. 1	H	H	H	H	H	K	k	SP	L	L
	No.105	H	H	H	H	H	H	k	SP	L	L

抗原菌株：蚤由來株 — 血清稀釋：101

免疫菌株		5	10	20	40	80	160	320	640	1280	K
人由來	1	H	H	H	H	H	K	SP	L	L	L
	24	H	H	H	H	H	K	k	SP	L	L
	52	H	H	H	H	H	fH	k	SP	L	L
	69	H	H	H	H	H	fH	k	SP	L	L
鼠由來	80	H	H	H	H	H	K	SP	SP	L	L
	65	H	H	H	H	H	K	k	SP	L	L
	100	H	H	H	H	H	fH	k	SP	L	L
蚤由來	101	H	H	H	H	H	fH	k	SP	L	L
	100	H	H	H	H	H	K	k	SP	L	L
虱由來	110	H	H	H	H	H	fH	K	k	SP	L
對照	No. 1	H	H	H	H	H	K	k	SP	L	L
	No.105	H	H	H	H	H	H	k	SP	L	L

537—29

　　　第3節　抗原構造ニ就テ
　由來ヲ異ニセル各菌株ノ間ニ抗原構造ノ差異ガアルカ否カヲ Castellani 氏吸收試驗ニヨツテ
檢査シタ。

實驗方法

　生理的食鹽水ヲ以テ5倍ニ稀釋シタ可檢血清ニ被檢菌株ノ普通寒天 37°C 45時間培養菌ノ
1cc約1g濃度ノ生理的食鹽水菌浮游液ヲ同量ニ加ヘ、45°Cノ恒溫水槽ニ6時間納メ大テ水
室ニ翌朝迄靜置シ、凝集ノ完結ヲ待チテ良ク遠心沈降シ、要スレバ更ニ其ノ上清ヲ取リ、之ニ
等量ノ濃厚菌液ヲ加ヘ、同上操作ヲ繰リ返シ十分吸收セシメ、最早吸收菌ニ對シテ凝集反應ヲ
起サナイコトヲ確メタ後、其ノ吸收血清ヲ以テ所要菌株ニ就テ凝集反應ヲ行ツタ。

實驗成績

　1株免疫血清及No.1株免疫血清ヲ1株、24株、52株、69株、80株、95株、100株、101株、106
株、110株、No.1株、No.105株ノ各株ヲ以テ吸收シ、其ノ吸收血清ニ對シテ1株、No.1株ヲ
以テ凝集反應ヲ行ヘルニ第17表ノ如キ成績ニシテ1株免疫血清及No.1株免疫血清中ニ産生ヲ
レタ凝集素ハ前述ノ各菌株ニヨツテ完全ニ吸收サレルコトヲ認メタ。

　次ニ1株、24株、52株、69株、80株、95株、100株、101株、106株、110株、No.1株、No.
105株等ノ各免疫血清ヲ1株或ヘNo.1株ヲ以テ吸收シ、其ノ各吸收血清ニ對シテ天々各菌株ヲ
以テ凝集反應ヲ行ヘルニ第18表ノ如キ成績ニシテ、前述ノ各菌株ノ免疫血清中ニ産生サレタ凝
集素ハ總テ1株或ヘNo.1株ニヨツテ完全ニ吸收サレルコトヲ認メタ。

537—30

第17表　吸　收　試　驗　（其ノ1）

血清	吸收菌	抗菌株／成原試	凝　集　價								
			20	40	80	160	320	640	1,280	2,560	K
1	1	1／No.1	±	—	—	—	—	—	—	—	—
	24	1／24	±	—	—	—	—	—	—	—	—
	52	1／52	±	—	—	—	—	—	—	—	—
	69	1／69	±	±	—	—	—	—	—	—	—
	80	1／80	±	±	—	—	—	—	—	—	—
	95	1／95	±	±	—	—	—	—	—	—	—
	100	1／100	±	±	—	—	—	—	—	—	—
	101	1／101	±	±	—	—	—	—	—	—	—
	106	1／106	±	±	—	—	—	—	—	—	—
	110	1／110	±	±	—	—	—	—	—	—	—
	No.1	1／No.1	±	±	—	—	—	—	—	—	—
	No.105	1／No.105	±	—	—	—	—	—	—	—	—
No.1	1	No.1／1	±	±	—	—	—	—	—	—	—
	24	No.1／24	±	±	—	—	—	—	—	—	—
	52	No.1／52	±	±	—	—	—	—	—	—	—
	69	No.1／69	±	±	—	—	—	—	—	—	—
	80	No.1／80	±	±	—	—	—	—	—	—	—
	95	No.1／95	±	±	—	—	—	—	—	—	—
	100	No.1／100	±	±	—	—	—	—	—	—	—
	101	No.1／101	±	—	—	—	—	—	—	—	—
	106	No.1／106	±	±	—	—	—	—	—	—	—
	110	No.1／110	±	±	—	—	—	—	—	—	—

第18表　吸　収　試　験（其ノ2）

血清	吸収菌	抗原菌株＼成績	凝　集　価								
			20	40	80	160	320	640	1,280	2,560	K
1	1	1 No.1	±	−	−	−	−	−	−	−	−
24	〃	24 1	±	−	−	−	−	−	−	−	−
52	〃	52 1	±	−	−	−	−	−	−	−	−
69	〃	69 1	±	±	−	−	−	−	−	−	−
80	〃	80 1	±	−	−	−	−	−	−	−	−
95	〃	95 1	±	±	−	−	−	−	−	−	−
100	〃	100 1	±	−	−	−	−	−	−	−	−
101	〃	101 1	±	±	−	−	−	−	−	−	−
106	〃	106 1	±	±	−	−	−	−	−	−	−
110	〃	110 1	±	−	−	−	−	−	−	−	−
No.1	〃	No.1 1	±	±	−	−	−	−	−	−	−
No.105	〃	No.105 1	±	−	−	−	−	−	−	−	−
1	No.1	1 No.1	±	±	−	−	−	−	−	−	−
24	〃	24 No.1	±	±	−	−	−	−	−	−	−
52	〃	52 No.1	±	−	−	−	−	−	−	−	−
69	〃	69 No.1	±	−	−	−	−	−	−	−	−
80	〃	80 No.1	±	−	−	−	−	−	−	−	−
95	〃	95 No.1	±	−	−	−	−	−	−	−	−
100	〃	100 No.1	±	±	−	−	−	−	−	−	−
101	〃	101 No.1	±	±	−	−	−	−	−	−	−
106	〃	106 No.1	±	±	−	−	−	−	−	−	−
110	〃	110 No.1	±	±	−	−	−	−	−	−	−

　以上ノ成績ヨリ1株、24株、52株、69株、80株、95株、100株、101株、106株、110株、No.1株、No.105株ハ孰レモ同一抗原ヲ有シ且其ノ免疫血清中ニハ同一抗體ヲ産生スルコト方判決ス。

　次ニ1株、24株、80株、101株、No.1株ノ各菌株ヨリ調製セル菌液ヲ生菌ノ儘及1.0％フォ

537—32

ルマリン殺菌、60°80分加熱殺菌、100°C30分煮沸殺菌シテ、1株免疫血清ニ就テ凝集反應ヲ檢査セル＝100°30分ニテ殺菌セル菌液ノミハ顆粒狀ノ凝集ヲ現スノヲ認メタ（第19表）、其處デ1株、No.1株ノ100°C30分ニテ殺菌セル菌液ヲ以テ1株免疫血清、No.1ノ株免疫血清ヲ夫々吸收シ、其ノ吸收血清ニ對シテ1株ノ生菌液及100°C30分殺菌菌液ヲ以テ凝集反應ヲ行ヘルニ第20表ノ如キ成績ニシテ生菌液ハ依然雲絮狀ノ凝集ヲナスニ拘ラズ、100°C30分殺菌菌液ハ全然凝集反應ヲ起サナイコトヲ認メタ、此ノ成績ヨリ「ペスト菌ハ耐熱性抗原ト易熱性抗原ヲ有シ、易熱性抗原ハ雲絮狀、耐熱性抗原ハ顆粒狀ノ凝集反應ヲ起シ、且「ペスト菌ノ免疫血清ノ中ニハ兩抗原ニ對スル免疫抗體ノ夫々產生セラレルノヲ認メタ、其ノ後「ペスト菌ノ非粘稠性變異ニ關スル研究ニヨリ耐熱性抗原ハ菌體抗原ニシテ易熱性抗原ハ Envelope 抗原デアルコトガ判ツタ。

第19表　殺菌處置ノ抗原性ニ及ス影響

血清	處方理法	成績 / 抗原菌株	凝 20	40	集 80	160	價 320	640	1,280	2,560	K
1	生菌	1	×××	××	××	×	⊥	—	—	—	—
		24	×××	××	××	×	⊥	—	—	—	—
		80	×××	××	××	××	×	⊥	—	—	—
		101	×××	××	××	×	⊥	—	—.	—	—
		No.1	×××	××	××	××	×	⊥	—	—	—
	1.0% フォルマリン殺菌	1	×××	××	××	×	⊥	—	—	—	—
		24	×××	××	××	×	⊥	—	⊥	—	—
		80	×××	×××	××	××	×	⊥	—	—	—
		101	×××	×××	××	××	×	⊥	—	—	—
		No.1	×××	××	××	×	⊥	—	—	—	—
	60°C 30分殺菌	1	×××	××	××	×	⊥	—	—	—	—
		24	×××	××	××	×	⊥	—	—	—	—
		80	×××	××	××	×	⊥	—	—	—	—
		101	×××	××	××	×	⊥	—	—	—	—
		No.1	×××	××	××	×	×	⊥	—	—	—
	100°C 30分殺菌	1	╫	＋	＋	＋	＋	⊥⊥⊥	⊥⊥	⊥	⊥
		24	╫	╫	＋	＋	⊥	⊥⊥⊥	⊥⊥	⊥	⊥
		80	╫	＋	＋	＋	⊥	⊥⊥⊥	⊥⊥	⊥	⊥
		101	╫	＋	＋	＋	⊥⊥⊥	⊥⊥	⊥	—	—
		No.1	╫	＋	＋	＋	⊥	⊥⊥	⊥	—	—

註　×ハ雲絮狀凝集、十ハ顆粒狀凝集ヲ表ハスモノトス。

第20表　吸収試験（其ノ2）

血清 吸収菌	抗原菌株	凝　集　価								
		20	40	80	160	320	640	1,280	2,560	K
1	$\frac{1}{(100°C30分)}$ ／ （生 菌）$\frac{1}{(100°C30分)}$	××× ⊥	×× ⊥	×× ⊥	⊥ ⊥	⊥ ⊥	— ⊥	— ⊥	— ⊥	— —
	No.1 $(100·C30分)$ ／ （生 菌）$\frac{1}{(100°C30分)}$	××× ⊥	×× ⊥	×× ⊥	× ⊥	⊥ ⊥	— ⊥	— ⊥	— ⊥	— —
No.1	$\frac{1}{(100"C30分)}$ ／ （生 菌）$\frac{1}{(100°C30分)}$	××× ⊥	××× ⊥	⊥ ⊥	⊥ ⊥	⊥ ⊥	— ⊥	— ⊥	— ⊥	— —
	No.1 $(100"C30分)$ ／ （生 菌）$\frac{1}{(100°C30分)}$	××× ⊥	×× ⊥	×× ⊥	× ⊥	⊥ ⊥	— ⊥	— ⊥	— ⊥	— —

第4章　総括及考察

今次流行ニ於テ「ペスト」患者ヨリ分離セル5株、「ペスト」屍體ヨリ分離セル66株、鼠ヨリ分離セル29株、蚤ヨリ分離セル9株、虱ヨリ分離セル1株、計110株ニ就テ其ノ生物學的並ニ血清學的性狀ヲ檢査セル成績ヲ總括シテ述ベレバ次ノ如クデアル。

1. 形態ハ「グラム」陰性ノ短桿菌ニシテ單染色ニテハ兩端濃染シ、鞭毛及芽胞ヲ有セズ、莢膜ハ認メラレナカツタ。

2. 普通寒天斜面ニ克ク發育シ、37°Cニテ培養セルモノハ其ノ菌苔粘稠性デアツタ。然ルニ高松株ノミハ37°C培養菌ニモ粘稠性ヲ缺除シ、所謂非粘稠性變異株デアルコトヲ認メタ。

3. 普通ブイヨン」ニ37°Cニテ培養スル時ハ培養液ハ一樣ニ潤濁シ、管底ニ沈殿物ヲ認メタガ、高松株ハ潤濁度ガ他ノ菌株ニ比シテ少ナク、微細顆粒狀ノ菌塊ノ浮游スルヲ認メ且沈殿物ノ多イノヲ認メタ。

4. 聚落ハ圓形ニシテ隆起シ、大、小ノ聚落ヲ混ズル菌株多ク、且聚落周圍ノ量ハ大キサ小ニ種々デアツタ。

5. 「インドール」反應ハ總テ陰性デアツタ。

6. 含水炭素分解性ヲ檢査セルニ各菌株ノ間ニハ其ノ分解性ニ差異ナク、流行株ハ總テ3〜4日ニテ「グリセリン」ヲ分解シ、倉內ノ所謂α型菌デアルコトガ判ツタ。

7. 海猽及家兔ノ働性血清ノ有スル「アレキシン」作用ニ對スル抵抗ヲ檢査セルニ流行株ハ鬩布セ二對シテ抵抗性ヲ有シ、其ノ中ニテ旺盛ニ增殖スルノヲ認メタ。

8. 流行株ノ中ヨリ人由來ノモノ、鼠由來ノモノ、蚤由來ノモノ、虱由來ノモノヲ適宜ニ抽出シテ海猽ニ對スル毒力ヲ檢査セルニ軟レモ毒力強クシテ、其ノ最少致死量ハ10^{-4}〜10^{-5}mgデアルノヲ認メタ。

9. 流行株ノ抗原性ニ就テ檢査セルニ流行株ハ「ペスト」菌免疫家兔血清（凝集價640倍）ニ對シテ軟

537—34

レモ被凝集性ヲ認メ、血清稀釋160～640倍迄凝集反應ヲ起シ、菌株ニヨツテ若干ノ差異ガ認メ
ラレタ。

沈降原性モ總テノ菌株ニ於テ認メラレ、前記家兎免疫血清ニ對シ、抗原稀釋4～32倍迄陽性
ニ現レ、菌株ニヨツテ若干ノ差異ガ認メラレタ。

補體結合反應ノ抗原性モ總テノ菌株ニ於テ認メラレ、前記家兎免疫血清ニ對シ血清稀釋40～
160倍完全溶血ヲ防止シ、菌株ニヨツテ若干ノ差異ガ認メラレタ。

尚被凝集性、沈降原性及補體結合反應ノ抗原性ノ間ニハ孰レモ併行セル關係ハ認メラレナカ
ツタ。

10. 流行株ノ内ヨリ代表的ナ菌株ヲ選定シ、其ヲ以テ家兎ヲ免疫シ、免疫抗體ノ産生能ニ差異ガ
アルカ否カヲ檢査シタ結果、孰レノ菌株モ凝集素、沈降素、補體結合反應抗體ヲ同程度ニ産生
スル能力ヲ有スルコトヲ認メタ。

11. 由來ヲ異ニセル菌株ノ間ニ抗原構造ノ差異ガアルカ否カヲ Castellani 氏吸收試驗ニヨツテ檢
査シタ結果、各菌株ハ孰レモ同一抗原ヲ有スルコトヲ認メタ。尚各株ハ孰レモ耐熱性抗原ト易
熱性抗原ヲ有スルコトヲ明カニシタ。

結 言

同一流行ニ於テ由來ヲ異ニシテ分離サレタ110株ノ「ベスト菌ノ生物學的並ニ血清學的性状ヲ檢
査シタ結果孰レノ菌株モ同一性状ヲ有スルヰトヲ明カニシタ、唯一株ニ就テ非粘稠性變異株ヲ檢
出スルコトガ出來タ。

文 獻

1) Dieudonne, A. & Otto, R. : "Handbuch der pathogenen Microorganismen," (1928),
III. Aufl., 4, 179. 2) 倉内：滿洲醫學雜誌、(昭. 5), 12, 827., 13, 53. 3) 倉内：
細菌學雜誌、(昭. 12), 493, 121. 4) 倉内：東京醫事新誌、(昭. 12), 3020, 447. 5)
Tsuchia, K. & Li Te Chuan：Jl. Orient. Med., (1929), 10, 33. 6) 西村：滿洲醫
學雜誌、(昭. 5), 13, 71.

4.2.7　昭和 15 年農安及新京ニ発生セル「ペスト」流行ニ就テ　第 5 編 流行ニ於ケル防疫実施ノ概況

資料出处：日本国立国会図書館関西館蔵、博士論文。

内容点评：本资料为《陆军军医学校防疫研究报告》第 2 部第 538 号《关于昭和 15 年农安和新京发生的鼠疫流行　第 5 编　关于流行中防疫实施的概况》，1943 年 4 月 12 日提交。

陸軍軍醫學校防疫研究報告
第2部　第538號

昭和15年農安及新京ニ發生セル「ペスト」
流行ニ就テ
第5編　流行ニ於ケル防疫實施ノ概況

陸軍軍醫學校軍陣防疫學教室(主任　增田大佐)
陸軍軍醫少佐　高　橋　正　彦

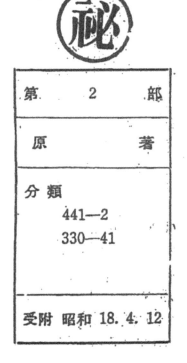

第　　2　　部		
原　　　　著		
分　類		
441—2		
330—41		
受附　昭和 18. 4. 12		

538—2

擔任指導　陸軍軍醫少佐　石　井　四　郎

緒　　言

昭和15年9月下旬滿洲國首都新京ニ「ペスト」ノ流行發生スルヤ、其ノ當初ハ市當局ガ專ラ防疫ニ當ツタケレドモ、流行蔓延ノ徴アリ、且重大事態ヲ惹起スル俱ガアツタノデ10月5日ヨリ軍ガ主體トナリ、軍官民ヲ一體トスル防疫態勢ヲ整ヘテ、流行ノ撲滅ヲ期スルニ到リ、其ヨリ11月中旬ニ至ル迄徹底的ニ「ペスト」防疫ガ實施サレタ、其ノ間ニ行ハレタ防疫業務ハ極メテ複雜多岐ニ亙ルノデ其ノ一々ニ就テ述ベルコトハ困難デアルガ、其ノ中デ將來ノ「ペスト」防疫上參考トナル樣ナ事項ニ就テ茲ニ記述スル次第デアル。

第1章　防疫機關ノ編成

今次流行ニ於テ臨時ニ編成サレタ「ペスト防疫隊ハ加茂部隊ノ人員ヲ主體トシ、其ニ滿洲內2.3ノ陸軍病院ヨリ派遣サレタ軍醫、衛生將校、衛生下士官ỏ衛生兵等ヲ加ヘテ編成シタモノデ、編成人員ノ概要ヲ示セバ第1表ノ如クデアル。

538

第1表 「ペスト」防疫隊ノ編成

区分		人員	将校	下士官	兵	計	摘要
防疫部	本部	庶務	2	4	14	20	別働隊トシテ診療班（3人）、警備班（10人）、經理班（8人）、輸送班（48人）ヲ有ス。
		企劃	3	3	2	8	
		情報	2	2	6	10	別働隊トシテ宣傳班（15人）、寫眞班（6人）ヲ有ス。
		資材	2	9	8	19	
		研究	4	8	16	28	
		教育	2	2	4	8	
檢疫部	檢疫	防疫斥候	3	3	10	16	
		撲滅	2	1	10	13	
		檢診	25	5	30	60	別働隊トシテ檢挍班（20人）、豫防接種班（30人）、收容班（15人）ヲ有ス。
	試術毒	消毒	1	1	10	12	別働隊トシテ瓦斯班（20人）ヲ有ス。
		檢索	10	13	36	59	
		病理	2	4	4	10	
		隔離診療	2	2	10	14	
1人 2人			60	57	160	277	総計 729人

以上ノ他防疫隊長ハ民政部保健司、新京市衞生處、新京市衞生試驗所、滿洲國赤十字社、滿鐵臨時防疫委員會ヲ區處シ、新京憲兵隊、野副部隊警備隊、獨立憲兵隊（滿憲）、首都警察廳、新京鐵道警護隊、協和會首都本部等ノ協力ヲ得テ、軍官民一體ノ防疫態勢ヲ備ヘ、以テ「ペスト」防疫ノ完遂ヲ期シタ。

此ノ他ニ裝備ノ概要ヲ述ベル必要ガアルケレドモ、之ハ各班ニヨツテ差異ガアリ、而モ稍メテ複雑多岐ニ互ルノデ省略スル。

第2章　防疫施設ノ概要

防疫隊本部ニハ始メノ期間ハ滿洲電業會社ノ管理局ヲ使用シ、其ノ後ハ國防會館ヲ使用シタ。本部ニ於テハ人ノ出入劇シキタメニ病毒傳播ノ機會ヲ作ルコトノナイ様ニ出入人員ノ消毒ヲ勵行ニシタ。

隔離病舎ハ市立傳染病院（千早病院）內ニ設備シ、尙其ノ1棟ニ健康隔離所ヲ設備シタ。此等ノ建物ハ人員收容以前ニ除鼠及除蚤的清掃ヲ行ヒ且鼠族ノ出入ヲ防止スルタメニ厼ニ光防鼠設備ヲ行ツタ。

菌檢索所ニハ始メハ千早病院內ノ菌檢索室ヲ使用シタガ後ニハ馬疫研究所ヲ使用シタ、是等ノ既設ノ設備ヲ以テ概ネ檢索業務ヲ遂行スルコトガ出來タ、「ペスト」菌ノ檢索ニハ特別ナ設備ヲ必要トシナイケレドモ動物試驗室ハ必ズ設備スル必要ガアル、之ハ鼠族及昆蟲ノ出入ヲ防止又ハ設備ヲ有スルモノデナケレバナラナイ、以上ノ他ニ鼠族及昆蟲ノ分類及檢査ヲスル室ヲ別ニ設備スル必要ガアル。

病理解剖ニハ千早病院附屬ノ病理解剖室ヲ使用シタ。

538—4

屍體ノ燒却ニハ市立火葬場ヲ使用シタ。

防疫從業員ノ宿舎ニハ兵舎ヲ使用シ、尚一部ノモノノ爲ニハ市內ニアル宿屋ヲ借上ゲテ使用シタ。

第3章 防疫實施業務ノ概要
第1節 防 疫 要 領

I. 防疫本部ノ業務

1. 庶 務 班

　庶務班ハ主トシテ命令、會報ノ傳達、報告、通報ノ作製發送、發來輸ノ整理、宿營ニ關スル事項、各種勤務ノ割出、隊內外ニ關スル連絡通報ニ關スル事項、軍事郵便ノ取扱、人事ニ關スル事項等ヲ業務トシタ。

　別勤隊トシテ診療班、警備班、經理班、輸送班ヲ有シ、診療班ハ隊員ノ診療、警備班ハ部隊ノ警備及軍紀ノ取締ヲナシ、經理班ハ隊員ノ諸給與、給養、調辨、支拂業務ヲ實施シ、殊ニ資材班ト密接ニ連絡シテ各種材料ノ購買業務ヲ遺憾ナカラシメ、輸送班ハ人員、資材ノ輸送、捕鼠ノ蒐集、患者、行路病者及屍體ノ收容及運搬、各班ノ業務連絡等ヲ行ツタ。

2. 企 劃 班

　各種企圖ニ基ク計劃、命令、會報ノ起案、區處下團體並ニ協力團體トノ連絡、外部トノ交涉、日々ノ防疫對策ノ起案、患者及有菌鼠發生地域ノ隔離及解除ニ關スル計畫、交通遮斷ニ關スル事項、晨安附近「ペスト」防疫計畫、防疫隊解散ニ關スル事項等ニ就キ夫々計畫シ、又編成裝備ニ關スル事項、功績ニ關スル事項ヲ取扱ツタ、尚必要ト認メルコトニ就テハ其ノ實施狀況ヲ檢閲シタ。

　交通遮斷ハ警察隊ヲシテ之ヲナサシメ、自治區團ヲシテ之ニ協力セシメタ。

3. 情 報 班

　「ペスト」ニ關スル情報ノ蒐集ニ努メ防疫計畫ノ樹立ニ資スルヲ第一ノ任務トシタ、尚報道業務(新聞、「ラジオ」、「パンフレツト」、「ポスター」、講演)ヲ統制シ、民衆ノ敎育及啓發、流言ノ防止ニ努メタ。

　次ニ防疫會報ヲ司會シ、防疫關係各機關ノ連絡及防疫對策ノ打合セニ資シタ。

　別勤隊トシテ宣撫班及寫眞班ヲ有シ、宣撫班ハ民衆ニ對スル衛生思想ノ普及及徹底、民衆ノ宣撫等ヲ行ヒ、寫眞班ハ防疫業務ノ記錄撮影ヲナシ、尚宣撫班ノ業務ヲ援助シタ。

4. 資 材 班

　防疫用資材ノ蒐集及關係各機關ヘノ補給ヲ第一任務トシタ。補給上最モ困難ヲ感ジタモノハ「ペスト防菌衣、「ゴム長靴」、「ゴム手袋デアツタ、尚蚤取粉、除蟲菊等ハ著シク不足シテ個人防疫上寒心ニ耐ヘナイモノガアツタ、補給シタ特殊資材トシテ擧ゲラレルモノハ捕鼠器、豫防接種液、「クロールピクリン」、「コクソール」、實驗動物等デアツタ、以上ノ他ニ代

538+5

用防疫材料ノ考案、機械及器具ノ修理等ヲ行ツタ。

5. 研 究 班

「ペスト」發生家屋及「ペスト」發生地域ノ環境衛生學的調査ヲ行ヒ、以テ將來ノ「ペスト」防疫對策ヲ考究シタ。

鼠族ノ習性及食性ノ檢査ヲ行ツタ。

「ペスト」流行史ノ調査及今次流行ノ疫學的研究ヲナシタ。

毒瓦斯ノ殺鼠及殺蚤效果ヲ檢査シ、尚其ノ效果檢定法ニ關スル研究ヲ行ツタ。

流行地域ノ水質及地質學的研究ヲ行ツタ。

「ペスト」症ノ病理組織學的檢査ヲ行ツタ。

6. 敎 育 班

防疫從業員ノ敎育、流行地域ノ指導者階級ニ對スル敎育等ヲ行ツタ、尚宣撫班ト連絡シテ民衆ノ敎育ヲ行ツタ。

Ⅲ. 防疫實施機關ノ業務

防疫實施機關ハ防疫ノ初期ニハ隊長ニ直屬シテ業務ヲ實施シテキタガ後ニハ是等防疫實施機關ノ業務ヲ統制區處スル爲ニ撲滅部ガ編成サレ、撲滅部長ノ命令ニヨツテ業務ヲ實施シタ。

1. 防疫斥候隊

流行發生原因ノ調査(病毒搬入經路ノ調査)、傳染源ノ調査、傳染經路ノ調査ヲ行ツタ、即チ小池班ハ初發患者ノ感染經路及續發患者ノ感染經路ヲ調査シ、主トシテ患者ノ發生狀況ヨリ流行發生原因ノ究明、傳染源ノ究明及傳播經路ノ究明ニ任ジ、尚新京市內全般ヲ偵察シ、疑ハシキ患者及死因不明ノ病死者或ハ行路病者及行路病死者ノ摘出ニ努メ、及檢査材料ヲ取得シ、病毒ノ傳播ヲ未然ニ察知シ、流行ノ蔓延ヲ防止スルコトニ努メタ。

長花班ハ流行發生地域及其ノ附近ノ鼠族ヲ蒐集シ、其ノ種類及數量ヲ檢査シ、尚鼠體附着昆蟲ノ種類及數量ヲ檢査シ、或ハ家屋內或ハ塵埃內ニ遊離シテキル蚤ノ狀況及荷物ニ附着シアル蚤ノ狀況等ヲ調査シ、其ノ調査成績ト鼠族及昆蟲ニ就テノ菌檢索成績ニヨリ流行發生原因ノ究明、傳染源ノ究明及傳播經路ノ究明ヲナシタ、尚新京市內各地域ノ鼠族及鼠體附着昆蟲ノ種類及數量ヲ廣ク調査シ、各地域ノ「ペスト」發生素因ノ有無ヲ明カニシタ。

宮崎班ハ自體防諜竝ニ敵性行爲ノ有無、ノ聯ヘノ反響、流言蜚語ノ調査ニ任ジ、主トシテ謀略的見地ヨリ流行發生ノ原因ヲ調査シタ。

2. 撲 滅 隊

流行地域一帶ノ鼠族ノ撲滅及病毒傳播ノ虞アル動物ノ撲滅ヲ主任務トシタ。

鼠族撲滅ノ方法トシテハ凡ユル手段ヲ使用シタ、即チ捕鼠器ヲ使用スルイロイロノ方法ト殺鼠劑ヲ使用スルイロイロナ方法ヲ併用シ、或ハ鼠巢ヲ探求シテ鼠ヲ捕殺シタ、蒐集シタ鼠ハ之ヲ菌檢索班ニ送付シタ。

以上ノ他各家屋ニ適スル防鼠設備ヲナシ或ハ鼠穴ヲ充塡シ、或ハ住民ニ鼠ノ習性ヲ知得セ

538－6

シメ、凡ユル手段ヲ用ヒテ人ト鼠トノ接腸ヲ絶ツ様ニ努メサセタ尚種々ノ手段ニヨツテ鼠及蚤ノ驅除ヲ期シ難イ様ナ患者發生家屋ノ燒却ヲ行ツタ。

3. 檢 診 除

多數ノ檢疹班ヲ編成シテ夫々擔當地域ヲ定メ、「ペスト汚染地帯ノ檢病的戸口調査ヲ行ヒ、或ハ防疫偵察ヲ實施シ、速カニ「ペスト患者及同容疑者ヲ摘發シ、或ハ死因疑ハシキ病死者ヲ摘出シ、之ヲ收容班ニ連絡シテ隔離病舍ニ收容サセタ、之ハ傳染源ヲ芟除スル爲ト病毒傳播ノ狀況ヲ知ル爲ニ役立ツタ。

「ペスト容疑者ハ體溫ノ上昇(38°C以上ヲ標準トス)、脈搏ノ頻數、壓痛アル腺腫、顏貌ノ疲憊狀態、步行踉蹌等ニ注意シテ摘發シタ。

尚警察除及自治團體ト協力シテ交通遮斷區域ノ監視及監督ヲナシ、又同區域内ノ住民ニ對スル物資ノ配給等ヲ指導シタ。

別勵除トシテ檢疫班、豫防接種班、收容班ヲ編成シテ夫々次ノ如キ業務ヲ分擔サセタ。

檢疫班、　新京ニ於テ農安流行方面ヨリノ降車客ヲ檢診シ、以テ病毒ノ搬入ヲ防止シ、尚新京驛ヨリノ乘車客ヲ檢診シ、病毒ノ搬出ヲ防止シタ。

豫防接種班、　流行發生地域ヲ中心トシテ市民全般ノ豫防接種ノ徹底ヲ計ツタ、尚豫防接種ノ普及ヲ徹底セシメル爲ニ「ペスト豫防注射證ヲ發行シテ之ヲ所持セシメ、之ヲ所持シナイ者ニハ交通ヲ禁止スル如クシタ。

收容班、　各檢診班及防疫斥候除ト連繫シ、「ペスト患者及同容疑者或ハ行路病者ノ收容隔離ヲナシ、又所要人員ノ健康隔離ヲナシタ、尚防疫斥候除及各檢診班ト連繫シ、行路病死者或ハ死因疑ハシキ病死者ヲ收容シ、之ヲ病理解剖班ニ交付シタ。

以上ノ他ハ檢診除ハ一部ヲ以テ長春縣「ペスト偵察除ヲ編成シ、長春縣ニ於ケル「ペスト」發生狀況ヲ調査シタ。

4. 消 毒 除

患者發生家屋及有菌鼠發見家屋ノ消毒及該家屋内ノ汚染物件ノ消毒ヲナシタ。

尚健康隔離者ノ消毒、汚染地區通過人員、車輛及物件ノ消毒ヲナシタ。

大ニ自體防疫ノタメ防疫從業員ノ消毒、使用セル防菌衣及物件ノ消毒ヲナシ、尚各作業班ニ必要ナ消毒藥ノ調製及交付ヲシタ。

此ノ期間ニ使用シタ主要藥物ハ「クレゾール石鹼液414,000ｇ、石炭酸184,500ｇ、「ピレトリン液180,000ｇ、酒精18,000ｇ、蚤取粉7,500ｇデアツタ。

以上ノ他昆蟲ノ撲滅ヲ任務トシタ、而シテ蚤ヲ驅除スル方法トシテハ大掃除ヲシテ塵埃ヲ燒却セシメ、居室ヲ清潔ニシテ蚤ノ發生ヲ防止シ、尚蚤取粉、除蟲菊ヲ撒布サセテ之ヲ殺蟲シ或ハ蚤ノ刺戟ヨリ防止シ、又衣服、寢具等ヲ日光ニ曝干シ或ハ饅頭蒸利用ニヨル消毒ヲ行ハセタ、其ノ他入浴其ノ他ニヨリ身體ノ保清ニ努メサセタ。

尚患者發生家屋及有菌鼠發見家屋ハ５％クレゾール石鹼液ノ消毒ヲ以テ殺菌及殺蟲ノ目的

690

538一瓦

ヲ達シタ。

別勤隊トシテ瓦斯班ヲ有シ、所要ノ家屋ニ就テ毒瓦斯ニヨル鼠及蚤ノ撲滅ヲ行ツタ。

5. 検　索　隊

「ペスト容疑者トシテ隔離病舎ニ收容サレタ患者ニ就テ菌検索ヲ行ヒ、「ペスト症ナルカ否カヲ決定シ、尚流行發生地域ノ住民ノ喀痰、血液等ニ就テ菌検索ヲ行ヒ、菌保有者ノ検出ニ努メタ。

病理解剖班ト連絡シテ行路病死者及死因不明ノ病死者ノ屍體ニ就テ菌検索ヲ行ヒ、其ノ死因ヲ明カニシタ。

流行發生地域ヨリ蒐集セル鼠及昆蟲或ハ新京市全般ヨリ蒐集セル鼠及昆蟲ニ就テ菌検索ヲ行ヒ、病毒ノ傳播ノ範圍及病毒侵径ノ程度ヲ知ルニ努メタ。

其ノ他病毒傳播ノ疑アル動物、昆蟲及物件ニ就テ菌検索ヲ行ヒ、病毒傳播經路ノ究明ニ對シ有益ナ資料ヲ提供シタ。

6. 病理解剖隊

行路病死者及死因不明ノ病死者ヲ解剖シテ其ノ死因ノ究明ニ努メタ。

尚「ペスト」ニテ死亡セルモノノ屍體解剖ヲ行ヒ、「ペスト症ノ病理解剖學的所見及病理組織學的所見ヲ検査シタ。

7. 隔離診療隊

隔離病舎ニ收容サレタ「ペスト患者及「ペスト容疑者トシテ收容サレタ患者ノ診斷的治療ヲシタ、尚健康隔離者ノ收容監視ヲシタ。

以上ノ他「ペスト症ニ就テノ臨床的觀察並ニ臨床的検査ヲシタ。

別勤隊トシテ外科治療班及「レントゲン班ガアリ、外科治療班ハ腺ペスト患者ノ外科的治療ヲ行ヒ、「レントゲン班ハ各型ノ「ペスト患者ノ「レントゲン學的検査ヲナシタ。

8. 其　ノ　他

交通遮斷ハ警察隊ヲシテ行ハセ、自治團體(義勇奉公隊)ヲシテ之ニ協力セシメタ。

尚交通遮斷區域內ノ物資ノ配給ハ自治團體(協和會、義勇奉公隊、青年團、國防婦人會)ヲシテ行ハセタ。

市內ノ大清掃ニハ官衙、會社ヲ休務セシメ、全市民ヲ協力セシメタ。

豫防接種ノ普及ニハ市內開業醫ヲ協力セシメタ。

第2節　感染經路及傳染經路ノ究明

今次「ペスト」ノ流行ニ於テ病毒ガ何處ヨリ如何ナル經路ニヨリ擴大セラレ、如何ニシテ傳播ガ行ハレタモノデアルカニ關シテ防疫斥候隊ハ初發患者ノ感染經路及續發患者ノ發生狀況等ヲ詳細ニ調査シ、併セテ謀略的行爲ノ有無ヲ調査シ、尚流行發生地域ノ鼠屍ノ狀況及有菌鼠ノ検出狀況等ヲ考究シタ結果、今次ノ流行ハ「ペスト流行地域(農安方面)ヨリ病毒ガ直接ニ三角地域ニ搬

691

538～8

入セラレ、此處ニ鼠ペスト」ノ流行ヲ惹起シ、遂ニ人ペスト」ノ流行ヲ惹起スルニ至ツタモノデア
ルト推論スルニ足ル資料ヲ獲得スルコトガ出来タ。此ノ事ハ流行地域内ノ鼠族及昆蟲ノ菌検索ノ
結果ヨリモ明カニシテ、今次人ペスト」ノ直接ノ傳染源ハ流行地域内ノ「ドブネズミ」間ニ傳播サ
レタ病毒ニシテ、大部分ハ有菌鼠ヨリ蚤ヲ介シテ人ニ傳播サレタモノデ人ヨリ人ヘノ直接ノ傳播
ハ例外的ノモノデアルコトヲ明カニシタ、併シナガラ病毒搬入ノ時期及搬入ノ方法ニ就テハ不明
デアツタ。

　上述ノ結論ヲ得ル爲ニ調査サレタコトニ就テ項目別ニ述ベレバ大體次ノ如クデアル。

1. 流行ノ初期ニ發生シタ「ペスト患者ノ發病前10日間ニ於ケル行動特ニ流行地域トノ交通或ハ流
　行地ニ交通アル人トノ交通關係ノ有無

2. 三角地域内ニ於ケル斃鼠ノ發見狀況

3. 農安ニ於ケル「ペスト患者ノ發生狀況及之ニ對スル檢疫實施ノ概況

4. 農安方面ト新京トノ人的，物的ノ交通狀況

5. 三角地域内居住民ノ行動調査、特ニ流行地（農安方面）トノ交通ノ有無

6. 流行發生前ニ於ケル三角地域ヲ中心トスル新京市内ノ行路病死者及死亡者ノ死因調査

7. 田島犬猫病院出入獸畜ニ關スル調査、特ニ其ノ獸畜所有家庭ノ狀況及其ノ獸畜所有者ノ流行
　地域トノ關係（獸畜ヲ携行シテ農安方面ノ流行地ニ出入セルコトナキヤ。）

8. 患者相互間ノ交通關係ノ有無

9. 「ペスト菌ヲ取扱フ研究機關關係者ニ關スル調査

10. 新京市内ニ於ケル細菌用具ノ販賣狀況

11. 田島犬猫病院ト外人トノ關係

12. 流行發生前ニ於ケル思想的容疑者ノ動靜

13. 流行發生前ニ於ケル新京來往外人ノ狀況

14. 流行地域ニテ捕獲セル鼠族及昆蟲ノ菌検索

　　　　第2節　傳染源ノ究明

　防疫ノ要締ハ傳染源ヲ速カニ發見シテ之ヲ芟除スルコトデアル、今次流行ニ於テハ鼠ペスト」
ノ先行シテキルコトガ明瞭デアツタノデ先ヅ病毒ガ如何ナル範圍ニ如何ナル程度ニ侵淫シテキル
カヲ究明スル爲ニ全市内ヨリ蒐集シタ鼠族ニ就テ菌検索ヲ行ツタ、其ノ結果流行ノ初期ハ三角地
域ニ相當ニ高率ニ有菌鼠ヲ發見シ、其ヨリ次第ニ周圍鼠族ヨリ菌ヲ検出シ。其ノ成績ヨリ鼠族間
ノ病毒ガ三角地域ヲ中心トシテ次第ニ周圍ニ傳播セル狀況ヲ明カニスルコトガ出来タ、尚鼠體ニ
附着シテキル「ケオピス鼠蚤及「アニズス鼠蚤ヨリ菌ヲ検出シ、其ノ成績ヨリ鼠ヨリ人ニ病毒ヲ傳
播スルノハ鼠蚤デアルコトヲ明カニスルコトガ出来タ。

　次ニ二次的傳染源トナル慮ノアル「ペスト患者ノ早期發見ニ努メタ、之ニ就テハ流行地域内デ
ハ検診隊ガ專ラ之ニ當リ、其ノ他ノ地域デハ防疫斥候隊ガ之ニ當ツタ、摘出シタ「ペスト患者及

692

537-29

同容疑者ハ速カニ之ヲ隔離病舎ニ收容シタ、尚行路病者及行路病死者或ハ死因不明ノ病死者ヲ防疫所候験、檢診隊ニヨツテ摘出シ、隔離所ニ收容シ、或ハ病理解剖隊ニ送付シテ菌檢索ノ結果共ノ病名及死因ヲ決定シ、病毒傳播ノ狀況ヲ察知スル資料ニシタ。

尚患者ノ發見ヲ容易ニスルタメニ死因疑ハシキ病死者ハ其ノ家族或ハ診療セル醫師ヲシテ申告セシメ、尚市民一般ニ「ペスト患者ヲ陰蔽スルコトガ恐ルベキ結果ヲ惹起スルコトヲ宣傳シ、或ハ指導階級ニ「ペスト」ニ關スル敎育ヲナシ、「ペスト患者及同死亡者ノ陰蔽ガ行ハレナイ樣ニシテ傳染源ノ究明ニ努メタ。

第4節　傳染源ノ剿滅

「ペスト流行ノ傳染源トナルベキモノハ「ペスト患者及「ペスト屍體、有菌鼠及有菌蚤、病毒汚染物件等デアル、從ツテ流行ヲ終熄セシメル爲ニハ是等ノ傳染源ヲ剿滅スルコトガ必要デアルノデ玆ニ今次流行ニ於テ行ツタ傳染源剿滅ノ方法ニ就テ述ベル。

二次的傳染源トシテ重要ナ意義ヲモツ「ペスト患者ニ就テハ速カニ之ヲ摘出シテ隔離病舎ニ隔離シ、其ノ排泄物ハ嚴重ニ消毒シテ病毒ノ傳播ヲ防ギ、又死亡セル際ハ火葬ニ附シテ病毒ノ絶滅ヲ期シタ。

行路病死者及死因不明ノ病死者ハ收容シテ剖檢シ、其ノ死因ヲ明カニシタ後夫々適當ニ處理ヲシタ。

人ペスト」ノ直接源トシテ最モ大キナ意義ヲ有ツ鼠族ノ撲滅ニ關シテハ撲滅隊ヲシテ之ニ當ラセ、凡ユル手段ヲ使用シタ、卽チ捕鼠ニ關シテハ從來用ヒラレテ來タ捕鼠器ヲ多數募集シ、各家庭ニ貸與シテ捕鼠作業ニ協力サセタ、其ノ他種々ノ捕鼠方法ヲ民衆ニ考案セシメ之ヲ實施シ之ヲ、又捕鼠器ノ使用方法ヲ新聞、「ラジオ」等ヲ以テ民衆ニ敎育シ、尚指導員ヲ派シテ捕鼠ヲ指導セシメ、又新京ノ鼠ノ食性及習性ヲ調査シテ餌トシテハ油揚、牛肉等ガ良好デアルコトヲ知リ又捕鼠能率ノ向上ヲ計リ、或ハ鼠ヲ買上ゲル方法及多數鼠ヲ捕獲セルモノニハ償金ヲ出ス方法等ヲ採用シ、或ハ强制的ニ鼠ヲ捕ラセル等ノ凡ユル手段ヲ盡シテ捕鼠ヲナサシメタ、殊ニ流行發生地域及其ノ周圍ノ地域ニ於テハ捕鼠ニヨル鼠族ノ撲滅ニ重點ヲ置イタ。

殺鼠劑ニヨル撲滅法ニ關シテモ凡ユル藥物ヲ使用シテ效果ヲ擧ゲルコトニ努メタ、殺鼠劑ニヨル時ハ鼠ガ斃死セル後ニ鼠體ニ附着シテヰル蚤ヲ遊離スルノデ流行地域デハ有菌蚤ヲ遊離シテ反ツテ危險ナ場合ガアルノデ、主トシテ流行地域以外ノ地域ニ於テ此ノ方法ニ重點ヲ置イタ、尚鼠ヲ鼠穴內ニテ斃死セシメル目的ニテ鼠穴ノ中ニ殺鼠劑ヲ入レ、外ヨリ其ノ鼠穴ヲ閉塞スル方法ヲ採ツタ、之ハ蚤ヲ遊離セシメル俱ガナイノデ極メテ良好ナ驅除法デアルト考ヘラレル、殺鼠劑ニヨル驅除モ民衆ノ協力ヲ俟ツコトガ大部分デアルノデ殺鼠劑ニヨル驅除法ニ就テハ新聞、「ラジオ」ヲ通ジテ敎育スルノミナラズ、指導員ヲ派シテ指導シタ、殺鼠劑ハ鼠ノ嗜好ニ適スル食物ニ附ケテ置イテ、其ヲ用ヒル時ニハ放事場、下水溝、塵埃捨場等ヲ淸潔ニシテ食物ノ接近ガ敢テ在テキナイ樣ニセネバナラナイコトヲ特ニ强調シタ。

693

538—10

次ニ「クロールピクリン」、「コクゾール」等ノ毒瓦斯ガ鼠族ノ驅除ニ極メテ有效ニシテ且確實デアルコトヲ確メタノデ、必要ヲ認メル家屋ニ對シテハ是等ノ藥物ヲ使用シテ徹底的ナ鼠族ノ驅除ヲ行ツタ、即チ氣密度ノ良好ナ良ク密閉サレタ家屋デハ 10～15g/m³ ヲ用ヒ、20時間ニテ概ネ殺鼠、殺蚤ヲ完全ニ行フコトガ出來タ。併シナガラ氣密粗惡ナ滿人家屋ニ於テハ縱ヘ戸障子ニ目張ヲ施シテモ屋根、壁ニ隙間多ク、20g/m³ ヲ使用シテモ尚效果ヲ期シ難キコトヲ認メタ。

以上ノ他ニ家屋內ノ鼠巢ヲ探索シテ鼠ヲ捕殺スルコトニ努メタ。

次ニ「鼠ペスト」ヲ人ニ傳播スルモノハ鼠體ニ附着シテヰル「ケオピス鼠蚤及「アニズス鼠蚤ニシテ、而モ其ガ家屋內ニ遊離シ、衣服、寢具ニ附着シ、或ハ塵埃ニ粉レ込ンデヰルコトガ明カデアルノデ、之ヲ驅除スルコドガ極メテ必要デアル。

昆蟲ヲ驅除スル方法ハイロイロアルガ、今次流行ニ於テ實施シタ方法ヲ述ベレバ次ノ如クデアル、即チ流行地域ノ家屋ヲ始メ全市ニ亙ツテ大掃除ヲ行ヒ、其ノ區埃ヲ燒却シテ遊離蚤ノ絶滅ヲ計リ、尚常ニ屋內ヲ淸潔ニシ、疊下ニ古新聞ヲ敷イテ蚤ノ發生ヲ防止シタ、次ニ各家庭ニ於テ被服、寢具、敷物類ヲ屢ミ直射日光ニ曝シテ蚤ノ殺滅ヲ行ハセタ。

藥物ニヨル蚤ノ驅除法トシテハ個人用トシテ流行地域內ノ住民ニハ除蟲菊ヲ使用セシメ、之ヲ寢具、襦袢等ニ撒布セシメテ蚤ノ刺螫ヨリ身體ヲ保護サセタ、尚室ノ隅ミニ撒布シテ蚤ノ近接ヲ防止セシメタ。

患者發生家屋ノ家材、寢具、被服、其ノ他ノ物件ニハ 5％クレゾール石鹸液ヲ多量ニ噴霧シテ殺菌竝ニ殺蚤ノ目的ヲ達シタ。

尚必要ト認ムル家屋ニ就テハ前述セル如ク室ヲ密閉シテ「クロールピクリン」、「コクゾール」等毒瓦斯ニヨリ長時間燻蒸ニヨリ家屋內ノ昆蟲ノ絶滅ヲ計ツタ。

又患者ノ被服、寢具等ハ蒸氣消毒ヲ行ツテ殺菌及殺蚤ノ目的ヲ達シタ、其ノ他必要ト認メルモノハ燒却滅菌シタ。

患者發生家屋ハ上述ノ如キ「クレゾール石鹸液ニヨル消毒ヲ行ツタ後「クロールピクリン」或ハ「コクゾール」ニヨル燻蒸消毒ヲ行ヒ、然ル後ニ海狽及白鼠ニヨル蚤吸着試驗ヲ行ツテ、其ニ依ツテ完全ニ除蚤サレテヰルカ否カヲ檢査シ、其ノ結果以上ノ如キ消毒方法ニテハ完全ニハ除鼠、除蚤ノ目的ガ達セラレナイト考ヘラレタモノハ家屋ノ周圍ヲ鐡板ニテ圍ヒ、鼠族ノ逃亡ヲ防グ如クシタ後ニ燒却處分ニ附シタ。

　　　　第5節　傳染經路ノ杜絶

病毒ノ傳播ヲ防グ爲ニハ傳染經路ヲ杜絶スルコトガ必要デアル、今次流行ニ於テハ傳染經路ヲ杜絶スル目的ヲ以テ次ニ述ベル如キコトガ行ハレタ。

1. 患者及關係者ノ隔離

　　二次的傳染源トナル「ペスト患者ヲ速カニ隔離病舍ニ隔離シ、尚檢診中ニ要ハシイ患者ヲ發見シタ時ハ速カニ之ヲ隔離病舍ニ收容シタ。尚患者ノ發生セル家族或ハ患者ト交通ノアツタモ

538—11

ノハ濃厚ニ汚染サレテキルモノトシテ、之ヲ健康隔離所(隔離病舎トハ別棟ニ設ケル)ニ收容シ
タ、隔離期間ハ患者ニアリテハ完全ニ治癒シ、他ニ病毒ヲ傳播スル危險ノ全クナクナル迄隔離
シ、患者關係者ノ隔離期間ハ隔離ヲナシ、消毒ヲ完了シタ時ヨリ起算シテ滿14日トシタ。

以上ノ期間隔離シタ後嚴重ナ檢診ヲ行ヒ、身體ヲ消毒シ、衣服, 持物等ノ消毒ヲ完了シタ後
ニ隔離ヲ解除シタ。

2. 交通遮斷

「ペスト患者ノ發生シタ地域或ハ有菌鼠ヲ發見シタ地域ハ直チニ適當ナ地域ヲ劃シテ交通遮
斷ヲ行ヒ、其ノ地域内ノ住民ト他地域ノ住民トノ間ノ交通ヲ禁止シタ、斯クシテ交通遮斷區域
内ノ消毒、鼠族及昆蟲ノ驅除ヲ徹底的ニ行ツタ。

交通遮斷ノ期間ハ其ノ地域内ニ於ケル發生狀況鮮明シ、最早ヤ流行ノ處ナキニ至ツタ時ヨリ
(最終患者ノ發生セル時)起算シテ滿14日間トシタ。

尚病毒傳播ノ機會ヲ少クスルタメ學校ノ休業ヲナシ、或ハ娛樂機關ノ制限或ハ交通制限等ヲ
シタ。

3. 檢 疫

最安方面ヨリノ病毒搬入ヲ防止スルタメ新京驛ニ於テ最安方面ヨリノ降車客ノ檢診及消毒ヲ
行ヒ、又新京ヨリ他地域ヘノ病毒ノ搬出ヲ防止スル爲ニ乘車客ノ檢疫ヲ行ツタ。

4. 防疫設備

鼠ニヨル病毒ノ傳播ヲ防止スルニハ鼠間ノ交通ヲ杜絶シ、鼠ト人トノ交通ヲ杜絶スルコトガ
必要デアル、之ガ爲ニハ家屋ニ防鼠設備ヲスル必要ガアル、其處デ家屋ノ入口ニ鐵板ヲ低ク張
ツテ鼠ノ出入ヲ防止シ、又鼠ノ通路トナル様ナ箇所(溝渠トノ通路及壁、天上等ノ穴)ハ塗ヲ閉
塞シ、或ハ金網ヲ張ツテ鼠ノ出入ヲ防止シタ、又屋内ヲ清潔ニシ、殊ニ食物ノ残渣ノナイ様ニ
シテ鼠ノ出入ヲ防止シタ。

尚必要ヲ認メタ建物ハ亞鉛鐵ヲ圍繞シ、下様ヲ深ク地中ニ埋メ、鼠ノ出入ヲ防止シタ。

5. 貨物運搬ノ禁止及制限

最安方面ニ「ペスト」ノ流行發生スルヤ被服、毛布、綿類等ノ新京市内ヘノ搬入ハ禁止サレテ
キタケレドモ尚其ノ實施ガ不十分デアツタノデ、以上ノ他家具、寢具、穀類等ノ搬入ヲ禁止シ
タ。

以上述ベタ様ナ荷物ニハ鼠或ハ蚤ガ紛レ込ンデ運搬サレル危險ガ大デアルノデ流行地域ヨリ
ノ搬出モ禁止シタ。

第6節 個人防疫法

1. 豫防接種ノ普及

「ペスト・ワクチン」ハ他ノ「ワクチン」ニ比シテ極メテ有效ナモノニシテ、而モ「ワクチン」接
種ニヨル所謂陰性期ハ認メラレズ即チ流行發生セル後ニ豫防接種ヲスルモ全然害ハ認メラレナ

538—12

イノデ假防接種班アンテ豫防接種ヲ行ハセ、又市内開業醫ヲ動員シテ豫防接種ニ協力セシメ
タ、尚豫防接種ノ普及徹底ヲ計ル爲ニ「ペスト豫防接種證ヲ發行シ、之ヲ所持シナイモノへ通
行ヲ禁止スル如クシタ。

2. 「マスク」ノ使用

　　流行ノ末期ニハ敗血症型ペスト」發生シ、此等ノ患者ニハ著明ナ肺症狀ヲ起シテ飛沫傳染ノ
危險ガアリ、且寒氣ノ襲來ト共ニ肺ペスト」ノ流行ヲ惹起スル虞ガアツタノデ市民ニハ外出時
必ズ「マスク」ヲ使用サセタ。

3. 身體ノ保溫ニ努メサセ、又皮膚等ヲ損傷サセナイ樣ニ注意シタ、又蚤其ノ他ノ吸血昆蟲ニ刺
螫サレナイ樣ニ被服、寢具ニ除蟲菊粉ヲ撒布セシメタ。

4. 民衆ノ教育特ニ指導者階級ニ對スル防疫知識ノ向上ニ努メタ(「ラジオ」、新聞、「ポスター」、
「パンフレツト」、講演、映畫、展覽會等ニヨル方法)。

　　　第7節　防疫實施人員ノ自衞

　　患者ノ檢診、收容、看護、細菌檢索、病理解剖、消毒、驅鼠、除鼠等ノ作業ニ從事シタ防疫實
施員ハ自衞ノ爲次ノ事項ニ注意シタ。

1. 患者又ハ病毒汚染ノ場所及物件ニ接觸セントスル時ハ頭巾、「マスク」、豫防衣及「ゴム長靴ヲ
着テ、手ニハ「ゴム手袋ヲ使用シタ。

2. 消毒、檢診、治療等ニ用ヒタ器具、器械、被服類ハ其ノ都度嚴重ニ消毒シタ。

3. 鼠族及昆蟲類ヲ驅除スル場合ニハ常ニ鼠族ニ附着セル蚤又ハ附近ニ潛伏シテキル蚤、南京蟲、
虱等ヲ身邊ニ附着セシメナイ樣ニ注射シタ、又萬一附着シタ蚤類ガ衣服內ニ潛入シナイ樣ニ扮
裝ノ要所ヲ緊縛シ、其ノ部分ニ除蟲菊ヲ撒布シタ。

4. 皮膚ニ微細ナ傷デモ負ハナイ樣ニ注意シタ、若シ損傷ノアル時ハ速カニ治療ノ方法ヲ講ジ、又
病毒ノ侵入ヲ防止スルタメ損傷部位ニ繃帶ヲ施シ、或ハ絆創膏ヲ貼附スル等ノ適宜ナ處理ヲ取
ツタ。

5. 作業終了後ハ成ルベク入浴シテ身體ヲ淸潔ニシ、淸潔ナ衣服ニ更へ、含嗽ヲ勵行シ、併セテ
日常粘膜ヲ損傷シナイ樣ニ注意シタ。

　　斯クシテ防疫業務ヲ終了シ、防疫隊ヲ解散スル際ニハ防疫從業員全員ノ檢疫ヲ行ヒ、10日間
隔離シテ、異常ノナイコトヲ觀察セル後ニ夫々原所屬ニ復歸サセタ。

　　　　總　　　括

1. 今次流行ニ於ケル軍官民ヲ一體トスル、防疫機關ノ編成ノ概要ニ就テ述ベタ。

2. 今次流行ニ於ケル防疫施設ノ概要ニ就テ述ベタ。

3. 防疫ノ實施要領ニ就テ述べ、次ニ感染經路ノ究明、傳染源ノ究明、傳染源ノ剿滅、傳染經路
ノ杜絶、個人防禦法、防疫實施人員ノ自衞等ニ就テ實施シタ具體的手段ト其ノ效果ニ就テ述べ

538—13

タ。

之ヲ要スルニ今次ノ「ペスト」防疫ハ軍官民ヲ一體トシタ防疫態勢ニ於テ實施サレタコトニ特徴ヲ有スルモノニシテ、一朝有事ノ際ニハ斯カル高度防疫態勢ヲ必要トスルコトハ想像ニ難タナイノデ、斯様ナ際ニ何等カノ参考ニナラバト思ヒ不備ヲ顧ミズ、此ノ記述ヲナシタ次第デアル。

文　　　献

1) 滿鐵衛生課：「ペスト」防疫指針、(康德2年6月)　　2) 阿部：大陸醫學、(昭. 16, 1, 3.
3) Dieudonne, A. & Otto, R.："Handbuch der pathogenen Microorganismen," (1928).
III, aufl., 4, 179.

4.2 附录 ペスト防疫報告書（1940 年）（节选）

资料出处：日本贸易振興機構（JETRO）亚洲经济研究所藏、FA011033。

内容点评：本资料为南满铁道株式会社"新京"临时防疫委员会的《鼠疫防疫报告书》，选取其中第二编"总务班"第十二章"农安派遣队"、第四编"检疫班"第五章"防疫费"和第六章"效果"。日军 731 部队于 1940 年 6 月对农安等地散布鼠疫跳蚤后，"新京"9 月 27 日爆发鼠疫流行，"新京"临时防疫委员会于 10 月 12 日成立。

目　次

目 次

二

目　次 (二)

四

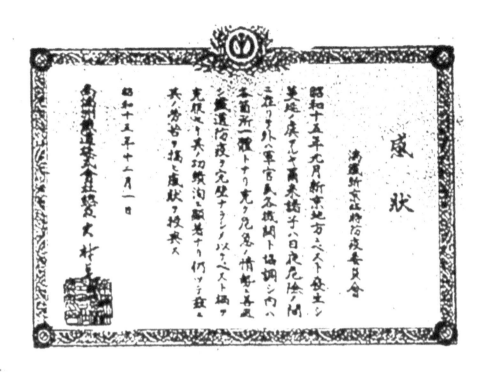

感　謝　狀

感　狀　授　與　式（於新京支社）

ムルトコロデアリマシテ致方アリマセンカ滿鐵會社社員デアリマス各位ニ對シテハ決シテ隔離中ハ勿論隔離後ノコトニ就テモ心配イタナイ

樣會社ニ於テ處置シ各位ノ出勤ヲ待ツテ居ルノテアリマス

卽チ隔離出勤不能中ト雖會社ニ出勤ト同樣ノ給料手當ハ支給スル外尚出來ルダケノコトハスルツモリデアリマス

何ウカ各位ハ臭々モ心配セス完氣テ健康ニ氣ヲ付ケ良ク保管�指示ニ從ヘレ防疫ニ注意スル樣希望シマス

昭和十五年十月十八日

新京支社長

午島理事

第十二章　農安派遣隊

第一項　編成出發迄

十月十五日非公式ニ新京支社長宛軍早川少佐ヨリ新京附近ニ於ケル病源地帶ニシテ新京防疫ニ應接關係ヲ有スル農

安縣城附近「ベスト」撲滅ヲ期ス爲、軍、滿洲國、滿鐵、滿赤合同ニテ之ノ力防疫ヲ實施スルニ付協力方申入レアリ且同

日軍會報常上ニ於テ之ノ力防疫隊編成並滿鐵トシテ協力スヘキ水項卽チ防疫隊員ノ輸送手配宿營用トシテノ列車及自動

車（從業員ヲ含ム）ノ供出等協議セリ。

翌十六日關係者ノ會合協議ノ結果ニ依リ不取敢左記非項手配方總局宛連絡セリ。

（前記之力處置ハ運輸班第二章第六項參照）

記

（一）隊編成期間　十月十九日ヨリ約二週間

（二）人　員　約二、一〇〇名

第二項　總務班

四三

第二編　總務班

四四

（三）隊員物資ノ輸送竝宿營ノタメ客車二二輛（ロ ホ二、ハネ五、ハ一五）貨車一三（ヤ一一、ム二〇）十九日八時迄ニ

新京驛ニ集結供出ノコト

（四）提安驛構内側線ニ前號客貨車ヲ廻入シ宿營竝診擦施設ヲ爲ス

以テ左ノ諸項ヲ手配スルコト

イ、宿營用客車ニハ夜間通汽スルコト

ロ、驛貨物倉庫ヲ事務室トシテ提供スルコト

ハ、ロネニハ寢具一式入附ノコト

ニ、ハネニハ枕入附ノコト

ホ、ハノ座席ニ適當ノ板ヲ置キ各ボックスニ二名宛横臥可能ナル

如ク裝置スルコト

ヘ、宿營手配竝電話架設ノ爲メ檢車區員及電氣區員ヲ派遣スルコ

ト

（五）新京—提安間隊員竝物資輸送ノ臨時列車運轉ニ就テハ野鐵ヨ

リ別途通達アルニ付右ニ依リ處置ノコト

（六）自動車ヲ現地ニテ使用スルニ付左ニ依リ供出スルコト

イ、輛數　バス一〇、トラック一五、計二五輛（含附屬品）

ロ、半廂八十九日十二時迄ニ提安驛ニ集結ノコト

提安驛進出段階出發狀況

八、遞轉乎其ノ他所要人員ヲ十九日九時迄ニ新京支社前ニ集結ノコト

（七）本隊ニ加ハリ隊長ノ指揮下ニ入ル滿鐵社員ハ臨時軍屬ト爲ス旨關東軍トノ間ニ協議濟

殺イテ次ノ如ク正式ニ關東軍命令及關東軍臨時ペスト防疫隊本部ノ農安附近ペスト防疫計畫ニ接シタリ。

[備 考] 一

關作命甲第三八〇號

關 東 軍 命 令

一、軍ハ首都新京ノ防疫陣ヲ更ニ强化シ流行「ペスト」ノ早期絕滅ニ努ムルト共ニ一部ヲ以テ新京防疫ニ直接關係ヲ有
スル農安縣城附近「ペスト」病源地帶ノ防疫ヲ實施セントス

二、關東軍臨時「ペスト」防疫隊本部長ハ依然前任務ヲ賴行スルト共ニ一部ヲ以テ農安縣城附近「ペスト」病源地帶ノ防
疫ヲ實施スヘシ

右農安縣城附近「ペスト」病源地帶防疫實施ノ爲滿洲國民生部保健司ト長及滿鐵臨時防疫委員會委員長ヲ區處スヘシ

三、關東憲兵隊司令官ハ以然前任務ヲ賴行スヘシ

農安縣城附近「ペスト」病源地帶ノ防疫警察勤務ニ關シテハ滿洲國等務機關之ニ任ス

四、尾高、篤津部隊長ハ別紙ノ部隊ヲ臨時編成シ十月十九日十二時迄ニ新京ニ派遣シ關東軍臨時ペスト防疫隊本部長
ノ指揮下ニ入ラシムヘシ

五、新京陸軍病院長ハ現ニ補備教育中ノ短期現役軍醫全員及臨時教育要員大部ヲシテ十月十六日十八時以降關東軍臨

十月十六日十二時

新京軍司令部

第二編 總 務 班

四五

第二編　總務班

四六

六、哈爾濱陸軍病院長ハ關東軍衛生部下士官候補者教育部長ヲシテ現ニ教育中ノ衛生下士官候補者全員ヲ十月十七日
時「ペスト」防疫隊本部長ノ指揮下ニ入ラシムヘシ

十二時迄ニ新京ニ派遣シ關東軍臨時「ペスト」防疫隊本部長ノ指揮下ニ入ラシムヘシ

七、波田、安井部隊長及大連陸軍病院長ハ夫々左記衛生將校ヲ速ニ新京ニ派遣シ關東軍臨時「ペスト」防疫隊本部長ノ

指揮下ニ入ラシムヘシ

左　記

大連陸軍病院　　衛生大尉吉岡政夫

海拉爾第一陸軍病院　衛生中尉林田藤市

安東第一陸軍病院　衛生大尉佐藤鶴雄

八、　　隊長ハ第四及第六項ノ部隊、人員ノ新京ニ於ケル宿營給養ヲ擔任スヘシ

九、農安縣城附近「ペスト」病源地帶防疫實施ノ細項ニ關シテハ關東軍參謀長ヲシテ指示セシム

關東軍司令官　梅　津　大　將

下達法　要旨ヲ電報（命令受領者ニ口述）後印刷交付

配布先　尾高、鷲津、波田、安井、野副部隊、臨防疫、新京、哈爾濱、大連、安東、第一、海拉爾第

一、各陸軍病院、部內、最高顧問、滿洲國政府關係處司

別紙

臨時編成苦力隊派出區分表

部隊	編成基準	
第一防疫班	將校ノ指揮スル下士官四兵約八十名ヨリ成ル	尾高部隊
第二防疫班	將校ノ指揮スル下士官二兵約四十名ヨリ成ル	瀋津部隊
備考	一、下士官ハ成ルヘク衛生下士官ヲ充ツルモノトス 二、兵ハ概ネ三分ノ一ハ衛生兵トシ他ハ成ルヘク機關銃操縱兵ヲ充ツルモノトス 三、防疫班用諸資材ハ携行セサルモノトス 四、人員ハ駐屯地出發前ニ於テ成ルヘクペスト豫防接種ヲ實施スルモノトス	登出部隊

「備考」二

關作命甲第三八〇號ニ基キ左ノ如ク指示ス

　　　　指　　示

一、農安縣城附近「ペスト」病源地帶防疫實施開始ノ時期ハ一月二十日トシ約二週間ヲ以テ一應之カ終結ヲ圖ルモノトス

二、農安縣城附近「ペスト」病源地帶ノ防疫實施場所左ノ如シ

　　農安縣城及北ノ外郭「ペスト」發生部落

第二編　勤　務　班

四七

第二編　總　務　班

四八

揖家店附近

稔椹坨子附近

三、農安縣城附近「ペスト」病源地帶ノ防疫實施ノ為特ニ準據スヘキ事項左ノ如シ

1　防疫ノ實施ハ新京直接防疫ニ最モ關係ヲ有スル重要地域ヨリ開始スルヲ本則トス

2　防疫ノ實施ニ方リテハ特ニ民心ノ安定ニ努ムルト共ニ民衆ヲシテ自ラ進ンデ防疫ニ從事スル如ク利導スルコトニ努ムルモノトス

3　本防疫實施總結ニ伴ヒ滿洲國側獨自ノ機關ヲ以テ所要ノ期間首都新京ノ直接防疫ニ遺憾ナカラシムル恆久的對策ヲ講シ得ル如クスルモノトス

4　防疫從事員ノ本病感染ノ豫防對策ニ關シテハ特ニ萬遺憾ナカラシムルモノトス

四、關東軍臨時「ペスト」防疫隊本部長ハ關係機關ト協定シ防疫實施要領ヲ策定シ豫メ報告スルト共ニ關係機關ヘ通報スルモノトス

昭和十五年十月六日

關東軍臨時「ペスト」防疫隊本部長殿

關東軍參謀長　飯　村　中　將

「備　考」三

參考配布區分
憲司、勢剛憲隊、最添關間、部內、滿洲國政府關係官司

派遣軍校經由

關參一發第四四二二號

昭和十五年十月十七日

擬安附近ペスト防疫ノ爲車輛供出ニ關スル件

關東軍參謀長　飯　村　穰

南滿洲鐵道株式會社

鐵道總局長　佐藤應次郎　殿

擬安附近ペスト防疫業務實施ノ爲十月十九日ヨリ概ネ二週間機關車一、二等寢臺車二、三等寢臺車五、三等客車一

五有蓋貨車四無蓋貨車三（所要從事員ヲ含ム）ヲ擬安驛ニ留置シ軍ニ供用セシムルト共ニ之ニ伴ヒ擬安驛施設ノ一部ヲ

軍ニ使用セシメラレ度依命通牒ス

追而右ハペスト防疫ノ爲止ムヲ得サル處置ニシテ一般ニ適用スル儀ニアラサルモノト承知相成度

尚細部ニ關シテハ左記ニ據ラレ度申添フ

　　　　左　記

一、供出車輛ハ新京ヨリ擬安迄輸送スルペスト防疫隊員輸送列車ノモノヲ流用ス

但シ右輸送ハ野戰鐵道司令部ノ計畫スルトコロニ依ル

二、供出車輛ハ防疫隊員ノ宿泊ニ使用ス之カ爲三等客車ニハ簡單ナル給裝施設ヲナスモノトス

三、右列車宿泊ノ爲必要ナル鐵道從事員ハ本期間關東軍臨時ペスト防疫隊本部長ノ指揮ニ入ルモノトシ臨時乘局（但

シ無給トス）トス

第二印　軍　務　班

四九

第二輯　總務班

五〇

尚本期間ニ於ケル鐵道從事員ノ宿營、給養ハ軍ニ於テ擔任ス

四、供出車輛ノ專用料ハ軍、滿鐵間軍事輸送關係業務規定ニ據ルモノトス

五、農安縣施設中軍ノ使用ニ供スルハ關棧内ノ貨物倉庫トシ之ニ所要ノ電燈通信施設ヲナスモノトス

六、以上車輛ノ專用、驛、車輛等ニ實施スル施設ニ要スル經費ハ軍ニ於テ共實費ヲ負擔ス

七、以上實施ノ細部ニ關シテハ軍主任參謀ヲシテ連絡セシム

「備考」四

派遣將校經由關參一發第四四二三號

農安附近ペスト防疫ノ爲自動貨車差出ニ關スル件

昭和十五年十月十七日

關東軍參謀長・飯　村　　穰

南滿洲鐵道株式會社

鐵道總局長　佐藤應次郎殿

農安附近ペスト防疫實施ノ爲自動車十五輛パス一〇輛（運轉手共）ヲ十九日十二時迄ニ農安驛ニ差出シ關東軍臨時ペ

スト防疫隊本部長ノ指揮ヲ受ケシメラレ度依命通牒ス

追而右差出ノ細部ニ關シテハ左記ニ據ラレ度

左　　記

一差出期間ハ概ネ二週間トス

二、本期間ニ於ケル滿鐵從事員ノ身分ハ臨時軍屬（但シ無給トス）トシ其宿舍、給養ハ軍ニ於テ擔任ス

三、自動貨車及バスハ軍ノ借上トシ其料金及之ガ輸送、從事員ノ差出ニ要スル經費ニ關シテハ別途軍、貴社間ニテ協定スルトコロニ據リ軍ニ於テ負擔ス

「備考」五

二五部中第一六號

農安附近ペスト防疫計畫　關東軍臨時ペスト防疫隊本部

第一、方　針

農安附近傍ノペスト利源ヲ一擧ニ撲滅シ以テ國都新京ノペスト禍ヲ速ニ終熄セシム

特ニ防疫從事員ノペスト感染ノ豫防ニハ萬遺憾ナキヲ期ス

第二、要　領

一、先ツ目下患者多發シアル農安縣城附近ニ主點ヲ指向シ主力ヲ以テ農安縣城近傍各一部ヲ以テ果家店及楡樹坨子附近ノ防疫ヲ實施スル傍ラ所要ノ部落ニ對シ臨時一部ヲ派遣シ得ル如ク準備ス

二、滿洲國警察隊八十月十九日淀迄ニ農安縣城近傍果家店及楡樹坨子附近ノ交通遮斷ヲ實施ス

三、交通遮斷ノ配備完了ト共ニ防疫ノ趣旨ヲ住民ニ周知徹底セシメ以テ民心ノ恐慌不安ヲ防止ス

四、防疫部隊ノ主力ハ滿洲國警察隊ニ相踵イテ農安ニ到リ直ニ防疫ノ諸準備ニ着手ス

五、二十日朝ヨリ防疫ヲ開始ス

但シ當初果家店、楡樹坨子附近ニ對シテハ防疫序隊ノ派遣ニ止ム

第二班　勤　務　班

五一

第二編　總務班

六、後續防疫部隊ハ二十日七時十五分新京出發農安ニ追及シ防疫ニ參加ス

七、農安縣城內外裴家店及楡樹坨子附近ニ於テ防疫ヲ實施スル傍ヲ適時所要ノ地點ニ防疫斥候ヲ派遣シ患者發生ノ實況ヲ確ム

附表第一ノ如シ(缺表)

第三、防疫隊ノ編成並裝備

防疫實施要領別冊ノ如シ(缺冊)

第四、防疫實施

第五、交通遮斷

滿洲國警發隊ハ左記諸項ニ準據シ交通遮斷ヲ計劃實施スルモノトス。

記

一、防疫實施ノ初頭ニ於ケル交通遮斷地域附圖第一共ノ一ノ如シ、農安縣城ニ於ケル交通遮斷ノ現配備(附圖共ノ二)ハ依然現狀ノ儘トス

二、交通遮斷ハ十月十九日日沒迄共ノ配備ヲ完了スルモノトス.

三、裴家店、楡樹坨子等農安縣城ヨリ遠隔セル部落ノ交通遮斷ニ任スル隊員ノ裝備給養ニハ特ニ遺憾ナキヲ期シ其ノ不備、不充分ノ爲ニ感染ノ災禍ヲ招クカ如キコトナカラシム

四、患者發生ナキ部落ト雖濫リニ立入ルコトヲ禁止ス

第六、　署　　備

五二

野戰部隊ヨリ派遣セラルル警備部隊ハ農安附近防疫資施地域ニ於ケル全般ノ警備ニ任スル外所要ニ應シ防疫警察勤務ノ支援後據タルモノトス。

宿舍共ノ他ノ直接警戒ハ各機關緊密ナル連繫ノ下ニ自ラ之ニ當ルモノトス。

特ニ防諜ニ留意ス。

　　　第七、輸送

一、新京ヨリ農安方面ヘノ輸送ハ左表ニ據ルモノトス但シ列車運行ノ細部ハ野鐵ニ於テ計畫ス

新京農安間旅前輸送計畫

列車番號	輸送部隊	輸送時日	摘要
第一列車	滿洲闊東憲察隊　七六五名	新京發　十九日　一四時二〇分 農安著　十九日　一六時二〇分	宿營用車輛ヲ充當スルモノトス
第二列車	次 防疫隊主力 滿赤部設隊 滿部隊 電民電 貿	有蓋（內二兩業務隊）二二兩 フラツト	新京發　十九日　一五時四〇分 農安著　十九日　一八時〇二分	一、次車ハ宿營用車輛ヲ充當スルモノトス 二、貨車ハ主トシテ圓珠、宿營器具、消毒具ヲ搭載ス

第二後務班

第二編　總務編

第三列車		
第一及第二防疫隊二八名	新京發農安著	二十日 七時一五分 普通列車トス

五四

二、農安ヨリ晶家店及楡樹坨子間ノ發際隊員及防疫斥候ノ輸送ハ自動貨車ニ依ルモノトス

第八、通信連絡

一、新京農安間

1　滿鐵守備専用線ヲ使用シ左圖ノ如ク囘線ヲ構成ス

農安ノ端局施設ハ滿鐵、新京ニ於テハ紙司令部擔任トス

農安　　　　　　　　新京

X　　　　　　　　　X總本部（電電管理局）

本部（驛西側中學校）　軍司令部（第一課）

2　障碍時ハ臨機滿鐵ノ他ノ囘線若ハ電線ニ依ルモノトス

3　施設位置ノ細部ニ圖シテハ現地ニ於テ指示ス

4　施設時期

十月二十日十時迄ニ完了スルモノトス

三、農安縣城附近

1　防疫用

イ、施政ネベキ通信網附圖第二ノ如シ

715

ロ、施設勤任、電電トス

ハ、要　領

新京本社ヨリ所要ノ要員及資材ヲ十月十九日第二臨時列車ニテ新京發提安ニ輸送ス速ニ作業ヲ終了シ翌日嚴車

消毒ノ上歸京スルモノトス

施設後ノ維持竝防疫終了後ノ撤収作業ハ主トシテ現地電電社員ニテ實施スルモノトス

ニ、經　　費

軍負擔トス

2　警　察　用

警務司ニ於テ計畫施設スルモノトス

三、堀家店共ノ他ノ連絡施設

自動車、列車便、飛行機等ニ依リテ連絡スルヲ主眼トシ尚爲シ得レハ警務司、滿鐵、電電等ノ餘剰資材ヲ以テ電話回線ヲ搆成スルモノトス

第九、照　　明

一、施　　設

附圖三ノ如シ

二、掠　　任

電裝トス

第二編　總　務　班

五五

第二輯　總務班

五六

三、要　領

新京本社ヨリ所要ノ要員及資材ヲ十月十九日第二臨時列車ニテ新京發農安ニ輸送ス

速ニ作業ヲ終リ翌日嚴重ニ溝器ノ上鮎京スルモノトス

施設後ノ維持竝防疫終了後ノ搬收作業ハ主トシテ現地電業社員ヲシテ實施スルモノトス

四、經　費

軍負擔トス

宿營給養計畫

第十、宿　營　給　養

別冊ノ如シ。

第十一、宜　撫

左記要項ニ準據シ滿洲國側ニ於テ計畫實施スルモノトス

一、住民ノ逃走ヲ防止スル必要上防疫實施ヲ秘匿シ十月十九日夕憲察隊ヲ以テスル交通遮斷ノ配備完了ト共ニ一般ニ周知セシムルモノトス

二、交通遮斷ト共ニナルヘク速ニ防疫實施ノ趣旨ヲ了得セシメ以テ民心ヲ恐慌動搖セシメサル爲離般ノ手段ヲ講ス

別冊

一、農安停車場宿舍準備數左ノ如シ(容車充當)

二十噸等度客　四八名分(二平輔裝具附)

派遣部隊宿營給養計畫

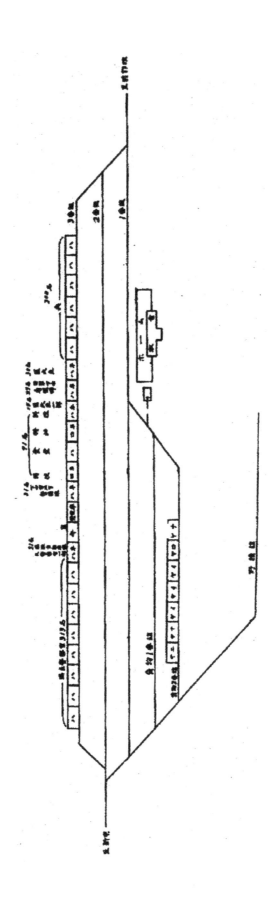

二、宿舎使用區分左ノ如シ

一、〇三〇分

六六二名分(一五車輛一輛四四名使用)

三二〇名分(五車輛)

夜間車内ハ蒸気煖房及發電ニ依リ點燈ヲ爲スモノトス。

計

三等客車

三等寝袋

使用區分／使用者	軍	満鐵	満洲國満	赤	警務署
二等寝袋	二五	一	三	六	一二

使用區分／使用者	軍	満鐵	満洲國満	赤	警務署
三等寝袋	一五〇	三〇	一〇	三〇	一八〇〇
三等客車	二〇〇	一	六二	一	二〇〇
計	三七五	三一	七四	三六	四〇三

備考

1 豫備三等寝袋 二二 三等客車 一〇〇

2 平ノ將校ニシテ三等車ヲ使用スルモノハ一瓦斯器ヲ四人ニテ使用シ上段ハ荷物置場ニ使用セシム

1 搭載、満亦ノ給養ハ車ニ於テ給ス

3 滿軍及事務處ハ獨立給養ヲ行フモノトス

第二回 勤務班

五七

719

第二編　總　務　班

　　　　　　　　　　　　　　　　　　　　　　　　　　　　　　　　五八

四、軍ノ給與次ノ如シ

1、イ、新京滯在間、

慈內居住下士官以下ノ宿營給養ハ野間部隊ノ撥任

ロ、其ノ他ノモノノ宿營ハ野間部隊ニ於テ撥任シ給養ハ臨滿旅發規定第五表定額內實費支辨トス

2　新京以外ニ出勤中ハ總テ臨滿旅費規定第五表定額內實費支辨トス

3　防疫遮斷間ニ於ケル食糧其ノ他ノ補給ニ遺憾ナカラシム

4　防疫實施上住民ニ被ラシメタル損害ハ努メテ之ヲ補償ス

5　防疫開始ト共ニ事實ヲ新聞其ノ他ニ發表シ不安疑惑ノ一掃ニ努ム

6　以上常ニ民心ノ安定ニ努ムルノミナラズ住民ヲシテ自主積極的ニ防疫ニ協力從事スル如ク利導スルモノトス

　　　　第十二、敎　育

農安附近防疫實施間ニ於ケル敎育ハ左記要領ニ據ルモノトス。

　　　　記

一、關東軍派遣衛生將校三名及短期軍醫三八名ノ敎育

十六日防疫隊ノ全般任務ニ就キ實施

十七日、十八日要員ヲ任務別ニ各班ニ配屬シ那門事項ヲ實地ニ習得セシム

二、十九日增配セラルヘキ關東軍派遣衛生部下士官候補者（約一二〇名）敎兵（一二〇名）ニ對スル敎育

1　現滿洲國ペスト發生狀況

2　ペスト防疫隊ノ任務編成裝備

3　ペスト病、ペスト按學ニ就テ

4　ペスト診断（ペスト菌ノ性状培養法、ペストノ早期診断）

5　ペストノ防疫並撲滅法ニ就テ

6　活動寫眞教育

十月十八日農安行臨時列車時刻モ十月十九日第一列車ハ新京驛第四ホーム發一四時一〇分農安着一六時十七分第二列車ハ同ジク一五時十分農安着十七時十七分ト決定シ夫々派遣人員ノ選定車輛供出連絡方法（毎日午前午後ノ二回定運時話）等準備完了シ十九日之等襲安派遣社員ハ新京支社第三會議ニ於テ委員長ヨリ見エサル故ト雖フ諸子ノ勞苦身ノ危險ハ實ニ御氣遣ニ堪エヌカ今回ノ撲滅隊ノ任務ノ重大性ニ鑑ミ滿鐵社員トシテ將一層ノ努力ヲ望ム旨懇篤ナル訓示アリ且亦社員會新京聯合會主催ニテ壯行令ヲ催シ尾崎聯合令長ハ特ニ先人ノ名ヲ辱シメサル様共ノ重責ヲ果シ無事歸還セラルヽ様神カケテ御祈リスル旨ノ激勵ノ辭ヲ述ヘ見送ルモノ見送ラル、モノ共ニ感激セリ。

派遣社員ノ武運長久ヲ祈リ新京神社ノ御守及マスクヲ贈呈シ溌溂タル二勇シク元氣旺盛一路襲安ニ向ケ出發シタリ。

派遣社員ノ名簿並自動車隊ノ編成左ノ如シ。

襲安ペスト防疫派遣員名簿

所	屬	査	格	職	名	氏	名	年	齢	記	事

第二監理所務班

| 洮南縣城内監理所 | 刷 | 參 | 事 | 監理所長 | 高橋勤一 | | 四四 | | | | |

第二課　雄機班

所属	役職	氏名	年齢
同	監理員	吉田政信固	三五
新京自動車區	助菜役員	有安英俊	三三
同	集菜員	小倉貞吉	三〇
同	運轉手	瀨川　英一	二九
同	同	宇都良英	四
哈爾濱自動車區	同	中村直一	二六
同	同	奥田勇次郎	三
同	同	小榮次郎	三
同	同	中島　一	二六
同	同	川越吉成	三四
同	同	鵜野正男	二七
同	同	若林正治	二一
敦化自動車區	同	小林恆松	二六
同	運轉手心得	堀口松五郎	二二
同	運轉手見習員	葛原快市	三〇
敦化自動車區明月溝自停	運轉手見習員	反田伊虎丸	三一
同	運轉手	森川淵三郎	〇
同	同	西森秀樹茂	二六
壯	同	渡邊　實	二六

所属	職	職名	氏名	番号
同	同	同	石本武夫	三五
魏南自動車区	同	運轉手	塔崎貨雄	二六
同	同	運轉手	矢野渡雄	三三
同	同	運轉手心得	廣瀬正平	三一
同	同	運轉手	沼部宮次	四
同	同	運轉手心得	隋山三次郎	五
同	同	運轉手	澗崎佑	八
牟天自動車区	同	運轉手心得	澗原正夫	三
同	同	運轉手	鈴木賈	〇
哈爾濱自動車区	同	同	藤岡伸夫	一
同	同	同	市川照一	六
同	同	運轉手	近藤金蔵	三
朝鮮鐵道自動車区	同	同	不松茂雄	八
新京鐵道局	同	運轉手兵器員	松元李治	六
同	健職	機關助士	松本勝英	〇
白城子檢車区	同	機關	希嫩満雄	三
同	職員	機關士員	中野英一郎	七
斉々哈爾檢車区	同	檢車員	桑原正三	二
三棵樹檢車区	同	車輌員	高田耕平	一
第二課勤務班			高橋芳雄	五

六一

第二編 總務班

同	同	軍手員李研案	三三

六二

農安派遣自動車班ハ之ヲ二箇分隊トシ第一分隊ハ三箇班十七名第二分隊ハ二箇班十二名トシ隊長以下三十一名ノ編成ナリ。

尚之等派遣員ハ十月二十三日夫々軍宛軍屬トシテノ手續ヲナシタリ。

第二項　農安ニ於ケル状況

第一　農安街ノ人口

農安街人口ハ左ノ如クナルカペスト發生後約三分ノ一ニ及フ住民ハ何レカ逃亡セルモノノ如シ。

記

日　系　　　二一一名

滿　系　　三二、八五五名

計　　　三三、〇六六名

第二　現在迄ノペスト發生状況竝防疫隊着後ノ状況

現在迄ニ於ケルペスト死亡者累計ハ農安縣城二六五名現患者數八二九名ナリシカ防疫隊着農後ノ状況ハ十二月十九日現在ニ於テ

一、ペスト患者ナシ

死亡累計

二九八名

治癒累計

二、對人防疫

　イ、檢診人員　二一、二一八名（有熱者ナシ）累計　九一八、一四九名

　ロ、健康隔離者　三名

三、對動物防疫

　ナシ。

第三　鐵道ニ於ケル防疫狀況

農安驛ニ於ケルペスト防疫對策トシテハ驛ペスト防疫要綱竝ニ交通遮斷班ノ編成及勤務要領ニ依リ之ニ協力スルノ外鐵道關係自體防疫ノ强化ニ努メ鐵等一致左記方法ニ依リ防疫ニ從事セリ。

記

一、鐵道防疫ノ編成

二、農安驛效等護隊農安分所ペスト防疫對策作成及之カ實施

三、驛ヨリ東方百米地點（農安街道）ニ於テ警護隊員效驛員ヲ以テ該箇所ノ出入者全員ニ對シ消毒及警戒ヲナス

四、驛北側（白城子寄）踏切ノ交通遮斷ハ警護隊員之ニ當ル

即チ槪略路農安驛ヲ中心ニ三百米以內ニ於ケル圈內ヲ農安鐵道防疫班活動地帶トシテ防疫ニ當レリ。

第四　關東軍ニ於ケル防疫情況

關東軍ペスト防疫隊八十九日十六時二十分詩ノ第一次防疫隊（警察官）七六五名先頭ニ第二次八十八時二二分防疫隊本

第二課　　勤　務　班

六三

第二編　總務班

六四

部員及満洲ノ三六〇名ニ二十日九時三十分着ノ第三次防疫隊（關東軍）ニ二八名ヲ最後トシ防疫隊本部ヲ不取敢城内小學校ニ迨キ關東軍之力統轄ニ當ルコトトナリ二十日各々調示アリタル後宜撫班ハ指導將校七名軍屬四十名ヲ以テ農安縣長、協和合、警察署長、街長等ヲ勵カシ細胞組織トシ一般ニ働キ掛ケ宜撫工作ノ徹底ヲ期スヘク十時三十分十二個分隊ヲ以テ寄任地域ヲ定メベスト發生地要圖ヲ作成十一時診掖班ハ軍醫二十二名看護婦二十八名ヲ以テ編成十二時四十分効疫斥候班ハ防疫上必要ナル偵察ヲナシ防疫對策ノ確立竝防疫ヲ有効ニ運用セシムル目的ヲ以テ十四時區習ニ就ケリ。

警官隊ハ到着後直チニ三筒大隊ニ分チ第一大隊ハ巽家店、第二大隊ハ縣城内、第三大隊ハ城外へ向ッテ出勤二十一時包園隊形ヲ完了セリ。

編成

イ、防疫斥候班
ロ、檢診班
ハ、消毒給水班
二、野犬野鼠撲滅班
ホ、検索班
へ、病理解剖班
ト、經理資材班
チ、宜撫班

り、交通監視隊

（満洲國警首隊ヲ以テ組織三大隊ニ分ツ）

尚彼安裏遣員ノ總指揮ニ當リタル高橋澆南鐡道監理所援ノ左ノ報告ニ詳細ヲ知ルヘシ、即チ、自動車隊ハ隊長以下三二一名ヲ以テ組成之ヲ二箇分隊八班ニ分チ夫々防疫隊各班ニ編入所屬班ノ任務遂行ニ當レリ。

隊員查材ノ輸送ハ勿論城內ニ部落ニ汚染地帶深ク進入シ或時ハ死體ヲ或時ハ患者ヲ隔離者、牧容運搬シ生々シキ現實ノ危險ニ曝サレツツ死ノ恐怖ヲモ忘レ只管防時ニ精進シ居ルモ時ニ危險ノ爲養食ヲ喫スル能ハス又雨後ノ泥路ニ惱マサルルアリ或ハ患家ノ探訪ニ奔养セラルルアリテ其ノ苦心ハ想像ニ絶スルモノアリ六時半起床、點呼、車隊ノ整備朝食出勤ト日沒迄目マクルシキ活動ノ連報ニモ拘ラス隊長以下元氣旺盛ニテ車ノ稱讚裡ニ各班ノ任務ヲ完遂セリ其ノ活勤狀況左ノ如シ。

一、檢　診　班

キハ四輛ヲ以テ宿營地ヨリ本部ヘ防疫隊員ヲ輸送本部ヨリ近ニ各目的地ヘ出勤スル檢診隊ノ輸送並其ノ日ノ活勤ヲ終ヘタル防疫隊員ヲ本部ヨリ宿營地迄輸送ス本班ハ特ニ危險ニ付各自ノ身體並車輛ノ消毒ハ入念ニ且自發的ニ何囘モ繰返セリ。

尚本班中ノ一輛ハ毎日不疑番ノ送迎ヲモ爲シ居リ深更一時ニ及フコト珍カラス。

二、撲　滅　班

國民高等學校ニ本部ヲ近キキト二輛ヲ以テ班員竝捕鼠用品、藥品等ヲ患者發生地帶ノ家屋迄輸送ス。

撲滅班ハペストノ媒介ヲ爲ス鼠蚤犬猫ノ驅除撲殺ヲ計ルヲ以テ目的トシ之等ニ必要ナル捕鼠用品藥品ノ配給竝捕鼠

ノ蒐集ヲ爲シ又滿人組長ヘノ鼠ノ捕獲方法等ヲ說明時ニ患者ノ收容患家ノ見舞等ヲ爲スコトアリ。

三、防疫本部附

國民高等學校ニ本部ヲ置キキキ一ヲ以テ本部員ノ連絡輸送竝各隔離所トノ連絡業務ニ從事ス又宣傳ビラ配布ノ爲城內ニ出勤シ或ハ爲眞班ト行動ヲ共ニスルコトアリ。

四、戰鬪司令所

キハ六輛ヲ以テ編成サレ縣警務科ニ本部ヲ置ク每日宿營地ヨリ本部迄ノ所員ノ輸送警察官隊ノ輸送竝各班トノ連絡ニ從事ス又每日一名舉家店ニ連絡員トシテ殘リ軍ト共ニ野營ヲ爲シ勤務ハ交番制ヲ採リ居レリ。

五、病理解剖班

キト三輛ヲ以テ編成ス最初一輛ナリシモ檢送多忙ノ爲途中ヨリ二輛ヲ增ス各部落ヨリ死體竝隔離收容者ノ輸送ニ從事ス檢診班ノ通報ニ基キ患家ヲ探シ患者竝健康者ノ收容ヲ爲スモ滿人ハ隔離所ヘ收容サレルヲ厭ヒ隱蔽スルヲ以テ飛テモナイ處ヲ敎ヘラレルコト等アリテ收容者ノ探索ニハ一方ナラヌ苦心ヲ爲セリ。

六、防疫斥候班

キハ二輛キト二輛ヲ以テ編成シ斥候班員ヲ檢送病家ノ調査探索ニ從事ス。

七、消毒給水班

キト二輛ヲ以テ編成サレ各班各箇所ニ於ケル消毒水ノ給水竝各部落ヘノ消毒水ノ輸送ヲ爲ス。

八、經理資材班

本部ヲ分遣隊舍ニ逬キキト一輛ヲ以テ各班ヘノ資材ノ輸送ニ從事ス。

第五　停留客車内宿泊人員

一、日軍下士以上　　　　　　　　　　　　三百名

一、哈爾濱陸醫大生　　　　　　　　　　　四十五名

一、哈爾濱赤十字社看護婦　　　　　　　　二十七名

一、将校(哈醫大教授ヲ含ム)　　　　　　七十一名

一、守備隊下士以下　　　　　　　　　　　三十一名

一、満系警察官(約半數ハ出勤)　　　　　三百十三名

一、自動車隊員　　　　　　　　　　　　　三十一名

計　　　　　　　　　　　　　　　　　　　八百十八名

第六　農安驛構内要圖及列車停留狀況(附圖參照)

第七　防疫隊ニ對シ施設供與

防疫隊到着後列車内ニ宿泊スル為特ニ之レカ為メノ諸施設(風呂便所)ノ供與並隊長室トシテ一、二等待合室食堂トシテ三等待合室又防疫隊將校用浴場施設場所トシテ裝甲軌道車庫内ノ一室ヲ提供セリ。

第八　到着荷物ノ處置

到着小荷物及貨物ノ引取リハ交通遮斷ニ依リ從來ヨリ困難ヲ來シ居リタルカ今般ノ防疫陣ノ強化ニ依リ之カ引取リハ一層至難ノ狀勢トナリ一方城内外住民ノ生活必需品ハ防疫陣ノ強化ニ比例シ缺乏ノ度ヲ加ヘオル情勢ニ鑑ミ之カ對策トシテ縣長ト懇談縣長ノ責任ニ於テ縣防疫班ノ名ニヲ以テ之カ運搬ヲナシ眞荷主ヘ引渡方辨旋ノコトニ協定ノ(配送

第二編　總務班

六七

荷物ノ荷受人印鑑ハ縣長代印ヲ承認ス）到着通知ハ縣公署庶務科ヘ通知スルコトトシ以テ引取ノ圓滑ト滯貨ノ防止ヲ期スルコトトセリ。

因ニ防疫隊來屯後右ニ依リ縣長ヘ引渡數量左ノ如シ

小荷物　　小荷物到着個數　　　　　　　　　　　　四四七個

　　　　　縣長印ニテ引渡シシタル數　　　　　　　一五〇個

貨　物　　貨物到着個數　　　　　　　　　　　　　二九一個

　　　　　防疫隊ヘ引渡シタル數　　貨小切口　　　一三九廳

　　　　　縣長印ニテ引渡シタル數　貨小切口　　　一六二七廳
　　　　　　　　　　　　　　　　　　　　　　　　　四五廳

　　　　　其ノ他引渡シタル數　　　貨小切口　　　一五九七廳
　　　　　　　　　　　　　　　　　　　　　　　　　二二廳
　　　　　　　　　　　　　　　　　　　　　　　　　三〇廳

第三項　軍引揚ケニ伴ヒ引殺キ滿洲國ヘ協力

農安ニ於ケル軍ノ行フ防疫ハ豫定通ノ二週間ヲ以テ十一月七日引揚ケト決定之ニ代リテ滿洲國ニ於テ引殺キ防疫ニ従事スルコトトナリタルヲ以テ軍同樣ニ協力スルコトトセリ。

民生部公函第一六四號（民保防第二三三號）

、康德七年十月三十一日

南滿洲鐵道株式會社　　　　　　民生部大臣　呂　榮　寰㊞

總裁　大村卓一殿

農安ペスト防疫ニ關スル施設引體方ニ關スル件

農安ペスト防疫ノ為現在貴社ヨリ關東軍ニ供與中ノ人員車輛等ハ防疫機構ヲ當部ニ於テ引體ク場合必要有之ニ付十一月二日以降常分ノ間現在關東軍ニ供與中ノ諸施設ヲ現狀ノ儘引繼キ當部ニ供與方特ニ御配慮相成度右及依頼追テ細部ニ關シテハ本部保健司長ト貴社鐵道總局長ニ於テ協定セシメ度ニ付爲念

民官房發第二五四五號（民保防第二五〇號）

康德七年十一月二十七日

民生部次長　土　肥　顯　圀　（印）

南滿洲鐵道株式會社

總裁　大村卓一　殿

農安附近ペスト防疫ニ關スル諸施設貸借契約方ノ件

農安附近ペスト防疫ニ關スル諸施設貸借契約方ノ件

十一月十四日附鐵總應四〇第五號八ノ五ヲ以テ御承認有之候首題ノ件別紙契約書ニ調印送付申上候ニ付一部折返シ回送相成度候

民生部次長土肥顯圀ト南滿洲鐵道株式會社鐵道總局長佐藤應次郎ノ間ニ左記ノ如ク協定ス

農安附近ペスト防疫ニ關スル滿洲國滿鐵間ノ協定書

記

一、滿鐵ノ派遣人員

機關區員　　三名（職員一、傭員二）

檢車區員　　五名（　　傭員　五）

第二回　總　務　歷

第二編　総務班

自動車區員　　三二名（職員　一、傭員三一）

計　　　　　四〇名（職員二、傭員三八）

右派遣員ノ派遣中及歸還後隔離中ニ於ケル身分ニ關シテハ滿洲國保障ス

二、人件費

滿鐵派遣社員ニ對スル人件費ハ滿鐵旅費規程ニ依リ支出シタル費用金額ヲ民生部負擔ス

三、車輛及自動車ノ供與数、使用料金及期間

イ、車種

車種	輛数	料金
機關車	一輛	一輛一日壹百五拾貳圓
二等寝臺車	二輛	一輛一日参拾金圓
三等寝臺車	四輛	一輛一日貳拾四圓壹角
三等客車	八輛	八輛一日ニ付壹百七拾壹圓八角五分

備考

最安現在三等客車

			貸與料金
「ハ1」型	二輛	一輛一日ニ付	
「ハ2」型	一輛	同	貳拾壹圓貳角五分
「ハ3」型	四輛	同	貳拾壹圓四角
「ハ5」型	一輛	同	貳拾貳圓六角五分
貨車	三輛	同	貳拾貳圓金角五分
發電車	一輛	同	拾七圓

七〇

自　動　車　　二五輌　　四　　　四拾四圓

但シ一日ハ十時間トシ作業時間カ十時間ヲ超過シタル場合ハ右超過時間一時間若ハ其ノ未満ニ就キ五圓五角ノ割増金ヲ加算スルモノトス

緊急設備使用料　　貳百八拾圓（貸與期間ヲ通シ二輌分）

ロ、前號ノ車輌供與期間ハ昭和十五年十一月七日ヨリ防疫隊引揚迄トス

四、自動車檢送運貨

八、自動車及發電車用ノガソリンハ民生部負擔トシ所要ノ油脂類ハ滿鐵負擔トス

農安驛ヨリ各自動車ノ所屬箇所迄ノ鐵道輸送運貨ハ民生部負擔トス

五、防疫隊引揚後滿鐵派遣員ノ隔離（隔離中支給スル旅費モ含ム）ニ要スル費用及車輌共ノ他ノ消毒ニ要シタル費用ハ民生部負擔トス

六、農安驛ノ施設ハ滿鐵ニ於テ能フ限リ民生部防疫隊ニ對シ便宜供與スルモノトス

七、復路輸送ハ一括之ヲ爲スモノトシ運貨料金ハ次ノ通トス

イ、旅　客
運貨ハ客車定員ニ對スル五割引トス但シ其ノ乗車人員カ客車定員五輌分以下ノ場合ハ客車五輌分ニ對スル五割引

ロ、代　物
貨車及發電車ノ廻送ニ要スル運貨料金ハ代物運送規則所定ニ依ル
但シ當該貨車ニ代物積載シタルトキハ當該貨物ノ車扱所定運貨料金ノミヲ收受スルモノトス

第二届　勤務班

七一

八、滿洲國ニ對シ滿鐵ヨリ前記ノ諸裝用貸料金ヲ請求スル際ハ民生部トス

九、本協定替ハ相互ニ各一通ヲ保有ス

康德　七　年十一月二十七日

昭和十五年十一月二十七日

鐵道總局長　　　　　　民生部次長　土　肥　題　國

南滿洲鐵道株式會社

佐　藤　應　次　郎　㊞

第四項　農安派遣隊ノ引揚

軍ニ引續キ實施シ來リタル滿洲國搜關ニ依ル防疫モ十一月二十七日滿洲國防疫委員會ニ於テ情勢ノ變化ニ伴ヒ農安

派遣中ノ警官隊ノ一部約三百名ヲ十一月三十日引揚クルコトニ決定セリ

從而現地使用中ノ車輛ハ三等寢臺車一、三等客車六、機關車一、發電車一、バス九、トラック二、計二〇ヲ殘置シ

他ノ車輛(二等寢臺車二、三等寢臺車三、三等客車一、バス六、トラック八、計二〇)ハ新京へ廻送シ直ニSK式消毒

ヲ實施スルコトトセリ。

右ニ伴ヒ殘置車輛要員ハ共ノ任務ノ重要性ニ鑑ミ特ニ殘留シ任務完了シタキ申出アリタル左記ノ者ヲシテ充當スル

コトトシ他ノ十九名ハ警官隊ト共ニ三十日農安發八一四列車ニテ歸遷セリ此ノ日聯頭ニハ神守委員長初メ各委員竝ニ

社員會新京聯合會ハ社員會旗ヲ先頭ニ出迎ヒ數十日ノ不自由而モ日夜危險ナル業務ニ タッサワリタル同僚社員ノ元氣

一杯且ツ規律アル動作ハ出迎ノ者ヲシテ感激セシメタリ一同下車整列スルヤ神守委員長ハ懇篤ナル慰勞ノ辭ヲ述ヘラ

レ、之ニ對シ平松班長ハ派遣中ノ報告ヲナシタル後社歌ヲ高ラカニ合唱シ滿鐵社員ノ意氣旺ナルヲ遺憾ナク具現セリ

直チニ社員宿泊所ニ至リ玆ニ於テ五日間ノ隔離ニ服シ此ノ間一同何等異狀ナク十二月四日二十四時豫定通リ之ヲ解除ヲ受ケ翌五日新京支社ニ於テ神守委員長代理トシテ北條總務班長ノ挨拶ヲ受ケ一同極メテ元氣ニテ解散夫々任地ニ歸還セリ

尚之ニ先タチ十一月十五日派遣日數及苦勞ヲ考慮シ一應全派遣社員ノ交代ヲ企圖セルモ全員進ンテ歸還ヲ肯セスベスト防疫ノ使命ヲ遂行センカ爲メ其ノ危險ナル業務ニ携リタルハ特記スヘキ事柄ナリ

記

自動車助役　有安美俊　川越吉之

巡轉手　　　埒川昇一　奧田勇次郎　森川源三郎

綱野正成　葛原快市　辻　寛

西森秀樹　渡邊茂

石本武夫　横山三次郎　濱崎侑

藤岡仲夫

松元秀治

機關助手　松本勝美　香城滿雄

車電員　　高橋芳雄

車手員　　李樹棠

第二班　總務班

七三

第二編　徳・鵜　班

而シテ残置自動車及留置客車及人員左ノ如シ

自動車残置輛数

防疫隊防疫班　　バス六輛　　トラック二輛

防疫諸業隊　　　バス三輛

計　　　　　　　十一輛

留置客車及人員

キ ハ 326	オ イ ヲ 271	ハ 32	ハ 3924	ハ 2047	ハ 3304	ハ 328	ハ 3587
		祭察	同	同	同	同	
日本軍 防諸 諸隊 軍							
一二 五七 二一 名名 名名 名	三 五 名名		三一 五名	二七 六名	三〇 名名	三六 名名	

十二月十三日満洲國防疫委員會ニ於テ更ニ廿九日一齊ニ提安移留防疫隊引揚ケ決定シタルニ付直ニ社内各關係箇所ニ連絡シ之カ處理ニ萬全ヲ期セリ而シテ十九日正午臨時列車組成ヲ以テ到着スルヤ一同聊カノ疲勞モ見セス元氣ニテ

七四

ホームニ降リ立チ神守委員長代理北條總務班長ノ挨拶ヲ受ケ直ニ社員宿泊所ニ至リ三日間ノ靜養（現地隔離ヲ終リ居

ルヲ以テ本回ハ何等制限ヲ受ケス）ヲナシ二十一日支社ニ於ケル解散式ニ特ニ尾崎社員會新京聯合會長ノ挨拶ヲ受ケ

夫々任地ニ歸還セリ

リ

本防按隊引揚ケニ依リ二十一日附ヲ以テ農安縣城ノ遮斷隔離並農安縣境ノ長春縣檢問所十三箇所ハ夫々解除セラレ

タリ

第二回　德　務　班

七五

第四編　検　疫

二四八

第五章　防　疫　費

新京ニ於ケル今次ノ流行ニ要セシ防疫費中新京臨時防疫委員會檢疫班關係左ノ如シ

人　件　費	二七、五〇〇・〇〇 ^門
物　件　費	一七六、五六九・六四
備　　　品	一七、九六三・四〇
藥　　　品	五五、七三三・〇〇
醫科理化	五、七九三・九四
消　耗　品	七三、七五三・一九
雑　　　費	二三、三三六・二一
合　　計	二〇四、〇六九・六四

第六章　效　　果

政治經済交通ノ中心地タル國都ニ於ケル「ペスト」發生ニ伴ヒ余等先ツ防疫班ヲ組織シ次テ十月十二日新京臨時防疫委員會ノ結成セラルルヤ檢疫班トシテ一五〇名ノ防疫員ヲ動員爾來三箇月眞性患者相次イテ發生シ恰モ烈風ニ煽揚セラレタル猛火ノ如ク疫勢一時ニ瀰蔓セルタメ防疫ノ特性タル焦眉ノ急務ヲ毅急相應シ能ク之ヲ處理ス

即チ・

豫防接種施行人員　　　　　　　二四一、〇九五名

列車乗込檢疫數　　　　　　　　　八四、九〇〇名

新京驛ニ於ケル望診人員　　　　一〇二、〇二三名

戶口檢診及特別檢診人員　　　　二五八、八九三名

捕　　殺　　數　　　　　　　　　二二、〇〇〇頭

瓦斯消毒容積　　　　　　　六五、二二二・八三立方米

「カルホール」放水式消毒施行面積　　四七、二五四平方米

之カ遂行ニ當リテハ恭風飛雪寒肌ヲ劈ク中ニ立ツモノアリ或ハ猛毒ナル瓦斯圈內ニアリテ不眠不休恕命セリ

殺上以テ今社機關ヲ死守シ鐵道運營ノ特異的自衞防疫ヲ完遂スルト共ニ他商來官各機關ヲ輔翼シ官民提携短日月ニ

之ヲ熄滅シ得タル　ハ昕决トスルトコロナリ

第四編　檢　　疫

二四九

5 远东国际军事法庭
国际检察局调查

5.1　2 Apr. 1947: IPS Documents No. 1895, 1896

资料出处：National Archives of the United States, R331, M690, #270.

内容点评：战后远东国际军事法庭国际检察局文件有关日军在华开展实施细菌战的证据材料第 1895 号文件下落不明。本资料为国际检察局内部相关文献编号文件。

1895

SUMMARY REPORT ON ORIGIN OF PLAGUE IN NORTHERN CHE
KIANG in 1940, signed by W.W. YUNG, Director of
Epidemic Prevention, National Health Administration
of China, 16 April 1946.

Bacteriological warfare in Ningpo and Chuhsien, China.

2 April 1947

FROM: Central Files Unit

TO: Chief, Document Division

SUBJECT: IPS Documents 1895, 1896

1. The subject documents were charged out to the Chinese Division on the 6th of November 1946 and have never been returned.

2. The Chinese Division say that these documents were turned over to the Philippine Division by them.

3. The Philippine Division claims that they turned the documents over to Mr. D.N. Sutton.

4. Mr. Sutton claims no knoledge of the documents what soever.

5. This matter is turned over to your office for action.

James B. Dodds
Central Files Unit

MEMORANDUM

TO   : Lt.OBERG,
             Assistant Chief of the Document Section.

FROM   : Lt.PETROV,

SUBJECT   : I.P.S. Documents 1895, 1896

Reference is made on your memorandum dated 3 April 1947. I hereby inform you that two documents on bacteriological warfare were once turned over to Gen. Vasiliev by the Chinese Division but the general is sure that these two were not the originals but the typed copies of the documents referred. We looked through our files but failed to find any traces of the originals of the two documents.

Lt. Petrov.

GENERAL HEADQUARTERS
SUPREME COMMANDER FOR THE ALLIED POWERS
INTERNATIONAL PROSECUTION SECTION

3 April 1947

MEMORANDUM FOR: Lt. Ohberg, Acting Chief of Document Division

FROM   : Mr. Lopez

SUBJECT   : IPS Documents 1895 and 1896.

    1. It is true that these documents covering bacteriolog-ical warfare in China were once turned over to me after Chief of Counsel had asked me to make a study on it but later those documents were turned over to Mr. Sutton, then back to the Chinese Division. My last recollection of them is that Mr. Chu of the Chinese Division took the documents to the Russian Division in order to sound the opinion of the Russian Associate Prosecutor whether two Japanese nationals who are in Russia could be made available for interrogation here.

Pedro Lopez
Associate Prosecutor

INTERNATIONAL PROSECUTION SECTION

Doc. No. 1895   14 June 1946

ANALYSIS OF DOCUMENTARY EVIDENCE

DESCRIPTION OF ATTACHED DOCUMENT.

Title and Nature: Summary Report on origin of plague in northern CHE KIANG in 1940, signed by W. W. YUNG, Director of Epidemic Prevention, National Health Administration of China.

Date: 16 Apr 46 Original (x) Copy ( ) Language: Eng.

Has it been translated? Yes ( ) No (x)
Has it been photostated? Yes ( ) No (x)

LOCATION OF ORIGINAL (also WITNESS if applicable):
Document Division

SOURCE OF ORIGINAL: Dr. Robert Pollitzer of Nat. Health Administration at NANKING.

PERSONS IMPLICATED:

CHARGES TO WHICH DOCUMENT APPLICABLE: Germicidal warfare in China. Violation of Rules of Land Warfare as exemplified by HAGUE and GENEVA Conventions.

SUMMARY OF RELEVANT POINTS:

Summary reveals that bubonic plague epidemics broke out in several towns previously entirely free from such infection, soon after Japanese planes had visited these places and had scattered considerable quantities of wheat and rice grains over the areas. Towns affected were NINGPO and CHUHSIEN. Japanese planes dropped yellowish granules over KINHWA and while no plague developed, tests of granules revealed findings characteristic of plague bacillus. Statement made in presence of Dr. Pollitzer.

Analyst: 2d Lt. Blumhagen   Doc. No. 1895

Not used

CHARGE OUT SLIP

DATE _6 Nov, 1946_

EVIDENTIARY DOC. NO. _1895_

TRIAL BRIEF_____

EXHIBIT NO._____

BACKGROUND DOC. NO._____

SIGNATURE _William Kaw_

ROOM NO. _328_

Never reproduced

Will receive memo from Chinese on this.

File

NOTE: See memo info in folder of Doc. 1896

5.2   IPS EVIDENTIARY DOCUMENT NUMBER 1896: Affidavit of HATABA, Osamu, on Bacterial Warfare carried on by EI 1644 Force in China, 1943

资料出处：National Archives of the United States, R331, M690, #271.

内容点评：战后远东国际军事法庭国际检察局有关日军在华开展细菌战的证据材料第 1896 号为中国在押日军战俘榛叶修讯问记录及本人亲笔供述。榛叶修为日军荣 1644（资料中误作 1664）细菌部队九江支队卫生兵，于 1944 年 3 月向中国方面投诚。美军情报部门对其进行了多次讯问。

INTERNATIONAL PROSECUTION SECTION

EVIDENTIARY DOCUMENT NUMBER ____1896____

TITLE: Affidavit of HATABA, Ouamu, on Bacterial Warfare carried on byy

____ EI 1664 Force in China, 1943.

SOURCE: HATABA, Osamu

MICROFILMING

Document __1896__   Source: HATABA, Osamu
hAs been microfilmed on __21 Oct__ 1948 for
permanent historical record.

(None) (Part) of this document had been extracted for court use.

F. MATTISON
File Unit
Document Division

Translated by: T. YAMAMOTO.

Testimony regarding crimes committed by a
Japanese Force.

The organization of the "EI" 1644 force, in Central China, a
Water Supply and Purification Unit was as follows:-

1. General Affairs Bureau.
2. Epidemic Prevention Section.
3. Material Section.
4. Physics and Chemistry Section.
5. Intendance Section.

The General Affairs Bureau was in charge of the office work, personnel affairs, education, instruction, etc. of the unit in general.

Epidemic Prevention Section was dealing with the examination and culture of microbes, prevention of contagious diseases and other general epidamic prevention work.

The Material Section was in charge of the various medical supplies, water supply materials and other work regarding material in general.

The Physics and Chemistry Section was working on the examination of poison, the culture of vaccines, examination of drinking water and on other scientific research.

The intendance Section was managing the accounts, supplies, etc. of the Unit.

The principal officers of the unit in September, 1943, were as follows:-

The Commander of the unit at Nanking, H.Q.:
Col. SATO Shunzo, Army Medical Corps.
The chief of the General Affairs Bureau at Nanking H.Q.:
Maj. AWAYA Ippo, Army Medical Corps.
The chief of the Epidemic Prevention Section at Nanking H.Q.:
Capt. OKOCHI Masao, Army Medical Corps.
The Comdr. of the detachment at Chinchiang : Maj. OKURA, A.M.C.
The chief of the Epidemic Prevention Section at Chiuchiang:
Lieut. SAITO Shichiro, A.M.C.

I do not remember the names of the others.

The original duties of this unit were to look after the health of Japanese soldiers, the prevention of the contagious diseases, the preventative examination and vaccination of the Japanese nationals. The unit was established for the purpose of preventing diseases. In operations they also supplied drinking water to the forces engaged in the operations by organizing water supply sections.

It is a fact that this unit cultured the microbes such as those mentioned below. However, even in the unit only the officers directly

Testimony regarding crimes committed by a Japanese Force (cont'd).

concerned with the matter knew and the matter was kept secret from the other officers, and men. It is a fact, though, that the following microbes were cultured during June, 1942. (1) Cholera, (2) Typhus, (3) Plague, (4) Dysentery.

All members of the Epidemic Prevention Section participated in culturing the microbes.

The diffusion of the microbes took place during June and July of 1942, but the number of times the diffusion took place or the quantity diffused is unknown. Microbes were spread in the area around Kinhwa of Chekiang prefecture, but as the withdrawal of Chinese Armies from the area was so rapid, the advancing Japanese Army entered the contaminated area. And as the Japanese made short rests or camped in the area and used the nearby water for drinking and cooking purposes, a large number of cases of contagious disease resulted.

A great number of Chinese inhabitants also suffered from the epidemics and died. It is not clear how the command for the culture of microbes was issued, but as I do not believe that the unit would take such measures at its own discretion. I believe that the orders came from some one like the Commander of the Army, (The Comdr. of the 11th Army SHIMOMURA Sadamu) or the Comdr. of the Division (Divisional Commander - SAKUMA Tameto). The object of such an operation is to diffuse the malignant microbes in the rear of the enemy and to spread the epidemics artificially in order to kill and to demoralize the enemy. It is an inhumane act which also badly affects the inhabitants. When I visited the Hangchow Military Hospital about the middle of September, 1943, it was overcrowded by Japanese soldiers suffering from contagious diseases and every day three to five men were dying. I was told that about August of the same year they accommodated thousands of cases by laying straw mats in the open yard of the Hospital.

According to the words of TATSUZAWA Tadao of Tokyo, a lance corporal of the Army Medical Corps of "EI" 1644 Force, he flew to the front lines to scatter the microbe from the aircraft. The unit had two or more aeroplanes for its own use.

I am one who was attached to the Epidemic Prevention Section of the Water Supply and Purification Corps, from May, 1942 to March, 1943, but who deserted from the unit upon discovering that under the name of "Sacred War" inhuman acts, such as I mentioned, were being committed. The Physics and Chemistry Dept. was also making researches on poisons.

Former member of Epidemic Prevention Section of "EI" 1644 Force.

April 17, 1946.

(Signed) HATABA Osamu.

Address; Shizuoka-ken, Ogasagun, Kawashiro-mura, Kurazawa, 358.

日本生物武器作战调查资料（全六册）

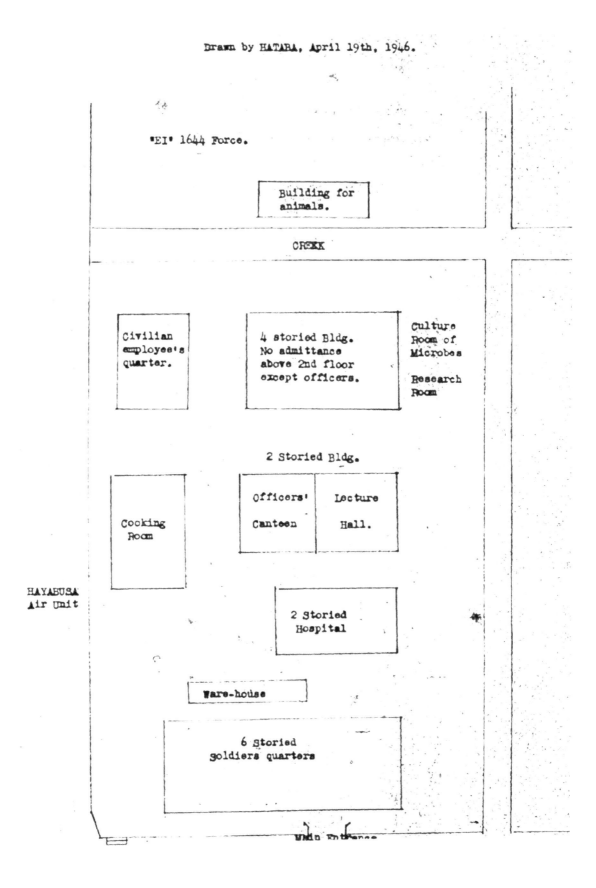

Drawn by HATABA, April 19th, 1946.

"EI" 1644 Force.

Building for animals.

CREEK

Civilian employee's quarter.

4 storied Bldg. No admittance above 2nd floor except officers.

Culture Room of Microbes

Research Room

2 Storied Bldg.

Cooking Room

Officers' Canteen

Lecture Hall.

HAYABUSA Air Unit

2 Storied Hospital

Ware-house

6 Storied soldiers quarters

Main Entrance

128 KUNSHAN Road, Shanghai.

A Committee for culture movements against Japan.

SHIZUOKAKEN, Ogasagun, Kawashiromura, Kurasawa, 358.

c/o TAKAFUJI Oenjiro.

Tokyo-to, Hongo-ku, Nishikatamachi, Tono 10

OKADA Yoshihoko.

Tokyo-to, Koishikawa-ku, Tanaka Bunkyo Do.

(Book store).

INTERNATIONAL PROSECUTION SECTION

Doc No 1896   14 June 1946

ANALYSIS OF DOCUMENTARY EVIDENCE

DESCRIPTION OF ATTACHED DOCUMENT

    Title and Nature: Affidavit of HATABA, Osamu on Bacterial Warfare carried on by EI 1664 Force in China 1943.

    Date: 17 Apr 46 Original (x) Copy ( ) Language Jap

    Has it been translated? Yes (x) No ( )
    Has it been photostated? Yes ( ) No (x)

LOCATION OF ORIGINAL: Document Division

SOURCE OF ORIGINAL: HATABA, Osamu

PERSONS IMPDICATED: Col. SATO, Shunzo; Maj AWAYA, Ippo, Capt OKOCHI, Masao.

CRIMES TO WHICH DOCUMENT APPLICABLE: Violation Hague Convention

SUMMARY OF RELEVANT POINTS:

    Affiant was member of the above Water Supply and Purification Unit in China Charges germ cultures were spread by plane and other means in Sept 1943 near KINHWA CHEKIANG Prefecture Some killed many Japanese soldiers as well as Chinese civilian population

Analyst: W. F. Wagner   Doc No 1896

GENERAL HEADQUARTERS SUPREME COMMAND ALLIED POWERS
INTERNATIONAL PROSECUTION SECTION

Not used

CHARGE OUT SLIP

DATE 6 *May* 1946

EVIDENTIARY DOC. NO. *1896*

TRIAL BRIEF

EXHIBIT NO.

BACKGROUND DOC. NO.

SIGNATURE *William Rice*

ROOM NO. *328*

Never reproduced

GENERAL HEADQUARTERS, SUPREME COMMAND ALLIED POWERS
INTERNATIONAL PROSECUTION SECTION

Document No. _____1896_____　　　　　　_12 June_ 1946

CERTIFICATE

I, _____William Kaw_____, hereby certify
th
that I am associated with the International Prosecution
Section, General Headquarters, Supreme Command Allied Powers
and that the attached document, consisting of _____ pages
and described as follows: _Testimony regarding_
Crimes committed by a Japanese Army

and dated _Kaw 17 april 1941_, was obtained by me on the
date above set forth in my above capacity and in the conduct
of my official business and in the following manner, to wit
(place and from whom obtained, including specific Japanese
archives, records and files involved, if any) _from_
Hatabo Osamu, a Japanese, at Shimura-ku
Ogasagun, Kawashin-mun Kurigawa, 558

_____William Kaw_____
NAME

_____CAF-6_____
RANK OR CAPACITY

_____
ASN

INTERNATIONAL PROSECUTION SECTION

Doc. No. 1696 Date: _____

ANALYSIS OF DOCUMENTARY EVIDENCE

DESCRIPTION OF ATTACHED DOCUMENT

Title and Nature: _Affidavit of HATABA, Osa____
on Bacterial Warfare Activities of El 66 _____

Date: 17 April 46 Original (X) Copy ( ) Language _____

Has it been translated? Yes (X) No ( )
Has it been photostated? Yes ( ) No (X)

LOCATION OF ORIGINAL (also WITNESS if applicable)

Pros Div

SOURCE OF ORIGINAL: HATABA, _____

PERSONS IMPLICATED:
Col. SATO, Shunzo, Maj. ARAYA, _____
Col. OKOCHI, _____

CRIMES TO WHICH DOCUMENT APPLICABLE:

Violation Hague Convention.

SUMMARY OF RELEVANT POINTS (with page references)

_Affiant was member of the above
Water Supply and Purification Unit which
Charges germ cultures were spread by ____
and other means in Sep 1943 near KIANGSI,
CHEKIANG Prefecture. ___ killed many Japanese
soldiers as well as Chinese civilian population_

Analyst: _____ Doc. No.

日軍罪業證明書

防疫即チ第四四部隊（六四部隊）ハ支那派遣日軍ノ一部（?）ニシテ次ノ通リデアツタ。

一　總務部　　　　一　防疫科

一　庶務科　　　　一　理化學科

一　經理科

總務部ハ部隊全般ノ事務、人事、敎育指導等ヲコトヲ管理シテイタ。

防疫科ハ細菌檢索ヲ始メ傳染病防疫其他一般防疫業務ヲ擔當シテイタ。

理化學科ハ各種衛生ナル科給水用器具其

…一般資材ヲ整備シテイタ。

理化學研究ハ、毒物瓦斯防止、銃彈製造…

水煙調査、其他、理化學的研究ヲ主トシテイタ。

經理ハ、部隊内ノ經理ヲ主管シテイタ。

當時昭和二十年九月、部隊ノ主要ナル責任者ハ、如クデアッタ。

部隊長	陸軍軍醫大佐	佐藤俊三
總務部長	同軍醫少佐	粟屋一步
防疫部長	同軍醫大尉	大河内雄天
防疫部隊長	軍醫少佐	大塚
江文部隊長	軍醫中尉	佐藤七郎

其他ノ人名ハ忘却シテ記憶ガナイ。

吉枝

（一般ニ一〇〇日ハ防疫給水ニ伝染病予防注射ヲ行フコト

伝染病予防ノ為ニ設置サレタルモノデアリ

伝染病予防止ノ為ニ設置サレタルモノデアリ

防疫給水ノ組織ヲ以テ作戦部隊ニ薄ク

ヲ施シタリ。

傳染病撲滅ヲ図ル如キ伝染病撲滅ヲ図ル一般ニ

直接関係セル将故

昭和十七年六月中

撲滅菌ヲ製造セシコト、事実ナリ。

部隊

係ハ防疫給員全部ナリ。

...ノ時期ハ昭和十七年六月ヨリ七月ニテ

...回数、数量等ハ不明ナリ。

散布区域ハ浙江省金華ヲ中心トセル地域ナリ。

此結果ハ中国軍撤退急ナリシ為進軍セ

ル日本軍ガ撒布地域ニ進出シ小休止又ハ宿泊

セシ結果、飲料水炊事等ニ附近水ヲ使用シ

...数多ノ伝染病患者ヲ出シタリ。

又中国住民中ニモ多数ノ患者ヲ出シ仕...

...定、命令系統詳細ハ不明デアルガ

...的ニ忘行為ヲ行ヘルモノデアル。

コレヲ行フモ、

コノ□八激烈ナル病原菌ヲ敵軍ニ撒布シテ人工的ニ伝染病ヲ拐頭セシメ、其ノ流行、蔓延ニ依リテ敵軍ヲ殲シ士気ヲ沮殺セシムルヲ目的トスルモ、一般住民ニ対シテモ殃及スル悪結果ヲ生ズルコトアルモ、陸海軍病院ニ收容シタルモノトス。

及ボス非人道的行為デアル。

昭和十八年九月中旬ニ自分ハ抗州陸軍病院ニ於テモ同病院ハ伝染病患者（国軍兵士）デ充満シテ居リ毎日五、六名ノ死亡者ヲ出シテ居リタリ。同年八月頃ハ同病院ニ患者五、六百名ヲ收容シタリ。

喜林．

安ヲ示サタ・

栄第一六四四部隊ノ衛生兵長立澤忠次大尉

ハ出兵ニ言ニ依レハ假ニ細行機ニ依テ前線

ニ病原菌撒布ニ出動セリト話シタ。

部隊ハ事用機カ最少二個有以上アリタ。

自分ハ昭和十七年五月ヨリ十八年三月マテ防

疫給水部防疫科ニ勤務セリタカ聊モナ

行ヲ知リテ部隊ヲ脱走セシ者テアル如キ非人道的行為ヲ

毒薬研究ナシモ行ナシテタ・

元栄一六四四部隊防疫科員

昭和二十年五月三十七日　　蔡

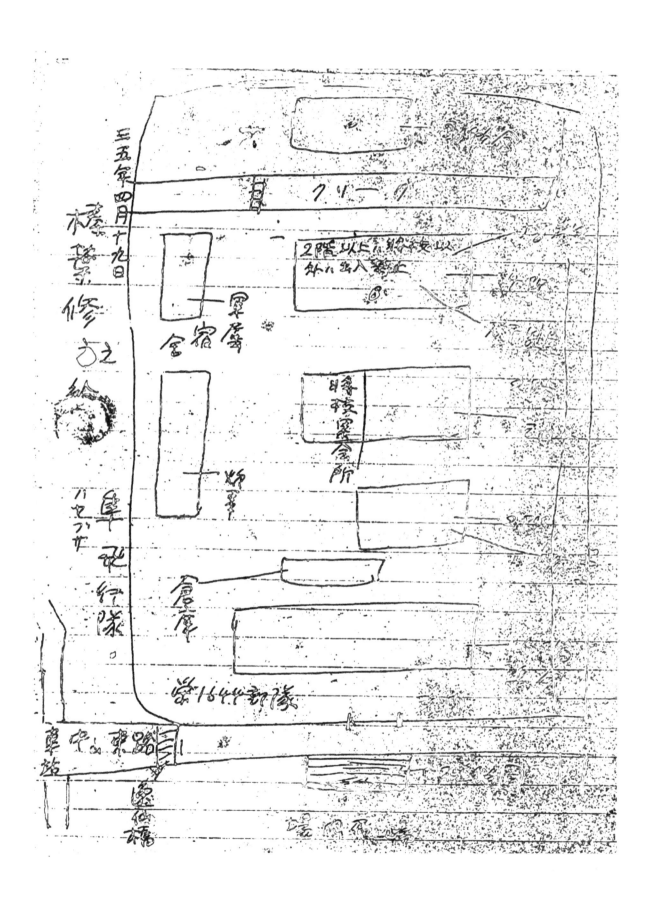

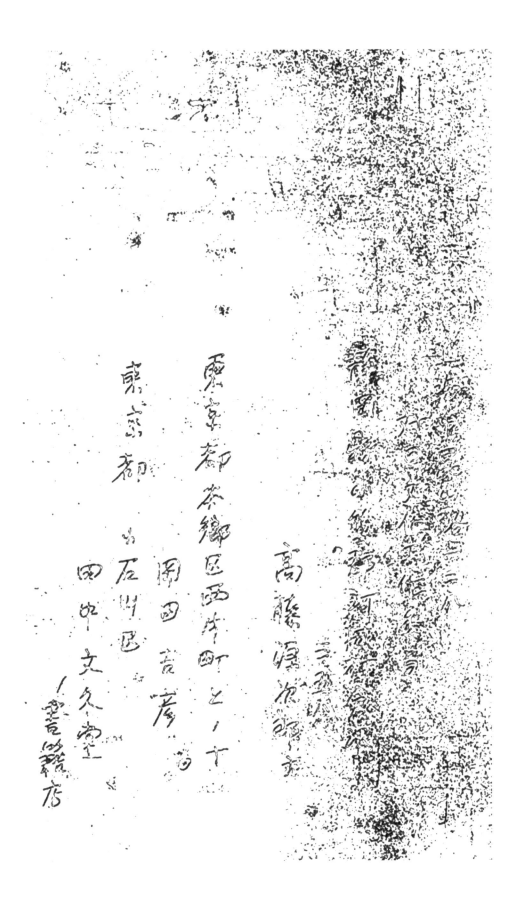

5.2 附录 1　3 Dec. 1944: SINTIC ITEM #185: Prisoner of War Interrogation, POW#229

　　资料出处： National Archives of the United States, R112, E295A, B11.

　　内容点评： 本资料为资料 5.2 附录 1：1944 年 12 月 3 日美军对日军荣 1644 细菌部队九江支队卫生兵榛叶修（俘虏号 #229）的讯问记录。榛叶修的供述证实日军配备专业细菌部队，并在中国战场实施了细菌武器攻击。

Extract from SINTIC ITEM #185 **SECRET**

HEADQUARTERS
UNITED STATES ARMY FORCES
CHINA THEATER
OFFICE OF THE ASST. C. OF S, G-2
APO 879

SINTIC ITEM #185   3 December 1944.

SUBJECT: Prisoner of War Interrogation.

RE: Water Supply and Purification Dept., etc.

SOURCE: POW#229, CHIMBA Isamu, Lance Cpl. Water Supply and Purification
            Depts at Nanking and Kiukiang; captured Mar. 1944 near Kiukiang,
            Preliminary interrogation at TUCHIAO, Szechwan, 29 Nov to 2 Dec
            1944.

RATING: B-2

NOTE: Remarks contained in square brakets / / were not made by POW,
            but are our own comments and additions.

_____

Prisoner's History:

POW #229, CHIMBA Isamu (   ), Lance Cpl.
Age 30; born Shizuoka-Kan; residence Nagoya City.
Graduate X-Ray Section, Medical College of Nagoya Imp. University.
Profession: X-Ray Specialist (physician)
Last Unit: Water Supply and Purification Dept., attached to 68 Div.
Captured March 1944.

Consceipted and trained as medical soldier (eiseihei) in Nagoya Army
Hosp., attached to 3 Div., in 1936/37 (before graduating from Med. Coll.)
No foreign service at this time.

Recalled June 1943, as first replacement (Dai-ichi hoju-hei), (phys. class
B-2), to NAGOYA Army Hospital. Was there 10 days, along with 420 men
called up as Med. Troops (eiseihei) at same time. These other men were
mostly also replacement men, and with the exception of about seven, none had
ever received any training.

From Nagoya, POW traveled to HANGCHOW, Chekiang Province, as follows:

All (about) 420 draftees left in one group, under command (transport commander) of 2 Lt. (Med) KOBAYASHI of Nagoya Army Hospital. From Nagoya by
train to SHIMONOSEKI; ferry boat to FUSAN; train (freight -- cars) by way
of MUKDEN, SHANGHAIKUAN, TIENTSIN, HSUCHOW, to P'UKOW. Freight-cars each

held   **SECRET**

SECRET

G-2 Comment:

1. There is a greater variety of materials, and other materials named, than would be required for the manufacture of the vaccines specifically mentioned.

2. There is a greater variety, and other kinds of animals, than the manufacture of the stated vaccines would require. These animals may have been used in experimental work.

3. There is nothing in the report, except the PWIs (SINTIC Rating B-2) statment, "The bacteria used in the CHEKIANG campaign in 1942 were produced at NANKING in building A, etc.", which is inconsistant with this institution being a large regional vaccine institute and central general laboratory for routine and perhaps for research purposes.

4. The facilities described could and may be used for the production of BW agents, but there is no conclusive evidence in this report xx that they were employed for this purpose. Investigation of this report is continuing.

Note: The CHEKIANG campaign was the largest undertaken in China in 1942 involved approximately 70,000 Jap troops and took place May - August. It followed the Doolittle raid of 18 April 1942. Items 187 and 188, noted in basic communication, have never been received.

SECRET

5.2 附录 2　4 Dec. 1944: Bacterial Warfare, JICA//10,596, JOSEPH K. DICKEY, Col. GSC, G-2, China Theater, U. S. Army Forces

资料出处：National Archives of the United States, R112, E295A, B11.

内容点评：本资料为资料 5.2 附录 2，是 1944 年 12 月 4 日美军中国战区情报部上校 Joseph K. Dickey 对重庆日军战俘 #230 和 #229 审讯报告，题目：细菌战。

日本生物武器作战调查资料（全六册）

CONFIDENTIAL

CONFIDENTIAL

G-2, CHINA THEATER REPORT

Country reported on: JAPAN.

Subject: Bacterial Warfare.

From: Chungking, China.   JICA # 10,596   4 December 1944.

Source: Japanese Prisoners of War.
Evaluation: B-2.

Summary:-

    Attached report lists instances in which bacteria have been used in warfare
in Central China by the Japanese Army. It also lists the location of a plant for
the cultivation of bacteria at Nanking. The specific location of this plant will
be determined and this report amplified as quickly as possible. For the immediate attention of the Chief, Chemical Warfare Service, and the Surgeon General.

    SOURCE: POW #230, Lance Cpl., 17 IMB, captured Dec. 1943 in Hunan;
               POW #229, Lance Cpl (Med), Water supply & purification Depts.,
               Nanking and Kiukiang, and other POWs interrogated 29 Nov 44 at
               TUCHIAO, Szechwan.

    RATING: B-2. (POW #230, who furnished the bulk of the information and
               also obtained some additional and confirmatory information from
               other POWs, is considered reliable. POW #229 is also considered
               reliable. Other information supplied by both, which could be
               checked, has been found correct).

- -

    Principal Informants:

        POW #230, Lance Cpl., Inf., 17 IMB, captured Dec 1943 in Hunan, parti-
        cipated both in the Chekiang-Kiangsi campaign in the spring of 1942,
        and in the Changte campaign in the fall of 1943.

        POW #229, Lance Cpl., Med Corps, Water Supply & Purification Depts.,
        Nanking, and Kiukiang, captured March 1944 near Kiukiang. (See SINTIC
        Item #184 for details).

    Note:

        This report of course covers only those instances of the use of
        bacteria in warfare by the Japanese definitely known to above pris-
        oners. This is only a preliminary report.

    USE OF BACTERIA IN WARFARE IN CENTRAL CHINA BY THE JAPANESE ARMY:

    1. The Water Supply & Purification Dept. Hq (Boeki Kyusui-Bu Honbu),
        code name NOBORI (   ) 1644, at NANKING, was known in the period
        July 1943 to Feb 1944 (the period when POW #229 was assigned there)
        to be cultivating bacteria, principally typhus, cholera, and dysen-
        tery bacilli.

Unnumbered

Dir Int 3
CWS 2
Med 2

                                              (JOSEPH K. DICKEY,
                                              Colonel, GSC,
                                              G-2, China Theater
                                              U. S. Army Forces.

Distribution:- War Department

CONFIDENTIAL

MIS NOTE: This report will not be reproduced in whole or in part, or distributed
to any agency or person other than those listed on the left hand margin above
without the approval of the Chief, MIS.

772

2. The fourth floor of the building near the Nanking airport occupied
    by this Hq was strictly guarded and access permitted to very few
    officers. POW #229, basing his belief on rumor and "various indi-
    cations", believes that on this floor was located the section res-
    ponsible for bacterial warfare in Central China.

3. Japanese troops were prevented to gain knowledge of the use of bacteria
    by the Japanese army. In the campaign against Kinhwa (Chekiang prov-
    ince) Japanese ground units, apparently advancing faster than the
    source of orders and planning for bacterial warfare in the area had
    anticipated, proceeded to enter a district still affected by bacteria
    dropped from the area. This reportedly resulted in considerable
    casualties on the side of the Japanese.

4. Known instances of use of bacterial warfare:

Campaign	Date Used	Location	Kind of Bacteria
Chekiang-Kiangsi	May 1942	Kiangsi Prov.	Typhus (Chibusu)
" "	" "	SHANGHSIAO (上 㦩,)	Dysentery (Sekiri)
" "	" "	Vicinity of KINHWA, Chekiang	Typhus, cholera, dysentery
Changte	Nov 1943	Vicinity of CHANGTE, Hunan	Cholera

5. In all the above instances, the bacteria were dropped from airplanes.
    (TN - No information has been secured so far as to quantities used, etc)

From: G-2, Chungking, China.   JICA # 10,596   4 December 1944.

DBG/wl   CONFIDENTIAL   Page 2

5.2 附录 3　6 Dec.1944: Water Supply and Purification Unit, Japanese Army, Report No. 10595, JOSEPH K. DICKEY, Col. GSC, G-2, China Theater, U. S. Army Forces

资料出处： National Archives of the United States, R112, E295A, B11.

内容点评： 本资料为资料 5.2 附录 3，是 1944 年 12 月 6 日美军中国战区情报部上校 Joseph K. Dickey 的报告：1944 年 11 月 29 日至 12 月 2 日战俘 Chimba Osamu（榛叶修）讯问记录。

SECRET

MILITARY INTELLIGENCE DIVISION W. D. G. S.

MILITARY ATTACHE REPORT

J. Y. (Country reported on)

Subject: Water Supply and Purification Unit, Japanese Army I. G. No. _____
(Brief descriptive title)

From M.A.A. Chungking   Report No. 10,595   Date 6 December 1944

Source and degree of reliability: Japanese Prisoner of War
Evaluation: B-2
Ref: G-2, China Theater rpt. JICA #10,596

SUMMARY.— Here enter careful summary of report, containing substance succinctly stated, include important facts, names, places, dates, etc.

Primarily order of battle on above-named organization but much information pertaining to the functions thereof are included. This report should be consulted with JICA Report No. 10,596, pertaining to BACTERIAL WARFARE. For the immediate attention of Chief, Chemical Warfare Service and The Surgeon General.

JOSEPH K. DICKEY,
Colonel, GSC,
G-2, China Theater,
U. S. Army Forces.

MIS NOTE: This report will not be reproduced in whole or in part, or distributed to any agency or person other than those listed on the left hand margin without the approval of the Chief, MIS.

DISTRIBUTION: War Department

and master

Unnumbered

Dir Int 3
CWS 2
Med 2

Distribution by originator _____

Routing space below for use in M. I. D. The section indicating the distribution will place a check mark in the lower part of the recipients' box in case one copy only is to go to him, or will indicate the number of copies in case more than one should be sent. The message center of the Intelligence Branch will draw a circle around the box of the recipient to which the particular copy is to go.

AGF	AAF	ASF	AC of S G-2	Chief IG	Eur.-Afr.	Far East	N. Amer.	Air	Dissem.	AIC	FLBR	OSS
MA Sec.	CIG	Rec. Sec.	ONI	BEW	CWS	ENG.	OPD	ORD	Sig.	State	QMG	

Enclosures:

1 copy to Dr Hudson.

SECRET

SOURCE: POW 229, CHIBA Isamu, Lance Cpl, Water Supply and Purification Depts at Nanking and Kiukiang; captured Mar. 1944 near Kiukiang. Preliminary interrogation at TUCHIAO, Szechwan, 29 Nov to 2 Dec 1944.

RATING: B-2

NOTE: Remarks contained in square brackets / / were not made by POW, but are our own comments and additions.

Prisoner's History:

POW 229, CHIBA Isamu (春葉勇   ), Lance Cpl.
Age 30; born Shizuoka-Ken; residence Nagoya City.
Graduate X-Ray Section, Medical College of Nagoya Imp. University.
Profession: X-Ray specialist (physician)
Last unit: Water Supply and Purification Dept., attached to 68 Div.
Captured March 1944.

Conscripted and trained as medical soldier (eiseihei) in Nagoya Army Hosp., attached to 3 Div., in 1936/37 (before graduating from Med. Coll.) No foreign service at this time.

Recalled June 1943, as first replacement (Dai-ichi hoju-hei), (phys.class B-2), to NAGOYA Army Hospital. Was there 10 days, along with 420 men called up as Med. Troops (eiseihei) at same time. These other men were mostly also replacement men, and with the exception of about seven, none had ever received any training.

From Nagoya, POW traveled to HANGCHOW, Chekiang Province, as follows:

All (about) 420 draftees left in one group, under command (transport commander) of 2 Lt (Med) KOBAYASHI of Nagoya Army Hospital. From Nagoya by train to SHIMONOSEKI; ferry boat to FUSAN; train (freight cars) by way of MUKDEN, SHANHAIKUAN, TIENTSIN, HSUCHOW, to P'UKOW. Freight-cars each held about 40 men. Train traveled mostly at night only, and trip took about one week. Soldiers were allowed outside cars, on platforms only, at stations, where prepared food ("bento") was handed them; no cooking on train.

About 16 medical troops left at HSUCHOW (徐州   ), Kiangsu Prov., to enter hospital there; about 40 (for NANKING #1 and 2 Army Hosp), at NANKING. Others left at NANKING* to proceed to HANKOW, to LUSHAN, etc.

As far as P'UKOW, same train also carried about 300 Transport Troops (unit unidentified) from GIFU, destined for YINGSHAN (应山), Hupeh Province; as well as about 300 infantry of C-3 unit from NAGOYA, apparently destined for HANKOW. Entire train, carrying about 1020 men, had about 30 cars. (Med. troops, inf. and transport traveled as separate groups however; each under its own transport commander).

From NANKING POW traveled to SHANGHAI by train, thence by train to HANGCHOW. About 60 medical troops off at SHANGHAI (for #1 and #2 Army Hosp. there); others at SOOCHOW (苏州), Some traveled on from HANGCHOW TO KINHWA (金华).

Arrival at HANGCHOW, on 15th June 1943; where POW and 12 others of group (all untrained except POW) entered HANGCHOW Army Hospital.

POW and 4 others (untrained) of same group were transferred beginning of July 1943 to Water Supply and Purification Headquarters (Boeki Kyusuibu Hombu), NANKING.

In Feb (10/2/44), POW only was transferred to Water Supply and Purification Dept., Branch, attached to 68 Div. at KIUKIANG (九江). POW was captured in March 1944 near KIUKIANG.

From G-2, China Theater, Chungking   Rpt. #10,595   Date: 6 December 1944

DRG:gas   Page 2

SECRET

PURIFICATION DEPT., HQ., NANKING (Hombu).

... iber 1943:   SAKAE (荣) 1644
... ..c. 1943:   NOBORI(登) 1644
/Note: OB book carries code 1644 as "Central China Water Supply & Purification Dept./
Change of code-name in December 1943 entailed a curtailment of jurisdiction of the Hq at Nanking. In February 1944 it was rumored that this Hq might be transferred to SHANGHAI.

C.O.: Col. (Med) SATO Shunji (佐藤俊二)   (- 2/44 -)
/1942 AL: C.O. S.China Water Pur.Dept (11/41)/

Gen. Affairs Dept (Somubu)
C.O: Major (Med) AMAYA Ippo (尼雅一步)   (- 2/44 -)
/1942 AL translation: Maj. AMAYA Kazuo, mistake for AMAYA Ippe in original. Position: Army Cent Met Sec (7/41)/

Atchd: Capt (Med) OKAMACHI (Or OKOCHI) Masao (大渕雅夫)(- 2/44 -)

2nd Lt (Med) SUZUKI   (鈴木)   (- 2/44 -)

2nd Lt (Med) WATANABE (渡邊)   (- 2/44 -)

Sanitation Section (Boeki-Ka)
/Above is standardized translation, which however seems unsuitable in this case. Epidemic Prevention Section more closely represents both Japanese name and purpose of the section/

C.O.: Capt (Med) OTA Yoshizo (太田由蔵)   (- 2/44 -)
/Not in 1942 AL/

Attached: 2nd Lt (Med) YAMAGUCHI Wataru (山口渉)   (- 2/44 -)
/Not in 1942 AL/

Water Supply Section (Kyusui-Ka)
C.O.: 1 Lt (Med) SAISHO Atsushi (税所篤)   (- 2/44 -)
/1942 AL: Atchd NANTO Army Hosp (7/41)/

Atchd: 2 Lt (Med) HIRATA Takeo (平田武夫)   "
/Not in 1942 AL/

Materials Section (Zaimu-Ka, 材務课)
C.O: 1 Lt (Med.)   (name unknown)

Attchd: 2 Lt (Med) KAMOTO   (河本)

Physico-Chemical Section
(Correct name may be Physico-Chemical Research Laboratory, i.e. Rikagaku Kenkyusho, but it was generally known as "Rikagaku" only)

C.O.: 1 Lt (Med) AKITA Torao (秋田虎雄)   (- 2/44 -)
/Not in 1942 AL/

Atchd: 1 Lt (Med) INUKAI (大饲)   "

Total strength of Hq.in Nanking: military personnel, about 400.

                        Gunzoku (Jap. civilians) about 200.

                        Chinese employees: about 40 (male and female; for menial work)

                        Total: approximately 640 (Feb. 1944).

From: G-2. China Theater. Chungking   Rpt. #10.595   Date SECRET 1944

SECRET

FUNCTIONS OF WATER SUPPLY & PURIFICATION DEPT. Hq:

(1) General Affairs Section (Somuka)

Administration, general and of personnel in Water Supply & Purification Units under Hq jurisdiction.

(2) Sanitation Section (Boeki-Ka) (Epidemic Prevention Section)

a. Manufacture of vaccines and serums for preventive injections. Quantity produced is sufficient to supply Japanese troops (and probably Japanese civilians) in Central China.

b. Laboratory examination of excreta. Both excreta of local Japanese military units as well as of civilian (Chinese) population is examined for indications of contagious diseases, etc.

c. Cultivation of bacteria. The principal categories of bacteria cultivated are cholera, typhus, and dysentery bacilli. PO. stated that large quantities of animals (guinea pigs, rats, etc) were used for experiments in this section, access to which was strictly forbidden to all unauthorized personnel.

d. Giving injections to population in case of epidemics.

e. Inspection of food and food stores in Nanking (possibly also adjacent localities)

(3) Water Supply Section (Kyusui-ka)

To purify water and supply it to Army units. /See SITTC item 135 regarding details of water purification equipment used/

(4) Materials Section (Zairuka)

Procures and supplies materials and repairs equipment for all sections of Water Supply & Purification Dept.

(5) Physico-Chemical (Laboratory) (Rikagaku..)

Examination of water characteristics in Central China.

Manufacture poisons and drugs. (Purpose not definitely known).

Organizes Kendokuhan (検毒班) for active operations. These sections, usually consisting of 6 men, test water found in operations zones to ascertain whether or not it contains poison or other injurious elements.

d. Organizes Dendodo Sokatsu - han (電導度調定班 Electric Conductivity Measuring Sections). These sections, usually consisting of a out 6 men, go ahead of Kendokuhan and, by means of electric conductivity t sts, investigate water, other liquids, foods, etc.) tests should indicate whether or not matter tests is pure. Elements found to contain impurities are turned over to Kendo-kuhan for analysis.

These two types of sections are organized for active campaigns.

(6) A nursery or garden (Noon 農園) is attached to the Physico-Chemical Section in Nanking. This is located adjacent to the building housing the Water Supply & Purif. Dept. Hq. In it are cultivated poisonous (alkaloid) plants. Supervision is in the hands of a corporal, who commands five Japanese soldiers and about 10 Chinese employees (gardeners). Area covers about 1000 Tsubo plus. /More than 4000 sq. yds./

From: G-2, Chungking, China.   Rpt. 10,095   Date: 6 December 1944

D.IG: ae   Page 4

SECRET

WATER SUPPLY & PURIFICATION DEPT., BRANCH DEPT., attend to 68 Div.,
(Ssui Ki Bu; 68 Shidan Zaizoku)

Location: KIUKIANG (九江)(- 3/44 -)

Code: HINOKI (檜) 1644.

C.O.: Maj (Med) HASIMOTO Kunio (橋本邦雄)   (- 3/44 -)
      /1942 AL: Capt (12/40), Med; C.O., Water Pur. Dept; 3/39/

Adj: 2 Lt (Med) KOBAYASHI Shintaro (小林新太郎)
      /Not in 1942 AL/
      This officer also has the concurrent job of
      C.O. of the Physico-Chemical Section.

Shomuka (General Affairs Section) (corresponding to somu-ku of HQ in Nanking),

C.O.: 2 Lt (Med) SUZUKI Hideya (鈴木秀也)   (- 3/44 -)
      /Not in 1942 AL/

Personnel & Awards Subsection (Jinji-Koseki):

      W/O SHIRAISHI Tomishiro (白石富四郎)

Sanitation Section (Bsocki-ka)

C.O.: 1 Lt (Med) SAITO Shichiro (齋藤七郎)
      /Not in 1942 AL/

Water Supply Section (Kyusuiku)   ) combined in one section
) called Zaimuka (Materials Section)
Materials Section (Zaimuka)   )

Physico-Chemical Section

C.O.: 2 Lt (Med) KOBAYASHI Shintaro; concurrently also adjutant.

This Branch Dept (Shibu), attached to the 68 Div, and taking its code name (Hinoki),
received its orders not from the 68 Div, but from the Water Supply & Purification
Dept., HQ, Nanking. PW states that apparently all such departments attached to
divisions at least in the area under the jurisdiction of the 13 Army (and possibly
all of Central China), were under jurisdiction of Nanking rather than the
divisions etc. to which they might be attached. They all had the code number 1644,
preceded by the code name of the division to which they are attached.

Strength of the Kiukiang Branch Dept (Hinoki 1644):   80 M. and officers
                                                      15 gunzoku (drivers etc).

Equipment (Vehicles) of Kiukiang Branch Dept., Water Supply & Purif. Dept:

      1 passenger car (for C.O.)
      1 water filtering and supply car (kyusuisha; see SECRET Item 136)
      5 trucks.

Interrogator's Remarks:

      PW 229 is considered trustworthy. He is well educated; his intelligence
      is above average, and it is believed he is sincere.

Data:

From: G-2, Chungking, China   Rpt. 10,595   Date: 6 December 1944

EAB:gaa   Page 5

779

~~SECRET~~

1. Officers' names are underlined where such officers are handly identified, or where their assignment according to this report differ from
that previously known to us.

2. Dates indicated in round brackets are the last date on which .G. knew
respective officers to hold job described. Dashes (-) before and
after dates indicate that officers concerned held jobs before date
indicated, and still held them when .G. last knew of them.

- - - -

SOURCE: PO., 229, Lance Cpl., water Supply & Purification Depts at Nanking (Hq)
and Kiukiang (Branch); captured Mar. 1944 near Kiukiang. For background
see SINTIC Item 185, Interrogated at TUCHIAO, Szechwan, 29 Nov to 2 Dec
1944.

RATING: B-2.

NOTE: Remarks contained in square brackets / / are our own.

The basic filtration equipment which the Japanese Army in Central China (and
probably elsewhere) uses is an apparatus which utilizes no chemical agents. It
was supposedly invented by Maj. Gen. ISHII Katsuya (石井勝也) /Not listed in
1942 Army List/.

It consists of a steel cylinder closed at both ends; a pump (operated either by
hand or over a chain drive), a revolving brush shafts running the length of the
cylinder, and about six porcelain tubes of porous texture built lengthwise into
the cylinder around the brush shaft, and revolving in opposite direction to the
latter.

Water is sucked into the cylinder at one end and held at a pressure of about 45
lbs. It penetrates the walls of the porcelain tubes. These tubes are made of a
porcelain called HODOGAYA Yakimono (保土ヶ谷焼物); possibly this
material is produced in HODOGAYA, Yokohama, or by a company of that name, (or
both). This is a grayish material and although it is porous, no pores are apparently visible to the naked eye.

The impurities that are deposited on the outer walls of these porcelainware tubes
are brushed off by the central rotating brush, the porcelain tubes themselves
rotating in opposite direction. A tightly covered opening at the side of the
cylinder can be opened to remove dirt periodically; one end of the cylinder can be
opened for thorough cleaning and change of tubes.

See attached sheet for sketch of apparatus.

Models: These filtration machines (rosuiki 濾水器) come in four different
sizes, viz:

(A) (甲) Largest size. 18 or 20 of these apparatuses are mounted on a special
truck (water supply car 給水車). Motive power for the pumps and
revolving brushes and tubes is supplied from the automobile engine when the
car is not in motion.
One such automobile will filtrate and supply about 40 metric tons of drinking
water per hour.

(B) (乙) Second size, somewhat smaller than (A). Six filter tubes only. It
weighs about 90 kgs; is normally operated by hand (by means of a handle pushed
left and right), and supplies about 1700 litres of water per hour. Usually
carried on trucks.

From: G-2, China Theater, Chungking Rpt. 10,595 Date: 6 December 1944

DAG:gae Page 6

SECRET ~~SECRET~~

(C) (丙) Third size. Weighs about 70 kgs, and can be carried by four men. Maximum capacity 1200 litres per hour. Usually hand-operated.

(D) (丁) Fourth size. For individual use. Length about 30 centimeters (one foot); capacity about 5 litres per hour. Not much used.

Cleaning: Model (A) requires "minor" cleaning at least once every 90 minutes. For this purpose a small door on the side of the cylinder is opened.

For period thorough cleaning and overhauls one end of the cylinder is opened.

Limitations: Although normally these filtration apparatuses operate very satisfactorily even on dirty creek water, and filter out all bacteria, they do not filter out poison.

Water pressure in cylinder must be watched. Normal operating pressure is 45 lbs / per square inch ?/. If pressure increases substantially, there is danger of fracture of filtering tubes.

Equipment of Japanese Army Units (Central China):

Each Japanese battalion usually has 1 or 2 model (B) apparatuses (normally called "Suiki-Otsu" 水素 乙). Smaller units have 1 model (C). These are normally hand-operated.

Water Supply & Purification Depts normally have one water supply truck with 18 - 20 Model (A) apparatuses (engine operated).

Interrogator's Remarks: No. 229 who supplied above information is considered trustworthy and fairly well informed.

Interrogator: JWS

Attcht: Sketch of SUIKI-OTSU.

From: G-2, China Theater, Chungking   Rpt. 10,595   Date: 6 December 1944

SECRET ~~SECRET~~

Sketch of water Filtration Apparatus Model (B) ("SUIKI-OTSU")

Capacity: 1700 litres per hour (hand operated or power operated)

Explanations:

A - steel cylinder, length about 100 cm., dia. about 45 cm
B - inlet tube (end of flexible hose attached to this can be dropped
    into creek etc.; i.e. into source of water supply)
C - outlet tube (for filtered water)
D - covered opening for frequent removal of impurities
E - removable end wall (removed for overhauls etc.)
F - pressure gauge
G - revolving brush, rubbing against outside walls of tube H.
H - porcelainware (Hodogaya-yakimono) tubes (porous), into which
    water filters. Rotate in opposite direction to G.

Later View:

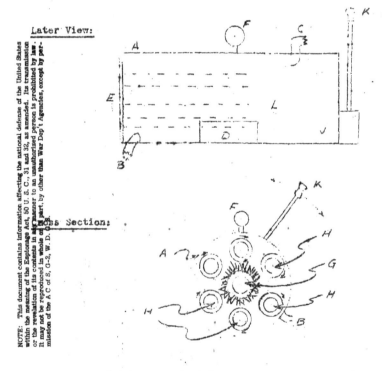

Cross Section:

J - pump (with chain wheel for power drive, and handle K for hand
    operation.
L - gears for rotation of revolving brush and tubes

From: G-2, China Theater, Chungking   Rpt. 10,595   Date: 6 December 1944

DRC:gac   SECRET   Page 3

5.2 附录 4 13 Dec. 1944: Japanese Chemical and Bacteriological Warfare in China, TO: JICA, HQ, USF, China Theater, Rear Echelon, FROM: JOHN A. BURDEN, Maj., A.U.S.

资料出处：National Archives of the United States, R112, E295A, B11.

内容点评：本资料为资料 5.2 附录 4，是 1944 年 12 月 13 日美国陆军少校 John A. Burden 提交美国中国战区司令部的报告，题目：日本在中国的化学战与细菌战——1944 年 12 月 11 日日军战俘 #229 再讯问记录。

CONFIDENTIAL

Refer to:
SINTIC Items #213,
214, 216, 217.

HEADQUARTERS
UNITED STATES FORCES
CHINA THEATER
OFFICE OF ASST. C OF S, G-2

93990

JAB/JWS/mh
A. P. O. 879
13 December 1944

SUBJECT: Japanese Chemical and Bacteriological Warfare in China.

TO : JICA, HQ, USF, China Theater, Rear Echelon, A.P.O. 627.

1. Attached are SINTIC Items #213, 214, 216 & 217, being compilations of additional information secured from prisoners of war through reinterrogation conducted on 11 Dec 1944.

2. These reports are submitted in supplementation of SINTIC Items #187 & 188 submitted on 4 December 1944.

For the A. C. of S, G-2.

JOHN A. BURDEN
Major, A.U.S.

4 encls.
as above.

CC: Theater Surgeon, HQ, USF, China Theater, Rear Echelon, A.P.O. 627.

CONFIDENTIAL

CONFIDENTIAL

HEADQUARTERS
UNITED STATES   ARMY FORCES
CHINA   THEATER
OFFICE OF THE A.C. OF S, G-2

JWS/
A. P. O. 879,
12 December 1944.

SINTIC ITEM #213.

SUBJECT: Japanese Preparations for Bacteriological Warfare in China.

SOURCE: POW#229, Lance Cpl. (Med), Water Supply and Purification Depts.,
Nanking, and Kiukiang. POW was with Hq at NANKING from July 1943
to Feb 1944; with Dept at KIUKIANG Feb to March 1944, when he
was captured. Reinterrogated at Tuchiao, Szechuan, 11 Dec 1944.

RATING: B-2.

NOTE: Refer to SINTIC Item #187 for report on preliminary interrogation
on Bacteriological Warfare; to SINTIC Item #185 for report on
Water Supply & Purification Dept. (Date

Supplementary Report to SINTIC Item #187, dated 3 Dec 1944:

1.   To POW's knowledge, the bacteria cultivated by the Research Department
of the Water Supply & Purification Dept. Hq in Nanking, are cholera,
typhus, dysentery; experiments with plague bacilli were under way in
Jan. 1944. There may be other bacteria that are cultivated there, but
POW has no knowledge thereof.

2.   Vaccines manufactured are "Yonshu Kongo -四種混合 ",(a mixture of
Para-typhoid A, Para-typhoid B, dysentery, and cholera vaccines; therefore called "Quadruple Mixture"), "and others" (not specified). The
quantity produced is sufficient to satisfy Japanese Army requirements
in Central China, as well as ample to use widely among civilians in
the area in case of incipient epidemic.

3.   The building in NANKING where the vaccines are produced and where
bacteria are cultivated is shown on the attached sketch as "A"; it is
the 4-story Research Dept (Kenkyushitsu) of the Water Supply & Purification Dept Hq. POW estimates length of building at about 40 meters;
width at about 20 meters.

4.   Raw materials used, in quantities which POW was unable to estimate, are
agar-agar, eggs, meat extracts, casein, animal blood, glucose, maltose,
powdered liver. Animals used (housed in building "B" on sketch) include
cows, horses, rabbits, goats, guinea pigs, mice, geese, marmots (?).

5.   Effluent from building is somewhat yellowish in color and has the odor
of putrid fish; it is mixed with waste steam and then disposed of into
the sewer.

- 1 -

213/1

CONFIDENTIAL

CONFIDENTIAL

6. Individuals working in the second to fourth stories of building "A" where bacteria are cultivated are said to wear rubber gloves and some kind of simple nose-mouth masks (probably similar to those worn commonly by many Japanese in winter in order to "guard against" colds). They "disinfect" before leaving building (washing with disinfectant soap etc). Every three months, they are required to take pills (POW does not know how many) which containing certain immunizing agents and are a substitute for injections. (Exact nature of these pills not known).

7. Access to second and upper floors of Building "A" is permitted only to Japanese army officers and warrant officers who have special permit for this building; other officers and noncommissioned officers etc. are not admitted under any circumstances. Admitted are also specially qualified "Gunzoku" (civilians employed by the Japanese army), who make up the bulk of the personnel in this building. Some of them are former Army surgeons, and many of them are rated the equivalent of majors and even higher-ranking officers.

8. Water Supply & Purification Dept Branch in KIUKIANG had a Research Dept cultivating bacteria, but this was on a very minor scale. POW thinks that other branches may have similar section. Vaccines for use of Japanese Army in North China are produced by Water Supply & Purification Dept in Peiping.

9. POW stated that Japanese soldiers as a rule have absolutely no knowledge of use of bacteria by their army. There is a standing order which forbids troops and civilians attached to the Water Supply & Purification Departments to mention to anyone in which section they work, to discuss the nature of their work, etc., and normally members of various departments do not know each other. POW believes that in case of a BW attack by Japanese army, possibly only commanders of divisions and independent units near the affected area would be notified, and such knowledge would be withheld from other officers and from all troops.

10. When Japanese troops overran an area in which a BW attack had been made during CHEKIANG campaign in 1942, casualties upward from 10,000 resulted within a very brief period of time. Diseases were particularly cholera, but also dysentery and pest. Victims were usually rushed to hospitals in rear, particularly the HANGCHOW Army Hospital, but cholera victims, usually being treated to late, mostly died. Statistics which POW saw at Water Supply and Purification Dept Hq at NANKING showed more than 1700 dead, chiefly from cholera; POW believes that actual deaths were considerably higher, "it being a common practice to pare down unpleasant figures".

11. POW believes incubation period in case of cholera infection was about a day; 3-4 days in case of typhus; about 10 days in case of para-typhoid. Most contagion apparently resulted from drinking water, but also from food.

- 2 -

213/2

CONFIDENTIAL

93990-3

786

CONFIDENTIAL

~~bacteria~~ used in the CHEKIANG campaign in 1942 were produced at NANKING in building "A" shown on attached sketch. They were spread from special airplanes attached to the Water Supply & Purification Dept Hq at NANKING. This Hq has three special planes attached to it, which are stationed at the airfield in front of the compound on which the Dept Hq's building stand. The plane or planes for the CHEKIANG bacteria attack took off from there. POW at the time heard that a 2 Lt. SUZUKI (given name not known) flew along in the attack.

13. POW is not certain how the bacteria are dropped. Has heard that for attacks, the planes carry four electric refrigerators filled with test-tubes containing bacteria, there being "tens of thousands" of tubes in a plane.

14. Some other Water Supply & Purification Depts in China (e.g. the one in PEIPING) also have special planes attached to them; end of 1943 a total of six planes was said to be attached to these departments in all China. These are apparently small (reconnaissance type?) planes and they always fly under fighter escort provided by the regular Air Corps.

Interrogator's Note:

POW himself, being a non-commissioned officer, did not work in the Research Dept. of the Water Purification and Supply Hq. He is therefore unable to supply more accurate and definite information than that stated in this report and in SINTIC Item #187. His information is based on statistics and reports he saw whilst assigned to another department of the said Hq, and to a small degree on observations and "general knowledge within the Hq". Prisoner is very intelligent and sincere and has had medical training at NAGOYA University Medical College as an X-Ray specialist. It is felt that his information can be accepted as reliable.

Interrogator: JWS.

- 3 -

213/3

CONFIDENTIAL

93790-A

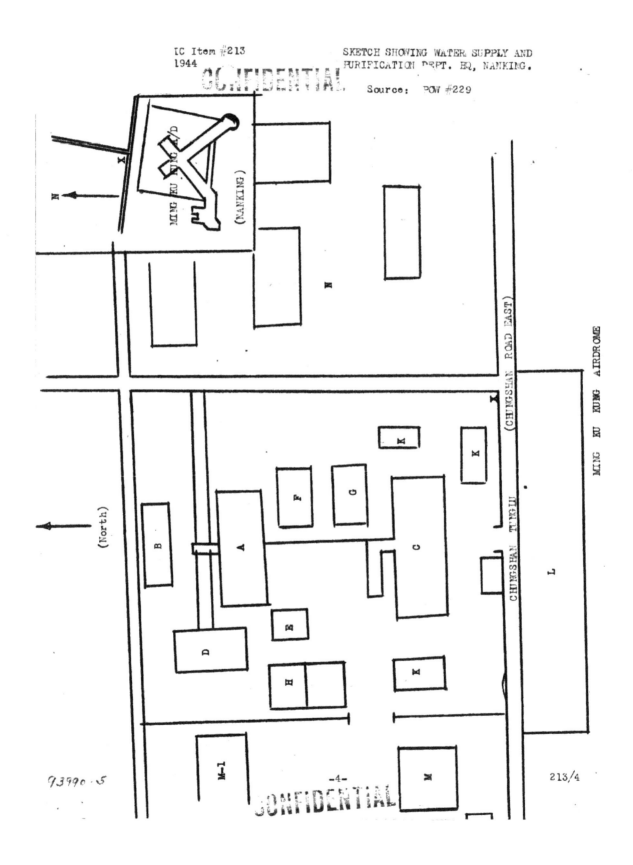

IC Item #213
1944

CONFIDENTIAL

SKETCH SHOWING WATER SUPPLY AND
PURIFICATION DEPT. HQ, NANKING.

Source: POW #229

CONFIDENTIAL

Enclc to SINTIC ITEM #213, 12 Dec 1944.
Explanation of Sketch Showing Water Supply & Purification Dept. Hq.
Installations, Nanking. (As of Feb 1944)

This sketch is not drawn to scale; relative size of buildings is not accurate.

The compound of the Water Supply & Purification Dept Hq is located directly north of MING KU KUNG Airdrome, NANKING, and north of CHUNG SHAN RD EAST; to the east of it is a compound with buildings of the Nanking (Puppet) Government Military Academy; to the west are barracks of an air unit.

Note point marked X on main sketch and on inset sketch for orientation. Inset sketch is drawn to scale from air photo and shows exact location of point X relative to location of MING KU KUNG A/D.

Explanation of Letters:

A - 4-story building housing Research Dept of Water Supply and Purification Dept Hq. (Bacteria cultivated here)

B - Animal house.

C - 6-story building, housing Dept Hq (offices); also used for barracks for Hq personnel, and storerooms.

D - Living quarters for "Gunzoku" employed at Hq, and some military personnel.

E - Boiler rooms.

F - 2-story building. Lecture hall.

G - 2-story building. Dispensary.

H - Garage; kitchen.

J - Tall smoke stack.

K - Warehouses of Water Supply & Purification Dept Hq.

L - Gardens of Water Supply & Purification Dept Hq; poisonous and alkaloid plants are cultivated here (See SINTIC Item #185).

M - Buildings used as barracks of an air unit.

M-1 - Air unit barracks, 4-story building.

N - Compound with buildings of Nanking (Puppet) Government Mil.Academy.

- 5 -

CONFIDENTIAL

213/5

5.2 附录 5　2 Jan. 1945: OSS, Reported Japanese Use of Disease Serums and Cultures, 9, Dec. 1944

资料出处： National Archives of the United States, R112, E295A, B11.

内容点评： 本资料为资料 5.2 附录 5：1945 年 1 月 2 日美军中国战区司令部战略情报局通报的 1944 年 12 月 9 日情报，题目：日本人使用疫病血清和细菌培养基——在浙赣会战第一期，日军飞机沿金华、兰溪间的交通要道，在空中散布伤寒、霍乱、痢疾病菌。

n.D.D.1837

OFFICE OF STRATEGIC SERVICES
WASHINGTON, D. C.

OFFICE OF STRATEGIC SERVICES
TECHNICAL INTELLIGENCE

DISTRIBUTED	2 January 1945	DISSEMINATION NO. A-47271
COUNTRY	China	ORIGINAL REPORT NO. Y-2167
SUBJECT	Reported Japanese Use of	DATE OF REPORT 9 December 1944
	Disease Serums and Cultures	EVALUATION F-0

CONFIRMATION)
SUPPLEMENT }
CORRECTION)

SOURCE
SUB SOURCE

DATE OF INFORMATION probably September
PLACE OF ORIGIN Kunming

NUMBER OF PAGES 1
ATTACHMENTS
THEATRE

The following information was received from Kiukiang 115° 55' E, 29° 45' N. The message was undated, but was believed to have been sent in September, and emanated from Tu-wei (杜微) which could not be located on the map.

According to a report by a Chinese soldier, formerly with the Japanese Department of Epidemic Defense and Water Supply branch at Kiukiang, who has now returned to the Chinese side, the mission of that department at the present time is to prepare disease serums and cultures. During the first period of the Chekiang-Kiangsi battle, the enemy spread cultures of typhoid, cholera, and dysentery by plane, in the pools and streams along the important communication lines between Kinhwa (金華) 119° 40' E, 29° 05' N, and Lan-ch'i (蘭谿) 119° 30' E, 29° 15' N. Their hope was to infect soldiers and civilians and thus weaken Allied fighting strength.

SECRET

791

SECRET

G-2 Comment:

The Chekiang - Kiangsi battle noted probably refers to the Chekiang campaing in the spring and summer of 1942 since both Kinhwa and Lanchi fugured in this campaign. However, since that time there has been some minor action in this same area.

Information from POW #229 (SINTIC item #213, 12 December 44, previously reported) also mentioned the use of choleria dysentery by the Japanese (which, according to POW, resulted in casualties among their own troops.

SECRET

5.2 附录 6　5 Mar. 1945: OSS, Jap "Anti-Epidemic & Water Supply Section", Bacteriological Warfare

资料出处: National Archives of the United States, R112, E295A, B11.

内容点评: 本资料为 5.2 附录 6，是 1945 年 3 月 5 日美军中国战区司令部战略情报局情报，题目：日军的防疫给水部队和细菌战——日军战俘榛叶修讯问报告。

OFFICE OF STRATEGIC SERVICES

INTELLIGENCE DISSEMINATION BID 0402.

COUNTRY   China   ORIGINAL RPT. YV-252

SUBJECT   Jap "Anti-Epedemic & Water Supply Section,   DATE OF INFO. 5 March 1945
           Bacteriological Warfare   DATE OF RPT. 22 Sept 1945
                                                           DISTRIBUTED

ORIGIN   Kunming
THEATRE   China   CONFIRMATION
                                                           SUPPLEMENT

SOURCE
SUB SOURCE   NO. OF PAGES 4
EVALUATION   ATTACHMENTS   0

        The following report is based on information secured by Chinese Army
interrogation of a prisoner who was captured by Chinese guerrilla troops
5 March 1944 in a small village, 8 Chinese li southeast of Kiukiang. The
prisoner, a graduate of the Imperial University, Department of Medicine
and specializing in X-Ray, was at the time of his capture serving as Chief
of the Epidemic Prevention Division of the Kiukiang Branch of the "Anti-
Epidemic and Water Supply Section" of the Japanese Army. In peacetime
this section is engaged in the study of bacteria, the prevention of epidemics
and providing safe water supply for the Japanese Army; in wartime one of its
primary tasks is bacteriological warfare.

History of Bacteriological Warfare Section

1. The Section known as the "Anti-Epidemic and Water Supply Section" was
established toward the close of 1938 with headquarters in the Central Hospital (Chung Yang Yuan) Nanking. (See para. 5) Originally it was attached
to the Japanese Expeditionary Force in China headquarters. In October 1943
it was converted into a special unit of the Thirteenth Army. During the
last six years branches have been successfully established throughout
occupied China. The mission of these establishments is to develop and breed
such bacteria cultures as dysentery, cholera, and typhoid and then to provide for their proper dissemination in wells and other sources of water supply
used by the Chinese Army. Thus in the early stages of the Chekiang-Kiangsi
campaign the Japanese sent aircraft especially equipped for the purpose of
contaminating the water supply of the Chinese Army. When the Japanese
pushed into a position evacuated by the Chinese troops, they reaped the har-
vest of their own labors and suffered several thousand chasualties from the
poisoned water supply.

Production of Bacteria

2. In the Nanking HQ of this unit a four-story building is devoted to the
preparation ob bacteria. On the first two floors, bacteria are isolated
and typed and on the two upper floors there are facilities for breeding
the bacteria in special broths at a temperature of between 37 and 38 degrees.
Special cases are used, each containing 5,000 tubes and each tube capable
of containing in the vicinity of 40 million bacteria when the process is
properly carried out. (Dimensions of cases: 1.2m. by 1m. by 1m.)

Dissemination of Bacteria by Plane

3. Special planes are used for dropping these tubes, which break upon

CONFIDENTIAL
CLASSIFICATION

MID	DNI	A-2	STATE	TREAS;	OWI	FEA	AMS	MC	FCC	JICA	L	JANAC		
			JICA DISTR:	JIARC;	SBC 290 (1)									
THEATRE DISTRIBUTION		G-2 CT 879 - 3	G-2 CCC 627 - 3	AF Hq 879 - 1	JICA KMG 2									

Hitting the water. Each plane can carry four of the special cases, that is, 20,000 tubes. A crew of five is used, consisting of a pilot, a radio-operator, and a major and two lts. observing and dropping germ cases. The plane is slightly larger than a reconnaissance plane and its fuselage is painted in three colors: khaki, yellow, and green. It is generally escorted into operations by two fighter planes. Nanking has four such planes, these planes being stationed at the MING KU KUNG (Ming Dynasty Former Palace) airfield. These belong to the headquarters organization and in addition the Number One Branch also in Nanking has two planes. The Shanghai Branch is allotted two, the Fengtien Branch four, the Mu Tan Chiang (   ) Branch four, and the Canton Branch two. This gives a total of 18 planes devoted to this type of operation.

4. Headquarters Organization and Personnel

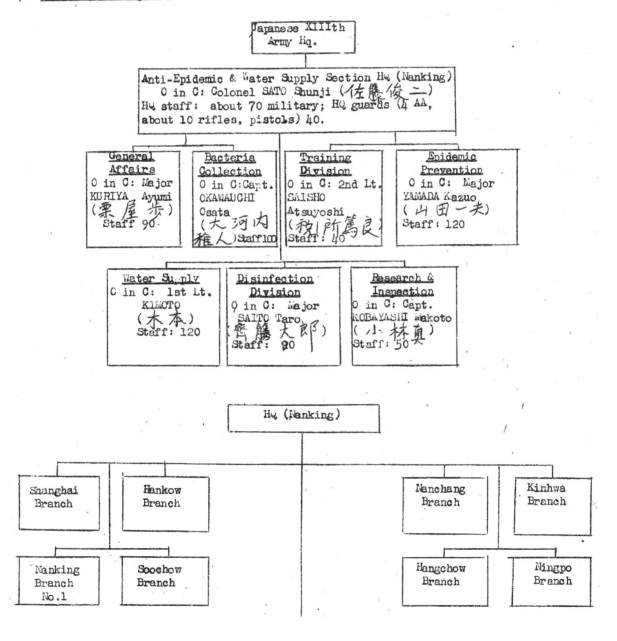

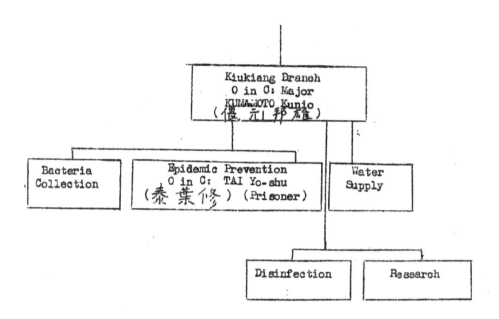

Remarks:

   (a) The exact number of staff members and equipment of above branches varies with local situation.

   (b) Branches are also believed to exist in Manchuria and North China as well as in South China but these apparently are not attached to the Thirteenth Army. The prisoner did not seem to be in command of sufficient facts to permit any generalization concerning germ warfare activities and organizations outside the Hankow-Nanking-Shanghai regions.

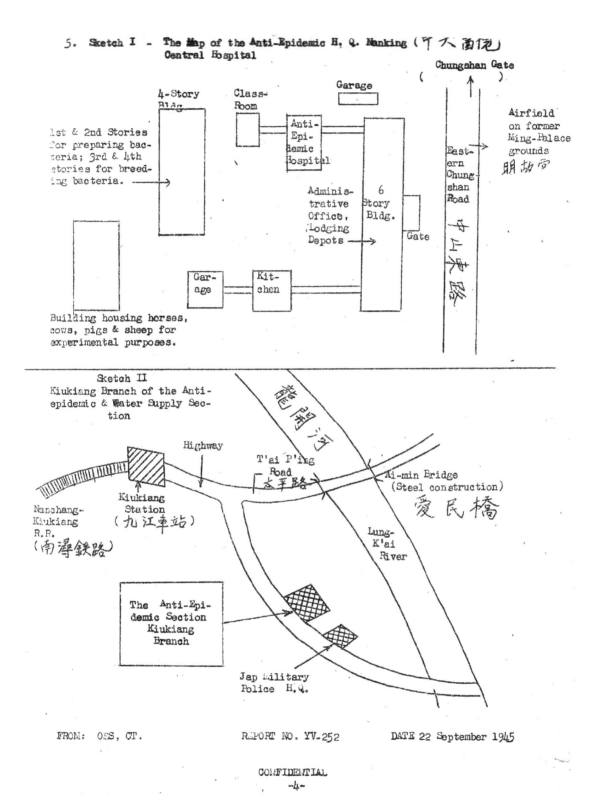

5. Sketch I - The Map of the Anti-Epidemic H. Q. Nanking (中大面貌)
Central Hospital

Chungshan Gate

Garage

4-Story Bldg

Class-Room

1st & 2nd Stories for preparing bacteria; 3rd & 4th stories for breeding bacteria.

Anti-Epidemic Hospital

Administrative Office, Lodging Depots

6 Story Bldg.

Gate

Eastern Chungshan Road 中正東路

Airfield on former Ming-Palace grounds 明故宫

Building housing horses, cows, pigs & sheep for experimental purposes.

Garage

Kitchen

Sketch II
Kiukiang Branch of the Anti-epidemic & Water Supply Section

Highway

T'ai P'ing Road 太平路

Ai-min Bridge (Steel construction) 愛民橋

Kiukiang Station （九江車站）

Nanchang-Kiukiang R.R. （南潯鐵路）

Lung-K'ai River

The Anti-Epidemic Section Kiukiang Branch

Jap Military Police H.Q.

FROM: OSS, CT.   REPORT NO. YV-252   DATE 22 September 1945

CONFIDENTIAL
-4-

797

5.3 美国检察官 Thomas H. Morrow 与 David N. Sutton 向首席检察官 Joseph B. Keenan 提交的有关报告

5.3.1 2 Mar. 1946: Sino-Japanese War, Memorandum to: Joseph B. Keenan, From Thomas H. Morrow, Col.

资料出处: National Archives of the United States, R331, E317.

内容点评: 远东国际军事法庭中国检察团于 1946 年 2 月初到达东京，中国检察官为向哲浚。国际检察局分工负责日本对中国军事侵略的为美国检察官 Thomas H. Morrow 上校。本资料为向哲浚等到达东京大约三星期后的 3 月 2 日，由 Morrow 向首席检察官 Joseph B. Keenan 提交的报告，其中提出日军违反国际法，在中国战场实施化学战和细菌战。

2 March 1946

Subject:　　　　Sino-Japanese War.

Memorandum to:　Joseph B. Keenan

From:　　　　　Thomas H. Morrow, Colonel.

　　　　The following memorandum is submitted as an indication of the scope of that part of the case involving the Sino-Japanese War. The undersigned has already requested of Mr. Mignone copies of certain documents from the Japanese Foreign Office which concern the diplomatic communications between the Japanese and Chinese ~~nation~~ preceding and throughout the war, and has also listed outstanding events which should be covered and concerning which the great volume of evidence will have to be obtained in China, as it presently appears. Those events are as follows, and while there are many other matters that might be included in evidence, these are the dramatic and outrageous acts of the Japanese which should be susceptible of proof:

　　　　First, the Marco Polo Incident, 7 July 1937. The skirmish at the Marco Polo Bridge in the outskirts of Peiping has all the earmarks of a deliberate attempt on the part of the Japanese to start trouble and embark upon an aggressive war with China.

　　　　Second, the so-called Shanghai Incident, 13 August 1937, whereby the Japanese inaugurated a large-scale invasion of central China by the use of both naval and army forces.

　　　　Third, the so-called Rape of Nanking, wherein the Japanese Army captured the city of Nanking and embarked upon an unrestrained orgy of rape and massacre. In the "Stars and Stripes," 22 February 1946, the Chinese War Crimes Commission is quoted as saying that the Rape of Nanking cost the lives of 500,000 Chinese who were hanged, murdered, burned or bombed. This newspaper report ~~indicates~~ that there, ~~was~~ a Chinese War Crimes Commission. The newspaper's statement asserts that this Commission has been investigating atrocities for several months, and it should be approached and the results of this investigation obtained.

Memo to Mr. Keenan, subj: Sino-Japanese War, 2 Mar 46.

General MATSUI, according to Vinacki's "History of Modern China," was relieved from command on account of the chorus of protests from foreign observers at Nanking. General MATSUI was in command of the army that invested Nanking and was to have reported at Sugamo Prison 1 March, 1946. He has been sick, it is claimed.

Fourth, the furious bombing and shelling of Canton and Hankow, Canton being taken 21 October and Hankow 27 October 1938, should also be developed in evidence. These cities were claimed by the Chinese to be unfortified and the bombing and shelling unnecessary.

As to General ITAGAKI, it is stated that in the occupation of Shun Shien he chained prisoners of war on the Ding Poo Highway to be bitten by ferocious dogs he let loose for that purpose. It is also stated that the army massacred 5,000 school students at Shoh Shoan. In this connection it should be noted that General ITAGAKI was involved in the plot to grab Manchuria, was engaged in aggressive war in central China and was later Minister of War in the first KONOYE Cabinet and also the HIRANUMA Cabinet from June 1938 to 30 August 1939, inclusive.

It should also be noted that there is proof that the Japanese imported Persian opium into China and it was claimed that they compelled Chinese farmers to grow the poppy for the manufacture of opium. The claim is made that this was part of an attempt to reduce the Chinese will to fight on the theory that if they were opium addicts they would not be likely to be interested in patriotic endeavor. The undersigned has made no study of this matter up to the present, however.

The matters set forth hereafter are merely memoranda indicating the course of events in China and the diplomatic moves made by the government of China which prove in general that the war was aggressive on the part of Japan and that the Chinese made frequent efforts to obtain a peaceful settlement of whatever disputes may have been alleged as causes for the beginning and continuation of the war.

- 2 -

Memo to Mr. Keenan, subj: Sino-Japanese War, 2 Mar 46.

12 July '37 - Chinese Minister of Foreign Affairs suggested to the Counsellor of Japanese Embassy immediate cessation of military movements on both sides, but there was no response from the Japanese government.

19 July '37 - Chinese Government formally in writing renewed proposal for simultaneous withdrawal of troops to their respective original positions. Also agreed to accept any pacific means of settlement.

26 July '37 - Text of ultimatum delivered 26 July, demanding withdrawal of Chinese troops from Peiping.

(Also in this connection, History of organization and actions of Peace Preservation Corps of Greater Shanghai, China).

(Copy of the Boxer Agreement, 1901, which gave Japan and other nations extra-territorial rights in China).

(Text of warnings by Chinese Government to municipal authorities of Shanghai and the Peace Preservation Corps to take especial precautions against trouble).

9 August '37 - Text of demands of Japanese upon Chinese Shanghai authorities, and Chinese version of killing of Japanese near airdrome, which brought about these demands.

(In this connection, copy of Shanghai Armistice Agreement of 1932, properly authenticated, should be procured).

(Get also copy of Paris Peace Pact, Nine Power Treaty, and Covenant of the League of Nations in this connection).

30 March 1940 - Authenticated copy of note from Dr. Wang Chung-hui, Minister of Foreign Affairs, to foreign governments concerning "National Government of Republic of China".

- 3 -

Memo to Mr. Keenan, subj: Sino-Japanese War, 2 Mar 46

1 Dec '40 - Declaration of Chinese Government concerning the puppet government (an authenticated copy).

30 Aug '37- China's appeal to League of Nations and Signatories of the Nine Power Treaty. (authenticated copy).

15 Sept '37-Text of Dr. Wellington Koo's speech before the Assembly of the League of Nations (authenticated copy).

22 Sept '37-Proceedings of League of Nations Advisory Committee on Mandate, properly authenticated.

27 Sept '37-Properly authenticated copy of resolution of Council of League of Nations concerning indiscriminate bombing of China.

5 Oct '37- Authenticated copies of two reports made by sub-committee to the Advisory Committee of League of Nations and referring in the second report to Article 7 of the Nine Power Treaty.

6 Oct '37- Resolution of the League of Nations Assembly, properly authenticated.

3 Nov '37- Authenticated copy of the proceedings of the Brussels Conference and copies of the two refusals of Japan to attend the consultation of representatives.

7 Nov '37- Authenticated copy of communication to the Japanese Government from the conference.

12 Nov '37- Authenticated copy of reply of the Japanese Government.

15 Nov '37- Authenticated copy of declaration of the conference.

24 Nov '37- Authenticated copy of resolution of the conference and authenticated copy of statement of Dr. Koo, Chief Chinese Delegate.

2 Feb '38 - Resolution of the League Council, calling attention to the Assembly's resolution of 6 October 1937, duly authenticated.

- 4 -

Memo to Mr. Keenan, subj: Sino-Japanese war, 2 Mar 46

2 Feb '38   - Statement of Dr. Koo on this date to the League
(cont'd)   Council, duly authenticated.

10 May '38 - Authenticated copy of proceedings of Council of
             League of Nations on this date, including Dr. Koo's
             speech, wherein he ~~~~~~~ that the Japanese were
             about to use poison gas.

14 May '38- Authenticated copy of resolution of Council of
            League of Nations concerning poison gas. Also
            authenticated copy of statement by Dr. Koo.

Sept. '38 - Authenticated copy of Dr. Koo's communication to
             Council of League of Nations.

19 Sept '38- Authenticated copy of text of telegram to the
             Japanese Government, extending an invitation to
             place dispute before the League.

22 Sept '38- Authenticated copy of Japanese Government's decli-
             nation.

30 Sept '38- Authenticated copy of resolution of Council of
             League of Nations concerning Japan's use of poison
             gas.

             Authenticated copy of report adopted by Council
             concerning Japanese aggression in China.

17 Jan '39 - Authenticated copy of Dr. Koo's appeal to the 104th
             session of the Council of the League of Nations.

20 Jan '39 - Authenticated copy of resolution of the League Coun-
             cil. Also authenticated copy of Dr. Koo's statement
             concerning the resolution.

22 May to - 105th Session of the League Council. Authenticated
27 May '39   copy of Dr. Koo's statement and two resolutions
             adopted on May 27, concerning the Japanese ag-
             gression.

             Authenticated copy of Dr. Koo's statement on reso-
             lutions, 27 May 1939.

19 Dec '39 - Authenticated copy of transactions of the League
             Council concerning Chinese Government's appeal on
             this date.

- 5 -

Memo to Mr. Keenan, subj: Sino-Japanese War, 2 Mar 46

9 Dec '41 - Authenticated copy of Chinese formal declaration
of war against Japan.

A history of the proceedings under the Treaty of China
with various foreign powers, including Japan, granting such
powers extra-territorial rights in China after Boxer Rebellion,
1901, and a properly authenticated copy of this Treaty should
be ready for introduction into evidence. It is particularly
desired that the delimitations of territory wherein the
Japanese troops were to be stationed from Tientsin to Peiping
be indicated by marked map or in some other graphic manner to
accompany this information. If there exists any agreement
between the Chinese and Japanese whereby Japanese soldiers were
given the right to hold maneuvers at a distance of three (3)
kilometers or more from the ____, an authenticated copy of this
is also desired. (Note: General KAWABE claims such an agreement is not in existence.)

An authenticated statement of the casualties, both civilian
and military, of China by reason of the Sino-Japanese War. (it
will be noted in this connection that the Japanese claim in the
Japan Year Book of 1941-42 that the estimated number of Chinese
killed was 2,015,000 from July 1937 to June 1941, inclusive,
and that the total loss, including also wounded and captives,
was 3,800,000. The report indicates that military and naval
casualties are meant. This report comes from the Army Information Section, Imperial Japanese Headquarters. It will also be
noted that Mr. Wendell Wilkie stated in October 1942 that the
Chinese military casualties were 5,000,000. If the Chinese
Government has any figures, same should be submitted, properly
authenticated, for evidence.

It is also recommended that Dr. Wellington Koo and Dr.
Alfred Sao-ke Sze would make important witnesses at the trial
and their presence should be obtained if possible.

It is recommended that former Ambassador Hsu Shih-Ying be
obtained as a witness also. If alive, General Sung Cheh-Yuan,
Chinese Commander in Hopei-Chakar, should also be obtained as a
witness.

If alive, the Mayor of Shanghai in August 1937 should be
interviewed for possible use as a witness.

- 6 -

Memo to Mr. Keenan, subj: Sino-Japanese War, 2 Mar 46

British Ambassador to China, Sir Hughe Knatchbull-Hugessen, should be located and statement procured as to the attempt by Japanese planes to kill him August 26, 1937.

Duly authenticated copy of Treaty of Non-aggression between China and Russia should be ready for production, if necessary.

Authenticated copy of the proclamation of blockade by the Japanese of the Chinese coast should be ready for production in evidence (5 December 1937).

Authenticated copy of Chinese formal acceptance through Foreign Minister Wang Chung-hui to the Nine Power conference in Brussels.

Chinese diplomatic and other papers concerning the puppet Mongol state called "Autonomous Government of Inner Mongolia," including any diplomatic interchange of notes with any other powers concerning this puppet state. This state established at Kweihua, 29 October 1937.

1 Nov '37 - Authenticated copy of statement of Chinese Foreign Affairs Minister concerning Japanese aggression.

20 Nov '37 - Authenticated copy of text of Chinese Government's announcement of removal from Nanking to Chungking.

9 Dec '37 - Authenticated copy of text of Japanese demand for surrender of Nanking and Chinese rejection.

12 Dec '37 - Authenticated copy of Chinese reports on bombing of the "Panay," "Lady Bird," and the "Bee."

14 Dec '37 - Authenticated copy of diplomatic correspondence concerning new puppet regime in Peiping, styled "Provisional Government of the Republic of China."

18 Jan '38 - Authenticated copy of statement of National Government declaring object of armed resistance against Japan.

23 Feb '38 - Authenticated copies of any Japanese reports indicating reason for, and circumstances surrounding, removal from command of General Iwane MATSUI, Commander in central China.

- 7 -

Memo to Mr. Keenan, subj: Sino-Japanese War, 2 Mar 46

39   13 March '38 - Authenticated copy of text of Chinese protest
of Germany's recognition of puppet regime in
Northeast Provinces.

40   28 March '38 - Authenticated copy of papers concerning new
Japanese puppet government called, "Reform
Government of the Republic of China," at Nanking.

41   21 May '38   - Authenticated copy of correspondence, if any,
concerning Hitler's order recalling German
advisors of the Chinese Army.

42   3 July '38   - Diplomatic correspondence, duly authenticated,
concerning French occupation of Paracel Islands,
Chinese possessions.

43   7 July '38   - Authenticated copy of Dr. Koo's correspondence
with the French concerning Paracel Islands.

It is suggested that the Chinese Ambassador
to England, Kuo Tai-chi, be located as possible witness.

44   26 Dec '38   - Authenticated copy of General Chiang Kai-shek's
speech concerning KONOYE's statement as to Sino-
Japanese War.

45   1 Jan '39   - Authenticated copy of report of expulsion of
Wang Ching-wei from the Kuomintang Committee.

46   11 Feb '39   - Authenticated copy of General Chiang Kai-shek's
statement concerning Japanese occupation of
Hainan Island.

47   8 June '39   - Authenticated copy of Mandate of Chinese Government ordering arrest and punishment of Wang Ching-
wei.

48   16 June '39 - Authenticated copy of Chinese-Russian Commercial
Treaty.

49   7 July '39   - Authenticated copy of General Chiang Kai-shek's
message to foreign powers concerning the war.

- 8 -

Memo to Mr. Keenan, subj: Sino-Japanese War, 2 Mar 46

18 Sept '39 - General Chian Kai-shek's statement to People's
                Political Council, authenticated copy.

10 Oct '39 - Authenticated copy of manifesto issued by National
                Government this date.

21 Jan '40   Authenticated copies of "Japan-Wang" secret treaty
 and 23 Jan   and General Chiang Kai-shek's statement concerning
   '40   same. Also authenticated copy of ratification of
                Chinese-Russian trade agreement.

30 March '40- Authenticated copy of Foreign Affairs Declaration
                against Nanking puppet government.

1 Oct '40 - Authenticated copy of statement that Chungking
                has created auxiliary capital.

2 Dec '40 - Authenticated copy of General Chiang Kai-shek's
                statement denouncing Wang-Japan Treaty, granting
                Japan control of certain rivers.

10 March '41- Authenticated copy of manifesto of first session
                of Second People's Political Council.

14 April '41- Authenticated copy of Foreign Minister Wang Chung-
                hui's declaration as to outer Mongolia and the
                Northeast Provinces.

1 July '41 - Authenticated copy of communications indicating
                that Chinese diplomats left Germany and Italy and
                China broke diplomatic relations with those two
                countries.

25 July '41 - Authenticated copy of Chinese Foreign Minister's
                statement about Japanese military occupation in
                Indo-China.

8 Dec '41 - Authenticated copy of Foreign Minister Sun Tai-chi's
                announcement of war declaration.

9 Dec '41 - Authenticated copy of Chinese declaration of war
                against Japan, Germany and Italy.

2 Jan '42 - Authenticated copy of Chinese announcement that
                Chinese troops entered Burma.

- 9 -

807

Memo to Mr. Keenan, subj: Sino-Japanese War, ? Mar 46

11 Jan '43 - Authenticated copy of new China-American and
China-British treaties.

24 Feb '43 - Authenticated copy of Chinese protest to Vichy
on Japanese occupation of Kwang-Chowwan.

20 May '43 - Authenticated copy of American and British treaty
ratifications.

- -

It will be noted that Dr. Koo warned the League of Nations
Council on 10 May 1938 that the Japanese were on the point of
using poison gas on a large scale in disregard of international
law and convention.

In that connection, the China Hand Book, 1937-1943, states
on page 356 that on June 23, 1938, "the Mateng Forts were be-
sieged and the attacking units employed gas." This was in
connection with operations referred to as the "Waen battle."
It was also stated in the same book, on page 357, that "in the
attacks poison gas was extensively used." Also on the same
page it is noted that on or about September 29, at Tienohiachen
Fort, "despite the enemy's aerial and naval bombardment and the
use of poison gas, the defenders checked them for days." Also,
September 19 to 23, 1939, in Hunan along the Sinchiang River,
"the enemy employed large quantities of gas in his attacks."
(See page 358, China Hand Book).

On 7 May, 1941, at Chiungh Sien, on the north bank of the
Yellow River, "the Japanese resorted to poison gas." (See page
362, China Hand Book).

In resisting the Japanese invasion of Burma in 1942, about
March 19th "poison gas used by the enemy suffocated many of the
defenders."

It is recommended that evidence be collected at once from
Chinese sources as to this use of poison gas by the Japanese.
In this connection, it is suggested that Dr. Koo may have information in his hands and he should be approached at once about
this matter. It is understood he is not in England but it seems
this matter should be important enough to bring him to Japan
when the trial commences and if his proofs are in China, it is
suggested that he indicate from London how we can obtain same
for preparation in this case.

- 10 -

Memo to Mr. Keenan, subj: Sino-Japanese War, 2 Mar 46

The Japanese were signers of the Treaty of Versailles and by that treaty the use of poisonous gases was prohibited. Also, a protocol prohibiting the use in war of asphyxiating, poisonous, or other gases and of bacteriological methods, was signed 17 June 1925 and duly accepted by numerous powers. The above information about poisonous gas, etc., is obtained from Hyde's "International Law," Volume 3, page 1820, but the powers who signed the protocol are not listed. Japan, however, was a party to the Treaty of Versailles, as above noted. Attention is also invited, in this connection, to "International Law," by L. Oppenheim, pages 271, 272, 273, 274 and 275.

It will be noted that the international prohibitions against use of gases began as early as the first Hague Conference, 29 July 1899. The prohibition against the use of gas only failed to be also included in the Treat of Washington, February 1922, because this clause was tied up with a controversial provision about submarine warfare. As far as known by the undersigned, however, there is no authenticated account of the use of poison gas in warfare since the Italian and Ethiopian War, except as used by the Japanese against the Chinese. Neither the Germans nor the Italians used gas in World War II.

Bacteriological Warfare

It will be noted that in the conditions above set forth, the protocol of 17 June 1925 prohibits bacteriological methods of warfare. At present I'm not able to say whether this protocol was signed by Japan or not, but will make further research. However, to complete this memorandum attention is invited to page 679 of the China Hand Book, wherein Dr. P. Z. King, on 9 April 1942, set forth that "reports submitted by Chinese and foreign medical experts definitely prove that on at least five occasions Japan resorted to bacteriological warfare in China." It is also stated that on 30 August 1942 a sixth attempt was made. On 27 October 1940 a quantity of wheat was dropped over Ningpo. An epidemic broke out soon and the diagnosis was definitely confirmed by tests. It appears that rice, wheat and fleas were scattered over certain towns and Bubonic Plague appeared soon after, causing a number of deaths.

It is recommended that if alive, Dr. King be procured for interrogation; also that the other experts who worked with him be located, with a view to presenting all these persons as witnesses at the trial. It is also recommended that a study be

- 11 -

Memo to Mr. Keenan, Subj: Sino-Japanese War, 2 Mar 46.

made to ascertain what assurances, if any, by treaty or otherwise, were given by Japan to refrain from either gas or bacteriological warfare.

In this connection, it is noted that the undersigned wrote to the Investigation Department of this Section, requesting that arrangements be made if possible to interrogate General ISHII. On 27 February 1946, the "Stars and Stripes" noted that this general was head of the Japanese Medical Research Institute and is charged with having conducted Bubonic Plague experiments on American and Chinese prisoners of war. It also stated that he admitted inventing a porcelain plague bomb and it appears that he has been conducting experiments in bacteriology, in conjunction with the Japanese Army, since 1941

This matter, as well as the poison gas episodes, assumes importance because of the obvious impossibility of developing such methods of warfare on the field of battle or through the resources of an army general in the field, and indicates that such prohibited methods of warfare were carried on by the Tokyo Government and not the field commanders.

THOMAS H. MORROW,
Colonel

Copies to:
      Judge Hsiang
      Mr. Henry Chieu

- 12 -

5.3.2 8 Mar. 1946: Report Assignment "B", TO: Mr. Joseph B. Keenan, Chief of Counsel, FROM: Col. Thomas H. Morrow

资料出处： National Archives of the United States, R331, E317.

内容点评： 本资料为远东国际军事法庭国际检察局美国检察官 Thomas H. Morrow 上校 1946 年 3 月 8 日再次向 Keenan 提交的报告，其中提及就细菌战讯问石井四郎的要求，未被许可。

GENERAL HEADQUARTERS
SUPREME COMMANDER FOR THE ALLIED POWERS
INTERNATIONAL PROSECUTION SECTION

8 March 1946

SUBJECT: Report Assignment "B"

TO : Mr. Joseph B. Keenan, Chief of Counsel

FROM : Col. Thomas H. Morrow

1. The status of this Assignment "B" subdivision at present is as
follows:

Judge Dell has been assigned to the Tribunal and will file a
report of his work up to date. He has been questioning HATA, Shrunruku,
Field Marshall, at Sugamo Prison. He has also been questioning Vice-
Admiral HAZAGAWA (who is not under arrest), and several men concerned in
the 26 Feb. 1936 mutiny have also been instructed to appear before him
for questioning.

Captain Harryman Dorsey is on special assignment with Lt. Col.
Brabner-Smith.

Mr. G. O. Hyde is interrogating OSHIMA, Hiroshi and will be busy
with him for some time.

Lt. Col. K. R. Parkinson is busy with ISHIDA, Otogoro who he is
questioning at Sugamo Prison, also YOKAYAMA, Yui at the same place, and
he has had assigned to him for questioning KUHARA, Fusanosuke and General
TANAKA.

Mr. E. E. O'Neill has been assigned to this "B" assignment, and
is at present helping Col. Parkinson.

Mr. W. C. Prout of the Investigation Department has been also
assigned to this Assignment "B" from Investigation Department. He is to
provide liaison with Army C.I.C. and C.I.S.

The undersigned has been engaged in the following work:

a. He has questioned ARAKI, Sadao, HATA, Shrunruku, KAWABE,
Shozo, ARITA, Hachiro and TANI, Hisao.

The status of these interrogations is as follows:

The questioning of ARAKI has been taken up by Mr. Hyder, and is nearing completion.

The questioning of HATA will have to be taken up by some one else, and where Judge Dell has left off.

KAWABE's questioning is complete.

The questioning of ARITA has not been completed and has not been carried out beyond the story of secret treaty 25 Nov. 1938 which was made by Japan and Germany at the same time as the Anti Comintern Pact. This questioning should be continued.

The questioning of General TANI, Hisao has been completed.

In connection with the above situations, the following recommendations are made to Lt. Col. Parkinson who will take charge of Assignment "B" during the absence of the undersigned:

That Colonel Parkinson continue his present inquiry.

That Judge Williams be asked to take up the following unfinished matters:

Questioning of the men concerned in the 26 February 1936 Incident. (Referred to this Assignment by Mr. Hyder.)

Questioning of HATA to be taken over from Judge Dell.

That Judge Williams confer with Mr. Hyder about the testimony of ARAKI, which should be submitted by ARAKI in writing, according to his own voluntary suggestion.

That the interrogation of ARITA be continued, having in mind events after 25 Nov. 1936.

In event that Judge Williams needs help, as appears, that another lawyer be assigned to help him.

This for the reason that the interrogation of MATSUI, Iwane should have priority over the above matters, as far as Judge Williams is concerned.

That if ITAGAKI is brought to this jurisdiction, his questioning also have a high priority.

- 2 -

It will be noted that on 25 February I wrote to Mr. Nathan asking that the requests for information concerning "B" Assignment, as contained in report of 11 January from self to Lt. Col. Sackett, be checked.

Captain Caine has obtained some of the documentary evidence requested, but there is much to be done beside this.

The undersigned saw Lt. Col. Thompson, with Col. D. S. Tait, G-2 Technical Intelligence, G.H.Q., in regard to Bacterial Warfare and the statement of activities of Lt. Gen. ISHII, as reported in a recent Stars and Stripes. This points to a connection with the alleged Bacterial Warfare reported in China Handbook 1937-42 (See Page 679).

The interview was negative in results. However, Thompson referred us to Col. Marshall, Chief Chemical Officer, G.H.Q., 5th floor, Mitzi Buchi Shoji Building.

The estimates of results of the questioning of persons by the undersigned will be submitted to Mr. Comyns-Carr's Committee.

THOMAS H. MORROW
Colonel

- 3 -

5.3.3　16 Apr. 1946: REPORT OF TRIP TO CHINA, TO: MR. JOSEPH B. KEENAN, FROM: THOS. H. MORROW

资料出处： National Archives of the United States, R331, E317.

内容点评： 1946 年 3 月 12 日，中国检察官向哲浚与美国检察官 Morrow、助理法务官 David N. Sutton 等赴中国调查，取得关于日军化学战、细菌战的第一手证据材料，4 月 12 日回到东京。本资料为 4 月 16 日 Morrow 向 Keenan 提交的中国调查报告。

TO   :   MR. JOSEPH B. WALKER

FROM   :   THOS. H. MORROW

SUBJECT: REPORT ON TRIP TO CHINA

Pages 1 -7   Report
      8 -9   Summary
      10-14   Recommendations
      15   Conclusion

23 April 1946

16 April 1946.

TO : MR. JOSEPH B. KEENAN, Chief Counsel.

FROM: THOS. H. MORROW.

SUBJECT: REPORT ON TRIP TO CHINA.

Judge C. C. HSIANG, Associate Prosecutor for China, Henry Chin LUI, Secretary, David Nelson SUTTON, Associate Counsel, International Prosecution Section and the undersigned, departed from Tokyo for China, arriving the afternoon of 12th March at Shanghai.

This was pursuant to orders from GHQ USAF PAC 7 Mar, 1946, to proceed to various points in China "for purpose interrogating witnesses, screening and analyzing documents, and obtaining evidence in connection with War Crimes".

The party five days later was met in Shanghai by Mr. Keenan and his party in Special Plane, and the following additional arrangements were made: Mr. Jack Crowley, in Mr. Keenan's party, was detailed to help in our work, and orders were requested detailing him on investigation work in China.

The following itinerary was followed:

    Shanghai to Peiping by plane;
    Peiping to Chunking by plane;
    Chungking to Nanking by plane;
    Nanking to Shanghai by Railroad train.

Mr. Sutton preceded the rest of the party from Chunking to Nanking in order to see a witness about to depart for Manchuria.

The party arrived in Shanghai on the return trip April 10th, 1946, and Mr. Sutton and the undersigned departed for Tokyo 12th April, 1946, leaving Mr. Crowley and Mr. Chin at Shanghai to get additional information and to await a special plane expected to be set up for China investigation.

The following matters were considered as deserving investigation, in connection in connection with the China case:

    A. Circumstances surrounding the 7 July 1937 so-called Marco Polo Bridge affair, which was the apparent spark that set off the Sino-Japanese conflagration 1937 to 1945 inclusive;

-1-

817

16-4-46 cont'd

B.   The planning and waging of continuous military
aggression of Japan against China;

C.   The economic exploitation of China by Japan.

D.   The attempted corruption of the Chinese nation by
the encouragement of sale of opium, morphine, heroin,
and other narcotics to the Chinese population;

E.   The use of toxic gas in warfare, contrary to international law;

F.   Bacteriological warfare, by the sowing of materiels
impregnated with Bubonic plague germs;

G.   German-Japanese intrigues, both during the time that
China and Germany were at peace prior to 1941, and
also after the collapse of Germany in 1945;

H.   Atrocities against the civilian population of China,
in violation of international law, and crimes against
humanity.

In addition to the search for testimony as to the above matters,
a list of seventy-eight (78) documents was submitted to the Chinese Authorities in Chungking and Nanking and which it was thought should be produced as evidence at the trial.

Of these documents, less than half have been obtained. It
should be stated that the Chinese Government records are being removed
from Chunking to Nanking, the new capital, and some are on a barge en route.
The Chinese Government has detailed a Mr. John YOUNG, of the Foreign Ministry, to help in the location of the documents yet to be obtained. In
this report, evidence is not referred to in detail because most of the documents in Chinese still await translation.

Results of the China trip thus far are set forth as follows:

1.   The events immediately preceding and surrounding the
Marco Polo Bridge affair, are well established. Formal statements
from the two Chinese officials, a civil magistrate and a General
of the Chinese Army concerned, and who actually conducted
negotiations with the Japanese at that time, are submitted(in the
Chinese language), and these men are available to testify at the
trial. Attention is invited in this connection to evidentiary

-2-

(16-4-46 cont'd)

Document No. 29 and which contains the "First Report of the Sub-Committee of the Far East Advisory Committee on 5 October 1937". (League of Nations Document A. 78. 1937 VII Geneva Oct 5th 1937.

The conclusions of the undersigned are in keeping with the findings of the League of Nations Sub-Committee, and the evidence gathered in China leads to such conclusion. In addition to the two witnesses above mentioned, a most valuable witness was located in the person of Colonel David BARRETT, Military Attache of the American Ambassador at Chunking who was at the Marco Polo Bridge the morning of 8 July, 1937, and made a report as to the situation. Generals STILWELL and DORN were also in Peping at the time, and would be valuable witnesses.

The conclusions above referred to are in effect that the clash was the result of Japanese aggression, and that the very manner in which the Japanese exploited the incident is cogent proof of that fact.

In this connection, it will be remembered that the armed Japanese forces were in China by virtue of certain treaty rights, but by no stretch of reasoning could their presence in large numbers be justified as suddenly appeared in vicinity of Tientsin and Peiping shortly after the Marco Polo Bridge incident. Troops were rushed in from Korea and other places, and within a month 80,000 Japanese troops were south of the Great Wall of China. This also appears from testimony collected.

The annotation in "Events Leading up to the World War II", from "Survey" (page 124) in substance constitutes the version of the Marco Polo affair that our testimony sets forth. Mr. Sutton and the undersigned visited the scene of the conflict at the Bridge.

B. The planning and waging of continuous military aggression by Japan against China is obvious from the celerity of the attack, the completeness of the several invasions, and the full equipment, readiness, and size of the large military and naval forces employed. A complete exposition of the documents in our possession, and to be furnished later, will prove this assertion.

C. The economic exploitation of China is covered by Mr. Sutton in an attached report.

D. The attempted corruption of the Chinese people by the encouragement of the narcotic trade is also subject of a report by Mr. Sutton attached hereto.

-3-

E. The use of toxic gas is considered to be well established, and in the following manner:

   1. Statement of Japanese prisoners that toxic gas was used;

   2. Statements of Chinese surgeons that they diagnosed and treated cases of Chinese soldiers who became battle casualties from poison gas;

   3. Identification of Japanese Gas weapons by curator of Museum of Fire Arms at TUNG KAI CHOW (near Chunking) where the weapons are on exhibition;

   4. Record of Gas Preventative Section Ministry of War, indicating 36968 casualties (2086 fatal) from Japanese Poison Gas, and containing photographs of victims of Japanese poison gas, showing mustard burns.

   5. Statement of Intelligence Officer, Gas Defense Administration, Chinese Army, that he analysed the contents of a shell collected on a Japanese Battlefield, saw casualties occasionally by gas at that battle, and witnessed a gas bombardment of Chinese troops by Japanese artillery in China.

   6. Statement of American Liaison Officer (Colonel John H. STODTER) with Chinese troops that he received training as a Gas Defense Officer in the American Army, and recognised a pocket of Tear gas in Burma, during the fighting there. He states a number of gas casualties were reported at the time to the Surgical units.

   7. Attention is invited to evidentiary Document No.558 wherein it is made plain that the Japanese possessed certain gas material.

   NOTE: The following comments are submitted on the use of Poison Gas, as disclosed by this investigation.

      a. The Chinese had no offensive gas material, and grossly inadequate gas defensive material, such as gas masks.
      b. Gas was used only as an emergency weapon, and generally when the Japanese were in a serious predicament.

      c. Gas Artillery and Mortar Shells, gas grenades, and bombs were used by the Japanese.

-4-

d. The following sorts of gas were employed by *adamsite*
the Japanese, according to Chinese: Mustard, Lewisite, ~~Adalsite~~,
Chloro Benzine, Playrene. Gas to cause sneezing and vomiting
was also referred to, without mention of its technical name.

e. While much of the evidence relates to tear gas, it
will be remembered that the various international prohibitions
of the use of gas in warfare make no distinction between the
use of tear gas and the more injurious kinds, such as phosgene
and mustard.

f. It is true that the American Army Investigating
Committee in China did not report use of gas by the Japanese.
It is also true that the Committee insisted on overwhelming
evidence, which was not reported to the Committee, as far as
appears.

In the opinion of the undersigned, the use of the poison
gas by Japanese in Sino-Japanese war is well established, and can be
further proved by a certain report on the use of Poison Gas sent to
Pacific War Council, 1943, by Dr. Wellington Koo, now the Chinese Ambassador to ~~China~~. The undersigned saw Koo in Chunking and Koo tried to
get the report, but was not successful. However the proof is now present
without this report.

F. The Bacteriological warfare charge is based upon a
report in China Hand Book 1937-1943, made by a Dr. P. Z. King.
Dr. King and his associates have been interviewed by Mr. Sutton
who is submitting an attached report on them.

G. German-Japanese Intrigues in China, involving the
German Ambassador STAHMER, among others, are subject of a separate
report by Mr. Sutton.

H. The atrocities developed are for the most part in
connection with the taking of Nanking. These atrocities were
committed against both military personnel and the civilian population.

a. Military Prisoners who were captured, and all men
suspected of former membership in the Chinese Army were herded
together by the thousands. These men were tied in groups of five
or six and shot down by machine guns or rifle fire. Thousands were
killed in this manner. Statements of survivors of those massacres,
who were eye witnesses, were obtained by the undersigned, and
are available as witnesses.

-5-

b. Civilians who witnessed rape of women, murder of civilians, men, women and children, and destruction of property of civilians have submitted written statements and will be available as witnesses.

c. Two burial societies in Nanking that are charitable organizations, have submitted through their officers, records indicating that in the months of December, 1937, January, February and March and April, 1938, they buried more than 160,000 persons in Nanking whose bodies for the most part lay in the streets, and were unknown and unclaimed by relatives. Most of these prisoners were killed by gunshot or bayonet wounds. These records are in our possession, and the officers of the societies are available as witnesses.

d. There are also certain signed statements of Japanese atrocities in Peiping.

e. The Japanese bombing of Chunking is shown by a chart.

f. The Chinese Ministry of War has submitted certain photographs showing Japanese atrocities.

g. In addition to the eye witnesses mentioned above, there is a volume of evidence derived from American missionaries who were present at Nanking from the time of the taking of the City by MATSUI'S Army 13 December 1937 until February 1938, when the outrage lessened in number and scope.

In this connection, Dr. Searle Bates, George Fitch and others were interviewed, including a H. J. Timperley who wrote a book "Japanese Terror in China" which he compiled from original sources of information, many of which are now destroyed. Mr. Timperley, and the others above referred to, are for the most part available as witnesses.

h. A.A. Durrance, now a Nanking manager of UNRRA, has submitted a statement concerning atrocities he personally witnessed in Hankow, and states that Admiral Glassford and his Staff were also witnesses.

i. There is much more to be developed in Shanghai concerning atrocities.

It will be remembered that the Japanese attacked Shanghai 28-29 January 1932, also 13 August 1937, and finally the International City on 8 December 1941.

Many atrocities were committed in connection with all three of these attacks, and Mr. Crowley and Henry Chin are at present in Shanghai procuring evidence as to this.

-6-

For instance, the torturing of J. B. Powell, an American and former editor of the China Weekly Review, and the terrible treatment of prisoners in the Bridge Prison Camp.

j. The Bombing of Canton, and outrages at the Baptist Mission there, are also to be developed.

k. The atrocities at Liuchow, Suchow, and Kweilin, have been referred to in testimony adduced thus far in China, but need further development, in order to prove what the undersigned believes to be a fact, namely: that violations of international law, atrocities, crimes against humanity, and other outrages committed by Japanese soldiers were of such a general nature and universal extent throughout the Sino Japanese War, as to indicate that the Japanese High Government officials deliberately embarked upon an orgy of frightful warfare in China or condoned or encouraged the same (if actually initiated by the various Army and lesser Commanders).

l. The treatment of American and British prisoners of war at Formosa and other places is also to be considered. There is some question as to whether this section desires to take up the Formosa situation, for instance, about 90% of the prisoners at Formosa were British, the remainder American. Mr. Sutton and the undersigned interviewed these prisoners and they tell a story of protracted semi-starvation, ill treatment and utter disregard for the ordinary rules of International Law governing custody of prisoners of war. For instance, there was no protection from Air Attacks, and no markings indicating that the prisoner of war camps were such. One camp, moreover, was adjacent to an airfield. Chinese prisoners of war were summarily executed, captured American pilots were ill treated, and then executed, but the ground forces Allied prisoners in Formosa were half starved, and set to work in unhealthy surroundings. Captain Gibbons and Cram, and Major Crossley, all of the British ground forces, stand ready at Shanghai to testify as to this, if their evidence is considered proper to be included in this case. They were prisoners for several years, having been taken at Singapore.

-7-

S U M M A R Y

The following propositions in the opinion of the undersigned, have been established by sufficient proof:

1. That the Marco Polo Bridge affair, which launched the war, was a deliberate attempt on the part of the Japanese to start trouble.

2. That the Nanking Atrocities persisted such a length of time after the taking of the city as to raise a presumption that the Tokyo Government at the time knew, or would have known the situation, but took no effective steps to stop the outrages, and that the members of such government are therefore responsible for such atrocities.

This statement is made because it seems beyond possibility that the Tokyo High Command and Ministry can adduce such rebutting evidence as that the Japanese Generals in China were beyond the control of Tokyo and fought the war there on their own.

The Nanking Atrocities include crimes against civilians and crimes against prisoners of war; and the evidence ranges from official documents to statements of victims and actual eye-witnesses.

3. That poison gas was employed by the Japanese in their operations against China. It was a weapon of last resort, (tear and sneezing gas were most often used), and its use was probably almost entirely discontinued after President Roosevelt's statement in 1941 threatening retaliation in case gas was used thereafter by the Japanese. However, when used, it was directed against civilians lacking any gas defense material and Chinese soldiers of whom a small proportion only were equipped with masks; and of whom 36,000 became casualties. Having joined in 1919 in a condemnation of gas warfare by the Responsibilities Commission of the Paris Peace Conference, the story of gas warfare by the Japanese becomes another instance of flagrant violation of a solemn international agreement. It is significant that gas warfare could not be waged without the knowledge and approval of the Japanese Ministry and High Command in Tokyo.

(a) Gas offensive material came from the Chemical Warfare Centre at Narashino, Japan, and could not be produced by a General in China, who must get his gas supplies from the homeland;

— A —

(b)　The Chinese had no gas offensive material, and it could not be said that the gas offensive material furnished by Japanese High Command was for retaliation;

(c)　Documents and testimony recently obtained by our Chemical Warfare Section, GHQ, shows that the High Command in Tokyo knew that gas was being used in China by Japanese Armies.

- - - - -

The above three phases of the case, outlined in Paragraphs "A", "B", and "H" on pages 1 and 2 of this report, are ready for presentation.

Mr. Sutton has indicated in his portion of the report what phases particularly developed by him are ready for presentation.

As to the remaining matter, it is recommended that no attempt be made to further develop the case for the purposes of this trial.

- - - -

RECOMMENDATIONS

The following recommendations are submitted:

1. That a special plane be obtained to afford transportation to Mr. Crowley and Henry Chin, now in Shanghai and engaged in obtaining further evidence. Also that the Chinese Committee of five, appointed by the Ministry of Foreign Affairs at Chunking, to gather evidence on atrocities, be afforded the facilities of the special plane.

2. That John B. POWELL, former editor of the China Weekly Review, be procured as a witness. He is now in America. His son in Shanghai, J. W. POWELL, has communicated with his father in my behalf, to discover if he is physically able to make the journey.

3. That the laws of the Chinese so-called "Puppet Government" concerning the drug traffic, be obtained.

4. That any reports of U. S. Consuls in China on sales of narcotics during the puppet Government Regime be gathered to show the large proportion of the drug traffic at that time, and in comparison to the lesser traffic before the installation of the puppet Government.

5. The Paramount Film Co. (I assume the address is Hollywood) has a film which is authentic and shows Japanese atrocities in China. Recommend that this film and the person who can verify the manner and place of the taking of the film pictures, be obtained for the trial.

6. It is recommended that Yates McDANIELS, now in charge of the Pacific Coast Bureau of the Associated Press, at San Francisco, be produced as a witness concerning the Chinese war. He has been recommended by the Editor of China Weekly Review as one who can tell about the situation in China during the war years, having been a Press representative at that time.

7. Norman SOONG is now in Tokyo as correspondent of the China Central News Agency, and can be reached at the Press Club. He was on the PANAY at the time of its bombing and can testify as to this, and events surrounding the Nanking capture. SOONG is available in Tokyo.

That being the case, it must be determined whether cumulative evidence from Mr. PAXTON, 1st Secretary of American Embassy at Nanking, and Ray MARSHALL, who were also on the PANAY should be attempted to be produced. PAXTON expects to go to the United States the end of this month to be gone for several months,

-10-

and MARSHALL is somewhere in the United States (to be reached through Colliers). In this connection, it should be remembered that George ATCHISON, of the State Department is now back in Tokyo, and can testify also as to the PANAY incident.

The "PANAY" incident is important in this respect only:
It constituted a brutal hint on the part of Japanese Military and Naval authorities that our gunboats had better get out of China. Also, the promises of the Japanese Governments to carefully respect American property in China, which were made concurrently with the apology, were not kept, according to Mr.Grew, the American Ambassador to Japan.

8. Dr. Robert LIM, Surgeon General of the Chinese Army, has promised to submit statistics as to casualties in the Chinese Army during the war. These were not available when the undersigned saw him, and it will be necessary to trace this promised documentary evidence.

9. Dr. George FITCH, Dr. Searle B.Tes, Mr. L.J. MILLS and other missionaires now in China can testify as to the Nanking capture and atrocities. FITCH is with UNRRA in China, the latter two are at Nanking. Others mentioned in TIMPERLEY's Book are also available, and the book is among our documents. They should appear as witnesses.

10. Mr. CROXLEY has been asked to interview General Robert I. McCLURE now at Nanking, who according to the Chinese War Minister, saw the devastation at KWEILIN, in company with General WEDEMEYER and SIMPSON.

11. There is a report in the League of Nations File according to the Chinese, on the use of Poison Gas by the Japanese, Japanese atrocities, and the opium and drug traffic when the Chinese Puppet Government was in existence.

These reports should be sent over from Geneva. They are not in Chinese Government Files.

12. Mr. I.K. LITTLE, American in charge of Chinese Customs in Shanghai, can testify as to the manner in which Japanese paralysed the Chinese Customs in North China before the war started in 1937, also as to what a fraud upon China was the East Hopei Autonomous Government. According to Colonel David D. Barrett, Military Attache, U.S.Army, at Chunking, LITTLE would be a good witness as to these matters. He should be called, if Mr. CROXLEY so recommends.

13. Colonel David BARRETT, address: c/o American Embassy, Chunking, was present at Marco Polo Bridge the morning after the initial skirmish 7 July 1937, speaks Chinese, has been in China for 16 years altogether, and it is recommended that he not only be called as a witness, but also to advise as to, and "line up" the Chinese witnesses. He knows China intimately.

14. It is recommended by the Dutch Ambassador to China that further evidence be obtained to show how General ARAKI corrupted the minds of school children when he was Minister of Education 1938 and 1939. The Ambassador states that the school books for children of tender age were illustrated with pictures of Japanese bayonetting and bombing the Chinese, glorifying war, and that if the libraries in unbombed towns like KYOTO were searched, or even the present schoolrooms, that copies of these school books would be found. Recommend that some such action be taken. Have already spoken to Mr. Hyder about this matter.

14. Dr. Wellington KOO in Chunking referred me to Report of the Pacific War Consul on use of Poison Gas in China in 1943, and asked the Foreign Office there to get me a copy. The Foreign Office could not find such copy. Recommend that Washington and London be traced for copies, which I would like to have.

15. Former Colonel A.A. TORRANCE, former member of Office of Strategic Services, filed a report on China to General WM. DONAVON. This report should now be in the hands of General John MAGRUDER who has succeeded General DONAVON in Washington. TORRANCE has been in China for some 30 years with the Standard Oil Co., is now head of UNRRA in Nanking, and has submitted a statement (now in file) as to atrocities in Hankow. Recommend that he be summoned as a witness and that his report be obtained from General MAGRUDER in Washington.

16. The failure to obtain so many documents from the Chinese Government presents a serious question. This matter has been referred to hitherto in this report.

The Chinese ministries were asked to furnish statements to the effect that the requested documents (which should have been in their files) were not located, but such statements were not obtained because Chunking office stated documents might be at NANKING (advance office) and Nanking stated that documents might be en route on a Barge.

It may be that the Court will allow counsel to make a professional statement to the effect that the documents were sought to be obtained where they should have been located, but could not

-12-

be found there, and that the prosecution be allowed to prove the same altitude.

In this connection, the newspaper L'Impartial at Chunking has copied most official correspondence of the Chinese Government since its stay in Chunking, and possibly such correspondence can be there obtained. Besides this, many statements in Chinese Hand Book 1937-1943, Chinese Year Books 1938, 1941 (which are printed in English) and the Japanese Year Books, and many purported copies of official documents in these books are no doubt accurate copies of the originals, and it will save much time and trouble if a foundation is laid for introduction of these books. This matter is submitted for consideration, with the recommendation that early efforts be made to lay a foundation for the introduction of year books and other secondary evidence.

17. State Department at Washington should be asked for a copy of President Roosevelt's statement in 1942, warning the Japanese that if they use poison gas against any of the Allies of the United States, that the United States will retaliate.

Also, any State or War Department reports on the use of poison gas by the Japanese in the Sino-Japanese War.

18. In connection with the Japanese attack on the Shanghai International City 8 December 1941, the records of our Naval Department as to the capture of the "WAKE" and treatment of the Wake prisoners should be produced to show the sneak tactics at Shanghai which were like those at Pearl Harbor and Singapore. This Shanghai attack has been generally disregarded because of the more serious Pearl Harbor attack at the same time. Suggest that Captain Robinson be approached about this for suggestions.

We had the "WAKE" at anchor in the River at Shanghai, and our consul and the Americans in the International City at that time, can testify as to their aggression. Mr. CROWLEY and Henry CHIN CHIU are developing this matter in Shanghai at this time.

19. It is recommended that some draftsmen from the Engineer Corps be detailed to work on some vivid sketches, to be identified and then introduced in evidence.

These can sometimes be drawn to scale, otherwise, and in some cases of necessity, will be approximate, but reveal relative positions of troops, natural objects, and geographical locations.

-13-

For instance, the undersigned desires Col. BARRETT to identify the Marco Polo Bridge and its environs, and it also seems important to show the City of Shanghai in connection with the three Japanese invasions of that place (1932, 1937, 1941) indicating location of the International City, the French Concession, Chapei, and the River.

20. It is recommended that Jack CROWLEY and Mr. Henry CHIU be transported by special plane to Kweilin, Liuchow, Suchow, Hankow, and Changsha, to gather further evidence. The desirability of sending Mr. Sutton and the undersigned again to China and to make a final check up of evidence, especially documentary, is also suggested.

21. The necessity of a plan to transport and house Chinese witnesses, when the trial is in progress, and has reached the time for introduction of evidence in the Chinese war period.

The witnesses will fall into the following categories:

a. Chinese Government Officials.

b. Chinese civilians and former soldiers (of humble origin generally).

c. American missionaries, Business men, and Army Officers now in China.

Suitable quarters will have to be provided upon their arrival here, also subsistence.

There may also be some witnesses from the United States such as Hallett ABEND, and General STILWELL. Provision must be made for them.

QUERY: SHOULD A SHIP FROM SHANGHAI IN TO TOKYO BE USED TO TRANSPORT WITNESSES FROM CHINA?

22. In view of the pre-trial program outlined in memorandum of Chief of Counsel 22 April 1946, and the distance involved between China and Tokyo, as well as the fact that we are having a third language (Chinese) to contend with, it is recommended that the special facilities above mentioned, be accorded to the sections charged with development of Japanese activities in China, and wherever possible.

The vastness of China, the large extent and length in years of the Sino-Japanese war, and the difficulties of communication, make such special facilities imperative.

-14-

CONCLUSION

The presence of Mr. Keenan at Shanghai, Peiping and Chunking, opened the way to information and evidence in a manner that greatly facilitated the task of Mr.Sutton, Mr.Crowley and Mr.Chiu, and the undersigned.

Mr. Keenan's calls upon General Li, Generalissimo Chiang Kai Shek, Premier T.V.Soong, Wellington Koo, paved the way to important acquisitions of evidence and information.

My investigation in China was largely carried out according to a plan formulated in consultation with Judge O. C. Hsiang, the Associate Prosecutor for China. Before my arrival at various places, Judge Hsiang made arrangements with individuals and institutions concerned which greatly facilitated my work. Mr. Henry Chiu, his secretary, and other members of the Chinese Government who were, through Judge Hsiang's arrangements, especially designated to collaborate with me, all gave me splendid cooperation.

Messrs. Sutton, Crowley and Chiu worked long hours and under trying conditions at times in order to carry out their mission, and exhibited a singular devotion to duty.

Respectfully Submitted,

THOS. D. MORROW,
COL.,   IGD.

-15-

5.3.4 23 Apr. 1946: REPORT FROM CHINA, BACTERIA WARFARE, David Nelson Sutton

资料出处: National Archives of the United States, R331, E317.

内容点评: 本资料为远东国际军事法庭国际检察局美国助理法务官 David N. Sutton 1946 年 4 月 23 日向首席检察官 Keenan 提交的中国调查报告中关于日军在中国战场实施细菌战的报告。

REPORT FROM CHINA

BACTERIA WARFARE

The China Handbook for 1937-1943, pages 679-682, recites instances of the use by Japan of bacteria warfare in China in 1940 and 1941. We tried to locate and secure statements from the persons mentioned in this report given in the China Handbook and to run down all available leads relative to the use by Japan of Bacterial warfare. At Chungking several conferences were held with Dr. P. Z. King, Director General of the National Health Administration of China, and with Dr. W. K. Chen, former head of the Department of Laboratory Medicine, Center Emergency Medical Service Training School and consultant for China Red Cross Medical Relief Corps, who is at present Medical Director of Methodist Union Hospital at Chungking.

While there were instances in which Japanese planes dropped grain and other foreign substances over Chinese cities and bubonic plague subsequently occurred, some of these instances being: (a) At Ningpo in Chekiang Province wheat having been dropped from planes October 27, 1940, and plague subsequently occurred. (b) At Chu-hsien in Chekiang Province rice and wheat grains and reportedly fleas having been dropped from a plane on October 4, 1940, and bubonic plague occurring November 12, 1940. No bubonic plague was ever previously known to have occurred in that city. (c) At Kinghwa granules were dropped from Japanese planes November 28, 1940, but no plague subsequently occurred.

Drs. King and Chen could not positively determine that the bubonic plague which occurred in these instances was caused from germs which had been dropped from the planes. There was, however, one other instance in which both of them are thoroughly satisfied that bacterial warfare was used. This was at Changteh in Hunan Province November 4, 1941, and the fact that both of these doctors are satisfied that the plague which

-1-

occurred at Changteh causes them to be of the opinion that in theother
instances Japan used or attempted to use bacterial warfare. At Changteh
the evidence indicates that a lone enemy plane flew very low over the
city November 4, 1941, dropping wheat and rice grains, pieces of paper
and cotton wadding and other unidentified particles in two sections of
the city. A statement in the official report signed by Mrs. E. J.
Bannon, R. N., who was at the time superintendent of the local Presbyterian Hospital, confirms this fact. Some of the grain was collected
and brought to the hospital and laboratory examinations showed bacillus
closely resembling that of plague. There had been no known instances
of previous cases of plague in that province. On November 11, 1941, the
first clinical case of plague came to notice at Changteh. Dr. W. K.
Chen and Dr. R. Pollitzer (concerning whom further information is hereafter given) went to Changteh and positively confirmed the fact that
persons there were suffering from and died of bubonic plague. Their
findings are set out in detail in the statements and reports submitted
herewith, and the investigation made by each of them on the ground led
them toward the firm conclusion that the plague which occurred at Changteh
and which was subsequently spread from there to other places was caused
from the substances which had been dropped from the enemy plane on
November 4, 1941.

Dr. R. Pollitzer, a native of Austria and a graduate of the Medical
School of Vienna University, has been in public health centers and plague
prevention work in China since 1921. A memorandum of his personal record
is as follows:

"PERSONAL RECORD OF DR. ROBERT POLLITZER

"Dr. R. Pollitzer was born in Vienna (Austria) in 1885. After having
finished his primary and middle school education he entered the Medical Faculty of Vienna University in 1903 and graduated in 1909 as
Doctor of Medicine.

"Having worked already as a student in the laboratory of the "Rudolph"
Hospital in Vienna, Dr. Pollitzer continued to do so until the end

-2-

834

of 1909, then entered the clinical services of the hospital, becoming eventually house-physician. He remained in this position until August, 1914, when he had to enter the army as a reserve officer in the Medical Corps.

"Becoming a prisoner of war at the Russian front in September, 1914. Dr. Pollitzer was transported to Eastern Siberia where he remained until early summer of 1920. He worked most of the time in war prison hospitals, usually as senior physician, and also had opportunities to give free aid to Russian patients suffering from infectious and other diseases.

"In summer 1920 Dr. Pollitzer joined the Austrian Red Cross Mission who had come to Vladivostok to help in repatriating the prisoners of war. The plan to return via Siberia and Russia to Austria could not be carried out and the mission had to return from the border of Soviet Russia to Vladivostok.

"Dr. Pollitzer decided to stay in Harbin where in January, 1921, he was offered to take charge of the Laboratory of the Manchurian Plague Prevention Service. He had thus an opportunity to assist in the investigation and control of the Manchurian pneumonic plague outbreak of 1920-21. Dr. Pollitzer remained in the Manchurian Plague Prevention Service until 1932, devoting his time to investigations on plague and cholera both in the laboratory and in the field.

"From 1932 until August, 1937, Dr. Pollitzer was with the National Quarantine Service in Shanghai, working mainly upon the problem of cholera and participating in the publication of manuals on cholera and plague.

"When the Quarantine Service had to close down upon outbreak of hostilities, Dr. Pollitzer worked for some months in an honorary capacity under the auspices of the Shanghai Municipal Council, first as Assist. Medical Officer for Refugees and then as Medical Officer for Refugees.

"In December, 1937, Dr. Pollitzer was invited to join the League of Nations Epidemic Commission in China and departed for the interior of China. As shown by the attached certificate, Dr. Pollitzer continued to work with this Commission until January 31st, 1941.

"Rejoining then the National Health Administration, Dr. Pollitzer was sent in the spring of 1941 to Chuhsien to help in investigating and controlling the plague outbreaks in that place and I-we. He was continued since then in anti-plague work in the field, working successively in Changteh (Hunan); Fukien, Chekiang and Kiangsi; Yunnan and again in Fukien and adjacent provinces. He is now being sent to Manchuria.

Submitted by

"April 3rd, 1946

/s/ DR. Pollitzer
Dr. R. Pollitzer"

While we were in Chungking it was learned that Dr. Pollitzer was at Nanking preparing to leave with Dr. Yung and others to investigate the

plague now spreading in Manchuria. D. N. Sutton went to Nanking on
April 2d ahead of the rest of the party in order to contact Dr. Pollitzer
and conferred with him on April 2d and April 3d.

Dr. Pollitzer has in his possession and furnished to us a copy of
a letter which he received from Aghnides, Under-Secretary of the League
of Nations, dated at Geneva, June 7, 1941, certifying that Dr. Pollitzer,
a former member of the Plague Prevention Bureau and subsequently attached
to the National Quarantine Service in China, had been employed by the
League of Nations in connection with its technical collaboration with
China from December 15, 1937, to January 31, 1941. The letter sets out
in detail the types of work performed by Dr. Pollitzer for the League
of Nations as bacteriologist and epidemiologist to a unit of the Anti-
Epidemic Commission in Kweichow and Hunan Provinces and in other parts
of China and recites, "During the whole period of the above-mentioned
activities, Dr. Pollitzer has proved himself to be a very capable and
extremely reliable expert, to whose excellent technical work, often
performed in very strenuous circumstances, a warm tribute should be
paid."

The official report made by Dr. P. Z. King, Director General, dated
March 31, 1942, to which is attached as Appendix 1, the statement of
E. J. Bannon, R. N., as Appendix 2, the report of Dr. R. Pollitzer; as
Appendix 3, 4 and 5, the report of Dr. W. K. Chen, are set out below.
There is also included a statement of "Plague in Chekiang Province" and a
copy of the certificate signed by I. C. Fang, Acting Director, National
Health Administration Department, April 4, 1946, certifying that these
several reports and statements are true and correct copies of the offi-
cial reports and documents on file in the National Health Administration
of the Republic of China.

-4-

"JAPANESE ATTEMPT AT BACTERIAL WARFARE IN CHINA

"Up to the present time the practicability of bacterial warfare
is little known to the public, because applicable experimental
results, if available, are usually kept as a military secret. In
the past, the artificial dissemination of diseased germs had been
done for military purposes. The pollution of drinking water supplies
by the introduction of diseased animals or other infected materials
into the wells had been practised by retreating armies with the
intention of causing epidemics of gastro-intestinal infections among
the opposing troops in pursuit. Fortunately, such water-born
infections can be controlled with relative ease by boiling of all
drinking water and disinfection by chemical means. Whether or not
other infectious diseases could be intentionally spread by artificial means with deadly results in a wide area had not been demon-
strated prior to the outbreak of the present Sino-Japanese War.
However, in the last two years sufficient circumstantial evidence
has been gathered to show that the Japanese have tried to use our
people as guinea pigs for experimentation on the practicability of
bacterial warfare. They have tried to produce epidemics of plague
in the Free China by scattering plague-infested materials with aeroplanes. The facts thus far collected are as follows:

"1. On October 29, 1940 bubonic plague for the first time
occurred in Ningpo of Chekiang Province. The epidemic lasted a
period of thirty-four days and claimed a total of ninty-nine victims.
It was reported that on Oct. 27, 1940 Japanese planes raided Ningpo
and scattered a considerable quantity of wheat grains over the port
city. Although it was a curious fact to find "grains from heaven,"
yet no one at the time seemed to appreciate the enemy's intention
and no thorough examination of the grains was made. All the plague
victims were local residents. The diagnosis of plague was definitely
confirmed by laboratory test. There was no excessive mortality among
rats noticed before the epidemic outbreak; and despite of careful
investigation no exogenous sources of infection could be discovered.

"2. On Oct. 4, 1940 a Japanese plane visited Chü-hsien of
Chekiang. After circling over the city for a short while, it scattered rice and wheat grains mixed with fleas over the western section
of the city. There were eye-witnesses, among whom was a man named
Han, who collected some grains and dead fleas from the street outside of his own house and sent them to the local Air-raid Precau-
tionary Corps for transmission to the Provincial Hygienic Laboratory
for examination. The laboratory examination result was that "there
were no pathogenic organisms found by bacteriological culture methods."
However, on Nov. 12, thirty-eight days after the Japanese plane's
visit, bubonic plague appeared in the same area where the grains and
fleas were found in abundance. The epidemic in Chü-hsien lasted.
twenty-four days resulting in twenty-one deaths. As far as available
records show, plague never occurred in Chü-hsien before. After careful investigation of the situation it was believed that the strange
visit of the enemy plane was the cause of the epidemic and the trans-
mitting agent was the rat fleas, presumably infected with the plague and
definitely dropped by the enemy plane. As plague is primarily a
disease of the rodents, the grains were probably used to attract the
rats and expose them to the infected fleas mixed therein. It was
regrettable that the fleas collected were not properly examined.

Owing to deficient laboratory facilities, an animal inoculation test was not performed; otherwise it could have been possible to show whether or not the fleas were plague-infected, and a positive result would have been an irrefutable evidence against Japan.

"3. On Nov. 28, 1940 when the plague epidemic in Ningpo and Chü-hsien, was still in progress, three Japanese planes came to Kinghwa, an important commercial center situated between Ningpo and Chü-hsien, and there they dropped a large quantity of small granules, about the size of shrimp-eggs. These strange objects were collected and examined in a local hospital. The granules were more or less round, about 1 mm. in diameter, of whitish-yellow tinge, somewhat translucent with a certain amount of glistening reflection from the surface. When brought into contact with a drop of water on a glass-slide, the granule began to swell to about twice its original size. In a small amount of water in a test-tube, with some agitation, it would break up into whitish flakes and later form a milky suspension. Microscopic examination of these granules revealed the presence of numerous gram-negative bacilli, with distinct bipolar staining in some of them and an abundance of involution forms, thus possessing the morphological characteristics of P. Pestis, the causative organism of plague. When cultured in agar medium these gram-negative bacilli showed no growth; and because of inadequacy of laboratory facilities animal inoculation test could not be performed. Upon the receipt of such startling report from Kinghwa, the National Health Administration despatched Dr. W. W. Yung, Director of the Department of Epidemic Prevention, Dr. H. M. Jettmar, epidemiologist, formerly of the League of Nations' Epidemic Commission, and other technical experts to investigate the situation. When arriving in Kinghwa early in January, 1941, they examined twenty-six of these granules and confirmed the previous observations, but inoculation test performed on guinea-pigs by Dr. Jettmar gave negative results. It is difficult to say whether or not the lapse of time and the method of preservation of the granules had something to do with the negative results from the animal inoculation test, which is a crucial test for P. pestis. At all events no plague o ccurred in Kinghwa and it indicated that this particular Japanese experiment on bacterial warfare ended in failure.

"4. On Nov. 4, 1941, at about 5 A.M. a lone enemy plane appeared over Changteh of Hunan Province, flying very low, the morning being rather misty. Instead of bombs, wheat and rice grains, pieces of paper, cotton wadding and some unidentified particles were dropped. There were many eye-witnesses, including Mrs. E. J. Bannon, R. N., Superintendent of the local Presbyterian Hospital and other foreign r esidents in Changteh. After the "all clear" signal had been sounded at 5 P.M., some of these strange gifts from the enemy were collected and sent by the police to the local Presbyterian Hospital for examination, which revealed the presence of micro-organisms reported to resemble P. Pestis. On Nov. 11, seven days later, the first clinical case of plague came to notice, then followed by five more cases within the same month, two cases in December, and the last case to date on January 13, 1942. The diagnosis of bubonic plague was definitely confirmed in one of the six cases in November by bacteriological culture method and animal inoculation test. According to the investigation of Dr. W. K. Chen, bacteriologist who had had special training in plague work in India and Dr. R. Pollitzer, epidemiologist o f the National Health Administration and formerly of the League of

-6-

Nations' Epidemic Commission, the Changteh plague epidemic was caused by enemy action because of the following strong circumstantial evidences:

"(a) That Changteh has never been, as far as is known, afflicted by plague. During previous pandemics and sever epidemics elsewhere in China, this part of Hunan, nay this part of Central China in general, has never been known to come under the scourge of the disease.

"(b) That the present outbreak may have been due to direct continuous spread from neighboring plague-infested districts is also untenable on epidemiological grounds. Epidemiologically, plague spreads along transport routes for grain on which the rats feed. The nearest epidemic center to Changteh is Chihsien in Chekiang, about 2,000 kilometers away by land or river communication. Furthermore, Changteh, being a rice producing district, supplies rice to other districts and does not receive rice from other cities. Besides, all the cases occuring in Changteh were native inhabitants who had not been away from the city or its immediate environs at all.

"(c) That all the cases came from the areas within the city where the strange objects dropped by enemy plane were found, and that among the wheat and rice grains and cotton rags there were most probably included infective vectors, probably fleas. The fleas were not noticed on the spot because they were not looked for and because the air-raid alarm lasted some twelve hours with the result that the fleas must have in the meantime escaped to other hiding places.

"(d) That there was no apparent evidence of any excessive rat mortality before and for sometime after the "aerial incident." About two hundred rats were caught and examined during the months of November, and December, but no evidence of plague was found. However, toward the end of January and the first part of February this year, among seventy-eight rats examined there were eighteen with definite plague infection. As plague is primarily a disease of the rodents, the usual sequence of events is that an epizootic preeds an epidemic; but that did not take place in the present case. The infected fleas from the enemy plane must have first attacked men and a little later the rats.

"(e) That all the first six human cases were infected within fifteen days after the "aerial incident" and the infected fleas are known to be able to survive under suitable conditions for weeks without feeding. The normal incubation period of bubonic plague is 3 to 7 days and may occasionally be prolonged to 8 or even 14 days. The timefactor is certainly also a strong circumstantial evidence.

"(5) A serious epidemic of plague occurring in Suiyuan, Ningsha and Shensi Provinces has been recently reported. From the last week of January this year to date there have been some six hundred cases. According to a recent communique from the local military in the northwestern frontier, 'a large number of sick rodents had been set free by the enemy in the epidemic area.' However, considering the fact that plague is known to be enzootic among the native rodents in the

-7-

Ordos region in Suiyuan, one must wait for confirmation of this report. Technical experts, including Dr. Y. N. Yang, Director of t he Weishengshu Northwest Epidemic Prevention Bureau, have been sent there to investigate and help to control the epidemic.

"The enumeration of facts thus far collected leads to the conclusion that the Japanese Army has attempted at bacterial warfare in China. In Chekiang and Hunan they had scattered from the air infective materials and succeeded in causing epidemic outbreaks of plague. Aside from temporary terrorization of the general population in the afflicted areas, this inhuman act of our enemy is most condemnable when one realizes that once the disease has taken root in the local rat population it will continue to infect men for many years to come. Fortunately, the mode of infection and the method of control of plague are known and it is possible to keep the disease in check by vigorous control measures. Our difficulty at present is the shortage of the anti-epidemic supplies required. The recent advance in chemotherapy has given us new drugs that are more or less effective for the treatment of plague cases, and they are sulfathiazole and allied sulphonamide compounds which China cannot as yet produce herself. For prevention, plague vaccine can be produced in considerable quantities by the Central Epidemic Prevention Bureau in Kunming and the Northwest Epidemic Prevention Bureau in L Lanchow, provided the raw materials required for vaccine production such as peptone and agar-agar are available. Rat-proofing of all buildings and eradication of rats are fundamental control measures, but under war conditions they cannot be satisfactorily carried out. If rat poisons such as cyanogas and barium carbonate can be obtained from abroad in large quantities, deratilization campaigns may be launched in cities where rats are a menace.

/s/ P.Z. King

P.Z. King, Director-General,

"March 31, 1942   NATIONAL HEALTH ADMINISTRATION"

"Appendix 1

"Presbyterian Hospital
"Changteh, Hunan, Dec. 18, 1941

"Dr. P. Z. King, Director-General
"National Health Administration
Chungking

"Dear Dr. King:

"Following the initial outbreak of plague there appears to have been a lull in the situation, at least I have only heard of one case being reported within the past few days. Dr. Chang Wei of the Provincial Health Bureau who himself examined this case assures me that the patient who died within a period of two days was a plague victim.

"The facts in connection with this outbreak appear to prove:

-8-

"1) That unhulled grain and wheat found on the streets and roofs
of houses in the city of Changteh following the visit of an
enemy plane on the morning of November 4th was dropped from
that plane. I might say in this connection that I watched
the flight of the plane closely that morning. In appearance
it was somewhat like an hydroplane and flew low over the city
--lower than any plane has yet flown in the more than 20 bomb-
ings I have witnessed here.

"2) That some of this grain was collected and brought to the hospital for examination.

"3) That the laboratory report showed bacillus closely resembling
that of plague.

"4) That some ten days after the grain was dropped a young girl
was brought to the hospital seriously ill, and that the symptoms indicated plague.

"5) Smears taken from the bubos, and from spleen and liver after
death, confirmed the diagnosis.

"6) That on succeeding days other patients were examined and treated
and that bacteriological examination showed plague bacilli present in each case.

"7) Dr. W. K. Chen's report of his investigations and experiments
appear to place the findings of plague bacilli beyond doubt.

"8) Finally I might add that this is the first occasion during my
long residence here (almost 30 years) that there has been an
outbreak of plague in this area, or if it has occurred it has
not been recognized as such.

"9) If the facts be true, as I believe they are, there can be only
one conclusion drawn and that is--that the enemy is now carrying on a ruthless and inhuman warfare against combatants and
non-combatants alike. Truly a new way of spreading Japanese
'culture.'

"Very sincerely yours,

"(Signed) E. J. BANNAN, R.N.

"Superintendent, Presbyterian Hospital, Changteh"

"Appendix 2

"Weishengshu Anti-Epidemic Unit No. 14
Changteh, Hunan, December 30, 1941

"Dr. P. Z. King, Director-General
National Health Administration
Chungking

"Dear Sir:

"I have the honour to report on the plague situation in
Changteh as follows:

"1) As unanimously stated by the inhabitants of Changteh, an enemy airplane, appearing in the morning of November 4th, 1941 and flying unusually low, scattered over certain parts of the city fairly large amounts of grain admixed to which were other materials as discussed below.

"2) On November 12th a girl, 12 years of age, was admitted to the local Missionary Hospital in a most serious condition with high fever and delirium. She died the next day. Post mortem examination revealed the presence of swollen lymphatic glands on the left side of the neck but since exceza was present in this region, a local infection of the skin might have been the cause of the gland swelling. Be this as it may, it is certain that numerous gram-negative bacilli, showing the microscopic appearance of plague bacilli, were found in her blood during life and in smears made after death from the spleen.

"3) This initial case was followed by six further plague cases confirmed by microscopical examination and in one instance also by culture and animal experiment, the last case being recorded on December 20th. Of these six patients five had inguinal buboes whilst the sixth presumably had septicaemic plague. All the above mentioned seven patients succumbed to the infection. They were all residents of Changteh.

"4) In addition a number of suspicious cases was recorded by subsequent investigations make it probable that only one of these patients, dying on November 19th, might have actually suffered from (?) septicaemic plague.

"5) Examination of small quantities of the grain dropped from the plane (the bulk of the grain had been collected and burnt as soon as possible) did not lead to definite results. I personally was shown on December 23rd two bouillon cultures made with this material. In smears from these cultures as well as from the subcultures made under my supervision, gram-positive bacilli and cocci preponderated whilst the minority of gram-negative bacilli present did not show appearances characteristic for P. pestis. A guinea-pig infected on December 23rd with the combined material from these cultures and subcultures, remained well to date.

"6) It might be emphasized, however, that these negative findings do by no means exclude a causal connection between the aerial attack on November 4th and the subsequent plague outbreak in Changteh. It should be noted in this connection that:

"(a) Plague bacilli are not fit to subsist for appreciable length of time on inanimate objects or to grow and survive when cultivated together with such microorganisms as found in the present instance. The fact that we failed to find plague bacilli in the cultures in question does therefore not exclude that they were originally present on the grain.

"(b) It must be moreover be kept in mind that the question whether or not the grain dropped from the plane was originally contaminated with plague bacilli, is not of such

-10-

paramount importance as it would seem at first glance.
the Indian Plague Commission and other investigators
after them had little or even no success when trying
to infect highly susceptible rodents including guinea-
pigs under optimal laboratory conditions through prolonged contact with plague-contaminated inanimate
objects or by feeding such animals with materials containing plentiful plague bacilli. That it would be
possible to obtain better results when trying to uti-
lise such methods in the case of human beings by throw-
in plague-contaminated materials from a plane, seems
not likely.

"On the other hand, it must be admitted that human
infections would be likely to occur if the material
dropped from the plane would serve as a vehicle for
plague-infected fleas. Hence there is no doubt that
the latter procedure would recommend itself to experts
who think it fit to participate in bacterial warfare
and I for one am led to assume that this method was used
in the present instance. Support for this assumption
is furnished by the statement made by several witnesses that the plane dropped besides grain also some
other material or materials variously described as
pieces of cotton or cloth, paper or pasteboard. Such
materials, especially the first two, would offer good
protection for fleas.

'7)   Further support for the assumption that the recent plague outbreak was due to enemy action is furnished by the following
considerations:

"(a)   Observations as to the time and place of the outbreak are well compatible with such assumption:

"We have seen that the first victim was admitted
to hospital on November 12th, i.e. 8 days after the
aerial attack--a period of reasonable length, especially
if infected fleas were involved which first had to seek
for individuals to feed upon. It is known on the other
hand that plague fleas may remain infective for weeks
or even months.

"The first six of the confirmed plague cases developed in persons living in two areas which had been
copiously sprinkled with the materials dropped from
the plane and only the seventh patient lived at some
distance from one of these areas.

"(b)   If we temporarily dismiss for the sake of argument the
assumption that the recent plague outbreak in Changteh
was due to enemy action, we would be rather at loss to
say how it could have originated. It must be noted in
this connection that

"(i)   No previous outbreak of plague in Hunan is on
record in modern times and the very intensive

-11-

anti-epidemic work done in this province since
the end of 1937 has shown no evidence whatso-
ever suggestive of plague.

"(ii) The nearest foci from which plague infection
could have been derived, are in Eastern Chekiang
and Southern Kiangsi. It takes at least about
10 days to reach Changteh from either of these
areas so that a person contracting plague infection in one of them and then starting on his
journey to Changteh would be likely to fall ill
before arrival. Such travellers have repeatedly
to change from one transport vehicle to another
and to stay overnight in the various stations
on route; they have to use their own bedding
during part of the journey at least. That they
would carry along infected fleas on their persons or in their effects is therefore unlikely.

"(iii) Changteh is situated on a river system entirely
different from those in Chekiang or Southern
Kiangsi so that direct traffic by boat which
might lead to the transport of infected rats
and/or fleas, is out of question.

"(iv) The Changteh region produces rice and cotton
so that it would be absurd to assume that such
commodities, infested with plague rats and/or
fleas would have been imported from elsewhere.

"(c) As recently confirmed by our observations in Chekiang
and Kiangsi, bubonic plague outbreaks in China are in
most, if not in all, instances ushered in by a very
considerable mortality of the local rats. No such
rat falls have been observed in Changteh and we have
not been able thus far to get any definite evidence
that the local rats have become infected.

"8) All the observations and considerations recorded above leave
little if any room for doubt that the recent plague outbreak
in Changteh was in causal connection with the aerial attack
of November 4th.

"9) It is reassuring that no further human case was reported during
the last ten days but this does not exclude the possibility
that further cases might occur.

"10) It is impossible to decide at present whether or not the rats
have become involved in the outbreak. As mentioned, so far
no definite evidence of rat plague was found and it appears
that the "Indian" rat fleas (X. cheopis) are infrequent at
the present junction and (b) Owing to untoward conditions
(inclement weather and constant air alarms) we have been able
so far to examine only limited numbers of rats. Prolonged
observation will be necessary to decide this most important
point.

-12-

"Respectfully submitted by
/s/ DR Pollitzer
(Signed) DR. R. POLLITZER

Epidemiologist,
NATIONAL HEALTH ADMINISTRATION"

"Appendix 2

"Clinical and Autopsy Notes of the Proven Case of
Bubonic Plague in Changteh

"Name of Patient: Hung Tsao-sheng
Date of Autopsy: November 25, 1941
Place: Isolation Hospital, Changteh
Operator: Dr. W. K. Chen
First Assistant: Dr. Y. K. Hsueh
2nd Assistant: Dr. B. Liu
Recorder: Dr. C. C. Lee

"Clinical History of the Patient:

"The patient, a male of 26, lived in a small lane in front of the Kwan Miao Temple, and used to work in a village outside Changteh. He returned to the city on November 19th, 1941, on account of the death of his mother six or seven days before. The cause of her death was not definitely known (? tuberculosis - long standing illness with severe emaciation). He felt unwell in the evening of November 23rd, and experienced feverishness and headache with malaise at about 11 p.m. The next morning he complained of pain and tenderness in the right groin for which a Chinese Plaster was applied. He vomitted once during the afternoon, and from then on his condition grew rapidly worse. Dr. C. C. Lee of the 4th Emergency Medical Service Training School & the 4th Sanitary Corps, was called in at 7 p.m. to see the patient, and found him to be dying. Important findings on examination were high fever, and enlarged and tender glands in the right inguinal region. Plague was strongly suspected. The patient was to have been sent to the Isolation Hospital, but he died at 8 P.M. before he could be removed. With the aid of the police, the body was brought to the Wei Sheng Yuan by 10 p.m. where disinfection of clothing and bedding was carried out in order to kill fleas. The plaster covering the groin was removed; cardiac puncture and aspiration of the right inguinal gland were performed for culture under sterile technique, and, since the light was inadequate, autopsy was postponed until the next morning. The body was laid in a coffin with the lid nailed down.

"Autopsy Findings:

"1. General Appearance: The cadaver was medium-sized and appeared very thin.

"2. Skin: Face was slightly blue, and lips cyanotic. No petechial spots or flea-bite wounds were seen. Lesions resembling scabies in the right popliteal region.

-13-

845

"3. Lymph Glands: The right inguinal glands were enlarged. Mesenteric lymph nodes also slightly enlarged.

"4. Chest Findings: Lungs normal in gross appearance. There was fluid estimated at 20 c. approximately in each pleural cavity. Pericardial effusion of about 20 cc. also present. Heart very flabby but not enlarged. Cardiac puncture through the right auricle performed under sterile technique and a few cc. of blood were obtained and inoculated on blood agar slant.

"5. Abdominal Findings: Liver firm. Spleen enlarged to twice its normal size. Kidneys normal. Haemorrhagic spots seen on the surface of liver, spleen and intestine. No free fluid in the adbomen.

"Bacteriological Findings:

"Specimen of right inguinal glands, liver, spleen and blood were taken for direct smears, culture and animal tests.

"1. Direct Smears: Carbol-thionin blue and Gram's method of staining were employed for all the smears. 50% ether in absolute alcohol was used for fixation. Under the microscope many oval-shaped Gram negative bacilli with their bipolar regions deeply stained were found.

"2. Cultivation: Under sterile technique, specimens of cardiac blood, inguinal glands, liver and spleen of the patient were inoculated on blood agar slant of pH 7.6 and incubated in a wide-mouth thermos bottle. Temperature was regulated at 37° centigrade. Twenty-four hours later, many minute greyish-white opaque colonies were found on the surface of the media. All were pure cultures. Smear examination showed Gram negative bipolar staining organisms.

"3. Animal Inoculation Test:

"A. Guinea-pig No. 1. The animal was artifically infected by smearing splenic substance of the cadaver on its right flank which was newly shaven at 3 p.m. on November 25, 1941. (The splenic substance was found to have contained many gram negative bipolar staining bacilli). The animal began to develop symptoms at 8 p.m. on November 26th, and was found dead in the early morning of November 28th. Thus the incubation period was not more than 29 hours, and the whole course of the disease ran at most 32 hours.

"Autopsy Findings:

"1. Skin: Swelling and redness at the
"2. Gland: site of inoculation. Bilateral enlargement of inguinal glands, more marked on the right side with congestion.

"3. Subcutaneous
Tissues: Edematous and congested. Haemorrhage at the site of inoculation.

-14-

"4. Chest Findings:　Not remarkable.

"5. Abdominal Findings: Spleen enlarged and congested.
Liver, kidneys and G. I. Tract
also congested.

"Specimens of heart blood, liver, spleen and inguinal
lymph glands were taken for smears and culture.

"Microscopic examination of the stained smears (Carbol-
thionin blue and Gram's stains) revealed Gram negative
bipolar staining bacilli similar to those seen in the
direct smears made of autopsy material from the patient.

"Culture of these specimens on blood agar slants at pH
7.6 was made. Twenty-four hours later, pure cultures
of similar organisms were found.

"B. Guinea-pig No. 2. This animal was similarly treated as
guinea-pig No. 1 at 9 a.m. on November 26th, but the
inguinal gland of the cadaver was used instead. Symptoms were first noticed at 8 a.m. on November 28th, an
incubation period of 47 hours. Death of the animal
occurred 44 hours later (in the morning of November 30th).

"Autopsy of th animal showed essentially the same gross
pathological changes as those of guinea-pig No. 1.
Direct smears of lymph glands, liver and spleen showed
similar findings.

"C. Guinea-pig No. 3. This time a pure culture of the organisms was used to smear on the newly shaven left flank of
the guinea pig. (The culture was obtained by growing the
cadaver's heart blood on blood agar slant at pH 7.6 for
24 hours.) The animal appeared to have become ill 45
hours later and was found dead in the early morning of
November 30th. The course of the disease of the animal
was, therefore, not more than 40 hours.

"On autopsy, gross pathological changes were found to
be similar to those of guinea-pigs Nos. 1 and 2 except
that changes of lymph-glands and spleen were more pro-
nounced.

"Smear examination of heart blood, lymph-gland, liver
and spleen yielded similar results.

"Conclusion:

"Clinical history, autopsy findings and bacteriological findings
prove the patient to be a case of bubonic plague, dying from septicaemic infection from Pasteurella Pestis.

"(Signed) W. K. CHEN, M.D.

Head, Department of Laboratory Medicine,
Emergency Medical Service Training School,
Ministry of War;
Consultant, Chinese Red Cross Medical Relief Corps

"Kweiyang.
December 12, 1941"

-15-

"Appendix A

"Clinical Notes of Cases in Changteh Suspected to be Plague

"Case No. 1 (Tsai Tao-erh)

"This patient, a girl of eleven living in Tsai Hung Sheng Char-
coal Dealer Shop (關廟街,蔡鴻勝炭鐔   ), Kwan Miao Street, was
said to have fallen ill on November 11, 1941 and was sent by the
police to the Kwangteh Hospital at 7 A.M. the next day for treatment. On admission she was seen by Dr. H. H. Tan and was found
delirious. Temperature 105.7° F. Eczema of the right ear. No
glandular enlargement or tenderness. Few rales were heard in the
chest. Abdominal findings were said to be normal. Blood smears
(Wright and Gram's stains) showed organisms resembling P. pestis
morphologically. Patient was then isolated and sulfanilamide treatment given. Her general condition turned from bad to worse in the
m orning of November 13th, when petechial spots of skin were noted.
Blood smear examination was repeated and revealed the same result
as before. At about 8 a.m. she died.

"Essential features of autopsy were enlarged left infra-auricular lymph nodes. No sign of pneumonia; liver and spleen enlarged
w ith hemorrhagic spots on their surfaces. Kidneys were also hemorr-
h agic. Splenic smear showed similar findings as the blood smear.
Culture of the splenic substances was done in the Kwangteh Hospital
but no definite report was obtained.

" Case No. 2 (Tsai Yü-chen)

"This was a woman of 27, living in Chang Ching Street (東門,長清
街   ), East Gate district; she was said to have had an abrupt
onset of fever on November 11th and died on the 13th. While her
cortage was passage Tehshan, Dr. Kent of Red Cross Medical Relief
Corps met it and made enquiry of the cause of her death. The above
information let him to suspect plague. Post mortem liver puncture
was done and smear examination showed organisms resembling P. pestis
morphologically.

"Case No. 3 (Nieh Shu-sheng)

"This was a man of 58 living in No. 1, 3rd Chia, 4thPao, Chi
Ming Cheng (東門,昭明鎮 四保三甲一户)East Gate district. Developed high fever in the evening of November 12th, complained of pain
and tenderness in the groin on November 13th. Aspiration of the
enlarged groin gland was done by Dr. P. K. Chien of Red Cross Medical
Relief Corps and smear examination (Wright stain) showed P. pestis
like organisms. The patient died the same evening.

"Case No. 4 (hsu Lao-san)

"The patient was a man of 25, living in No. 5, 5th Chia, 5th
P ao, Yun An Hsiang, Yang Chia Hsiang, East Gate district (東門 揚家巷 永安鄉
五保五甲五鐔). Became ill with fever and headache since November
12th. Seen by Dr. H. H. Tan and Dr. T. C. Fang, and found to have
t ender and enlarged groin lymph glands the next day. Aspiration
o f the gland was done in the Kwangteh Hospital and smear examination
(Wright's stain) showed P. pestis like organisms.

"Case No. 5 (Hu Chung-fa)

"A man living in Chung Fa Hospital, Kwan Miao Street (关庙街 鐘庵醫院). In the morning of November 19th, he went to the Wei Sheng Yuan complaing of being infected with plague and demanding treatment. He appeared, at that time, quite irritable and spoke somewhat incoherently. His pulse rate was rapid, but fever was not high. Groin glands were enlarged. Other findings were not recorded. He was immediately admitted to the Isolation Hospital. In the evening his temperature went up and he died.

"Autopsy by Drs. H. H. Tang and M. N. Shih showed bluish discoloration of the skin, more marked over the chest and abdomen. No enlargement of the lymph glands were noticed. Spleen was found to be slightly enlarged and other abdominal findings were not remarkable. Smear and culture of splenic material showed only Gram positive cocci and bacilli. It should be noted that Dr. Tan was working with inadequate culture media.

"(Signed) W. K. CHEN, M. D.

Head, Department of Laboratory Medicine
Emergency Medical Service Training School,
Ministry of War;
Consultant, Chinese Red Cross Medical Relief Corps

"Kweiyang
December 12, 1941"

"Appendix 5

"Notes on Examination of Grain Dropped by Enemy Plane

"Examination of a sample of grain dropped by the enemy plane over Changteh city on November 4, 5 a.m. 1941 and collected from the ground next morning and examined after an interval of fully 34 days.

"Gross Examination: The sample consists of barly, rice and unidentified plant seeds.

"Culture Examination: The sample was put into a sterile mortar and ground with 5 c.c. sterile saline. This mixture was cultivated on blood agar slants and copper sulphate agar slants (all pH 7.6). After incubation at 37° C. for 24-48 hours, only contaminating organisms of staphylocci, B. coli and unidentified Grampositive bacilli with central spores were found; no P. Pestis like organisms were found.

"Animal Inoculation: Two c.c. of the above mixture were injected subcutaneously into a guina-pig on Dec. 8th, 1941 at 9 a.m. The testing animal died in the evening of Dec. 11th after showing no sign of illness.

"Autopsy Findings: On the morning of Dec. 12th, autopsy of the dead animal was performed. Local inflamation, general congestion of subcutaneous tissue, inguinal lymph glands not enlarged, liver and spleen norman and not enlarged. Heart and lungs normal. Smears made from lymph gland, spleen and liver showed no P. pestis like organisms. Only Gram positive bacilli and some Gram negative bacilli were present.

"Culture of heart blood of the dead animal showed unidentified Gram postive bacilli with central spores. P. pestis not found. Culture from the lymph nodes, spleen and liver showed pure culture of B. coli only. P. pestis also not found.

"Conclusions: By culture and animal inoculation tests, P. pestis is not present in the sample.

"(Signed) W. K. CHEN, M.D.

Head, Department of Laboratory Medicine,
Emergency Medical Service Training School,
Ministry of War;
Consultant, Chinese Red Cross Medical Relief Corps

"Kweiyang,
December 12, 1941"

• • •

"Plague in Chekiang Province

"The official records of the Provincial Health Administration show the following plague incidence in (i) Ningpo; (ii) Chühsien; (iii) I-wu; (iv) Tungyany. It should be noted that the two last mentioned places derived infection from Chühsien.

"Year	Locality	Date of outbreak	No. cases	No. deaths
1940	Ningpo	Nov.-Dec.	99	97
	Chühsien	- " -	21	21
1941	Chühsien	March-July	195	184
	I-wu	Oct. - Dec.	153	118
	Tungyang	Nov. - Dec.	40	40
1942	Tungyany	May - ?	54	52
	I-wu	March - ?	135	126
1943	"	"	"	"
1944	I-wu	Feb.-March	20	13
Total 4 localities		1940-1944	717	651

-18-

"Recapitulation:

"Locality:	1940		1941		1942		1943		1944		Total	
	C.	D.	C.	D.	C.	D.	C.	D.	C.	D.	C.	D.
Ningpo	99	97	.								99	97
Chühsien	21	21	195	184	.		.				216	205
I-wu		.	153	118	195	126	.		20	13	308	257
Tungyang		.	40	40	54	52	.		.		94	92
Totals	120	118	388	342	189	178	.		20	13	717	651

"Plague infected rats in Chühsien, Chekiang, 1941.

"Month	Total No. of rats examined	Plague positive		Plague suspected	
		No.	%	No.	%
April	648	16	2.5	-	-
May	381	19	5.0	-	-
June	98	24	24.5	-	-
July	157	20	14.6	13	9.5
August	187	16	8.5	12	6.4
September	369	21	5.7	30	8.1
October	331	17	5.1	15	4.5
November	249	16	6.4	36	14.4
December	168	4	2.4	2	1.2

- - -

"WEI SHENG SHU
(NATIONAL HEALTH ADMINISTRATION)
THE REPUBLIC OF CHINA

" TELEGRAPHIC ADDRESS   Nanking
WEISHENGSHU OR "5898"

"The foregoing copies of Statement of Dr. P. Z. King dated March 31, 1942 with Appendices 1, 2, 3, 4 and 5 attached and statement of "Plague in Chekiang Province" are true and correct copies of the official reports and documents on file in the National Health Administration of the Republic of China.

"Witness my signature and seal this 4th day of April 1946

/s/ I. C. Fang

Acting Director, National Health Administration"

There was also secured from Dr. R. Pollitzer a statement dated April 3, 1946, on the total incidents of plague in Changteh and adjacent provinces from 1941 to 1943, a copy of which is as follows:

-19-

**"STATEMENT ON THE TOTAL INCIDENCE OF PLAGUE IN
CHANGTEH & ADJACENT PLACES (1941-1943)**

"1) As will be gathered from the documents dealing with the initial phase of the plague outbreak at Changteh, human plague was first diagnosed in one patient on Nov. 12th, 1941, who succumbed to the infection on the next day.

"Seven more instances of human plague were observed in Changteh during the rest of november and in December, all the patients succumbing to the infection.

"2) For various untoward reasons it was possible to examine only 35 rats and mice during the period Dec. 24th - Jan. 3, 1942, and no examinations could be carried out from the last mentioned date until January 30th. All the above mentioned 35 animals proved to be free from plague.

"Among 24 rats received on January 30th and 31st for examination from the central part of the city (i.e. one of the two areas over which the suspicious materials had been dispersed by the enemy plane on Nov. 4th, 1941), five were found to be plague-infected.

"Plague continued not only among the rodents in the central part of the city but on February 20th one rat obtained from the east end of the city (i.e. a place fairly near to the second area sprinkled by the enemy plane) was also found heavily infected.

"Further rat examinations showed not only continuing epizootics in the two above mentioned areas but it could be seen now rodent infection gradually spread to the other districts of the city. The total number of rodents examined in Changteh during 1942 was 5,520 amongst which 641, i.e. 11.61 per cent, were found plague-infected.

"Only 22 plague-infected animals were detected amongst the 368 rodents examined from January 1st to April 15th, 1943, the last plague rats being met with during the second half of February, 1943.

"3) Human plague reappeared in Changteh on March 25th, 1942 from which date until early July 30 victims to the infection were recorded. Actually, however, their number amounted presumably to at least 40 because of various untoward reasons not all patients could be found.

"4) Pneumonic plague infection was carried by a merchant who had visited Changteh, to his home in the Moolin Sub-District of Taoyuan County. Altogether 16 people succumbed to pneumonic plague in this locality during the period May 4th-30th, 1942.

"5) Bubonic plague infection was carried from Changteh to Shihkungchow and Chengtehchow, two villages to the north, leading first to infection of the local rats and then to human outbreaks. The total number of victims claimed in these villages in October and November, 1942, was 39. Only two of these patients could be saved.

"April 3rd, 1946

Submitted by,
/s/ DR Pollitzer"

A copy of "Report on Plague in Changteh, Hunan (Dec. 12th, 1941)" made by Dr. W. K. Chen together with a copy of the letter of transmittal from him to Dr. R. K. S. Lim, dated December 12, 1941, and a certificate of Dr. T. S. Sze, Head, Department of Preventive Medicine, Center Emergency Medical Service Training School, and of Dr. F. C. Lin, Senior Instructor, Department of Laboratory Medicine, Center Emergency Medical Service Training School, confirming and indorsing the conclusions arrived at by Dr. W. K. Chen in his report and a certificate secured by Dr. W. K. Chen, dated March 29, 1946, certifying to the conclusions of these reports is submitted herewith. (There is a sketch with the original report of t he city showing the area where the infected materials were found in greatest abundance and where the proven and suspicious cases appeared.)

"REPORT ON PLAGUE IN CHANGTEH, HUNAN

(Dec. 12th, 1941.)

Contents

"1. Preamble - Circumstances Leading to the Suspicion of Plague

"11. Report of Suspected Proven Cases of Bubonic Plague

"111. Information Gathered from Investigation and Enquiry

"1v. Appendices"

(Map)

"1. PREAMBLE - CIRCUMSTANCES LEADING TO THE SUSPICION OF PLAGUE:

"On November 4th, 1941, at about 5 a.m. a single enemy plane appeared over Changteh, flying very low, the morning being rather misty. Instead of bombs, wheat and rice grains, pieces of paper, cotton wadding and some unidentified particles were dropped. These materials fell chiefly in the Chi-ya-hsiang (鷄鴨巷) and Kwan-miao Street (関廟街) (Area "A" in map) and around the East Gate district (Area "B" in map) of the city. After the all clear signal (5 p.m.)., specimens of rice grains were collected and sent by the police to the Kwangteh Hospital (廣徳醫院) for examination, which revealed the presence of micro-organisms reported to resemble B. Pestis. (This was, however, shown to be erroneous by Dr. Chen Wen-Kwei later). Although the finding was by no means conclusive, suspicion that the enemy had scattered plague-infective material was in the mind of the medical workers who saw the incident on the spot.

-21-

"11. REPORT OF SUSPECTED AND PROVEN CASES OF BUBONIC PLAGUE:

"Nothing happened until November 11th, seven days after the 'aerial incident' when the first suspicious case of plague came to notice. This was a girl of eleven years old, living in Kwan-miao Street (Area "A" in map), complaining of high fever (105.7° F.) since November 11th. She was admitted to the Kwangteh Hospital. No other positive clinical finding war recorded but direct blood smear examination was said to have revealed the presence of P. pestis like organisms. She died on the 13th of November and post-mortem examination showed highly suspicious evidences of plague, smears from internal organs exhibiting similar organisms to those found in the blood (Case No. 1 Table).

"On November 13th another case was found dead. On enquiry the patient had high fever on November 11th and died on November 13th. Liver puncture was performed. Direct smear examination showed the presence of micro-organisms resembling plague Bacilli. This patient was living on Chang-Ching Street (长清衔) in the East Gate District (Area "B" in map) (Case No. 2, Table).

"Two more cases came to notice, both with high fever and enlargement of glands in the groin ('buboes') beginning on November 12th. Smear examination of gland puncture fluid showed the presence of plague-like micro-organisms in both cases. One died on the 13th and the other on the 14th. Both lived in the East Gate district. (Area "B" in map) (Case Nos. 3 and 4, Table).

"The fifth case, admitted to the Isolation Hospital on November 19th, had fallen ill with fever and delirium (and buboes) on November 18th. He died on the day of admission. Autopsy revealed apparently negative findings. (Case No. 5, Table).

"The Sixth case, a man of 28, living in Kwan-Miao Street (Area "A" in map) came down with fever, malaise and buboes on November 23rd, and died the next day. This case was proved by Dr. Chen Wen-Kwei, Head of the Dept. of Laboratory Medicine, Central Training School, who had just arrived from Kweiyang with an investigation unit, to be genuine bubonic plague by post-mortem findings, confirmed by culture and animal tests. (Case No. 6, Table and Appendix).

"All these cases were natives of Hunan and had liven in Changteh or in its immediate environs for years.

"Since then to date no fresh cases of plague have come to notice.

"CONCLUSION:
"The last case seen was proved to be bubonic plague. The clinical history and smears from five other cases leave little doubt that they were also cases of plague.

"111. INFORMATION GATHERED FROM INVESTIGATION AND ENQUIRY:

"a. General Information:

"Changteh is a city situated on the western shore of the Tung Ting Lake, directly on te northern bank of the Yuan River. Formerly, highway connections were available between this city and Hupeh Province in the north, Changsha in the east and Taoyuan and other cities in southwest Hunan. At present all the highway communications have been cut and the nearest highway is at Chengchieyi (60 Km.) to the southwest by river. River trafic to Chihchiang via the Yuan River is still open. At present, therefore, communication with Changteh is only possible by boat or by footpaths.

"Changteh has hot summers and cold winters which begin early in November. At the time of enquiry, atmospheric temperature ranged between 4 - 50 F.

"Changteh was an important business center in Northern Hunan but since the war its prosperity has been much reduced due to frequent enemy air-raids and the cutting off of highway communications.

"b. Medical Institutions at Changteh:

"1. Kwan Teh Hospital - a missionary hospital of 100 beds.
"2. Hsien Health Centre (Wei-Sheng-Yuan) holds out-patient clinics.
"3. An Isolation Hospital - of 50 beds was established after the outbreak of plague.

"c. Medical Statistics:

"Changteh has now a population of about 50,000. No mortality statistics are available. It is known to be an endemic centre of cholera and cholera epidemics have arisen from year to year.

"There has been no noticeable increase in human deaths prior to the 'aerial incident.'

"Since the first suspicious death from plague, records were kept of deaths in the city by the Hsien Health Centre, information being obtained from the police and coffin dealers. From November 12th-24th, 17 deaths were reported in all, including those suspected of plague. No information was available about the causes of the other deaths.

"d. Environmental Sanitation:

"General Sanitation of the city is rather poor. Frequent Air-raids have destroyed many houses. Most new houses are built of wood and provide easy assess to rats.

"Area "A". - Kwan-miao Street and Chi-ya-hsiang region (see map).

"This district is almost in the heart of the city and habilitations are over crowded. Streets are narrow and dirty. Several of the houses in which plague deaths had occurred were visited and found to have dark and poorly ventilated rooms with no floors. Garbage accumulations were commonly seen in the corner of the rooms. Rat holes were found everywhere. Other houses did not differ in general appearance from those described.

"Area "B". - East Gate region (see map).
"Although less crowded, this district was even less impressive being the living quarters of the poorer class. Environmental sanitation did not differ materially from Area "A".

"On enquiry it was elicited that no conspicuous increase of dead rats was found either prior to or during the present outbreak. An Indian wonder rat-trap was set in one of the plague-death houses for three successive nights but no rats were caught. Some 200 rats were 'bought' from the people and dissected but none of them showed any evidence of plague infection. These rats could not be traced to their place of origin. Many tangle-foot flea traps were also set in the houses in which plague death had occurred, but failed to catch any flea.

"IV. DISCUSSION AND CONCLUSIONS:

"1. Was plague present in Changteh?

"a. That plague was present in Changteh was proved by the case of bubonic plague investigated by Dr. Chen Wen-Kwei who had special training in plague work in India. This case, a man of 28 years old, was seen sick with high fever and 'buboes' on November 24th and died the same evening. He came to stay in the 'infected' area on November 19th and fell sick on November 23rd. On post-mortem examination he was found to have died of bubonic plague. Direct smear, culture and guinea-pig inoculation tests of material taken from groin lymph-nodes, spleen, liver and heart's blood all confirmed the diagnosés. (For detail protocal see Appendix1).

"b. Taht an epidemic outbreak of plague has taken place between November 11th and 24th was also evident from the discovery of five suspicious cases referred to above. It may be argued that none of these cases were bacteriologically confirmed by animal inoculation tests, but the clinical history with high fever, enlarged lymph-nodes in the groin ('buboes') and smears from either lymph-glands, liver or spleen being positive for P. pestis morphologically and their rapidly fatal course (death within 24-48 hours of the onset of the disease), leaves little or no doubt about their being actual cases of plague.

Moreover, most of the cases occurred at about
the same time. Hence an epidemic outbreak of
bubonic plague did exist beginning from November 11th, seven days after the 'aerial incident.'

"All smears were re-examined by Dr. Chen Wan-
Kwei who confirmed the finding of plague-like
bacilli.

"2. How did the plague outbreak arise? Could any connection be established between the outbreak and the alleged
infective material scattered by the enemy plane on November 4th, 1941?

"Three possibilities may be enquired into, namely:

"(1) Did plague exist prior to the 'aerial incident?'

"(2) Did plague come to Changteh from contiguous
districts known to be plague stricken?

"(3) Was the plague due to the scattering of infective material from the enemy plane on Nov.
4th, 1941?

"(1) That the present outbreak of plague may be due
to a local disease having suddenly broken out
into epidemic proportions is out of the question because Changteh has never been, as far
as is known, afflicted by plague. During
previous pandemics and severe epidemics elsewhere in China, this part of Hunan, say this
part of Central China in general, has never
been known to come under the scourge of the
disease. Spontaneous plague is not known.

"(2) That the present outbreak may have been due
to direct contiguous spread from neighboring
districts known to be plague stricken is also
untenable on epidemiological grounds. Epidemiologically, plague spreads along transport
routes for grain on which the rats feed.
Ships form good carriers of rats because they
contain cargo and from good harbourages for
these animals. Hence the coastal towns in
Fukien and Kwangtung Provinces were usually
the first to become infected by plague from
other plague-stricken ports, the disease gradually spreading inland later. Epidemic
foci now exist in certain districts of Fukien
and Chekiang and a few cities of Kiangsi
bordering the former two provinces. The
nearest city to Changteh where plague is now
severely epidemic, is Chuhsien in Chekiang
about 2,000 km. away by land or river communication. Incidentally it may be noted that
the plague in Chuhsien is also attributed to
infective material dropped by enemy planes

-25-

857

in 1940. With the existing state of cummuni-
cation it is not possible for plague to
spread from Chuhsien to Changteh. Besides,
all the cases occurring in Changteh were
native inhabitants of that city and as far
as can be ascertained, were not known to
have been away from the city or its immediate environs at all. Changteh, being a rice
producing district, furthermore supplies
rice to other districts and does not receive
rice from other cities. It is clear, therefore, that the present outbreak of bubonic
plague in Changteh is native in origin.

"(3) That enemy scattered plague infective material from the plane on November 4th, 1941 at
5 a.m. and caused the epidemic outbreak of
plague beginning on November 11th, is probable for the following reasons:

"1. All the cases came from the areas where
the grain, etc. dropped by enemy plane
was found.

"2. Among the wheat and rice grains and rags
of cotton and paper scattered there were
most probably included infective vectors,
probably fleas. The latter was not
found by those who swept and burned the
material, because:-

"a. Lay people did not know the possibility of dangerous fleas being scattered down and therefore did not
look for them.

"b. Air-raid alarm on November 4th
lasted from 5 a.m. to 5 p.m. with
the result that the fleas must have
in the meantime escaped from the
rags and grains and hid themselves
in nearby houses of more equable
temperature and humidity long before
the grains and rags were swept and
burnt after the all-clear signal.

"(3) Plague might be caused by infective material
in one of three ways:

"a. Grains thrown down may be infected
with plague organisms which when
eaten by local rats cause infection
among them. Later, the infection
is transmitted from the diseased
rats to the rat-fleas and these in
turn infect men through their bites.

"This was unlikely or unsuccessful
for two reasons:

-26-

858

"i. Grains collected and submitted
to cultural and animal inoculation tests have to date been
found negative for plague organisms
(Appendix 111).

"ii. There was apparently no evidence of any excessive rat
mortality since the 'aerial
incident.'

"b. Infected fleas may have been thrown
down together with the grain and
rags. The grain attracted the local
rats which offer refuge to the
infective fleas and thereby become
infected and further infect rats and
men.

"Apparently this did not take place
since:-

"i. All the human cases of plague
were infected within 15 days
after the 'aerial incident.'
Normally human plague cases
begin to appear at least two
weeks after the rat epizootic
which also takes time (Say
two weeks) to develop.

"ii. There was no apparent rat epizootic preceeding or during
the human outbreak as already
referred to.

"If infected fleas were released
from the plane, what prevented them
from starting an epidemic among the
local rats. In order that a rat
epizootic may take place, it is
necessary that the flea population
or rat-flea (Xenopsylla cheopis)
index should be high. Although no
data is available concerning the
normal rat-flea index in Changteh,
it is probable in view of the cold
weather, that it was not high enough
to cause rapid spread of the disease
among the rats. It is not yet known
whether the rats of Changteh have
become infected with plague. Further
research is necessary and only time
can tell.

"c. Infected fleas thrown down with the
grain, etc., may have bitten human
individuals directly and caused the
outbreak of plague.

"The evidence of this mode of transmission seems complete.

"i.   The normal incubation period
      of bubonic plague, i.e. the
      interval between the bite of
      the infective flea and the onset
      of disease, is 3 - 7 days but
      may occasionally be prolonged
      to 8 or even 14 days. Most of
      the cases seen had an incubation
      period of 7 - 8 days, which
      would indicate that these indi-
      viduals were bitten by the
      infective fleas very soon after
      they were released, probably on
      November 4th or 5th. Thus, the
      first case had its onset on
      November 11th, seven days after
      the 'aerial incident.' Simi-
      larly with the second case.
      The third and fourth cases fell
      ill on the 12th, eight days
      after the 'aerial incident.'
      The fifth case, about which the
      diagnosis was more doubtful
      than any other fell sick on
      November 18th (?). The proven
      case had been working in a
      nearby village (陳家咀   )
      and came into the city to live
      in one of the infected areas
      on November 19th. On November
      23rd five days after entering
      the infected area, and 15 days
      after the 'aerial incident,' he
      fell ill. Assuming he was
      bitten on the 19th, the question
      arises as to whether the infec-
      tive fleas could have survived
      from November 4th to November
      19th. The answer is in the
      affirmative, for it is known
      that infected fleas can live
      under suitable conditions for
      weeks without feeding.

"ii. All the human cases were inha-
      bitants of the area where grain,
      etc., dropped by the enemy plane
      were found.

"From the evidences presented the
following conclusions may be drawn:

"1.   That plague was epidemic in
      Changteh from November 11th to
      24th, 1941.

-28-

"2.　That the cause of the epidemic was due to the scattering of plague infective material, probably infective fleas, by an enemy plane on November 4th, 1941."

(In the original of this document there appears at this point a chart which should be referred to.)

"APPENDIX 1

"Clinical and Autopsy Notes of the Proven Case of Bubonic Plague

　　　"Name of Patient:　Kung Tsao-sheng (　龔操勝　)
　　　Date of Autopsy:　November 25th, 1941.
　　　Place:　　　　　　Isolation Hospital, Changteh

　　　Operator:　　　　Dr. W. K. Chen
　　　1st. Assistant:　Dr. Y. K. Hsueh
　　　2nd. Assistant:　Dr. B. Liu
　　　Recorder:　　　　Dr. C. C. Lee.

"Clinical History of the Patient:

　　　"The patient, a male of 28, lived in a small lane in front of the Kwan Miao Temple, and used to work in a village outside Changteh. He returned to the city on November 19th, 1941, on account of the death of his mother six or seven days before. The cause of her death was not definitely known (? tuberculosis - long standing illness with severe emaciation). He felt unwell in the evening of November 23rd, and experienced feverishness and headache with malaise at about 11 p.m. The next morning he complained of pain and tenderness in the right groin for which a Chinese plaster was applied. He vomited once in the afternoon, and from then on his condition grew rapidly worse. Dr. C. C. Lee of the 4th E.M.S.T.S. and the 4th Sanitary Corps, was called in at 7 p.m. to see the patient, and found him to be dying. Important findings on examination were high fever, and enlarged and tender glands in the right inguinal region. Plague was strongly suspected. The patient was to have been sent to the Isolation Hospital, but he died at 8 p.m. before he could be removed. With the aid of police the body was brought to Wei Sheng Yuan at 10 p.m. where disinfection of clothings and beddings were carried out in order to kill fleas. The plaster covering of the groin was removed; cardic puncture and aspiration of the right inguinal gland were performed for culture under sterile technique, and, since the light was inadequate, autopsy was postponed until the next morning. The body was laid in a coffin with the lid nailed down.

"Autopsy Findings:

"1.　General Appearance:　The cadaver was medium-sized and appeared very thin.

-29-

861

"2. Skin: Face was slightly blue and lips cyanotic.
            No petechial spots of flea bite wounds
            were seen. Lesions resembling scabies
            in the right popliteal region.

"3. Lymph Glands: The right inguinal glands were enlarged.
                    Mesenteric lymph nodes were also slightly
                    enlarged.

"4. Chest Findings: Lungs normal in gross appearance. There
                    was fluid estimated at 20 c.c. approxi-
                    mately in each pleural cavity. Pericar-
                    dial effusion of about 20 c.c. also pre-
                    sent. Heart very flabby but not enlarged.
                    Cardiac puncture through the right auricle
                    was performed under sterile technique and
                    a few c.c. of blood were obtained and ino-
                    culated in blood agar slant.

"5. Abdominal Findings: Liver firm. Spleen enlarged to twice its
                    normal size. Kidney normal. Hemorrhagic
                    spots were seen on the surfaces of liver,
                    spleen and intestine. No free fluid in
                    the abdomen.

"Bacteriological Findings:

    "Speciment of right inguinal glands, liver, spleen and blood
were taken for direct smears, culture and animal tests.

        "1. Direct Smears: Carbol-thionin blue and Gram's method
of staining were employed for all the smears. 50% ether in absolute
alcohol was used for fixation. Under the microscope many oval-
shaped Gram negative bacilli with their bipolar regions deeply
stained were found.

        "2. Cultivation: Under sterile technique, cardiac blood,
inguinal glands, liver and spleen of the patient were inoculated on
blood agar slant of pH 7.6 and incubated in a wide-mouth thermos
bottle. The temperature was regulated at 37 degrees C. Twenty four
hours later, many minute greyish-white opaque colonies were found on
the surfaces of the media. All were pure cultures. Smear examination showed Gram negative bipolar staining organisms.

"3. Animal Inoculation Test:

    "A. Guinea-pig No. 1. The animal was artificially infected by
        smearing splenic substance of the cadaver on the right
        flank of the animal, which was newly shaven at 3 p.m. on
        November 25th, 1941. (The splenic substance was found to
        have contained many Gram negative bipolar staining bacilli).
        The animal began to develop symptoms at 8 p.m. on November
        26th, and was found to be dead in the early morning of
        November 28th. Thus the incubation period was not more
        than 29 hours, and the whole course of the disease ran at
        most 32 hours.

        "Autopsy Findings:

"1.　Skin:　　　　　　　　Swelling and redness at the
　　　　　　　　　　　　site of inoculation.
"2.　Gland:　　　　　　　Bi-lateral enlargement of
　　　　　　　　　　　　inguinal glands, more marked
　　　　　　　　　　　　on the right side with conges-
　　　　　　　　　　　　tion.
"3.　Subcutaneous tissues:Edematous and congested,
　　　　　　　　　　　　hemorrhage at the site of ino-
　　　　　　　　　　　　culation.
"4.　Chest findings:　　Not remarkable.
"5.　Abdominal findings: Spleen enlarged and congested.
　　　　　　　　　　　　Liver, kidneys and G.I. tract
　　　　　　　　　　　　also congested.

"Specimen of heart blood, liver, spleen and inguinal
lymph gland were taken for smears and culture.

"Microscopic examination of the stained smears (Carbol-
thionin blue and Gram's stains) revealed Gram negative
bipolar staining bacilli similar to those seen in the
direct smears made of autopsy materials of the cadaver.

"Culture of these specimen on blood agar slant at pH. 7.6
was made.　Twenty four hours later, pure culture of similar organisms were found.

"B.　Guinea-pig No. 2. This animal was similarly treated as
guinea pig No. 1, at 9 a.m. on November 26th, but the
inguinal gland of the cadaver was used instead.　Symptoms
were first noticed at 8 a.m. on November 28th, an incubation period of 47 hours.　Death of the animal occurred
44 hours later (in the morning of November 30th).

"Autopsy of the animal showed the same gross pathological
changes as those of guinea pig No. 1.　Direct smear of
lymph gland, liver and spleen showed similar findings.

"C.　Guinea-pig No. 3. This time a pure culture of the organisms was used to smear on the newly shaven left flank of
the guinea pig.　(The culture was obtained by growing the
cadaver's blood on Blood agar slant of pH. 7.6 for 24
hours).　The animal appeared to have become ill 45 hours
later and was found dead in the early morning of November
30th.　The course of the disease of the animal was, therefore, not more than 40 hours.

"On autopsy, gross pathological changes were found to be
similar to those of guinea pig Nos. 1 and 2 except that
the changes of lymph glands and spleen were more pro-
nounced.

"Smear examination of heart blood, gland, liver and spleen
yielded similar results.

"Conclusion:

"Clinical history, autopsy findings and bacteriological
findings prove the patient to be a case of bubonic plague,
dying from septicaemic infection from Pasteurella pestis.

-31-

863

"APPENDIX II

"CLINICAL NOTES OF CASES SUSPECTED TO BE PLAGUE

"Case No. 1. (Tsai Pao-erh)

"This patient, a girl of 11, living in Tsai Hung-Sheng char-coal Dealer shop (蔡鴻勝炭號), Kwan Maio Street, was said to have fallen ill on November 11th, 1941 and was sent by the police to the Kwang-teh Hospital at 7 a.m. the next day for treatment. On admission she was seen by Dr. H. H. Tan and was found delirious. Temperature was 105.7 degrees F. There was exzema of the right ear. There were no glandular enlargement or tenderness. Few rales were heard in the chest. Abdominal findings were said to be normal. Blood smear (Wright and Gram's stains) showed organisms resembling P. pestis morphologically. Patient was then isolated and sulfanila-mide given. Her general condition turned from bad to worse in the morning of November 13th, when petechial spots of the skin were noted. Blood smear examination was repeated and revealed the same result as before. At about 8 a.m. she died.

"Essential features of autopsy were enlarged left infra-auricular lymph nodes. No sign of pneumonia; liver and spleen enlarged with hemorrhagic spots on their surfaces. Kidneys were also hemorrhagic. Splenic smear showed the same findings as the blood smear. Culture of the splenic substance was done in the Kwang-teh Hospital but no definite report was obtained.

"Case No. 2. (Tsai Yu-chen)

"This was woman of 27, living in the Chang-ching Street (長清街) East Gate district; she was said to have had an abrupt onset of fever on November 11th and died on the 13th. While her cortege was passing Tahshan, Dr. Kent of Red Cross Medical Relief Corps met it and made enquiry of the cause of her death. The above information led him to suspect plague. Post-mortem liver puncture was done and smear examination showed organisms resembling P. pestis morphologically.

"Case No. 3 (Nieh Shu-sheng)

"This was a man of 58, living in Nol, 3rd Chia, 4th Pao, Chi Ming Chen, East Gate district (東門磁明鎮四保坪一號). Developed high fever in the evening of November 12th, accompanied of pain and tenderness in the groin on November 13th. Aspiration of the enlarged groin glands was done by Dr. P. K. Chien of the Red Cross Medical Corps and smear examination (Wright Strain) showed P. pestis like organisms. The patient died in the same evening.

"Case No. 4 (Hsu Lao-san)

"The patient was a man of 25, living in No. 5, 5th Chia, 5th Pao, Yung An Hsiang, Yang Chia Hsing, East Gate district (東門,揚家巷永安鄉五保五甲五號). Became ill with fever and headache since November 12th. Seen by Dr. H. H. Tan and Dr. T. C. Fang, and found to have enlarged and tender groin lymph gland the next day. Aspiration of the gland was done in the Kwang-teh Hospital and smear examina-tion (Wright Strain) showed P. pestis like organisms.

-32-

"Case No. 5 (Hu Chung-fa)

"A man living in Chung Fa Hospital, Kwan Miao Street (关庙街 钟庆医院). In the morning of November 19th, he went to Wei Sheng Yuan complaining of being infected with plague and demanding treatment. He appeared at that time, quite irritable and spoke somewhat incoherently. His pulse rate was rapid, but fever was not high. Groin glands were enlarged. Other findings were not recorded. He was immediately admitted to the Isolation Hospital. In the evening his temperature went up and he died.

"Autopsy by Dr. H. H. Tan and Dr. M. N. Shih showed bluish discoloration of the skin, more marked over the chest and abdomen. No enlarged lymph glands were noticed. Spleen was found to be slightly enlarged and other findings in the abdomen were not remarkable. Smear and culture of splenic material showed only Gram positive cocci and bacilli. It should be noted that Dr. Tan was working with inadequate culture media."

"APPENDIX III

"Notes on Examination of Grain Dropped by Enemy Plane

"Examination of a sample of the grain dropped by the enemy plane over Chang-teh city on November 4th, 5 a.m. 1941 and collected from the ground next morning and examined after an interval of fully 34 days.

"Cross Examination: The sample consists of barley, rice and unidentified plants seeds.

"Culture Examination: The sample was put into a sterile mortar and ground with 5 c.c. sterile saline. This mixture was cultivated on blood agar slants and copper sulphate agar slants (all pH. 7.6). After incubation at 37 degrees C. for 24-48 hours, only contaminated organisms or staphylococci, B. Coli and unidentified Gram positive bacilli with central spores were found; no P. pestis like organisms were found.

"Animal Inoculation: Two c.c. of the above mixture were injected subcutaneously into a guinea pig on December 8th, 1941 at 9 a.m. The testing animal died in the evening of December 11th after showing no sign of illness.

"Autopsy Findings: On the morning of Dec. 12th, autopsy of the dead animal was performed. Local inflammation, general subcutaneous congestion, inguinal glands not enlarged, liver and spleen normal and not enlarged. Heart and lungs normal. Smears made from lymph glands, liver and spleen showed no P. pestis like organisms. Only Gram positive bacilli and some Gram negative bacilli were present.

"Culture of the heart blood of the dead animal showed unidentified Gram positive bacilli with central spores. P. pestis not found. Culture from the lymph nodes spleen and liver showed pure culture of B. coli only. P. pestis not found.

-33-

"**Conclusion:** By culture and animal inoculation tests, P. pestis is not present in the sample."

- - -

"I certify that the foregoing is a true copy of the official report prepared and submitted by me and that the facts therein recited are true to the best of my knowledge and belief.

"Witness my signature and seal this 29th day of March 1946.

/s/ W. K. Chen"

"Central Emergency Medical Service Training
School.
Dept. of Lab. Medicine,
Tuyunkwen, Kueiyang.

Dec. 12th, 1941.

"Dr. R. K. S. Lim,
Director, Central E.M.S.T.S. and C.R.C.M.R.C.
KUEIYANG.

"Dear Sir,

"I have the honour of submitting to you the attached report on the results of our investigation of the recent plague epidemic in Changteh, Hunan.

"By your order, an investigation unit consisting of Dr. B. Liu, Dr. Y. K. Hsueh (C.R.C.M.R.C.) and myself and technicians, C. L. Chu and C. L. Ting (E.M.S.T.S.) with field laboratory equipment, test animals, sulfathiazole and plague vaccine left Kueiyang on November 20th, arriving at Changteh on November 24th. The same night we started working on a human case just dead of plague-like infection. Autopsy findings together with bacteriological and animal tests, leave no doubt that we were dealing with a genuine case of bubonic plague with septicemia.

"The investigation was completed on November 30th. The handling of the outbreak was discussed with the local authorities in charge of the anti-epidemic measures. Vaccine and drugs of sufficient quantity were left in the hands of the medical units. As no fresh cases appeared, we left Changteh on December 2nd and returned to Kueiyang on December 6th. We brought back with us, the stained smears, pure culture of P. pestis which were isolated during this study and a sample of grains dropped from the enemy plane.

"Yours respectively,

/s/ W. K. Chen
W. K. Chen, M.D.
Head, Dept. of Laboratory Medicine
Central E.M.S.T.S.
Consultant, Chinese Red Cross Medical
Relief Corps."

"Dr. Chen's report and material have been examined by us and we have no hesitation in endorsing the conclusions arrived at in his report.

-34-

"T.S. Sze, M.B., B.S., D.T.M. & H., D.P.H., Dr. PH.
Head, Dept. of Preventive Medicine, Central
E.M.S.T.S.
Consultant, Chinese Red Cross Medical Relief Corps.

"F.C. Lin, M.D., B.S.
Senior Instructor, Dept. of Lab. Medicine,
     Central E.M.S.T.S.
Consultant Bacteriologist, C.R.C.M.R.C."

"I certify that the foregoing is a true copy of the official
report prepared and submitted by me together with a true copy of
the letter from me to Dr. R.K.S. Lim, Director, Central E.M.S.T.S.
and C.R.C.M.R.C. (now Surgeon-General and Director of Army Medical
Service of China) and of the certificate of Dr. Lin and Dr. Sze
endorsing the conclusions of this report and that the facts therein
recited are true to the best of my knowledge and belief.

"Witness my signature and seal this 29th day of March 1946.

                         /s/ W. K. Chen

                    "W. K. Chen, M.D.
                    Head of the Dept. of Laboratory Medicine
"Formerly: Central Emergency Medical Service Train-
                         ing School.
                    Consultant, Chinese Red Cross Medical
                         Relief Corps.

"Now: Medical Director,
                    Methodist Union Hospital,
                    Chungking, West China."

Mrs. E. J. Bannon is not now in China and we secured information

from the secretary of the Presbyterian Mission Board in Shanghai that

she is in the United States and could be located through the Presby-

terian Board of Foreign Missions, 156 Fifth Avenue, New York City.

Our informant, Mr. E. E. Walline, was the secretary of the China Coun-

cil Presbyterian Church in the United States and stated that he under-

stood the home address of Mrs. Bannon was Wooster, Ohio, but he wasn't

sure of this.

In Shanghai Dr. H. N. Jettmar was located and a conference was

held with him. Dr. Jettmar stated that his only investigation was in 1940 at Ningpo and Chuhsien. While the plague had appeared in those two places, in his opinion it could not be positively shown as having been caused as a result of the germs on grain or other substances dropped from an airplane. He stated that it was quite possible to develop the germs in large quantities and to put these germs on grain or other substances and scatter them from an airplane, that under good conditions the germs on grain would live for a long time and if this grain were eaten by rats they could become infective and fleas biting them would spread the disease. While his investigation was made some time after the foreign substances had been dropped from the airplane he was never able to positively confirm that the substances at the time he examined them contained plague germs. He stated that in Chuhsien there were delivered to him small globules about the size of spiders' eggs, very peculiar and unusual, which appeared to be mixed gelatin and agar and he was told by the citizens there that these had been gathered from the tops of 'richshaws and the roofs of houses after they had been dropped on the city by a Japanese plane. He didn't know definitely what types of germs these globules contained but at the time he examined them the germs which they then contained proved to be harmless when injected into guinea pigs. It is his opinion that the plague which occurred at Ningpo and Chuhsien in 1940 cannot be positively traced to germs dropped by Japanese planes. He is, however, at a loss to explain why Japanese planes would be dropping grain, globules and other substances on a Chinese city unless it were an effort to spread disease of some type. Dr. Jettmar is a scientist and was formerly with the League of Nations' Epidemic Commission. His evidence would be of no value to the trial.

It was impossible to contact Dr. W. W. Yung, Director of the Department of Epidemic Control, as he was at the time in Manchuria.

In the event that it is determined to develop in trial the use or attempted use of bacterial warfare by Japan, it is respectfully recommended:

1. That the following be secured as witnesses to testify in person:

    (a)　Dr. P. Z. King.

    (b)　Dr. W. K. Chen.

    (c)　Dr. Robert Pollitzer.

    (d)　Dr. W. W. Yung.

2. That Mrs. E. J. Bannon be secured as a witness or an affidavit be secured from her in the States giving full and complete details relative to the grain and other substances dropped from the plane in Changteh November 4, 1941, and 7 December before the outbreak of the plague in that city.

3. That other witnesses be secured or affidavits from other witnesses to testify to the fact that grain and other substances were actually dropped from Japanese planes in the cities in which the plague later appeared, the quantity of grain and other substances dropped from the planes, and other circumstances.

                         /s/ David Nelson Sutton
                             Associate Counsel
                  International Prosecution Section

23 April 1946

5.3.5　25 Apr.1946: Bacteria Warfare, TO: Mr. Joseph B. Keenan, Chief of Counsel, FROM: David Nelson Sutton

资料出处: National Archives of the United States, R331, E317.

内容点评: 本资料为 1946 年 4 月 25 日助理法务官 David N. Sutton 再次向首席检察官 Keenan 提交的关于日军细菌战的报告。

25 April 1946

TO   : Mr. Joseph B. Keenan
              Chief of Counsel

FROM   : David Nelson Sutton

SUBJECT   : Bacteria Warfare

In that section of the report from China relative to "bacteria warfare", the entire evidence secured in China on this subject was set out so that it would be available at one place to be used in determining whether or not to develop this phase of the case.

Dr. P. Z. King, Director General of the National Health Administration of China; Dr. W. K. Chen, now Medical Director of Methodist Union Hospital at Chunking; and Dr. Robert Pollitzer, who has been in public health and plague prevention work in China for 25 years and was formerly with the League of Nations Epidemic Commission in China, are entirely satisfied that the facts prove that the Japanese did make use of bacteria warfare. Dr. Chen and Dr. Pollitzer made personal investigations on the ground and detailed reports.

While the reports cover four places, the best investigation and report was made at Changteh in Hunan Province. That bubonic plague appeared in this city within seven days after a Japanese plane was reported to have dropped grain and other substances on the city on November 4, 1941, is definitely established. The weakness of the case is that we do not now have sufficient evidence to positively establish that grain or similar substances were dropped from a Japanese plane on this city on November 4, 1941.

On the present state of the record, it is respectfully recommended that no attempt be made to establish the use of bacteria warfare by the Japanese against China.

Should additional witnesses be located who can testify that grain or other substances were actually dropped from a Japanese plane on Changteh on November 4, 1941, then it would be proper to re-consider the matter in the light of additional evidence, for obviously the Japanese were not interested in providing "manna" for the Chinese people. Efforts are being made in China to secure additional evidence.

As the case now stands, in my opinion the evidence is not sufficient to justify the charge of bacteria warfare.

David Nelson Sutton

5.3.6　4 May 1946: Evidence of Japanese Use of Chemical Warfare agents in China, TO: Chief, Chemical Warfare Service, FROM: GEOFFREY MARSHALL, Col. CWS, Chief Chemical Officer

资料出处： National Archives of the United States, R331, E317.

内容点评： 本资料为 1946 年 5 月 4 日盟军总司令部化学战部队上校 Geoffrey Marshall 提交美军化学战部队长官的报告——1946 年 4 月 16 日 Morrow 上校向首席检察官 Keenan 提交的报告（资料 5.3.3）的摘要，题目：日本在中国使用化学武器的证据。内容包括日本细菌武器的使用。

CONFIDENTIAL

GENERAL HEADQUARTERS
UNITED STATES ARMY FORCES, PACIFIC
OFFICE OF THE CHIEF CHEMICAL OFFICER

APO 500
4 May 1946

SUBJECT: Evidence of Japanese use of Chemical Warfare agents in China.

TO : Chief, Chemical Warfare Service, Washington 25, D. C. (Attention: Chief, Intelligence Branch).

Inclosed herewith are extracts from the report of Colonel Thomas H. Morrow to Mr. Joseph B. Keenan, Chief International Prosecution Section relative to evidence developed by Colonel Morrow concerning the Japanese use of Chemical Warfare agents in China.

GEOFFREY MARSHALL
Colonel, CWS
Chief Chemical Officer

Incl Extracts from "Report of Trip to China", 16 April 1946.

CONFIDENTIAL

CONFIDENTIAL

C+310

Extracts from "Report of Trip to China", 16 April 1946.

* * * * *

The following matters were considered as deserving investigation, in connection with the China case:

* * * * *

E. The use of Toxic gas in warfare, contrary to international law;

F. Bacteriological warfare, by the sowing of materials impregnated with Bubonic plague germs;

* * * * *

Results of the China trip thus far are set forth as follows:

* * * * *

E. The use of toxic gas is considered to be well extablished, and in the following manner:

1. Statement of Japanese prisoners that toxic gas was used;

2. Statements of Chinese surgeons that they diagnosed and treated cases of Chinese soldiers who became battle casualties from poison gas;

3. Identification of Japanese Gas weapons by curator of Museum of Fire Arms at TUNG KAI CHOW (near Chunking) where the weapons are on exhibition;

4. Records of Gas Preventative Section Ministry of War, indicating 36968 casualties (2086 fatal) from Japanese Poison Gas, and containing photographs of victims of Japanese poison gas, showing mustard burns.

5. Statement of Intelligence Officer, Gas Defense Administration, Chinese Army, that he analysed the contents of a shell collected on a Japanese Battlefield, saw casualties occasioned by gas at that battle, and witnessed a gas bombardment of Chinese troops by Japanese artillery in China.

CONFIDENTIAL

-1-

CONFIDENTIAL

6. Statement of American Liaison Officer (Colonel John H. STODTER) with Chinese troops that he received training as a Gas Defense Officer in the American Army, and recognized a pocket of Tear gas in Burma, during the fighting there. He states a number of gas casualties were reported at the time to the Surgical units.

7. Attention is invited to Evidentiary Document No. 558 wherein it is made plain that the Japanese possessed certain gas material.

NOTE: The following comments are submitted on the use of Poison Gas, as disclosed by this investigation.

a. The Chinese had no offensive gas material, and grossly inadequate gas defensive material, such as gas masks.

b. Gas was used only as an emergency weapon, and generally when the Japanese were in a serious predicament.

c. Gas Artillery and Mortar Shells, gas grenades, and bombs were used by the Japanese.

d. The following sorts of gas were employed by the Japanese, according to Chinese: Mustard, Lewisite, Adamsite, Chloro Benzine, Picyrone. Gas to cause sneezing and vomiting was also referred to, without mention of its technical name.

e. While much of the evidence relates to tear gas, it will be remembered that the various international prohibitions of the use of gas in warfare make no distinction between the use of tear gas and the more injurious kinds, such as phosgene and mustard.

f. It is true that the American Army Investigating Committee in China did not report use of gas by the Japanese. It is also true that the Committee insisted on overwhelming evidence, which was not reported to the Committee, as far as appears.

In the opinion of the undersigned, the use of poison gas by Japanese in Sino-Japanese war is well established, and can be further proved by a certain report on the use of Poison Gas sent to Pacific War Council, 1943, by Dr. Wellington Koo, now the Chinese Ambassodor to England. The undersigned saw Koo in Chunking and Koo tried to get the report, but was not successful. However the proof is now present without this report.

CONFIDENTIAL
-2-

CONFIDENTIAL

F. The Bacteriological warfare charge is based upon a report in China Hand Book 1937-1943, made by a Dr. P. Z. King. Dr. King and his associates have been interviewed by Mr. Sutton who is submitting an attached report on them.

* * * * *

S U M M A R Y

The following propositions in the opinion of the undersigned, have been established by sufficient proof:

* * * * *

3. That poison gas was employed by the Japanese in their operations against China. It was a weapon of last resort, (tear and sneezing gas were most often used), and its use was probably almost entirely discontinued after President Roosevelt's statement in 1941 threatening retaliation in case gas was used thereafter by the Japanese. However, when used, it was directed against civilians lacking any gas defense material and Chinese soldiers of whom a small proportion only were equipped with masks; and of whom 36,000 became casualties. Having joined in 1919 in a condemnation of gas warfare by the Responsibilities Commission of the Paris Peace Conference, the story of gas warfare by the Japanese becomes another instance of flagrant violation of a solemn international agreement. It is significant that gas warfare could not be waged without the knowledge and approval of the Japanese Ministry and High Command in Tokyo.

(a) Gas offensive material came from the Chemical Warfare Centre at Narashino, Japan, and could not be produced by a General in China, who must get his gas supplies from the homeland;

(b) The Chinese had no gas offensive material, and it could not be said that the gas offensive material furnished by Japanese High Command was for retaliation;

(c) Documents and testimony recently obtained by our Chemical Warfare Section, GHQ, shows that the High Command in Tokyo knew that gas was being used in China by Japanese Armies.

The above three phases of the case, outlined in Paragraphs "A", "B", and "H" on pages 1 and 2 of this report, are ready for presentation.

* * * * *

CONFIDENTIAL

-3-

CONFIDENTIAL

RECOMMENDATIONS

The following recommendations are submitted:

* * * * *

11. There is a report in the League of Nations File according to the Chinese, on the use of Poison Gas by the Japanese, Japanese atrocities, and the opium and drug traffic when the Chinese Puppet Government was in existence.

These reports should be sent over from Geneva. They are not in Chinese Government Files.

* * * * *

14. Dr. Wellington KOO in Chunking referred me to Report of the Pacific War Consul on use of Poison Gas in China in 1943, and asked the Foreign Office there to get me a copy. The Foreign Office could not find such copy. Recommend that Washington and London be traced for copies, which I would like to have.

* * * * *

17. State Department at Washington should be asked for a copy of President Roosevelt's statement in 1942, warning the Japanese that if they use poison gas against any of the Allies of the United States, that the United States will retaliate.

Also, any State or War Department reports on the use of poison gas by the Japanese in the Sino-Japanese War.

* * * * *

Respectfully Submitted,

THOS. H. MORROW,
COL.   IGD.

CONFIDENTIAL

-4-

5.3.7　8 May 1946: Japanese Use of Chemical and Bacteriological Warfare Agents in China, TO: Chief, Chemical Warfare Service, FROM: GEOFFREY MARSHALL, Col. CWS, Chief Chemical Officer

资料出处: National Archives of the United States, R331, E317.

内容点评: 本资料为 1946 年 5 月 8 日盟军总司令部化学战部队上校 Geoffrey Marshall 提交美军化学战部队长官的报告，题目：日本在中国使用化学武器和细菌武器。该文件附件不全。

CONFIDENTIAL

C#340

GENERAL HEADQUARTERS
UNITED STATES ARMY FORCES, PACIFIC
OFFICE OF THE CHIEF CHEMICAL OFFICER

APO 500
8 May 1946

SUBJECT:　Japanese Use of Chemical and Bacteriological Warfare
　　　　　Agents in China.

TO　　　:　Chief, Chemical Warfare Service, Washington 25, D. C.
　　　　　(Attention:　Chief, Intelligence Branch).

　　　1.　Reference paragraph 5, letter this office, 23 April 1946,
subject:　"Japanese Bacteriological Warfare."

　　　2.　Inclosed herewith are:

　　　　　a.　Extracts from the report of Colonel T. H. Morrow to
Mr. Joseph B. Keenan relative to Japanese use of chemical warfare
agents.

　　　　　b.　Extracts from the Indictment presented to the International Military Tribunal for the Far East, 3 and 4 May 1946.

　　　　　c.　Report of Mr. D. N. Sutton relative to Japanese use of
bacteriological warfare agents.

　　　3.　It is noted in this connection that the use of poison gas
against the Chinese is alleged and included in Appendix D to the
indictment against the major war criminals.

　　　　　　　　　　　　　　　　　　GEOFFREY MARSHALL
　　　　　　　　　　　　　　　　　　Colonel, CWS
　　　　　　　　　　　　　　　　　　Chief Chemical Officer

3 Incls.
　Incl 1.　Extracts frm report
　　　　　of Col. T. H. Morrow
　　　　　to Mr. J. B. Keenan.
　Incl 2.　Extracts frm Indictment.
　Incl 3.　Report of Mr. D. N.
　　　　　Sutton.

CONFIDENTIAL

Extracts from the Indictment Presented to the International Military Tribunal for the Far East, 3 and 4 May 1946.

* * * * *

APPENDIX D

INCORPORATED IN GROUP THREE

The Laws and Customs of War are established partly by the practice of civilised Nations, and partly by Conventions and Assurances, which are either directly binding upon the parties thereto, or evidence of the established and recognised rules. The Conventions and Assurances hereinafter mentioned in any part of this Appendix will be relied upon as a whole for both purposes, only the most material Articles being quoted herein.

* * * * *

PARTICULARS OF BREACHES

All the offences are breaches of the Laws and Customs of War, and in Addition to, and as proved in part by, the several Articles of the Conventions and assurances specifically mentioned.

* * * * *

SECTION NINE

Employing poison, contrary to the International Declaration respecting Asphyxiating Gases signed by (inter Alia) Japan and China at the Hague on the 29th July, 1899, and to Article 23(a) of the said Annex to the said Hague Convention, and to Article 171 of the Treaty of Versailles:

In the wars of Japan against the Republic of China, poison gas was used. This allegation is confined to that country.

5.3.8　18 May 1946: Thomas H. Morrow

资料出处：National Archives of the United States, R331, E317.

内容点评：本资料日期为 1946 年 5 月 18 日，是远东国际军事法庭国际检察局美国检察官 Thomas H. Morrow 的履历。

18 May 1946

Born - Cincinnati, Ohio

Father, W. B. Morrow - Mother, Caroline C. Morrow

B.A. - University of Colorado, 1909
L.L.B. - University of Cincinnati 1911

Member of Ohio Bar since 1911 and United States Attorney,
Southern District of Ohio 1922-1923. Prosecuted George Remus,
et al. Special assistant to Attorney General of the United
States 1924. Democratic Candidate for Attorney General of Ohio
1924 (defeated).

Judge Common Pleas Court, First Judicial District of Ohio
1927-1942 (now absent on leave without pay).

Military Record

World War I - 1917-1918, Captain Co. K 148th Infantry, 37th
Division, served in France. Recommended for promotion for
"leadership in the presence of the enemy." Silver Star
Decoration awarded for "Gallantry in action" during Argonne
offensive.

World War II - 1942-43-44-45-46 - Lt. Col. and Executive 98th
Heavy Bomb. Group, Ninth Air Force. Colonel and Inspector
General IX Air Force Service Command. Served in Middle East,
Normandy, Belgium, Luxembourg, and Germany. Decorations:
Legion of Merit, Bronze Star, French Croix de Guerre with the
Palm, and Luxembourg Croix de Guerre.

Family - Widower with two sons. W. B. Morrow at Kenyon College,
Ohio, and Thomas V. Morrow, 1st Lt., Signal Corps, stationed at
Tokyo, Japan.

5.3.9   4 Jun. 1946: MEMORANDUM, Subject: Interrogations, by JOSEPH B. KEENAN, Chief of Counsel to the staff of the International Prosecution Section

资料出处： The University of Virginia Law Library, the Papers of David Nelson Sutton, Box 1.

内容点评： 本资料为 1946 年 6 月 4 日首席检察官 Keenan 向国际检察局成员发布的备忘录，题目：讯问。提及，中央讯问中心在日本成立，任何日本和外国国籍人士的讯问均由盟军占领军最高司令部 G–2 副参谋长直接掌管并指导。

GENERAL HEADQUARTERS
SUPREME COMMANDER FOR THE ALLIED POWERS
INTERNATIONAL PROSECUTION SECTION

4 June 1946

MEMORANDUM

TO   :   The Staff

FROM   :   The Chief of Counsel

SUBJECT: Interrogations

A Central Interrogation Center has been established under the control and direction of the Assistant Chief of staff, G-2, GHQ, SCAP to regulate interrogations of Japanese and foreign nationals in Japan, in accordance with existing War Department policies.

Hereafter no interrogations of Japanese or other enemy aliens will be performed in Japan by agencies of any country, except by prior authority of and under the direct supervision of the Assistant Chief of Staff, G-2, General Headquarters.

All requests by members of the International Prosecution Section for authority to conduct interrogations will be made in writing (an original and one carbon copy) to Miss Abilock, Room 300, and shall contain the name of the person to be interrogated and his or her address, or last known position of employment, together with a short description of the purpose of the interrogation. Clearance with G-2 will be obtained by the office of Mr. Morgan, and arrangements will be made for a date of interrogation with the person desired. American intelligence officers and interpreters will be present to assist in all authorized interrogations.

Three (3) copies of each interrogation will be furnished to Miss Abilock for forwarding to G-2.

This order applies to all interrogations wherever conducted.

JOSEPH B. KEENAN
Chief of Counsel

5.3.10　13 Dec. 1946: MEMORANDUM FOR MAJOR-GENERAL A. N. VASILIYEV, Subject: Bacteriological Warfare, Frank S. Tavenner, Jr.

资料出处： The University of Virginia Law Library, the Personal Papers of Frank S. Tavenner, Jr. and Official Records from the IMTFE, 1945-1948, Box 3.

内容点评： 本资料为 1946 年 12 月 13 日检察官 Frank S. Tavenner, Jr. 发给苏联检察官 A. N. Vasiliyev 少将的备忘录，题目：细菌战。提及数位检察官仔细审阅了柄泽（Karazawa）少佐、川岛（Kawashima）少将关于石井部队进行攻击性细菌武器实验活动的证词，目前的证据尚不足以立罪，没有必要要求苏联提交证人。

13 December 1946

MEMORANDUM FOR MAJOR-GENERAL A. N. VASILYEV

Subject: Bacteriological Warfare

Several members of our staff, including Justice A. J. Mansfield who is chargeable with the duty of presenting evidence relating to Class "B" and "C" offenses, have given careful consideration to the statements of Major Karazawa and Major-General Kawashima regarding the activities of the Ishii Detachment in experimenting with bacteria as a means of attack.

Upon directing investigation of Japanese records and reports on the subject of bacteriological warfare, I learned that an experienced investigator was sent directly from the United States to Japan where he conducted a seven-week investigation of this detachment, and no evidence was brought to light which would indicate that these experiments were being made at the direction of the General Staff in Tokyo or that any reports have been received relating to these experiments.

The Tribunal has made it very clear as to the evidence relating to atrocities and prisoners of war, that such evidence will not be received in the absence of an assurance by the Prosecution that the accused or some of them could be associated with the acts charged. We do not consider that the evidence now available is sufficient to justify an assurance that any of the accused can be associated with this activity by any of the criteria adopted by the Court with reference to atrocities and prisoner of war offenses. Although our investigation will continue for the purpose of obtaining additional evidence, the chance of success in the light of the investigation already made is so slight that it is not considered wise or reasonable to request the U.S.S.R. to produce the witnesses under these circumstances.

Frank S. Tavenner, Jr.

5.3.11 2 Sep. 1947: List of Attorneys-IPS

资料出处：National Archives of the United States, R331, E317.

内容点评：本资料日期为 1947 年 9 月 2 日，是远东国际军事法庭国际检察局在任、离任美国法务官名单。

RG 331, Entry 317
IPS File, Roll/Box

2 Sep 47

List of Attorneys - IPS

On Duty

Name	Date of Arrival	
Mr. Willis Mahoney	15 April	1946
Mr. Solis Horwitz	7 Dec	1945
Mr. Gilbert Woolworth	6 Dec	1945
Mr. Joseph F. English	7 Dec	1945
Mr. Arthur Sandusky	23 Jan	1946
Mr. David Nelson Sutton	13 Feb	1946
Mr. Frank S. Tavenner	14 Feb	1946
Mr. Guido Pignatelli	13 Mar	1946
Mr. Pedro Lopez	2 Apr	1946
Mr. William E. Edwards	3 Feb	1947
Mr. Robert L. Wiley	10 Feb	1947
Mr. Lester C. Dunigan	11 Feb	1947
Mr. Floyd W. Cunningham	24 Feb	1947
Mr. Smith N. Crowe, Jr.	28 Feb	1947
Mr. T. Ronald Delaney	20 Mar	1947
Mr. Robert M. Vote	25 Mar	1947
Capt. James J. Robinson	9 Dec	1945
Commander Charles T. Cole	21 Aug	1946
Col. Rowland W. Fixel	3 Mar	1947
1st Lt. Kurt Steiner	18 Mar	1946

Returned to US or left Section

Name	Date of Arrival	Date of Departure	
Mr. Edward H. Dell	7 Dec 1945		26 Mar 46
Mr. Robert M. Donihi	7 Dec 1945		12 Aug 46
Mr. Henry A. Hauxhurst	7 Dec 1945		21 Sep 46
Mr. Elton M. Hyder	7 Dec 1945		12 Aug 46
Mrs. Grace K. Llewellyn	7 Dec 1945		11 Sep 46
Mr. Otto Lowe	7 Dec 1945		18 Jul 46
Mr. A. Frederick Mignone	7 Dec 1945		31 Aug 46
Mr. Ernest E. Danly	7 Dec 1945		18 Sep 46
Mr. John Darsey	7 Dec 1945		5 Sep 46
Mr. John W. Fihelly	7 Dec 1945		6 Dec 46
Mr. Valentine C. Hammack	7 Dec 1945		5 Aug 46
Mr. Carlisle W. Higgins	7 Dec 1945		1 Mar 47
Mr. G. Osmond Hyde	7 Dec 1945		19 Dec 46
Mr. Worth E. McKinney	7 Dec 1945	(Dec'd)	24 Jan 47
Mr. Henry R. Sackett	7 Dec 1945		5 Sep 46
Mr. Amos W. W. Woodcock	7 Dec 1945		1 Mar 46
Col. Thomas H. Morrow	7 Dec 1945		12 Aug 46
Capt. Harryman Dorsey	7 Dec 1945		13 Aug 46